CATALOGUE OF G. B. SHAW PAPERS

Photograph of Shaw during rehearsals, 1914. Add. MS. 50582, f. 38.

Shaw himself annotated this photograph 'taken at the rehearsals of Pygmalion. H.M. Theatre 1913'. In fact these rehearsals took place between February and April 1914.

THE BRITISH LIBRARY
CATALOGUE OF
GEORGE BERNARD SHAW
PAPERS

THE BRITISH LIBRARY
2005

© 2005 The British Library Board

Published by the British Library
96 Euston Road, London NW1 2DB

British Library Cataloguing in Publication Data
is available from the British Library

ISBN 0 7123 4887 5

Printed in England
by St Edmundsbury Press
Bury St Edmunds

TABLE OF CONTENTS

FOREWORD

The Introduction to this Catalogue describes how, over a period of seven decades, the Department of Manuscripts at the British Library has acquired its existing holdings of the correspondence and papers of George Bernard Shaw. Here it falls to me to make visible the many pairs of curatorial hands which silently worked to make these collections accessible to researchers; and also to acknowledge the expertise and generosity of national and international Shavian scholars whose support and advice have been constant and invaluable.

Chief among the former are Alison M. Brown and T. J. Brown who, with the assistance of Marjorie L. Hoyle, carried out the major task of sorting into over 230 volumes the collections which are listed below as the Principal Series (I and II) of Shaw papers. These came to the Department, through Shaw's own bequest and through a purchase made possible by the Shaw Fund, in the decade after Shaw's death, and were made publicly available with exemplary speed. Further research on the dating of literary and political texts, and virtually all the groundwork for item-level indexing, was carried out by Yvonne Harvey, Margaret Nickson and Liz Duthie. The editor of the present Catalogue is Anne Summers, who with the assistance of William Frame, was able to take advantage of the Department's transition to the era of automated cataloguing; they are deeply indebted to the technical knowledge and editorial skills of the Department's present Head of Cataloguing, Rachel Stockdale. They are also very grateful to their colleague Richard Price who compiled Appendix I.

Looking outside the British Library, cataloguers have been able to turn for assistance to the curators of 'Shaw's Corner' at Ayot St. Lawrence, to the officers of the Society of Authors, and to those of the Public Trustee. Above all the scholarly help and encouragement of Dan H. Laurence and Michael Holroyd are warmly acknowledged. All belong to that legion of Shaw's friends and colleagues of whom he wrote in his will: '[they] have not only made my career possible but hallowed it with kindly human relations'.

April 2005   Dr. C. J. Wright
                                               Head of Manuscripts

INTRODUCTION

1. THE CORRESPONDENCE AND PAPERS OF
GEORGE BERNARD SHAW
IN THE DEPARTMENT OF MANUSCRIPTS
AT THE BRITISH LIBRARY

George Bernard Shaw, playwright and socialist (1856-1950), was a largely self-educated man. Arriving in London from his native Dublin at the age of twenty, he soon found his temple of learning at Bloomsbury, in the reading rooms of the British Museum. [1] In his will he designated the British Museum (together with the Royal Academy of Dramatic Art and the National Gallery of Ireland) as a residuary legatee 'in acknowledgment of the incalculable value to me of my daily resort to the Reading Room of that institution at the beginning of my career'. The services provided by the Bloomsbury Reading Room, in conjunction with the Departments of Printed Books and Manuscripts, are now, of course, the responsibility of a successor institution, the British Library. The bust of Shaw [2] which presides over readers consulting the collections of the Department of Manuscripts in the relocated and transformed new British Library at St. Pancras, commemorates a relationship which commenced in the mid-1870s, and symbolises its continuity, in a great variety of forms, in the present century.

Shaw's bequests, in addition to the income from royalties and investments, included a significant quantity of manuscript materials, for which several different dispositions were made. From the papers in his possession, predominantly letters, which were written by others, and in which he therefore owned no copyright, he bequeathed 'such letters and documents as might be worth preserving in a public collection such as that of the British Museum'. The domestic and family papers of Charlotte Frances Shaw née Payne-Townshend, whom he married in 1898, and who predeceased him in 1943, were to be offered to her surviving relatives. Other non-copyright material, particularly that relating to matters of business, was to be offered to the library of the London School of Economics, in whose establishment he and Charlotte had played a significant role. Shaw, who died childless, assigned copyright materials —

letters, papers, playscripts, drafts, etc., of which he was author — to his Executor, the Public Trustee. [3]

As will be seen from the first section of descriptive listings in this Catalogue, Shaw had in fact begun donating both copyright and non-copyright materials to the Department of Manuscripts while he was still alive. After his death, the non-copyright materials now listed as Series I of the 'Principal Series' of Shaw papers arrived in successive consignments at the Department, where they were by 1959 separated from the business correspondence and papers thought to belong more properly to the L.S.E. [4] Copyright materials were also sent to the Department for sorting over this period. During this first decade following Shaw's death, the claims of the three Residuary Legatees on his estate were complicated by those clauses of his will relating to the provision of funding for the introduction of a phonetic alphabet. A settlement was reached by 1958 which enabled the British Museum to proceed with the valuation and purchase of the copyright materials from the estate, and from the two other Legatees. [5] These materials are now listed as Series II of the 'Principal Series'. Both Series I and Series II were in 1961 'incorporated' in the Department's collections: that is to say, registered in their final arrangement into 236 volumes, each with a permanent accession number. [6]

From the 1930s to the present, Shaw manuscripts have continued to come into the Department via a number of routes. In the first place, there are Shaw's own donations, and those made by his correspondents and their descendants. Shaw presented Ellen Terry's letters to him, and Charlotte's correspondence with T. E. Lawrence. Letters written by Shaw himself figure largely in, for example, the papers of William Archer, John Burns, Sir Johnston Forbes-Robertson and Sir Isaac James Pitman, which were all presented by respective family members. The Department has also continued to acquire materials by purchase, often with the aid of the Shaw Fund. Thirty-seven volumes of the correspondence and papers of Charlotte Shaw were thus acquired in 1971, supplemented in 1982 by a further twenty-five volumes of papers of husband and wife transferred from 'Shaw's Corner' at Ayot St. Lawrence by the National Trust. Other purchases containing substantial Shaw materials include the Ashley Manuscripts from the library of T. J. Wise, purchased in 1938 (see descriptive lists, Section 5); the archive of the Society of Authors — very much Shaw's 'trade union', to whose affairs he committed much time and labour — incorporated in 1971; and that of G. K. Chesterton, one of Shaw's more heavyweight literary and philosophical sparring partners, purchased in 1990.

A most important source of Shaw manuscripts, listed as 'Lord Chamberlain's Plays' and 'Lord Chamberlain's Correspondence', deserves separate mention. In 1965 and 1988 the Department incorporated two series of playscripts which had been submitted to the Lord Chamberlain's Office for licence for public performance. These were presented to the Department by the Office, whose functions in this area were wound up with the abolition of censorship in 1968. Although it would have been possible to include these in the section of the Catalogue for Departmental Accessions 1961-2004, it has been thought more helpful to list this collection separately, together with the related collection of Lord Chamberlain's Correspondence; the latter has not been assigned Departmental accession numbers.

This enormous and heavily consulted theatrical archive contains many Shaw scripts, often annotated either by the playwright's or the Censor's pen. The L.C.P. Correspondence section is particularly rich where some of the more controversial titles (*Mrs. Warren's Profession*, as might be imagined; more surprisingly, perhaps, *The Shewing-Up of Blanco Posnet* and *Geneva*) are concerned. Reports from the Lord Chamberlain's Office, opinions commissioned from literary, diplomatic, political and even Palace advisers, letters from clerical advocates (or prosecutors), from theatrical managers and from Shaw himself offer an exceptional insight into the history of the works in performance.

Elsewhere in the Shaw collections are further rich seams to be mined on the subject of the performance history of the plays. The Shaw sections of the archive of the Society of Authors show the playwright discussing casting options and performing rights; and the extensive photographic collections show casts and sets from the early 1900s to the Hollywood film productions of the 1940s. Both the correspondence and the photographs illustrate the quite extraordinary universalism of Shaw's appeal to audiences. It is often forgotten that the first production of *Pygmalion* took place in German translation in Vienna in 1913, and that of *The Apple Cart* in Polish translation in Warsaw in 1929. *Pygmalion* was a success in Vienna, Warsaw, Paris and Moscow; *Mrs. Warren's Profession* in Rome and Paris. *St. Joan* can be studied in Hungarian and Japanese stage settings, and Shaw's general correspondence contains such rarities as an English translation of the Foreword to the Urdu translation of *St. Joan* by Dr. S. M. Q. Zoor of Secunderabad.

The extraordinary extent of Shaw's international influence is still an underresearched subject, a comment perhaps on our own lack of genuine international interchange in a supposedly global age. [7] It is a matter for regret that a part of the correspondence and papers which illustrates the production, distribution and exchange of the commodity which was Shaw's oeuvre, was by the provisions of his will separated from the manuscript texts of his plays, books and articles. However, since there are many separate collections of Shaw materials (see Appendix III, below) researchers will always need to be aware of the demands placed upon them by the fact of this dispersion. The general correspondence volumes in Series I of the 'Principal Series', containing as they do letters from both the English and non-English speaking world, should, if consulted as a chronological series rather than merely as a source for documents of particular

individuals, stimulate and inspire new perspectives on the diffusion of knowledge and cultural values in the nineteenth and twentieth centuries.

While not a year passes without a production, in this country at least, of one
of Shaw's plays, his political writings have suffered something of an eclipse.
The last generation of readers, from housebound mothers to bored National
Servicemen, who educated themselves by reading Shaw's works on municipal,
national and international politics, as well as his essays on art and music, has
practically passed away. Shaw began to inform, instruct, persuade and provoke
political audiences some years before he began to conquer audiences in the
theatre. He joined the Fabian Society in his late twenties and soon became a
leading member. In his eagerness to arrive at analyses of national and international capitalism he did not shun responsibilities closer to home, even when
his literary career blossomed. He represented the London parish (later borough)
of St. Pancras from 1897 to 1904, the years in which his dramatic successes
included *The Devil's Disciple, Caesar and Cleopatra, Captain Brassbound's
Conversion, Man and Superman* and *John Bull's Other Island.*

It is hard for us now to realise how powerful a voice Shaw's was for the
exercise of rationality in human affairs: how much of his life he devoted to
finding a politics which would reconcile individual freedom and responsibility
with collective obligation; and how naturally it came to the members of his
public to write to him with their ideas, questions and problems. Shaw the social
and political thinker is currently overshadowed for us by Shaw the humourist
and satirist; there seems, indeed, to have been no subject (except cruelty to
animals) which he could not treat as a legitimate subject for mirth; more even
than Shakespeare's Beatrice, he seems to have 'often dreamt of unhappiness, and
wak'd [him]self with laughing'.

In September 1948 the first Prime Minister of India, Jawaharlal Nehru, wrote
to Shaw that he would shortly be visiting England and hoped very much to have
the opportunity of a personal meeting:

'Forty years ago, when I was 18 and an undergraduate at Cambridge, I heard
you address a meeting there. I have not seen you again since, nor have I ever
written to you. But, like many of my generation, we have grown up in company with your writings and books. I suppose a part of myself, such as I am
today, has been moulded by that reading. I do not know if that would do you
any credit ... If I have the privilege to meet you for a while, it will be to
treasure a memory which will make me a little richer than I am'. [8]

The collections described and indexed in this Catalogue make it possible for us
to see more clearly the Shaw to whom Nehru wrote: Shaw the author of
Commonsense About the War (1914) and *The Intelligent Woman's Guide To
Socialism and Capitalism* (1928), willing to sacrifice his popularity to his
beliefs, and indefatigable in the support of his chosen causes. Add. MS. 50701,

for example, is a remarkable collection of cards and handbills, dating from 1886 to 1928, for meetings, debates and Sunday and evening classes addressed by Shaw. We see him making his way from Bloomsbury Socialist Society to Sunday Social Gatherings for the People in Tunbridge Wells, from open-air rallies of trade unions to meetings of the St. Pancras Vestry, from protests against compulsory vaccination to protests against forcible feeding of suffragettes, tirelessly engaging with the liberals and progressives, radicals and socialists, feminists, freethinkers and self-improvers of a world of intellectual ferment which our own age has largely lost to the professionalisation of knowledge and the routinization of party politics.

It is astonishing to think that all this public speaking was in addition to the hours of writing and routine attendance at committees which Shaw put into the business of St. Pancras, the Fabian Society and the Society of Authors. The eclectic nature of the British Library's Shaw collections certainly mirrors his own life. One of the best ways to get a measure of the unsparing use Shaw made of his energies is to turn to the Index of this Catalogue, where dramatic works, literary and musical criticism, Fabian papers, writings on Ireland and the Soviet Union, and political writings more generally, are listed in separate chronological sequences. They show us how extraordinarily productive Shaw was across a range of subjects and genres simultaneously, the creation of works of the imagination going hand in hand with political analysis, party polemic, and attention to the prosaic details of administrative procedure. That generosity of spirit and commitment to the public good which enriched so many lives and which are evident in the clauses of his will, are also revealed on every page of Shaw's archive.

Notes

[1]   For biographies of Shaw, the reader is referred to the three volumes published by Michael Holroyd, (London, Chatto & Windus 1988-1991) and his two subsequent volumes, *The Shaw Companion* (1992); Dan H. Laurence, ed., *Bernard Shaw: Collected Letters,* 4 vols. (London, Max Reinhardt, 1965-1988); and A. M. Gibbs, *A Bernard Shaw Chronology* (London, Palgrave, 2001).

[2]   The bust, executed by J. Coplans in 1955, was presented to the British Library by the Trustees of the British Museum.

[3]   Successive drafts of Shaw's will are to be found in Additional MS. 50712.

[4]   The transferred material included correspondence with publishers, translators and literary agents.

[5]   This vexed issue is partly covered in Additional MS. 71615, a volume from the papers of the economist Sir Roy Harrod. In 1956 Harrod was asked by the Residuary Legatees to depose to an Affidavit on the possible

economic consequences of a new alphabet. On the other side of the case, Additional MS. 79493 comprises a volume of papers, for the same period, of the scheme's principal supporter, Sir Isaac James Pitman.

(6)   It should be noted that, as with nearly all the manuscripts in its physical possession, the British Library does not own copyright in the Shaw Papers. This is vested in the Public Trustee, represented by the Society of Authors, 84 Drayton Gardens, London SW10 9SB; [0]208-7373-6642; www.societyofauthors.net

(7)   See 'Shaw in Translation' in *Shaw: The Annual of Bernard Shaw Studies, Vol. 20* (Pennsylvania State University Press, 2000), pp. 177-247; A. Summers, 'Gaps in the Record: Hidden Internationalisms', in *History Workshop Journal* 52, 2001, pp. 217-227.

(8)   Add. MS. 50526 B, f. 431, Nehru to Shaw, 4 September 1948.

2. HOW TO USE THIS CATALOGUE

In a digital age, it might be asked why it has been thought appropriate to produce a hard-copy version of this Catalogue. The Department of Manuscripts at the British Library has, indeed, been a pioneer of the automated cataloguing of manuscript materials, and most of its conventionally published catalogues have been retrospectively converted. The online searchable catalogue of indexes and descriptive listings can be accessed at http://molcat.bl.uk (address current at the time of going to press, although a new integrated catalogue is under development). The reader is referred to this source (or its successor) for all accessions of Shaw materials subsequent to the present publication.

Manuscripts Online Catalogue is a wonderful resource for keyword and name searches, date ranges, specific occupations and much else besides, but where an author such as Shaw is concerned, the sheer volume of entries under his name in the index makes search results unwieldy. Shaw's correspondents included so large a proportion of his most eminent literary, dramatic, musical, artistic and political contemporaries that few personal archives whose dates span the most active period of his career do not include some of his writings, and the British Library's holdings of those contemporaries' archives are very extensive.

Hard-copy publication has made it possible to edit and structure some 4,000 index entries relating to Shaw under additional headings which will, it is hoped, facilitate some of the more important lines of research in the field. Shaw's own entries are grouped as follows. Under the first heading, 'Dramatic Works', the plays are listed alphabetically, and for each play there is a listing, in chronological sequence, of all the relevant material in the collections, from early shorthand drafts through correspondence with censors, producers, performers, translators, etc., to photographs of different productions and stills from the Hollywood versions. To find all references to a named literary work, users are advised to consult this structured portion of the index, since cross-references within the descriptive lists have only been made selectively.

This section is followed by listings of novels and other literary works, including sketches and collaborations, also in chronological sequence, as are all the listings under the following headings: writings on art, literature and drama; writings on music; Fabian writings and papers; writings on Ireland; writings on the Soviet Union; general political and economic writings and papers; autobiographical, biographical and personal correspondence, notes and papers; general correspondence and miscellaneous papers; and photographs, portraits and caricatures.

The major proportion of the Library's holdings of Shaw's correspondence consists of letters to, rather than from Shaw. In either case, with few exceptions, it is alphabetically indexed under the name of Shaw's correspondent. Names of places and organisations, and some subject headings for correspondence on topics such as 'Vaccination' are also included in this alphabetical sequence. Two subject headings to note are Artworks and Photographs, under which are listed a great variety of images of Shaw and his contemporaries. In each case the listing is in date order (as it is for all index entries). The Photographs list contains entries which are also to be found for individual plays under the heading 'Dramatic Works', and under the names (where known) of their subjects and photographers.

In the Department of Manuscripts' published Catalogues of Manuscripts, it is traditional for 'Descriptions' to precede the 'Index Section'. As it has been very common for researchers, even in the pre-computer age, to concentrate on the latter almost to the exclusion of the former, the function of the 'Descriptions' merits explanation. These descriptive listings supplement the index entries in a number of important ways. They provide information about the provenance of manuscripts, recording when, whence and by what means they were acquired. They indicate whether manuscripts came to the Department in the volumes and sequences described, or whether they subsequently underwent re-arrangement. They also indicate whether manuscripts have been re-arranged since the Department's provisional sorting which first made them available to scholars.

Most importantly, descriptive listings provide intellectual context for the documents in which a particular researcher is interested. For example, it may be enlightening to discover whether a piece of writing emanates from a literary or a political context; and a lively Shavian exchange may be an enclosure within the archive of another personage. It is important to know when a text relates, not only to the immediate correspondent, or to the direct sponsoring or publishing organisation, but also to the personal or institutional originator of the larger collection within which it is located. For example, the Index will show that in 1918 the social reformer Beatrice Webb wrote to the future Lord Chancellor R. B. Haldane on the subject of *Mrs. Warren's Profession*; the Descriptions will show that their correspondence took place in connection with the proceedings of the national system of stage censorship operated by the Lord Chamberlain's Office.

A reader who looks for the name of a particular individual in the Index will find in the entry the date of the text or item of correspondence and the 'state' of the item. Autograph and English language are default; copy, printed, duplicate, typewritten, shorthand, etc. are indicated, as are foreign languages and physical fragmentation (happily rare). The reader will also find the accession number of the volume in which the item is to be found, as well as the folio reference (foliation differs from pagination in that only the first side of a page is numbered; the second side is noted as, e.g., f. 15v, or verso). On turning to the descriptive listings, the reader will find the accession numbers of the main volumes in numerical sequence, reflecting the chronological order of their acquisition by the Department in Sections 1-4. These Sections are followed by 5-7, listings of manuscripts which retain different numeration sequences. (The only exception is Section 7, Lord Chamberlain's Plays, for reasons stated above, p. x). On locating the accession number cited in the index entry, the reader will find the provenance and archival context of the item.

A non-traditional feature of this Catalogue can be found in Appendices I and II, containing details of non-manuscript material. Appendix I is the Handlist of the British Library's Rare Books collection of works owned by G. B. Shaw, and includes, among other publications, presentation copies from translators and privately printed rehearsal copies of plays. Many of the latter are first rehearsal copies, but there are also revised printings, and all should be consulted in connection with the versions of the same texts held in the manuscript collections. From time to time addenda to this collection are identified; for information supplementary to this Catalogue it is, as with the manuscript holdings, always worth making inquiries in the relevant Department. This is also true in respect of sound recordings of Shaw, for which guidance should be sought from the Sound Archive (see Appendix II). The electronic addresses cited in Appendix III for collections held outside the British Library are valid at the time of going to press. Users should note that copies of Shaw manuscripts obtained by the British Library under export licensing regulations are not included in the present catalogue.

DESCRIPTIVE LISTS

ACCESSIONS 1934-1960

43800-43802. Letters of Ellen Terry to G. B. Shaw, together with drawings of Shaw by her daughter and son Edith and Edward Gordon Craig, and a letter to Shaw of Sir Henry Irving; 1892-1922 (mainly 1895-1903). Most of the correspondence is published in *Ellen Terry and Bernard Shaw: a Correspondence*, ed. Christopher St. John (1931). Shaw's memorandum on his reasons for preserving the letters, at 43800 ff. i-ii, is published in *British Museum Quarterly*, ix, 1934-1935, pp. 81-83. Presented by Shaw in November 1934.

Five further, unpublished, letters of Terry to Shaw are in 46172, ff. 39-49; Shaw's letters to Terry are in 71068, with *rotograph* copies in Facs. 496. Shaw's letter to T. J. Wise of 1933 concerning the correspondence is at Ashley A4011, f. 113.

> **43800.** (ff. ii+269). 29 June 1892-30 Jan. 1897.
>
> **43801.** (ff. 307). 5 Feb. 1897-25 April 1898.
>
> **43802.** (ff. 288). 12 May 1898-6 May 1922.

The Ashley Manuscripts. The manuscript sections of the Ashley Library of Thomas James Wise, book collector, purchased in 1938, cover the most important poetic writers in English in the nineteenth century, and include correspondence with writers, critics and bibliographers. Numerous items of Shaw correspondence, both with Wise and others, are listed in detail in section 5 of the present Catalogue, and in the Index.

45296. (ff. 278). Correspondence of G. B. Shaw with William Archer; 1885-1924, n.d., with a note of G. B. Shaw of 1928. Includes letters of C. F. Shaw. Partly *typewritten copy*; partly *printed*. Partly *French* and *German*. Volume VII in the series 45290-45297, a collection of William Archer's correspondence presented to the Department by his brother, Lt.-Col. Charles Archer, in 1939. See also 50528, ff. 29-83.

45903, 45904. Letters of T. E. Lawrence to C. F. Shaw, including a few addressed to G. B. Shaw and others, with some letters of other writers, included in the Index; 1923-1935. Bequeathed to the Department of Manuscripts by Mrs. C. F. Shaw, and presented by G. B. Shaw in February 1944. See also 45922; 56495-56497.

> **45903.** (ff. 206). Jan. 1923-April 1928. Folios 100, 170 are *fragments*; folios 187-189 partly *typewritten*.

> **45904.** (ff. 228). May 1928-Jan. 1935. Folios 2, 17, 80 and 228 are addressed to G. B. Shaw. Partly *typewritten*.

45922. (ff. ii+123) Letters of C. F. Shaw to T. E. Lawrence; 1922-1935. ff. 59-123 are *typewritten copies* of the preceding folios. At ff. 56-58 are *fragments* of three letters; 1927-1928. At f. 54 is a letter of Mrs. Sydney Smith; 20 May 1935. Presented by G. B. Shaw in May 1944. Shaw's letter of presentation to the Keeper of Manuscripts is at f. i and his annotations of the letters are at ff. 56, 58, 86, 91, 101, 106, 111. See also 56497, ff. 1-66.

45923. (ff. iii+101). 'St. Joan', with Preface; 1923-1924, 1944. *Shorthand*, with occasional phrases and names of characters in full. The Preface follows the playscript at f. 69. At ff. i-iii are a postcard and notes to the then Keeper of Manuscripts in the British Museum, describing working methods and giving the dates of the composition of different sections of the work. Presented by G. B. Shaw in June 1944. See also 50633; 50634; 50644.

46172 G. Letters of Ellen Terry to G. B. Shaw; 1896-1904, n.d. At ff. 39-49 of a volume of miscellaneous Departmental acquisitions. Shaw's note of presentation is at f. 37, and he has annotated ff. 44 and 44v. The first of Terry's letters is written by an amanuensis and addressed 'Dear Julia', probably an allusion to the Julia mentioned in Shaw's letter to Terry of 8 Sept. 1897, now at 71068, f. 109. See the editorial notes of C. St. John in the published *Correspondence* (1931), pp. 205, 251. Presented by Shaw in February 1945, and supplementing Terry's letters in 43800-43802 and in the published *Correspondence*. See also 71068 and Facs. 496.

46287. (ff. 309v-339v). Correspondence of G. B. Shaw with John Burns; 1890-1928. Partly *typewritten*. Most letters are those of Shaw; there are two letters of Burns and two of C. F. Shaw to Burns. Part of Vol. VII of the series 46281-

46345, a collection of the personal and official correspondence and papers of John Burns, presented to the Department by his brother David Burns and his niece Alice Alexandra Fuller in 1946.

46505-46507. Letters of G. B. Shaw to Charlotte Frances Payne-Townshend afterwards Shaw; 1896-1934. Presented by G. B. Shaw in May 1948; his letter accompanying the gift is at 46505, f. i.

> **46505.** (ff. i+153). Letters and lettercards written before marriage; 21 Sept. 1896-4 May 1898. Included at ff. 93-143 are 51 leaves from an engagement-pad, giving a daily record of engagements and activities; 12 March-1 May 1898.

> **46506.** (ff. 157). Letters and postcards; 1912-1934. These include letters from motoring tours in Germany and France in 1912-1913, notes on the Inter-Allied Socialist and Labour Conference of 1917, and letters written during Shaw's visit to the Soviet Union in 1931.

> **46507.** (ff. ii+246). *Typewritten copies* of the letters contained in the previous two volumes. See also 50550.

48201. (ff. i+16). 'Why She Would Not: a Little Comedy'; July 1950. *Typewritten carbon copy*. This play in five scenes, although set up in type as No. LIV of the Standard Edition of the Works of Bernard Shaw (1931-1950), was suppressed by Shaw before publication. A set of proofs is in the Archibald Henderson Collection in the University of North Carolina Library. See A. Henderson, *George Bernard Shaw: Man of the Century* (1956), pp. 664-665, and E. Farley and M. Carlson, *George Bernard Shaw: A Selected Bibliography, 1945-1955* (1959), p. 323. Presented by the Public Trustee, in whom copyright is vested, in 1953.

50483 G. Letter of Arthur Davies to G. B. Shaw asking if he believed in ghosts, with Shaw's answer written on the same sheet; 5, 21 Jan. 1949. At ff. 48-49 of a volume of miscellaneous Departmental acquisitions. Presented by Mr. Davies in 1960.

50483 I. 'Common Sense about the War'; 1915. Items relating to a proposed reprint, at ff. 78-91 of a volume of miscellaneous Departmental acquisitions.
> ff. 78-88. 'A Word Concerning the 1915 Reprint': printer's copy of the preface to a projected reprint of Shaw's *Common Sense about the War*

(1915), of which the British Library holds a proof copy (Cup. 400. B. 31);
November 1915. *Typewritten*, with *autograph* corrections.

ff. 89-91. Two letters of Shaw to Clifford Sharp, editor of the *New States-
man*, relating to the project; 1, 4 Dec. 1915. Folio 91 is annotated by
Rennie Byles, a publisher and business manager of the *New Statesman*.
Mr. Byles bequeathed the documents to Mrs. Phyllis M. C. Pearce, from
whom they were purchased. Transferred from the Department of Printed
Books, May 1960. See also 50668; 50669 A, B; 50770.

PRINCIPAL SERIES OF SHAW PAPERS

There are two principal series of G. B. Shaw Papers consisting of two hundred and thirty-six volumes (50508-50743).

SERIES I.

50508-50592. Bequeathed by G. B. Shaw and incorporated in the Department of Manuscripts 8 March 1961. This series comprises materials in which Shaw did not own copyright.

Eighty-six volumes classified as follows:

A.   General Correspondence: 50508-50527.

B.   Special Correspondence: 50528-50565.

C.   Works by Other Authors: 50566-50581.

D.   Photographs relating to Shaw: 50582-50592.

A.   GENERAL CORRESPONDENCE.

50508. (ff. 306). 1857-1880.
50509. (ff. 279). 1881-1882.
50510. (ff. 337). 1883-1884.
50511. (ff. 371). 1885-1887.
50512. (ff. 308). 1888-1892.
50513. (ff. 267). 1892-1900.
50514. (ff. 389). 1901-1906.
50515. (ff. 456). 1907-1910.
50516. (ff. 435). 1911-1913.
50517. (ff. 452). 1914-1916.
50518. (ff. 343). 1917-1922.

50519. (ff. 399). 1923-1929.
50520. (ff. 258). 1930-1934.
50521. (ff. 372). 1935-1937.
50522. (ff. 477). 1938-1942.
50523. (ff. 184). 1943.
50524. (ff. 381). 1944-1945.
50525. (ff. 400). Feb.-July 1946.
50526 A. (ff. 1-256v). 1 Aug.-15 Sept. 1946.
50526 B. (ff. 257-516). 17 Sept. 1946-7 Sept. 1950.
50527. (ff. 279). Undated correspondence.

B.   SPECIAL CORRESPONDENCE.

50528. (ff. 110).
1.   ff. 1-28v. Sir George Alexander; 1900-1913, n.d. Partly *draft* and *signed*.

2.   ff. 29-83. William Archer (correspondence of and concerning); 1885-1924. Partly *shorthand* and *typewritten draft*; partly *signed*.
3.   ff. 84-98. Lena Ashwell; 1912, n.d.
4.   ff. 99-110v. Nancy, Viscountess Astor; 1930-1946, n.d. Partly *typewritten copy*.

50529. (ff. 212).
1.   ff. 1-14. Sir James Barrie, Bart.; 1901-1913, n.d. Partly *typewritten copy*.
2.   ff. 15-58. Max Beerbohm; 1898-1935. Partly *copy*.
3.   ff. 59-67. Annie Besant; 1885-1919.
4.   ff. 68-87v. Rutland Boughton (correspondence of and concerning); 1912-1945? Partly *typewritten*. See also 52365.
5.   ff. 88-128v. Hon. Sylvia Brett; 1910-1914.
6.   ff. 129-145. Robert Bridges; 1910?-1926. Partly *typewritten draft*.
7.   ff. 146-178. Lionel Britton (correspondence of and concerning); 1934-1943. Partly *printed*.
8.   ff. 179-212. Robert Williams Buchanan; 1891-1896.

50530. (ff. 228). Pakenham Thomas Beatty; 1878-1889, n.d.

50531. (ff. 166).
1.   ff. 1-41. Sir Hall Caine; 1904-1928.
2.   ff. 42-53v. Mrs. Patrick Campbell (correspondence of and concerning); 1901-1939.
3.   ff. 54-58v. Sir Lewis Casson and Dame Sybil Thorndike; 1925-1946.
4.   ff. 59-104v. Sir Sydney Cockerell; 1897-1950.
5.   ff. 105-125v. Walter Crane; 1885-1904.
6.   ff. 126-166v. Robert Bontine Cunninghame Graham; 1888-1913.

50532. (ff. i+338). Letters from Shaw to Charles Charrington and his wife, Janet Achurch; 1889-1924, n.d. *Typewritten copies.*

50533. (ff. 169).
1.   ff. 1-28v. John Davidson; 1901-1908.
2.   ff. 29-83. Lord Alfred Douglas; 1931-1944.
3.   ff. 84-102. Henry Havelock Ellis; 1888. Partly *shorthand draft*.
4.   ff. 103-116. Florence Emery *née* Farr (correspondence of and concerning); 1905-1916, n.d. Partly *printed*.
5.   ff. 117-169v. St. John Ervine; 1916-1948.

50534. (ff. 216).
1.   ff. 1-21. John Farleigh; 1933-1938.

2.   ff. 22-69. Sir Johnston Forbes-Robertson; 1897-1935.

3.   ff. 70-85. Curtis P. Freshel; 1937-1950.

4.   ff. 86-100. Roger Fry; 1912-1926.

5.   ff. 101-170v. Harley Granville Barker and his first wife, Lillah McCarthy; 1905-1943.

6.   ff. 171-216v. Lady Gregory; 1909-1925, n.d.

50535-50537. Letters of Elinor Huddart.

    50535. (ff. 305). 1878-1882.

    50536. (ff. 230). 1883.

    50537. (ff. 162). 1884-1894.

50538. (ff. 216).

1.   ff. 1-7. Lord Haldane; 1900-1919.

2.   ff. 8-17v. Rev. James Hannay *al.* 'George A. Birmingham'; 1908-1912.

3.   ff. 18-27v. Keir Hardie; 1906-1914.

4.   ff. 28-56. Frank Harris and his widow Helen (Nellie) Harris (correspondence of and concerning); 1898-1941.

5.   ff. 57-74. Austin Harrison; 1910-1912. Mainly *typewritten copies* of Shaw's letters to Harrison.

6.   ff. 75-88v. Annie E. F. Horniman (correspondence of and concerning); 1907-1912, 1937.

7.   ff. 89-152v. Henry Mayers Hyndman (correspondence of and concerning); 1884-1921. Partly *draft* and *copy.*

8.   ff. 153-199v. Dean W. R. Inge and his wife Mary Catherine Inge; 1921-1950.

9.   ff. 200-216. Laurence Irving, younger son of Sir Henry Irving, and other members of the Irving family; 1896-1946.

50539. (ff. 208).

1.   ff. 1-27v. Frederick Jackson; 1910-1914. Partly *copy.*

2.   ff. 28-38. Augustus John; 1915-1944.

3.   ff. 39-102v. Gertrude Kingston; 1912-1916.

4.   ff. 103-146v. Correspondence between Shaw, Lawrence Langner, and other members of the Theatre Guild of New York, concerning productions of 'Back to Methuselah' and 'St. Joan'; 1921-1943. Mainly *typewritten copies.*

5.   ff. 147-164. Roy Limbert; 1938-1949.

6.   ff. 165-174. Emil Ludwig and his wife Elga; 1932-1948, n.d.

7.   ff. 175-208v. Hon. Mrs. Alfred Lyttelton; 1909-1913, n.d. Partly *typewritten.*

50540. (ff. 100). Letters (and *copies* of same) of Shaw to T. E. Lawrence; 1922-1924; together with papers relating to Lawrence; 1935-1945. See also 56497, ff. 67-96.

50541. (ff. 99).
1. ff. 1-30. William Morris (correspondence of and concerning); 1884-1896. Partly *printed*.
2. ff. 31-99. May Morris, daughter of William Morris; 1885-1913.

50542. (ff. 90). Letters to Shaw from Professor Gilbert Murray and his wife Lady Mary Murray; 1900-1950.

50543. (ff. 207).
1. ff. 1-30v. Charles Alfred McEvoy; 1907-1927.
2. ff. 31-54. Dame Laurentia McLachlan; 1930-1950.
3. ff. 55-87v. Richard Mansfield; 1895-1898.
4. ff. 88-93. John Masefield; 1907-1946.
5. ff. 94v-102. Henry William Massingham; 1887-1900, n.d.
6. ff. 103-108. Sean O'Casey; 1940-1950.
7. ff. 109-207. Sydney Olivier (correspondence of and concerning); 1887-1944.

50544, 50545. Letters of Mrs. Jenny Paterson.

 50544. (ff. 190). 1882-1886.

 50545. (ff. 183). 1887-1888.

50546. (ff. 79). Letters of and concerning Mrs. Kate Perugini; 1927-1943.

50547. (ff. 195).
1. ff. 1-13. Hesketh Pearson; 1938-1944. Partly *fragment* and *typewritten copy*.
2. ff. 14-53. Marjory Davidson afterwards Pease; 1888-1946.
3. ff. 54-125. Sir Arthur Pinero; 1908-1917.
4. ff. 126-181. Sir Horace Plunkett; 1915-1920. Partly *shorthand* and *typewritten drafts* and *copies?*
5. ff. 182-195v. William Poel; 1909-1919. Partly *typewritten copy* and *shorthand draft*.

50548. (ff. 200).
1. ff. 1-44v. Ada Rehan and Lady Christine Barrington; 1904, 1905.
2. ff. 45-114. Charles Ricketts; 1907-1926, n.d.

3.   ff. 115-133. J. M. Robertson; 1885-1927.
4.   ff. 134-176. Correspondence of Auguste Rodin with G. B. and C. F. Shaw; 1906-1914. *French.* Partly *draft.* Preceded by *typewritten copies* of letters of Rainer Maria Rilke.
5.   ff. 177-182. Romain Rolland and his wife Marie; 1914-1919, 1949. *French.*
6.   ff. 183-200. George William Russell *al.* 'A. E.'; 1914-1934.

50549. (ff. 245).
1.   ff. 1-50. Henry Stephens Salt (correspondence of and concerning); 1889-1950.
2.   ff. 51-93. Henri Seiffert; 1888-1920.
3.   ff. 94-115. Upton Sinclair and his wife Mary; 1911-1942.
4.   ff. 116-210v. Letters of Alfred Charles *al.* 'Pharall' Smith, his wife and daughter; 1890-1941.
5.   ff. 211-228. W. T. Stead; 1887-1911.
6.   ff. 229-245. Henry Sweet; 1901-1911.

50550. (ff. i+246). Letters of Shaw to his wife Charlotte Frances; 1896-1934. *Typewritten copies.* The originals are 46505, 46506.

50551. (ff. 117).
1.   ff. 1-36. Molly Tompkins and her husband Laurence Tompkins; 1933?-1946.
2.   ff. 37-78. Sir Herbert Beerbohm Tree, his daughter Viola Tree, and his widow Lady Maud Tree; 1892-1935.
3.   ff. 79-89v. Frederick Herbert Trench; 1908-1917.
4.   ff. 90-117. George Sylvester Viereck and his son Peter Viereck; 1924-1947.

50552. (ff. 70). Correspondence of H. G. Wells with G. B. and C. F. Shaw; 1901-1941.

50553. (ff. 168).
1.   ff. 1-29. Graham Wallas; 1889?-1929.
2.   ff. 30-64. Diana Watts; 1923-1950.
3.   ff. 65-108. Sidney Webb, Baron Passfield; 1883-1938. Partly *copy.*
4.   ff. 109-117v. Beatrice Webb, Lady Passfield; 1913-1942.
5.   ff. 118-131. Sir Almroth Edward Wright; 1906-1943.
6.   ff. 132-141v. Sir Charles Wyndham; 1895-1911.
7.   ff. 142-167. W. B. Yeats; 1901-1932. Partly *typewritten copy.* A letter from Richard Ellmann of 1946 is at f. 168.

50554-50556. Letters and papers relating to phonetics and spelling reform.

    50554. (ff. 257). 1852-1942.

    50555. (ff. 140). 1943-1945.

    50556. (ff. 242). 1946-1956, n.d.

50557. (ff. 317). Letters and papers relating to the Fabian Society; 1884-1944.

50558-50560. Shorthand drafts of letters by Shaw.

    50558. (ff. 183). 1886-June 1908.

    50559 A. (ff. 1-196). Nov. 1908-23 March 1909.

    50559 B. (ff. 197-395). 25 March 1909- Jan. 1910.

    50560. (ff. 250). Feb. 1910-1917, n.d.

50561, 50562. Ashley Dukes Copies. Selection of letters made by Ashley Dukes, dramatist, theatre manager, and friend of Shaw, from the collection of originals in the possession of Gabriel Wells, dealer in rare books and manuscripts. The selection was intended for publication, but the project had lapsed by 1929, when Shaw made it clear that he would not allow his letters to be published in his lifetime. *Typewritten copies.*

    50561. (ff. 157). 1888-1900.

    50562. (ff. 235). 1901-1928.

50563. (ff. 39). Greeting cards, etc.; 1877-1950.

50564, 50565. Letters and memoranda of Shaw's biographers.

    50564. (ff. 138). Correspondence of Shaw with Professor Archibald Henderson; 1905-1946. Professor Henderson's publications relating to Shaw include: *Interpreters of Life and the Modern Spirit* (1911), *European Dramatists* (1914), *Contemporary Immortals* (1930), *Bernard Shaw, Playboy and Prophet* (1932), and *G. B. Shaw: Man of the Century* (1956).

    50565. (ff. 285).
    1.   ff. 1-119. Correspondence of Shaw with Professor Demetrius O'Bolger; 1910-1922. Professor O'Bolger died in 1923, some months after Shaw had refused to endorse his manuscript biography for publication.
    2.   ff. 120-285. Miscellaneous letters to Dr. F. E. Loewenstein, and

memoranda relating to Shaw; 1946-1948. Towards the end of Shaw's life, Dr. Loewenstein acted as his literary secretary. He published *Bernard Shaw through the Camera* (1948), *The Pictorial Record of the Life of Bernard Shaw* (1950), and *The Rehearsal Copies of Bernard Shaw's Plays* (1950).

C.   WORKS BY OTHER AUTHORS.

50566. (ff. i+117). James Bridie, 'It Depends What You Mean'; play, 1944 (published 1948). *Typewritten.*

50567. (ff. i+148). Rosie Dobbs, sister of Beatrice Webb, untitled autobiography; written between 1943-1947. *Typewritten.*

50568. (ff. 54). Harley Granville-Barker, 'Vote by Ballot'; play, 1914 (published in 'Three Short Plays', 1917). *Typewritten*; ff. 1-4, *MS.* notes.

50569-50575. Works in *French* by Augustin Frédéric Hamon, translator of Shaw's works; partly in collaboration with his wife Henriette Hamon.

> **50569.** (ff. 96). 'Le Testament d'Yves Lecoz'; n.d. Unpublished play. *Typewritten.*

> **50570.** (ff. 113). 'Le Mariage'; n.d. *Translation,* with Henriette Hamon, of Shaw's 'Getting Married', written in 1908. *Typewritten.*

> **50571.** (ff. 188). 'Pygmalion', n.d. *Translation*, with Henriette Hamon, of Shaw's play, written 1912-1913. Two *copies.*
> 1.   ff. 1-98. *Typewritten*, with *MS. amendments.*
> 2.   ff. 99-188. *Typewritten.*

> **50572.** (ff. 42). 'La Grande Catherine'; n.d. *Translation* of Shaw's play 'Great Catherine', written in 1913. *Typewritten*, with *MS. amendments.* Shaw's own amendments are at ff. 3-8.

> **50573.** (ff. 396). *Translation* of *The Intelligent Woman's Guide to Socialism*, written by Shaw in 1928. Part II only. *Typewritten.*

> **50574.** (ff. 238). Lectures on: 'The Devil's Disciple'; 'Caesar and Cleopatra'; 'You Never Can Tell'; 'John Bull's Other Island'; 'Man and Superman'; 'Widowers' Houses'; given at the Sorbonne 1910-1912. *Typewritten,* with Hamon's *MS. notes.*

> **50575.** (ff. 85). 'La Comédie'. Lectures given at Birkbeck College, London; 1916. *Typewritten.*

50576. (ff. 201). Frank Harris, 'On the Trail' (published 1930). *Typewritten.*

50577. (ff. 202). Frank Herbert Hayward, section of an unpublished book on Shaw; n.d. *Typewritten.*

50578. (ff. 16). Lawrence Langner, 'St. Bernard and St. Joan'; 1924. Unpublished play. *Typewritten.*

50579. (ff. 38). Untitled play by the children of Beacon Hill School, near Bath; 1940. *Typewritten.* Preceded by a letter to Shaw of Dora Russell.

50580. (ff. i+48). Marie Stopes, 'Antigone Awakened'; 1946. Unpublished play. *Typewritten.* Preceded by an *autograph* note to Shaw and an introductory essay on the subject of drama.

50581. (ff. 80). Siegfried Trebitsch, 'Ein Muttersohn'. Play in English *translation*, (published in Berlin, 1911). *Typewritten.*

D.   PHOTOGRAPHS RELATING TO SHAW.

50582 A, B. (ff. 173). Photographs mainly of G. B. Shaw; 1878?-1950, n.d. Including *printed extracts* from newspapers and periodicals.

 50582 A. (ff. 1-83). 1878?-1932, n.d.

 50582 B. (ff. 84-173). 1932-1950, n.d.

50583. (ff. i+15). Shaw's family; *circa* 1800-1937.

50584, 50585. Shaw's friends; 1887-1950, n.d. The albums have been laid out in roughly alphabetical order.

 50584 A. (ff. 1-87). A-I.

 50584 B. (ff. 88-147). J-N.

 50585. (ff. 132). O-Y and unidentified.

50586. (ff. 96).
1. ff. 1-42. Shaw's visit to Russia; 1931.
2. ff. 43-96. Other journeys, and places in Ireland associated with Shaw; 1908-1950, n.d.

50587. (ff. 30). Illustrations for 'Sixteen Self Sketches'; published 1949.

50588-50592. Productions of Shaw's plays. For names of persons represented, names of photographers, titles of plays and dates of productions, see Index.

> **50588.** (ff. 119). 'Androcles and the Lion', 'Arms and the Man', 'Back to Methuselah', 'Caesar and Cleopatra', 'Candida', 'Captain Brassbound's Conversion', and Anatole France, 'The Man who Married a Dumb Wife'; 1915?-1950.
>
> **50589.** (ff. 150). 'The Devil's Disciple', 'The Doctor's Dilemma', 'Heartbreak House', 'Major Barbara', 'Man and Superman'; 1915-1950.
>
> **50590.** (ff. 47). 'The Philanderer', 'Pygmalion', 'St. Joan', 'Shakes versus Shav'; 1914-1949.
>
> **50591.** (ff. 22). 'St. Joan' at Budapest; 1936.
>
> **50592.** (ff. 20).
> 1.   ff. 1-11. Fourth Annual Midsummer Drama Festival, Pasadena; 1938.
> 2.   ff. 12-18. Tsukiji Theatre, [Kobe?], Japan; 1926, 1927. Followed by unidentified material.

PRINCIPAL SERIES OF SHAW PAPERS

50593-50743. Purchased from the residuary legatees of G. B. Shaw, 9 April 1960, and incorporated in the Department of Manuscripts 8 March 1961.
   One hundred and fifty volumes classified as follows:

A.   Plays of G. B. Shaw: 50593-50649.

B.   Poems, Novels and Short Stories: 50650-50658.

C.   Critical Writings and Essays: 50659-50679.

D.   Fabian Society: 50680-50690.

E.   Newspaper and Periodical Articles: 50691-50699.

F.   Lectures: 50700-50705.

G.   Autobiographical Writings and Biographical Memoranda: 50706-50718.

H.   Notebooks and Drafts: 50719-50739.

I.   Miscellanea: 50740-50743.

A.   PLAYS OF G. B. SHAW.

In autograph longhand unless otherwise stated, and in chronological order.

50593. (ff. i+76). Passion Play; 1878.

50594. (ff. 102). 'Widowers' Houses'; 1884. *Shorthand.*

50595 A, B. 'The Cassone'; 1889-1890.

> **50595 A.** (ff. 93). At ff. 92v-80v, reading from the end, are notes for a review of F. Fyles's and D. Belasco's 'The Girl I Left Behind Me'; 1895.

> **50595 B.** (ff. 24). *Typewritten.*

50596 A-G. (ff. 100, 61, 80, 56, 83, 48, i+47). 'The Philanderer'; 1892-1893.

50597. (ff. 45). *The Philanderer* (1906). *Published* copy, with *autograph* rehearsal notes; n.d.

50598 A-C. (ff. 103, 74, 57). 'Mrs. Warren's Profession'; 1893.

50599. (ff. 74). 'Mrs. Warren's Profession'; proofs, etc. for the *Collected Edition of the Works of Bernard Shaw,* Vol. 7 (1930). Pages 179-180 of the publication contain additional material not present in this volume. Folios 13, 77-79 are corrected in another hand.
1. ff. 1-42. Playscript; 1894. *Printed,* with *autograph* revisions.
2. ff. 43–53v. Preface, 'Mainly About Myself'; 1898. *Printed* and *typewritten,* with *autograph* revisions.
3. ff. 54–74. Preface and 'Author's Apology'; *typewritten* insertions of 1930, together with *printed* texts of 1902 and 1907; all with *autograph* corrections. See also 50664, ff. 1-4.
This volume was rearranged and refoliated in 2002-2003.

50600. (ff. i+135). *Plays: Pleasant and Unpleasant,* Vol. 1 (1900). At ff. 96v-131v, 'Mrs. Warren's Profession' is annotated with *autograph* rehearsal notes; n.d.

50601 A-C. (ff. 81, 80, 40). 'Arms and the Man'; 1893. At ff. 40v-37v, reading from the end, are political lecture notes; n.d. See also 50643, ff. 1-47.

50602. (ff. 40). *Arms and the Man* (1905). *Published* copy, with *autograph* rehearsal notes; n.d.

50603 A-C. (ff. 69, 56, 53). 'Candida'; 1894.

50604. (ff. 116). 'The Man of Destiny'; 1895.

50605 A-C. (ff. 94, 94, 122). 'You Never Can Tell'; 1895.

50606 A-D. 'The Devil's Disciple'; 1896-1897.

50606 A. (ff. 5). Scenario, mainly *shorthand.*

50606 B-D. (ff. 60, 59, 66). *Autograph* playscript.

50607. (ff. 108). 'The Devil's Disciple', producer's copy, Queen's Theatre, 1907. *MS.* (hand unidentified), interleaved with *printed* and *typewritten* text, all with *MS.* amendments. See also 50643, ff. 48-54.

50608. (ff. iv+46). 'The Gadfly or, the Son of the Cardinal', dramatisation of novel by Ethel Voynich; 1898. *Typewritten,* with a few *autograph* production notes.

50609 A-D. (ff. 58, 61, 95, 17). 'Caesar and Cleopatra'; 1898.

50610. (ff. 164). 'Caesar and Cleopatra'.
1.   ff. 1-106. Parts of Caesar, Cleopatra, the Centurion and Ptolemy; 1899? *Typewritten.*
2.   ff. 107-123. Prologue; 1912. *Shorthand.*
3.   ff. 124-135v. Prologue; 1912. *Printed*, with *autograph* corrections.
4.   ff. 136-141. Prologue; 1930. *Printed,* with a few *autograph* notes.
5.   ff. 142-152. Prologue; 1926, n.d. *Typewritten,* with *autograph* amendments.
6.   ff. 153-164. Notes for film production; 1944-1945. *Typewritten,* with *autograph* amendments.

50611. (ff. 67). *Caesar and Cleopatra* (1904). *Published* copy, with *autograph* rehearsal notes; n.d.

50612 A-C. (ff. 61, 73, 62). 'Captain Brassbound's Conversion'; 1899.

50613. (ff. 45). 'The Admirable Bashville', prompt book for Stage Society performances; 1903. *Typewritten,* with some *autograph* rehearsal notes.

50614. (ff. 51). 'How he lied to her husband'; 1904.

50615. (ff. 60). 'John Bull's Other Island'.
1.   ff. 1-6. 'Instructions to the Producer'; 1904.
2.   ff. 7-60. Preface to the Home Rule edition; 1912. *Shorthand* (ff. 7-15), *typewritten* and *printed,* with *autograph* revisions.

50616 A-E. (ff. 80, 80, 58, 58, 52). 'Major Barbara'; 1905.

50617. (ff. 306). 'Major Barbara', filmscript; 1940-1941. Mainly *typewritten,* with *MS.* additions in Shaw's and others' hands. Includes some *fragments* and *shorthand*. At f. 21 Shaw's personal prologue, written as a trailer to the film, and relating to the progress of World War II, is reproduced in a cutting from *Variety*. At ff. 301-306 is a *copy* of the Ode, 'We forge our own destruction', arranged from 'Dall tuo stellato soglio' in the finale of Rossini's opera 'Il Mosé in Egitto'.

50618. (ff. 238). 'Major Barbara', screen version prepared for publication; 1941. Folios 2-15 are *printed* galley proofs in a different font, and with some different wording from the published versions of 1945-1949. Folios 16-150 are page proofs for pp. i-xxxvii and 1-147 of the 1945 edition. Folios 151-238 are the published playscript, *circa* 1930, with *autograph* corrections subsequently incorporated in the published screen version.

50619 A-D. (ff. i+61, 57, 61, 71). 'The Doctor's Dilemma'; 1906. See also 50643, ff. 77-97.

50620. (ff. 131). 'The Doctor's Dilemma', draft film script; n.d. *Typewritten.*

50621. (ff. 24). 'Getting Married', etc.; 1908. See also 50643, ff. 110-144.
1.   ff. 1-18. 'Getting Married'; *shorthand.*
2.   f. 19. Notes for preface to 'Fabian Essays'; *shorthand.*
3.   ff. 20-24. Miscellaneous notes, partly *fragment* and *shorthand.*

50622. (ff. 61).
1.   ff. 1-13. 'The Shewing up of Blanco Posnet'; 1909. *Shorthand* and *incomplete.* See also 50643, ff. 145-150.
2.   ff. 13*-60. 'Press Cuttings'; 1909. *Shorthand,* written in forward and reverse sequence. Miscellaneous notes are at f. 61.

50623. (ff. ii+98). 'Press Cuttings'; 1909? Two *typewritten* copies. The first, at ff. 1-49, has *MS.* additions and corrections in another hand; the second, at ff. 50-98, contains a slightly altered version of the preceding text.

50624. (ff. 47).
1.   ff. 1-44. 'Misalliance'; 1909. *Shorthand,* written in forward and reverse sequence. See also 50643, f. 181.
2.   ff. 45v-44v. Incomplete notes for a review; 1909? *Shorthand.* Miscellaneous notes are at ff. 46-47.

50625. (ff. 11). 'The Glimpse of Reality'; 1910. *Shorthand* and *incomplete.*

50626. (ff. 16).
1. ff. 1-10. 'The Dark Lady of the Sonnets'; 1914. *Printed proof* of 1910 with *autograph* corrections and additions.
2. ff. 11-16. Poem, 'The Dark Lady', author unknown; 1934. *Printed proof* with unidentified *MS.* amendments.

50627. (ff. 17). 'Androcles and the Lion', film scenario; 1950. *Typewritten.*

50628. (ff. 35). 'Pygmalion'.
1. ff. 1-4. Preface; 1916. *Typewritten draft* with *autograph* amendments, and *shorthand.*
2. ff. 5-35. Film scenario; 1934.

50629. (ff. 44). 'Pygmalion'; 1913 performing copy. *Printed* with *autograph* rehearsal notes; 1914?

50630. (ff. 19). 'Annajanska: the Wild Grand Duchess'; 1917. *Typewritten* with *autograph* corrections.

50631. (ff. 235). 'Back to Methuselah'; 1919-1945.
1. ff. 1-127. Preface and playscript; 1919-1920. *Shorthand.*
2. ff. 128-129. Lists of amendments to the Preface; 1921, n.d. *Autograph* and *typewritten.*
3. ff. 130-131. Blurb for Penguin book jacket; 1938. *Typewritten* with *autograph* corrections.
4. ff. 132-186. Preface; 1944-1945. *Printed* proof with *autograph* amendments.
5. ff. 187-192v. 'Introductory Note for Oxford University Press'; 1944. *Shorthand.*
6. ff. 193-228. Postscript; 1944. Two copies, *typewritten* with *autograph* alterations.
7. ff. 229-235. Cards to G. B. Shaw from Oxford University Press accompanying proofs; 1944-1945.
This volume was refoliated in 2002-2003, but the bound sequence is unchanged.

50632. (ff. 180). 'Back to Methuselah'; 1927-1928. *Printed* edition of 1927, with *autograph* amendments for the 1928 revival at ff. 65-91.

50633. (ff. 84). 'St. Joan'; 1923-1948, n.d.
1. ff. 1-28. *Fragments* of playscript and preface sent for publication; 1923. Mainly *typewritten* with *autograph* alterations. Folios 1-2 are brief *autograph* notes concerning their place and time of composition; 1926, 1944?

2.   ff. 29-41.   Transcript of B.B.C. Radio Schools broadcast on 'St. Joan';
      1942. Mainly *duplicated typescript.*
3.   ff. 42-46. B.B.C. broadcast; 1948. *Shorthand draft.*
4.   ff. 47-49. *Autograph* and *shorthand* note relating to, and *typewritten copy*
      of a letter of Monsignor M. Barbera, S.J., concerning the conditions on
      which the Catholic Authorities would not object to the showing of the
      film; 1935.
5.   ff. 50-53. *Autograph* pencil notes, apparently relating to the film script; n.d.
6.   ff. 54-84. Miscellaneous notes, some *autograph,* some in unidentified
      hands, together with postcards, etc., relating to Joan of Arc; n.d. At f. 64
      is a 'Domrémy medal' and at ff. 75-84 are further notes by Shaw on the
      history of the composition and performance of the play; *circa* 1944.

50634. (ff. 296). 'St. Joan', two copies of the film scenario; 1934? *Typewritten*
with *MS.* alterations in unidentified hands. Folios 1-168 are *typewritten* only,
and the text is almost identical to that beginning at f. 169; the latter has an
additional variant of the last sequence before the Epilogue and, at ff. 295-296,
the scenario for the 1920 canonisation. Some *MS.* additions appear to be dir-
ectorial; others relate to historical and canonical accuracy. See 50633, ff. 47-49.

50635. (ff. i+259). 'Too True to be Good'; 1931. *Shorthand* and *typewritten*
with *autograph* corrections.

50636. (ff. 44). 'Too True to be Good'; 1931. *Printed* rough proof with *autograph* corrections. Pages 9 and 10 have been excised and replaced by a printed
sheet bearing variant text (cf. 80808).

50637. (ff. i+55). 'The Simpleton [of the Unexpected Isles]'; 1934. *Shorthand.*
Folios 48-55 contain Shaw's reply, written for the Malvern Festival programme,
to the American critic Joseph Wood Krutch; 1935. *Printed proofs* with *autograph* corrections.

50638. (ff. i+31). 'The Millionairess'; 1934-1942.
1.   ff. 1-24. Playscript, mainly under the provisional title 'His Tragic Clients';
      1934. *Shorthand.*
2.   ff. 25-26. Alternative ending written speculatively for Soviet audiences;
      1936. *Typewritten* with *shorthand* additions.
3.   ff. 27-31. Narrator's opening for B.B.C. radio broadcast; 1942. *Type-
      written* with *autograph* alterations.

50639. (ff. 38). 'The Millionairess'. *Printed* rehearsal copy of 1940 with *autograph* revisions for B.B.C. production; 1942.

50640. (ff. 70). 'Geneva'. *Printed* rehearsal copy of 1938 revised in C. F. Shaw's hand. See also 50643, ff. 192-199.

50641. (ff. 162). 'Buoyant Billions'; 1936-1949.
1.   ff. 1-16. Prefaces; 1947-1949. *Shorthand, typewritten* with *autograph* revisions, and *printed proof* with *autograph* revisions. Two versions, dated 1947 and beginning at f. 2 and f. 11, preserve an earlier title, 'The World Betterer's Courtship'.
2.   ff. 17-60. Playscript; 1945. *Shorthand.*
3.   ff. 61-162. Playscript; dated 17/2/36 at f. 62, and 13/7/47 at f. 152. Entitled 'The World Betterer'. *Typewritten* with *autograph* revisions.

50642. (ff. 43). 'Farfetched Fables'; 1948.
1.   ff. 1-32. *Shorthand.*
2.   ff. 33-43. *Typewritten* with *autograph* amendments. Partly *fragment.*

50643. (ff. 203). Collection of miscellaneous material relating to plays, arranged in chronological order of the original date of composition.
1.   ff. 1-47. 'Arms and the Man'; 1923-1945.
   i.   ff. 1-8. Costume designs; line and coloured drawings; 1941?
   ii.   f. 9. Offstage dialogue for Act I; 1941?
   iii.   ff. 10-13. 'Instructions to Producer'; 1923. *Shorthand.*
   iv.   f. 14. Note by G. B. Shaw for Malvern Festival programme; 1932. *Printed proof* with *autograph* corrections.
   v.   ff. 15-26. Film sequences; 1941. *Shorthand.*
   vi.   ff. 27-42. Film sequences; 1941. *Typewritten* with *autograph* additions.
   vii.   ff. 43-47. Plot summary; 1945. *Typewritten* with *autograph* additions.
2.   ff. 48-54. 'The Devil's Disciple', film sequences; 1939. *Typewritten* with *autograph* additions.
3.   ff. 55-71. 'Man and Superman'; 1902.
   i.   ff. 55-70. Draft aphorisms for 'Maxims for Revolutionists'.
   ii.   ff. 71-71v. Fragment of dialogue.
4.   ff. 72-76v. 'Passion, Poison and Petrifaction, or the Fatal Gasolene'; 1905. Four illustrations in pen and ink wash by Harry Furniss, for his *Annual*; together with other pencil and ink sketches by Furniss.
5.   ff. 77-97. 'The Doctor's Dilemma', section of Preface; 1910. *Shorthand.*
6.   ff. 98-109v. 'The Inauguration Speech: An Interlude'; 1907. Written for Cyril Maude's opening of the Playhouse Theatre, and published in 1927 as 'The Interlude at the Playhouse'.
7.   ff. 110-144. 'Getting Married', Preface; 1910. *Shorthand.*

8.   ff. 145-150. 'The Shewing-up of Blanco Posnet', 'Memorandum for Censorship Committee' written for Preface; 1909. *Shorthand,* and *typewritten* with *autograph* alterations.

9.   ff. 151-161. 'Winifred', later re-titled 'The Fascinating Foundling'; 1909. *Shorthand.*

10.   ff. 162-180. Scenario for G. K. Chesterton; 1909. *Duplicated autograph*, followed by *typescript.* An *autograph* note at f. 162 indicates that the latter copy was made in 1938.

11.   f. 181. 'Misalliance', corrections for prompt copy; 1910? *Autograph carbon copy.*

12.   ff. 182-185. Sketches by J. M. Barrie; 1914. *Typewritten carbon copies.*

13.   ff. 186-189v. 'Glastonbury Skit [Gag]'; 1916.

14.   f. 190. 'Jitta's Atonement', plan of stage arrangement; 1923?

15.   ff. 191-191v. 'On the Rocks', list of characters; 1933? On *verso* are notes on pronunciation under the headings 'Major Elliott's broadcast' and 'Phonetics'; 1930s?

16.   ff. 192-199. 'Geneva'.
   i.   ff. 192-193. Note by G. B. Shaw for Malvern Festival programme; 1938. *Printed proof* with *autograph* corrections.
   ii.   ff. 194-195. 'Televised introduction to Act III'; 1939. *Typewritten* with *autograph* amendments.
   iii.   ff. 196-199. G. B. Shaw, 'Further Meditations on Shaw's Geneva'; 1939? *Typewritten.*

17.   ff. 200-203. Miscellany.
   i.   ff. 200-200v. Cast lists for copyright performance of 'The Philanderer', 'Mrs. Warren's Profession', 'The Gadfly' and 'You Never Can Tell'; 1898. Unidentified hand.
   ii.   ff. 201-202. *Fragment* of dialogue; 1940. *Typewritten.*
   iii.   f. 203. Suggested cast for 'Business', [unwritten play?]; 1920s? *Typewritten* with *autograph* additions.

50644-50648. Rehearsal notes; 1911-1937, n.d. See also 50730-50736, and 50739.

   50644. (ff. 356).
   1.   ff. 1-8. 'Arms and the Man'; 1911.
   2.   ff. 9-22. 'Fanny's First Play', Kingsway Theatre; 1915. *Typewritten copy.*
   3.   ff. 23-30. 'Augustus Does His Bit'; 1917. *Typewritten copy.*
   4.   ff. 31-32. 'The Inca of Perusalem'; 1917. *Typewritten copy.*
   5.   ff. 33-35. 'Annajanska' [here 'Anneganeka']; 1918. *Typewritten copy.*
   6.   ff. 36-55. 'Pygmalion', Strand Theatre; 1920.

7.   ff. 56-59. 'Candida', Holborn Empire; 1920. Ends halfway down the page.

8.   ff. 59-60. 'Pygmalion', Academy of Dramatic Art; 1920. Ends halfway down the page.

9.   ff. 60-66. 'The Shewing up of Blanco Posnet', Royal Academy of Dramatic Art; 1923.

10.   ff. 67-69. 'Great Catherine'; n.d., followed by 'You Never Can Tell'; 1920. *Typewritten copy.*

11.   ff. 70-101. 'John Bull's Other Island', Court Theatre; 1921. *Typewritten copy.*

12.   ff. 102-126. 'Heartbreak House'; 1921. Ends halfway down the page.

13.   ff. 126-129. 'Getting Married', Everyman Theatre; 1922.

14.   ff. 130-166. 'St. Joan'; 1924.

15.   ff. 167-182. 'Caesar and Cleopatra', Birmingham; 1925. Ends halfway down the page.

16.   ff. 177v, 180v-183v. Dialogue under the heading 'Lewis's Jazz Comedy, Everyman Theatre, Hampstead, 18/2/27'. In reverse sequence.

17.   ff. 182-206. 'Mrs. Warren's Profession', Strand Theatre; 1926. f. 197 includes 'Gags for Fanny's First Play, p. 210'.

18.   ff. 207-211. Shakespeare's 'Macbeth'; 1926.

19.   ff. 212-219. 'Major Barbara', Wyndham's Theatre; 1929.

20.   ff. 220-222. 'Back to Methuselah', Old Vic for Malvern; 1929. Ends halfway down the page.

21.   ff. 222-226. 'Heartbreak House', Old Vic; 1929.

22.   ff. 227-237. 'Heartbreak House', the Queen's Theatre; 1932.

23.   ff. 238-254. 'Too True To Be Good', Old Vic for Malvern Festival; 1932.

24.   ff. 255-286. 'On the Rocks'; 1933.

25.   ff. 287-295. 'The Six of Calais' and 'Androcles and the Lion', Regent's Park; 1934. Notes on both plays on most of these folios.

26.   ff. 296-298. 'Major Barbara', Old Vic; 1935.

27.   ff. 299-302. 'St. Joan', Birmingham for Malvern Festival; 1936.

28.   ff. 303-308. 'Pygmalion', Birmingham for Malvern Festival; 1936. The second half of f. 305, with f. 306, contains notes for 'On the Rocks' at the same theatre.

29.   ff. 309-310. 'The Millionairess', Malvern; 1937.

30.   ff. 311-313. 'The Apple Cart', Malvern; 1937.

31.   ff. 314-356. 'Great Catherine'; 1921. *Photocopied autograph.*

This volume was rearranged and refoliated in 2002-2003.

50645-50647. (ff. 60, 37+i, 35). 'The Apple Cart', 'Back to Methuselah', 'Heartbreak House', 'Caesar and Cleopatra'; 1929. Three notebooks used in forward and reverse sequence.

50648. (ff. i+19). 'Misalliance'; 1930?

50649. (ii+61). Notebook containing lists of theatrical companies permitted to perform Shaw's plays between 1897 and 1925, apparently commenced in 1915. Mainly in the hand of Ann Elder, with a few additions by Blanche Patch and by Shaw, and including a small quantity of correspondence. See also 56627-56637.

B.   POEMS, NOVELS AND SHORT STORIES.

50650. (ff. 121). Poems, epigrams and notes on novels; 1883-1946, n.d.
1.   ff. 1-20. Poems; 1883-1943, n.d. Partly *typewritten*. Folio 5 is in another hand.
2.   ff. 21-97. Epigrams and aphorisms; 1939, n.d. Mainly *typewritten*.
3.   ff. 98-121. Notes on manuscript novels presented to the National Library of Ireland in 1946. Partly *shorthand* and *typewritten*.

50651-50653. 'Immaturity'. See also 50650, ff. 98-121 *passim*; 50721 A, ff. 110v-112v; 55410, ff. 161-162; 55934, pp. 131-133.

   50651. (ff. i+49). Preface; 1930. *Typewritten*, with *autograph* note at f. i.

   50652. (ff. ii+323). Books I – II; n.d. *Typewritten*.

   50653. (ff. ii+365). Books III – IV; n.d. *Typewritten*.

50654. (ff. 36). 'The Irrational Knot', Preface; 1905. See also 50650, ff. 98-121 *passim*; 50721 A, ff. 100v-103; 55935, p. 34.

50655 A, B. (ff. ii+32, 101). 'Cashel Byron's Profession'; 1882-1883. *Shorthand.* See also 50650, ff. 98-121 *passim*; 50721 A, ff. 76v-78v, 86v-90.

50656. (ff. 103). 'An Unsocial Socialist'; 1883. *Shorthand.* See also 50721 A, ff. 82v-83.

50657. (ff. i+52). Unfinished novel; n.d. *Typewritten.*

50658. (ff. 163). Short stories, etc.; 1885-1937.
1.   ff. 1-108v. Stories Nos. 1-6 of 'Short Stories, Scraps and Shavings', (1932); 1885-1916. Partly *typewritten* and *printed*.

2. ff. 109-154. 'The Black Girl's Search for God' (published as *The Adventures of the Black Girl in her Search for God*); 1932. Mainly *shorthand*. At ff. 152-154 are *pencil* drawings by Shaw.
3. ff. 155-163v. Letters of Shaw to John Farleigh concerning illustrations for 'The Black Girl'; 1932. Printed in 'The London Mercury', March 1937.

C.   CRITICAL WRITINGS AND ESSAYS

50659. (ff. ii+90). *The Quintessence of Ibsenism* (1891); *published* copy with *autograph* corrections.

50660. (ff. 182). 'The Quintessence of Ibsenism'; 1890-1913.
1. ff. 1-22v. Letters to Shaw concerning Ibsen; 1890-1897.
2. ff. 25-182. Additions and corrections for the 1913 edition. *Shorthand, and typewritten* with *autograph* corrections.
This volume was refoliated in 2002-2003, but the bound sequence is unchanged.

50661. (ff. 99). Fabian lecture material; 1890-1906.
1. ff. 1-44. Material discarded from Shaw's Fabian lectures on Ibsen when publishing 'The Quintessence of Ibsenism'; 1890. *Typewritten* with *autograph* corrections.
2. ff. 45-99. Material discarded from Shaw's Fabian lectures on Darwin when publishing the Preface to 'Back to Methuselah'; 1906, n.d. *Typewritten* with *autograph* corrections.

50662. (ff. vii+136). Musical articles, etc., collected for an anthology; 1885-1945. Of these, only 'Critical Report on the Bands of the Salvation Army', at ff. 116-134, had not been previously published. Partly *shorthand, typewritten* and *printed*. At ff. ii-vii are C. F. Shaw's notes on publication details.

50663. (ff. 149). 'Religion and Religions', articles collected by Shaw for a publication which was not completed; 1896-1931, n.d. Only the following, written in 1922, had not been previously published: ff. 25-38, 'The Infancy of God'; ff. 39-66, 'On Ritual, Religion, & the Intolerableness of Tolerance'; ff. 67-92, 'The Church versus Religion'. *Typewritten* and *printed* with *autograph* corrections.

50664. (ff. 161). Prefaces by Shaw to his own works, and miscellaneous essays; 1906-1947, n.d. Partly *shorthand, typewritten* and *printed* with *autograph* corrections.
1. ff. 1-4. 'The Author's Apology'; 1906. See also 50599, ff. 54-79.
2. ff. 5-14. Preface to 'The Sanity of Art'; 1907.
3. ff. 15-74. Preface to the Collected Edition of 1921.

4.   ff. 75-105v. Materials prepared for the published edition of the corre-
      spondence of G. B. Shaw with Ellen Terry; *circa* 1929.
5.   ff. 106-116. Materials relating to the prospectus of the W. H. Wise
      Collected Edition; 1929-1931.
6.   ff. 117-134. Prefaces and postscripts; 1933-1935.
7.   ff. 135-142. Essays for the Malvern Festival; 1933-1939.
8.   ff. 143-145. Biographical essay on Florence Farr; 1941.
9.   ff. 146-151. 'Improving the National Anthem'; 1942, n.d.
10.   ff. 152-157. 'Pugilism', Prefatory Note; 1947, n.d.
11.   ff. 158-161. 'Pictures', Prefatory Note; 1940s?

50665. (ff. 310). Contributions and prefaces by Shaw to works by others;
1894-1942? Partly *shorthand, typewritten* and *printed*.
1.   ff. 1-18. Preface to 'The Theatrical "World" for 1894'.
2.   ff. 19-36. Chapter XXVII of Cyril Maude's 'The Haymarket Theatre'
      (1903); 1902.
3.   ff. 37-47. Preface to W. H. Davies, 'Autobiography of a Supertramp'
      (1908); 1907.
4.   ff. 48-60. Notes on Brieux and French drama; *circa* 1909-1911. See also
      50666.
5.   ff. 61-88. Preface to 'The W.E.A. Education Year Book 1918'.
6.   ff. 89-170. Preface to S. and B. Webb, 'English Prisons under Local
      Government'; 1921-1922.
7.   ff. 171-174. 'Mrs. Besant's Passage Through Fabian Socialism'; 1924?
8.   ff. 175-214. 'How William Archer Impressed Bernard Shaw'; 1926.
9.   ff. 215-227. Preface to G. H. Thring, 'The Marketing of Literary
      Property'; 1932.
10.   ff. 228-286. 'Morris as I Knew Him'; 1936. Marginal annotations in
      pencil between f. 268 and f. 286 are by William Morris's daughter May.
11.   ff. 287-302. Preface to Dickens, 'Great Expectations'; 1937?
12.   ff. 303-305. 'Ensor Walters'; 1937.
13.   ff. 306-308. Preface to MARS [Modern Architectural Research] Group
      catalogue, 'New Architecture' (1938); 1937.
14.   ff. 309-310. Comments on Moscow Trials drafted for, but not used in
      preface to S. and B. Webb, 'The Truth about Soviet Russia'; 1940?-1942.
This volume was refoliated in 2002-2003, but the bound sequence is unchanged.

50666. (ff. 59). Preface to Brieux's 'Three Plays'; 1909. *Shorthand.* See also
50665, ff. 48-60.

50667. (ff. i+125). 'Technical Socialism', 'a book which was never published';
circa 1900. Partly *typewritten.*

50668. (ff. 150). 'Common Sense about the War'; 1914-1915. *Shorthand* and *typewritten* with *autograph* corrections. The preface to the (unpublished) 1915 reprint is at ff. 146-150. See also 50483, ff. 78-88.

50669 A, B. (ff. 164, 161). 'More Commonsense about the War'; *circa* 1915-1918. *Shorthand* and *typewritten* with *autograph* corrections.

50670. (ff. 47). 'What I really said in the War'; 1930? Partly *shorthand;* mainly *typewritten* with *autograph* corrections.

50671 A, B. (ff. 121, 98). 'Peace Conference Hints', with, at f. 114, the preface to the French edition; 1918, 1919. *Shorthand* and *typewritten* with *autograph* corrections.

50672. (ff. 272). 'The Intelligent Woman's Guide to Socialism'; 1924-1927. Mainly *shorthand,* with some *typewritten* and *autograph* corrections.

50673. (ff. 61). 'The Intelligent Woman's Guide to Socialism', synopsis; 1925. At ff. 54v-60, in reverse sequence, are notes relating to the Collected Edition; 1929, 1930.

50674. (ff. ii+272). *The Intelligent Woman's Guide to Socialism and Capitalism* (1928). Published volume with *autograph* and *typewritten* corrections and insertions.

50675 A, B. 'Everybody's Political What's What?'; 1942-1944. *Typewritten* with *autograph* corrections.

    50675 A. (ff. 1-300).

    50675 B. (ff. 301-627).

50676. (ff. 90). 'The Rationalization of Russia', preface and first chapter only; 1932. Mainly *typewritten* with *autograph* corrections.

50677 A, B. Articles, lectures, etc., mainly *drafts; circa* 1889-1918.

    50677 A. (ff. 165).
       1.   ff. 1-25. 'Socialism, Utopian and Scientific'; 1892?
       2.   ff. 26-37. 'The Social Danger of Inequality; 1889?
       3.   ff. 38-57. 'Socialism and Property'; 1889?
       4.   ff. 58-63v. Answers to a questionnaire on socialism; 1892. *French.*
       5.   ff. 64-77. 'Advanced Socialism for Intelligent People'; 1909. Partly *shorthand* and *typewritten.*

6.   ff. 78-87. Drafts for a booklet on 'Equality'; n.d.

7.   ff. 88-92. Jotted notes for lectures on socialism; n.d.

8.   ff. 93-117. 'How to Settle the Irish Question', newspaper articles and pamphlet version; 1917.

9.   ff. 118-125. 'England's Extremity is Ireland's Opportunity'; 1916. *Typewritten.*

10.   ff. 138-165. 'War Issues for Irishmen: an open letter to Col. Arthur Lynch'; 1918. *Typewritten.*

50677 B. (ff. 30). Notebook containing draft chapter on education; n.d.

50678. (ff. 294). Miscellaneous correspondence and papers; 1892-1948.

1.   ff. 1-102. Correspondence and papers relating to vivisection; 1892-1948. Partly *printed, copy* and *draft.*

2.   ff. 103-168. Correspondence and papers relating to St. Pancras Vestry; 1894-1901, n.d. Partly *printed* and *typewritten draft.*

3.   ff. 169-230. Notes and reports on motor tours; 1909-1925. Partly *shorthand*, and *printed* and *typewritten copy.*

4.   ff. 231-294. Correspondence and papers relating to Roger Casement; 1916-1922. Including, at ff. 247v-254, Casement's *autograph* notes on G. B. Shaw's *typewritten* 'Rex vs. Casement', 1916; at ff. 265-275v is Shaw's *printed* pamphlet of 1922, 'A discarded defence of Roger Casement'.

50679. (ff. 399). Miscellaneous correspondence and papers; 1908-1950.

1.   ff. 1-125. Papers relating to the Society of Authors; 1908-1946.

2.   ff. 126-164. Papers relating to the Dramatists' Club; 1909, 1914, n.d. Partly *printed* and *shorthand.*

3.   ff. 165-318. Correspondence and papers relating to the Shakespeare Memorial National Theatre; 1908-1942. Partly *printed* and *typewritten copy.*

4.   ff. 319v-324. Papers of the B.B.C's Advisory Committee on Spoken English; 1931, 1936. *Typewritten.*

5.   ff. 325-374. Letters and papers relating to shorthand, phonetics and spelling reform; 1941-1948, n.d. Partly *printed.*

6.   ff. 375-385. 'Sixty Years in Business as an Author'; 1945. *Shorthand*, followed by *typewritten* with *autograph* corrections.

7.   ff. 386, 387. *Printed* subscription note of the Shaw Society, undated, and *typewritten draft* of G. B. Shaw relating to the American Shaw Society; 1950.

8.   ff. 388-399. Draft prospectus by G. B. Shaw for the British Music Society; 1918. *Shorthand.*

The sequence of the volume, from f. 351 onwards, was altered in 2002-2003.

D. FABIAN SOCIETY.

50680-50682. Memoranda, reports, ephemera, etc., of G. B. Shaw and others, relating to the affairs of the Fabian Society. Partly *printed, typewritten,* and *draft.*

> **50680.** (ff. 265). 1888-1906.
>
> **50681.** (ff. 337). 1907-1920, n.d.
>
> **50682.** (ff. i+52). 1903-1907.

50683-50688. Lectures by Shaw, given to or arranged by the Fabian Society. See also 50661; 50677 A, B.

> **50683.** (ff. i+173). 1885-1890.
>
> **50684.** (ff. 221). 1895-1907.
>
> **50685.** (ff. 269). 1908-1910.
>
> **50686.** (ff. 185). 1911-1913.
> *This volume was refoliated in 2002-2003, but the bound sequence is unchanged.*
>
> **50687.** (ff. 258). 1914-1916.
>
> **50688.** (ff. 285). 1917-1933, n.d.

50689. (ff. 209). Miscellaneous Fabian writings of G. B. Shaw, including, at ff. 20-39, prefaces to successive editions of *Fabian Essays*; 1888-1948, n.d. Partly *draft* and *printed.* See also 50621.

50690. (ff. 250). Fabian publications by Shaw and others; 1884-1930. Mainly *printed.*
1.   ff. 1-36v. Annual Reports for 1890, 1891, 1906, 1909.
2.   ff. 37-87. Report of the Special Committee appointed in 1906. Shaw's *autograph* underlinings and annotations are to be found between ff. 41v and 68. See also 50682.
3.   ff. 88-250. Fabian 'Tracts', Manifestos, etc.; 1884-1930.
The sequence of the volume, from f. 37 onwards, was altered in 2002-2003.

E. NEWSPAPER AND PERIODICAL ARTICLES.

50691. (ff. 109). Contributions to *The Hornet, The Dramatic Review,* and *The World*; 1876-1889. *Printed.*

50692. (ff. 79). Contributions to *The Pall Mall Gazette*; 1885-1888. *Printed.*

50693-50699. Other contributions on miscellaneous subjects, written for or published in newspapers and periodicals. Partly *shorthand, typewritten* and *printed.*

50693. (ff. 293). 1879-1901.	**50697.** (ff. 351). 1920-1932.
50694. (ff. 297). 1902-1907.	**50698.** (ff. 279). 1933-1943.
50695. (ff. 282). 1908-1915.	**50699.** (ff. 383). 1944-1950. n.d.
50696. (ff. 328). 1916-1919, n.d.	

F.   LECTURES.

50700-50705. Cards, handbills, notes and drafts for lectures and public addresses by Shaw, excluding those given for the Fabian Society, together with newspaper reports of speeches and meetings.

50700. (ff. 294). Cards; 1884-1888, n.d. *Printed.*

50701. (ff. 264). Bills and advertisements; 1886-1928, n.d. *Printed,* with *autograph* notes.

50702-50704. Drafts, notes, newspaper reports. Partly *printed* and *typewritten* with *autograph* amendments.

50702. (ff. 282). 1884?-1890.

50703. (ff. 237). 1892-1912.

50704. (ff. 278). 1913-1933, n.d.

50705. (ff. 129). Broadcasts; 1928-1947. Partly *shorthand, printed* and *typewritten* with *autograph* amendments.

G.   AUTOBIOGRAPHICAL WRITINGS AND BIOGRAPHICAL MEMORANDA.

50706. (ff. 180). 'Shaw Gives Himself Away'; 1939. Galley *proofs* and *type-written* with extensive *autograph* additions. *Incomplete.* Folios 167-180 comprise extracts from 'Bernard Shaw as a Clerk' (1908) not quoted in this publication.

50707 A, B, 50708. 'Sixteen Self Sketches'; 1949.

50707 A. (ff. 1-181). Preliminary draft. Mainly *typewritten* with *auto-graph* amendments; *incomplete.*

50707 B. (ff. 182-364). Preliminary draft. Partly *shorthand, typewritten* and *printed; incomplete.*

50708. (ff. 61). Galley proofs of preliminary draft (*incomplete*), with some *autograph* amendments and corrections.

50709. (ff. 152). Material discarded from 'Sixteen Self Sketches'. *Typewritten* with some *autograph* amendments.

50710 A, B.

50710 A. (ff. i+26). Autobiographical notes, etc.; 1877-1889, n.d. Partly *shorthand.* Bound notebook; ff. 18-26v are written in reverse sequence.

50710 B. (ff. 3). Autobiographical notes; 1876-1892. Partly *newsprint.*

50711 A, B.

50711 A. (ff. 231). Family history notes, medical reports, certificates of membership and other ephemera; 1889-1950? Partly *printed.*

50711 B. (ff. 170).
1.   ff. 1-130. Cheque-book stubs; 1911-1933.
2.   ff. 131-170. Motoring and travel documents; 1909-1947. Mainly *printed.*

50712. (ff. 140). Copies of Shaw's wills; 1901-1950. Partly *typewritten,* with *autograph* notes.

50713. (ff. 45). Form postcards and letters as sent by Shaw to correspondents; 1906-1944, n.d. *Printed* with some *typewritten drafts.*

50714. (ff. 282). Daily lists of correspondence to be dealt with, usually written by Shaw's secretaries but including some by Shaw; 1913, 1929-1941, n.d.

50715-50718. Address books, partly annotated in *shorthand.* The date ranges indicated are derived from Shaw's insertions.

50715. (ff. 135). 1887-1902.

50716. (ff. 54). 1883; 1891-1913.

50717. (ff. 54). 1912-1930.

50718. (ff. 56). 1932-1950. Folios 42-56 are miscellaneous loose lists and cards found elsewhere in the collection and inserted here during the course of the arrangement, including, at f. 42, a list of names, possibly guests, of 1903; and, at ff. 48-55, an undated 'Press List for theatrical paragraphs'.

H.   NOTEBOOKS AND DRAFTS.

50719. (ff. i+22). Juvenile drawings; 1871-1874, n.d.

50720. (ff. ii+13). Draft poem and personal memoranda; undated, included in *printed* diary for 1873.

50721 A, B. (ff. 123, 68). Draft poems, articles, letters, synopses of novels, printed leaflets, notes on music, shorthand exercises, etc.; 1877-1884, n.d. *Now bound together in one volume with two foliation sequences.*

50722. (ff. 74). Draft articles, lectures, letters and Fabian Society tracts, etc.; 1883-1889, n.d. Mainly *shorthand.*

50723. (ff. 26). Notes on miscellaneous subjects, arranged alphabetically, with *printed*, etc., inserts; 1886-1897, n.d.

50724. (ff. 24). Notes on the history of the socialist movement; *circa* 1890.

50725. (ff. ii+6). Draft poem and personal memoranda; 1892. Partly *shorthand.*

50726 A-C. (ff. ii+70, ii+79, 13). German exercises; 1893, n.d. Partly *type-written* and *printed.* 50726 A, ff. 45v-42v contain, in reverse sequence, a draft review of Henry James's play 'Guy Domville'; 1895.

50727. (ff. i+6). Miscellaneous notes and draft letter to the press; *circa* 1890.

50728. (ff. ii+32). Memoranda, list of photographs taken in France, etc.; at ff. 2-11 are rehearsal notes for 'The Man of Destiny'; at ff. 30-27, notes for 'The Revolutionist's Handbook'; 1901, n.d. Written in forward and reverse sequence.

50729. (ff. 25).
1.   ff. 1-14. Notes on vaccination; 1902, n.d.
2.   ff. 12v-24v. Notes on the Boer war; 1901? Written in reverse sequence.

50730. (ff. i+10). Personal memoranda, etc.; n.d. Notes on vaccination are at ff. 1-4; rehearsal notes for 'Mrs. Warren's Profession' at ff. 5v-6v.

50731. (ff. ii+39). Personal memoranda, and rehearsal notes as follows: ff. 6-17v, 18v, 'You Never Can Tell'; — f. 18, 'John Bull's Other Island'; — ff. ii, 33-19v, 'Candida'; 1904, n.d. Written in forward and reverse sequence.

50732. (ff. i+39). Miscellaneous notes and memoranda, together with: ff. 1-4v, rehearsal notes for 'John Bull's Other Island'; — ff. 6-7, 'The Philanderer'; — ff. 8-12, 'How he lied to her Husband'; — ff. 16-30, 38v-31v, 'You Never Can Tell'; — ff. 10v-8v, 28v- 16v, 30v, 31-35, 'Man and Superman'; — ff. 36-37, draft letter to Robert Loraine on the casting of 'Man and Superman'; *circa* 1903-1906. Written in forward and reverse sequence.

50733. (ff. 41). Personal memoranda, notes on discussions, etc., together with:. ff. 2-8, draft 'Maxims for Revolutionists', published in 1903; — f. 8v, notes for the preface to 'John Bull's Other Island'; — ff. 9-11, notes on Darwin and Marx 1905, n.d.; — ff. 14-22, 29v-16v, rehearsal notes for 'Major Barbara'; — ff. 36v-30v, rehearsal notes for 'Man and Superman'. Mainly n.d. Written in forward and reverse sequence.

50734. (ff. 88). Notes on debates, etc., and rehearsal notes, including: ff. 1v-2, 19v-21v, 27v-52 *passim*, 'The Philanderer'; — ff. 3-17, 21-25v, 'You Never Can Tell' ; — ff. 15v-19, 24-29, 33v-41v, 80-85, 'The Doctor's Dilemma'; — ff. 67v-53v, 'Captain Brassbound's Conversion'; — ff. 68v-72v, 75v-82v, 'Man and Superman'; — ff. 2v-4v, 78-74, draft letter to *The Daily Express*; 1909? Mainly n.d. Written in forward and reverse sequence.

50735. (ff. 42). Folios 1-21, rehearsal notes for 'Man and Superman' 1907; — ff. 21v-25v, draft letter to *The Times*, ('The Censor's Revenge'), 1909 (mainly *shorthand*); — ff. 22-33, draft preface to W. H. Davies, 'Autobiography of a Supertramp', 1908; — ff. 42v-34v, notes for 'Don Juan in Hell', 1907? Written in forward and reverse sequence.

50736. (ff. 42). Folios 1-39, Draft article, 'A Nation of Villagers'; — ff. 37v-30v, rehearsal notes for 'John Bull's Other Island'; — ff. 42v-38v, 30v-18v, rehearsal notes for 'The Devil's Disciple'; 1907, n.d. Written in forward and reverse sequence.

50737. (ff. 8). Memoranda, notes on own publications, draft letter to the press; *circa* 1908.

50738. (ff. ii+18). Folios 1-3, additional dialogue for 'Back to Methuselah', 1923; — ff. 4-14, notes on motoring in Scotland, n.d.; — ff. 15, 16, draft letters, 1927; — ff. 17, 18, list of prefaces, 1933.

50739. (ff. 13).   Letter in *shorthand draft, fragments* of dialogue and rehearsal notes; n.d.

I.   MISCELLANEA.

50740, 50741. Newscuttings, printed ephemera, etc., relating to Shaw but also to a variety of political, theatrical and medical topics.   Partly *French* and *German.*

> **50740.** (ff. 201). 1887-1930.

> **50741.** (ff. 309). 1875-1946, n.d. Not in strict chronological sequence.

50742. (ff. 234). Volume of miscellaneous pamphlets, discussion notes, etc., by writers other than Shaw; 1891-1948, n.d.   Partly *printed, duplicated,* and *typewritten.* Partly *German* and *Italian.*

50743 A, B. Volumes of miscellaneous notes and memoranda.

> **50743 A.** (ff. 1-218). 1883-1907?, n.d. Mainly on political and economic topics. Partly *shorthand.* Not in strict chronological sequence.

> **50743 B.** (ff. 219-447). 1883-1944, n.d. At ff. 363-367 are drawings thought to be stage sets for 'John Bull's Other Island'; f. 368 is a plan of scene for 'How He Lied to Her Husband'. Partly *shorthand.* Not in strict chronological sequence.

ACCESSIONS 1961-2004

Including further purchases from the residuary legatees, and gifts from the National Trust at Shaw's Corner, Ayot St. Lawrence.

50849 G. A sheet of *MS.* comments on drama, dated 1900, in which Shaw's handwriting has been imitated (f. 63). Part of a collection of forgeries (ff. 49-71v of a volume of miscellaneous Departmental acquisitions), presented by Sidney Hodgson, F.S.A., in 1961. See also 56364.

52365. (ff. 89). Correspondence of G. B. Shaw with Rutland Boughton; 1908-1950. Partly *draft, copy, typewritten* and *signed.* Includes one letter of C. F. Shaw, and a note of Constable & Co. of 1951. Volume II of the series 52364-52366, purchased in 1964 from Mrs. Kathleen Boughton. See also 50529, ff. 68-87v.

52556. Folios 143-169 are letters of G. B. and C. F. Shaw to Christabel Mary Melville, wife of Henry Duncan McLaren, 2nd Baron Aberconway; 1925-1930. They are part of Vol. VII of the series 52550-52556, presented by Lady Aberconway in 1959 and thereafter.

52752. Folios 212-324 are letters of and relating to G. B. and C. F. Shaw to Sir Sydney Carlyle Cockerell, Director of the Fitzwilliam Museum, Cambridge; 1901-1951. Partly *printed.* Part of volume CXXX of the series 52623-52773, the archive of diaries, correspondence and papers of Cockerell presented to the Department by Wilfrid Jasper Walter Blunt and Professor Francis Wormald in 1965. Correspondence with various members of Shaw's circle is to be found throughout the archive, covering the period 1923-1961. All writers are entered individually in the Index.

52929-53701. Playscripts from the Lord Chamberlain's office; 1851-1899. Including plays submitted for performing licence by Shaw himself, or by theatre managers on his behalf. For a later series, see 65534-68881. The plays by Shaw are listed in Section 7, Lord Chamberlain's Plays and Correspondence, below. Incorporated in 1965.

54786-56035. Correspondence and papers of the publishing firm of Macmillan and Company, purchased from the company in July 1967; 19th-20th cent. The locations of correspondence with Shaw 1880-1937, and readers' reports on manuscripts submitted by him 1880-1885, are detailed in the Index, in the entry for Macmillan & Co., and under the heading Shaw: Novels, Poems and Short Stories, in alphabetical order of title.

56105 J. Letters and postcards from G. B. Shaw to Professor William Alexander Robson of the London School of Economics and Dorothy Robson, his sister; 1912-1930. At ff. 67-76 of a volume of miscellaneous Departmental acquisitions. Presented by Professor Robson in April 1970.

56105 S. Letter from Evelyne D. Scott to G. B. Shaw, endorsed with his reply; 1938. There is an error in the date of Miss Scott's letter. At f. 125 of the same miscellaneous volume as the preceding. Presented by Miss Scott in March 1970.

56364. (ff. 16). Forgeries of Shaw's handwriting, with related material; 1876-1945. Purchased from T. G. R. Lawrence & Son, May 1970. See also 50849.
1. ff. 1-3. Letter of the pianist Annette Essipoff, 1876, followed by G. B. Shaw's note of 1940 describing her musicianship and explaining his use of her surname for a pseudonymous article in the *Daily Herald* of 1930.
2. ff. 4, 5. Forged MS. of this article, to which Shaw has appended a note concerning its inauthenticity; 1940.
3. f. 6. *Daily Herald* article, 'Bernard Shaw's Russian'; 7 April 1930. *Newsprint.*
4. ff. 7-16. Correspondence with booksellers, together with five further sheets of forged MSS., etc.; 1945-1970, n.d.

CHARLOTTE SHAW PAPERS.

56490-56526. Correspondence and papers of and concerning Charlotte Frances Shaw, *née* Payne-Townshend; 1822-1946, n.d. Thirty-seven volumes. Purchased from the residuary legatees of G. B. Shaw, 27 Feb. 1971. See also 63179-63203.

56490-56494. General correspondence of C. F. Shaw; 23 Dec. 1877-29 May 1943, n.d. Includes a few items addressed to G. B. Shaw, or to Mr. and Mrs. Shaw jointly.

> **56490.** (ff. 170). 23 Dec. 1877-12 May 1898, n.d.

> **56491.** (ff. 270). 21 June 1898-18 Dec. 1917.

> **56492.** (ff. 230). 9 Feb. 1918-23 Dec. 1931, n.d.; with enclosures dated 1914-1917.

> **56493.** (ff. 205). 10 Jan. 1932-2 May 1937.

> **56494.** (ff. 227). 6 June 1938-29 May 1943, n.d.

56495-56499. Correspondence and papers relating to T. E. Lawrence; *circa* 1921-1938.

> **56495, 56496.** *Typewritten copies* of letters from T. E. Lawrence to C. F. Shaw, together with some from T. E. Lawrence to G. B. Shaw, of which the originals are 45903, 45904; 8 Jan. 1923-31 Jan. 1935. Included are copies of two letters, 15 March 1928 and 26 Nov. 1930, of which the originals are missing. Letters to G. B. Shaw of 7 May and 19 July 1928 have been cut from the typescript.

>> **56495.** (ff. 297). 8 Jan. 1923-26 April 1928.

>> **56496.** (ff. 303). 2 May 1928-31 Jan. 1935.

56497. (ff. i+96).
1.   ff. 1-66. *Typewritten copies* of letters from C. F. Shaw to T. E. Lawrence, of which the originals, together with another set of typewritten copies, are 45922; 31 Dec. 1922-7 April 1935, n.d. At ff. 63-66 are fragments of three letters; 1926?-1928. At f. 60 is a letter of Mrs. Sydney Smith; 20 May 1935. *Annotations* by G. B. Shaw are at ff. 2, 29, 34, 44, 49, 56.
2.   ff. 67-96. *Typewritten copies* of letters from T. E. Lawrence to G. B. Shaw, of which the originals and top typewritten copies are 50540, ff. 1-60; 17 Aug. 1922-14. Jan. 1924.

56498. (ff. ii+66). Notebook of C. F. Shaw containing suggested amendments to the proofs of *The Seven Pillars of Wisdom*; *circa* 1921. At f. 55 is a diary summary for the year 1875; for earlier and subsequent summaries see 56500; 63189 H ff. 1-10v; 63189 I.

56499. (ff. 337). Miscellaneous papers relating to T. E. Lawrence.
1.   ff. 1-4v.   Corrected and annotated proofs of T. E. Lawrence's introduction to the 1924 edition of Richard Garnett, *The Twilight of the Gods.*
2.   ff. 5-12.   Prospectuses for T. E. Lawrence's *Revolt in the Desert* (1927), *T. E. Lawrence: By his friends* (1937), and for a projected edition of his letters, the last two to be edited by his brother A. W. Lawrence. *Printed* with *autograph notes* by A. W. Lawrence.
3.   ff. 13-32.   Proofs of 'Makik' by Maj. Hubert Winthrop Young, D.S.O., sent to T. E. Lawrence; 1926. *Printed* and *inscribed* by Maj. Young.
4.   ff. 33-337.   Photographs, press-cuttings, reviews etc.; circa 1924-1938.

56500-56524. Diaries, commonplace books, theosophical and literary notebooks and papers of C. F. Shaw; 1876-1936, n.d.

56500. (ff. 106). Diary summaries for the years 1876-1919, with a *typewritten copy*; compiled 1920?

56501. (ff. 35). Journal of a tour in Scotland; 29 Aug.-16 Sept. 1880.

56502 A-D. (ff. 47, ii+29, i+6, 44). Personal memoranda book, lists of books and poems; n.d.

56503. (ff. 109). Commonplace book, mostly of poetry; 1876-1926, n.d.

56504. (ff. i+73). Commonplace book; 1884-1916, n.d.

56505. (ff. 14). Extracts from the unpublished part of Oscar Wilde's *De Profundis* (now 50141 A, B); followed by extracts from other authors, including a copy of Rudyard Kipling's then unpublished poem, 'The Vampire'; *circa* 1897.

56506. (ff. 15). Jokes and anecdotes; 1886, 1887, n.d.

56507. (ff. iii+22). Notes on French, German and Egyptian history; 1882.

56508. (ff. 25). Notes on Petr Demyanovich Uspensky, *Tertium Organum* (1911), with other notes and extracts; 1936-1937?, n.d. See also 63195 B-E; 63196.

56509. (ff. 29). Extracts from P. D. Uspensky, *A New Model of the Universe* (1931); 1934. *Typewritten.* See also 63195 A.

56510. (ff. i+59). Theosophical notebook, annotated in 1950 by G. B. Shaw: 'Apparently these are notes for a synopsis of the doctrine of a Theosophist who edited The Quest'; 1930s?

56511. (ff. i+90). Theosophical notes, including lecture summaries, inscribed 'MS. of "Knowledge"'; 1913, n.d.

56512. (ff. i+66). Notes on theosophical lectures; 1917-1919, n.d. See also 63193 E, F; 63196.

56513. (ff. i+7). Notes on spiritual and psychical subconsciousness; n.d.

56514. (ff. i+30). Summary of Henry Drummond, *Natural Law in the Spiritual World* (1902), with other notes; 1931, n.d.

56515. (ff. 10). Notes on 'The Rule of Phase'; n.d.

56516. (ff. i+57). Notes on *The Yoga Sutras of Patanjali* (1912), with other notes; aft. 1915.

56517. (ff. 23). 'Sayings from the Bhagavad Gita', with other notes; n.d.

56518. (ff. i+37). 'Outline of the Sophia Mythos'; n.d. Mainly *typewritten.*

56519. (ff. 16). Commonplaces and poems on spiritual and moral themes; n.d.

56520. (ff. 24). Notes on palmistry; 1884.

56521. (ff. 99). Essays by C. F. Shaw; 1877-1879.

56522. (ff. i+18). Translated extracts from Théophile Gautier, *Mademoiselle de Maupin*; 1871.

56523. (ff. 126). Papers relating to the dramatist Eugène Brieux.
1.   ff. 1-88. Parts of the translation by C. F. Shaw of E. Brieux, 'La Femme Seule', published as *Woman on Her Own* (1916). *Drafts*, with a section in *shorthand.*
2.   ff. 89-98. Corrected proofs of the foreword by C. F. Shaw and preface by G. B. Shaw to the third edition of *Three Plays by Brieux* (1914).
3.   ff. 99-126. Undated shorthand notes by G. B. Shaw relating to 'La Femme Seule', with press-cuttings relating to Brieux productions, etc.; 1903?-1917.

56524 A, B. Miscellaneous papers; *circa* 1890-1941. Partly *typewritten* and *printed.*

56524 A. (ff. 110). Draft correspondence, press-cuttings and papers on social and political questions; *circa* 1897-1921. 'Letter on Maternity without Marriage', 1905, at ff. 20-31, appears to be *dictated* by G. B. Shaw.

56524 B. (ff. i+156). Literary, metaphysical and personal papers and drafts of correspondence; *circa* 1890-1941. Includes, at ff. 55-89, 'The Dream of a Spring Morning', C. F. Shaw's translation of Gabriele d'Annunzio's 'Sogno d'un mattino di primavera', *circa* 1897-1898; a note at f. 59 records a contribution by G. B. Shaw.

56525, 56526. Papers of the Payne-Townsend and related families; 1822-1891?, n.d.

56525. (ff. i+101). Financial memorandum book of Horace Payne-Townsend, with additional notes in other hands; 1856-1887, n.d.

56526. (ff. 10). Miscellaneous papers; 1822-1891?
1. f. 1. Memorandum of agreement between the Rev. Horatio Townsend and Daniel Conolly, of Derry; 1822.
2. ff. 2-3. Letter from J. R. Wolfenden to Lt. Col. Thomas Cox Kirby; 1840.
3. ff. 4-5. Memorial of Lt. Col. T. C. Kirby to the Duke of Wellington requesting service on full pay; 1844. *Copy.*
4. ff. 6-8. Papers relating to the commissioning of Franklin Knight Kirby in the Army; 1854.
5. ff. 9-10v. Prospectus for the Clonakilty and Rosscarbery Light Railway, co. Cork; 1891?

56627-56637. Correspondence, etc. of the Society of Authors of and concerning G. B. Shaw and C. F. Shaw; 1909-1961, n.d. This portion of the Society's Archive, in which the Shaw sequence comprises Vols. LIII-LXIII, was purchased in March 1969, and incorporated in 1971.

56627-56633. General correspondence relating to the affairs of the Society, to publications and translations of Shaw's works and to licences for performing the plays worldwide: containing many items written or annotated by Shaw. This correspondence overlaps to some extent with that in 56634-56637, below.

56627. (ff. 187). 1909-1916.

56628. (ff. 225). 1917-1929.

56629. (ff. 203). 1930-1936.

56630. (ff. 209). 1937-1942.

56631. (ff. 215). 1943-July 1947.

56632. (ff. 207). Aug. 1947-1949.

56633. (ff. 221).
1.   ff. 1-97. 1950, n.d.
2.   ff. 98-221. C. F. Shaw, 1917-1961. See also 63197.

56634-56637. Letters relating almost exclusively to licensing of Shaw's plays, containing very little correspondence of G. B. Shaw himself. See also 50649.

56634. (ff. 247). Sept. 1944-June 1947. *The foliation sequence of this volume, from f. 136 onwards, was altered in 2002-2003.* See also 56631.

56635. (ff. 183). July 1947-June 1948. See also 56631; 56632.

56636. (ff. 152). July 1948-Aug. 1949, n.d. See also 56632.

56637. (ff. 2). Graphic survey of productions of Shaw's plays, Feb.-May 1946.

57786, ff. 39-46. Letters of G. B. Shaw to the music critic Cecil William Turpie Gray; 1916-1946. Part of Vol. XIII of the series 57774-57803, the correspondence, papers and musical compositions of Gray, purchased from his executors in 1973.

58090, 58091. Vols. VI and VII of the series 58085-58118, the correspondence and papers of Charles de Sousy Ricketts, R.A. and Charles Haslewood Shannon, R.A., presented by Mrs. Marie Sturge Moore and members of her family in 1955, and reserved from use until February 1974. Within these two volumes of general correspondence are numerous letters of G. B. Shaw to Ricketts; 1907-1921. Details are given in the index.

58432, 58433. Cornwallis-West Papers: material relating to Major George Frederick Myddleton Cornwallis-West (b.1874, d.1951) and G. B. Shaw, together with a few associated items; 1914-1961. Presented by Miss Eileen Quelch of Canterbury, former secretary to Cornwallis-West, in January 1975.

> **58432.** (ff. iii+150). Play by Cornwallis-West entitled 'The Woman who stopped War'; 1933. *Typewritten carbon copy*, with *autograph* alterations and notes by G. B. Shaw, to whom the play was sent for criticism. See Eileen Quelch, *Perfect Darling: the life and times of George Cornwallis-West* (1972), pp. 173-180. 'The Woman who stopped War' was never produced, but was rewritten as a novel by Cornwallis-West and published in 1935.

> **58433.** (ff. 27).
> 1. ff. 1-21v. Sixteen letters from G. B. Shaw to Cornwallis-West; 1914-1941. Partly *signed*.
> 2. ff. 22-22v. Corrected proof of 'Commonsense about "[The?]Daily Worker"' by Shaw, from 'Forward'; 1 Feb. 1941. *Printed*, with *autograph annotations*.
> 3. ff. 23-24. Letter from Shaw to Clarence Henry Norman; 21 March 1917. *Typewritten copy*.
> 4. f. 25. *Typewritten* letter from Cornwallis-West to Eileen Quelch, concerning his bequest to her of the Shaw letters, etc.; 7 April 1942. *Imperfect. Facsimile copy.*
> 5. ff. 26-27v. Two letters from Shaw's former secretary, Blanche Patch, to Eileen Quelch; 25 Aug., 21 Oct. 1961.

58493. (ff. 111). Correspondence of Dr. Marie Charlotte Carmichael Stopes with and concerning G. B. Shaw; 1916-1952. Volume XLVII in the series 58447-58770, the archive of Dr. Stopes which she bequeathed to the Library and which was incorporated in May 1975.

59620 A - 59621 B. Papers of the journalist and author Wilfred Partington relating to the book dealer Thomas James Wise, purchased from Mrs. Audrey Ormrod in December 1975. This collection includes correspondence with G. B. Shaw and F. E. Loewenstein, detailed in the Index; 1939-1949. See also Section 5, the Ashley Manuscripts.

Other relevant content is as follows:

> **59620 C.** At folios 235-247, are Shaw's *autograph* marginal corrections and additions to pp. 13, 14, 61, 71, 144 and 278 of Partington's *Forging Ahead* (New York, 1939), together with a prefatory note and postscripts; 1940. *Photocopies*. In the British edition of this work, published in

London in 1946 under the title *Thomas Wise in the Original Cloth*, Shaw's comments are printed as an Appendix.

59620 D. Folios 19-32 are the *printed* proofs of this Appendix, with further *autograph* amendments by Shaw; 1945.

59621 A. Folios 125-143 are three sets of *printed* proofs of the Appendix, incorporating Shaw's amendments, with further alterations in Partington's hand; 1945.

59784. (ff. 15). Ten letters of G. B. Shaw to Edward Reynolds Pease, Secretary of the Fabian Society 1890-1913; 1890-1900. Purchased at Sotheby's, July 1976. See also 50557; 50680; 50681.

59892 U. Letters, cards, photographs, compliments slips, etc. of G. B. Shaw; 1892-1950. Partly *printed*. At ff. 125-144 of a volume of miscellaneous Departmental acquisitions. Between ff. 125 and 141 are to be found notes to: J. B. Glasier, J. Magny, S. D. Shallard, Clifford Sharp, C. Keane, Huntly Carter, S. C. Cockerell, A. Friars, L. N. Parker and J. C. Squire, on which further details are to be found in the Index. At f. 136 is a *typewritten* questionnaire of 1942 on Ireland and disarmament by W. R. Titterton, with Shaw's *autograph* answers. Photographs of Shaw are at ff. 139v-143v; 1921-1950. Bequeathed by Richard Vincent Hughes, 1978.

59901. (ff. 193). 'Heartbreak House'; 1917. *Typewritten*, with extensive *autograph* revisions and additions in longhand. At ff. 189-191 are three half sheets of revisions in *autograph shorthand*. The original shorthand draft of the script is presumed to have been destroyed. Purchased at Christie's, March 1978.

60391 Y. Postcard from G. B. Shaw to Dr. J. Kingston Barton announcing the death of his father, George Carr Shaw, and signed 'An Orphan'; 1885. At f. 158 of a volume of miscellaneous departmental acquisitions. Purchased from Quaritch, June 1979.

61891 D. Letter from G. B. Shaw to the Director of the B.B.C., complaining about a broadcast of 'Candida'; 1949. *Typewritten*, with *autograph* additions, but unsigned. At f. 33 of a volume of miscellaneous Departmental acquisitions. Purchased at Sotheby's, March 1980.

61891 L. Four letters of G. B. Shaw to Henry Havelock Ellis; 1888, 1889. The letters, the first of which is incomplete, relate to a proposed work on political economy by Shaw which remained unwritten. At ff. 80-87 of the same volume of miscellaneous Departmental acquisitions as the preceding. Purchased from Lawrence of Crewkerne, February 1981.

61998. (ff. 31). Letters and postcards of G. B. Shaw to Sir Johnston Forbes-Robertson (b.1853, d.1937), his wife Mary Gertrude *née* Elliott, and their daughter Jean; 1903-1946. Partly *signed.* Presented by Mrs. Vincent Sheean and Mrs. F. G. Miles, daughters of Sir Johnston and Lady Forbes-Robertson, July 1981.

62992. (ff. 23). Letters, etc., from G. B. Shaw and H. G. Wells to Holbrook Jackson, relating to disputes and elections in the Fabian Society; 1906-1907. Partly *printed* and *signed.* Including, at ff. 3-8, *galley proofs* of the speech, 'Reconstruction of the Fabian Society', delivered by Wells at the meeting of 7 Dec. 1906. Purchased from Bertram Rota, June 1982. See also 50514; 50515; 50557.

PAPERS FROM SHAW'S CORNER.

63179-63203. Papers of G. B. Shaw and C. F. Shaw; 1876-1950, n.d. Transferred by the National Trust from Shaw's Corner, Ayot St. Lawrence, February 1982. See also 56490-56526.

63179, 63180. (ff. 207, 207). G. B. Shaw, 'More Common Sense about the War'; 1915. Two *typewritten copies*, with annotations both *autograph* and by C. F. Shaw. See also 50668 and 50669 A, B.

63181. (ff. 6). Diary of G. B. Shaw; 1917. *Autograph*, mainly *shorthand*, and *printed.* Containing entries for 1-10 January only.

63182. (ff. 177).
1.   ff. 1-6. Notes for 'St. Joan'; n.d. *Autograph.*
2.   ff. 7-15. Notebook with *autograph* draft for parts of 'Bernard Shaw's Rhyming Picture Guide to Ayot Saint Lawrence'; 1950.
3.   ff. 16-25. 'The Limitation Conference II: After you, sir'. *Typewritten* with substantial *autograph* additions and amendments; 1921?

4. ff. 26-177. *Printed* proofs and articles by Shaw, with some *autograph* corrections; 1888-1948.
This volume has been rearranged and refoliated since the 1984 BL arrangement.

63183. (ff. 64). Miscellaneous notes, printed ephemera, etc., of Shaw; 1895-1947, n.d. *Autograph*, partly *shorthand*, *typewritten* and *printed*.

63184. (ff. 132). Corrected worksheets for the Pelman Institute course in Spanish and Italian, in the name of Miss Blanche Patch, but completed in Shaw's hand; 1924, 1928. *Autograph* and *printed*. Mainly *Spanish* and *Italian*.

63185. (ff. 116). 'Le métier de Madame Warren', *French* translation, mainly *typewritten*, of 'Mrs. Warren's Profession'; n.d. Not the same as Augustin and Henriette Hamon, 'La Profession de Mme. Warren' (Paris, 1913).

63186. (ff. 251). Miscellaneous correspondence of G. B. Shaw; 1905-1949, n.d. Partly *autograph*.

63187. (ff. 154). Accounts, letters, etc., relating to the Shaws' tenancy of a flat in Whitehall Court; 1934-1943, n.d. Mainly *typewritten* and *printed*.

63188-63192. Diaries of C. F. Shaw for 1876-1890 and 1903-1942, with annuary notes for the years 1868 and 1874-1892. *Autograph* and *printed*.

63188 A-H. 1876-1883.

63188 A. (ff. i+110). 1876.	**63188 E.** (ff. v+149). 1880.
63188 B. (ff. i+122). 1877.	**63188 F.** (ff. i+97). 1881.
63188 C. (ff. i+122). 1878.	**63188 G.** (ff. ii+100). 1882.
63188 D. (ff. ii+124). 1879.	**63188 H.** (ff. ii+85). 1883.

63189 A-I. 1884-1890. Followed by notes and annuaries for 1868-1892.

63189 A. (ff. ii+90). 1884.	**63189 D.** (ff. i+52). 1887.
See also 63193 D.	**63189 E.** (ff. i+83). 1888.
63189 B. (ff. ii+91). 1885.	**63189 F.** (ff. ii+74). 1889.
63189 C. (ff. i+131). 1886.	**63189 G.** (ff. i+91). 1890.

63189 H. (ff. 24). Annuary notes for 1868 and 1874-1887 are at ff. 1-10v. Notes on Old Testament reading are written from the end of the notebook at ff. 23v-11v.

63189 I. (ff. 50). Biographical notes, and annuary 1876-1892.

63190 A-M. 1903-1915.

63190 A. (ff. 76). 1903.	**63190 D.** (ff. ii+82). 1906.
63190 B. (ff. i+82). 1904.	**63190 E.** (ff. i+83). 1907.
63190 C. (ff. i+82). 1905.	**63190 F.** (ff. 82). 1908.
	63190 G. (ff. ii+82). 1909.

63190 H. (ff. ii+82). 1910.
63190 I. (ff. ii+82). 1911.
63190 J. (ff. i+87). 1912.

63190 K. (ff. ii+86). 1913.
63190 L. (ff. ii+87). 1914.
63190 M. (ff. i+87). 1915.

63191 A-M. 1916-1928.

63191 A. (ff. iii+87). 1916.
63191 B. (ff. i+87). 1917.
63191 C. (ff. iii+87). 1918.
63191 D. (ff. i+80). 1919.
63191 E. (ff. ii+81). 1920.
63191 F. (ff. ii+80). 1921.
63191 G. (ff. ii+81). 1922.

63191 H. (ff. ii+82). 1923.
63191 I. (ff. ii+78). 1924.
63191 J. (ff. i+79). 1925.
63191 K. (ff. ii+82). 1926.
63191 L. (ff. i+79). 1927.
63191 M. (ff. i+81). 1928.

63192 A-N. 1929-1942.

63192 A. (ff. iii+82). 1929.
63192 B. (ff. iii+80). 1930.
63192 C. (ff. ii+81). 1931.
63192 D. (ff. ii+81). 1932.
63192 E. (ff. i+79). 1933.
63192 F. (ff. i+81). 1934.
63192 G. (ff. i+81). 1935.
63192 H. (ff. i+80). 1936.

63192 I. (ff. i+81). 1937.
63192 J. (ff. i+81). 1938.
63192 K. (ff. i+81). 1939.
63192 L. (ff. 82). 1940.
63192 M. (ff. 82.) 1941. Entries up to 30 Aug. only.
63192 N. (ff. 80). 1942. Few entries.

63193-63196. Notebooks, etc., of C. F. Shaw; 1873-1941, n.d. Partly *typewritten* and *printed*.

63193 A-F. 1873-1923, n.d.

63193 A. (ff. 18). Notes on the German language; 1873.

63193 B. (ff. ii+6). 'List of owners of property through whose land it is proposed to take the Clonakilty-Rosscarbery Railway'; bef. 1876?

63193 C. (ff. 27). Latin notes; 1876.

63193 D. (ff. 48). Personal journal; 1884 Oct.-Nov., and n.d. See also 63189 A.

63193 E. (ff. i+47). Course notes on theosophy and Eastern religious texts; 1918-1919 and 1923. See also 56512.

63193 F. (ff. i+22). The same; 1920-1922, n.d.

63194 A-D. 1918? - aft. 1925.

63194 A-C. (ff. ii+47, i+47. ii+46). Spiritual notes; 1918?-1923?

63194 D. (ff. 56). Commonplace book; aft. 1925.

63195 A-E.   Notes on reading, principally on the writings of P. D. Uspensky; *circa* 1934-1937. See also 56508; 56509.

> **63195 A.** (ff. i+36). 1934.
>
> **63195 B.** (ff. i+40). 1934-1935.
>
> **63195 C.** (ff. 51). 1935?
>
> **63195 D.** (ff. i+57). 1936.
>
> **63195 E.** (ff. 1+3). 1937.

63196. (ff. i+130).
1. ff. 1-77. Meditations and notes on reading, particularly on Eastern religions; 1913, 1931, n.d.
2. ff. 78-94. J. C. Scholey, 'The Source of Life and Thought'; 1916. *Printed.*
3. ff. 95-116. Henry Bedinger Mitchell, 'Meditation'; n.d. *Printed.*
4. ff. 117-130. *Printed* fragments on spiritual topics, medical prescriptions, notes and memoranda; 1917-1937, n.d.

63197. (ff. 103). Miscellaneous correspondence of C. F. Shaw; 1893-1941, n.d. Partly *autograph* and *printed.*

63198 A - 63201.   Correspondence, accounts rendered, wills, inventories and other material relating to C. F. Shaw's financial affairs; 1849-1946, n.d. Partly *printed* and *typewritten.* Included is some material relating to G. B. Shaw's financial affairs.

> **63198 A.**   (ff. 162).   Papers relating to the property of the Payne-Townshend family and C. F. Shaw; 1849-1936, n.d.

63198 B. (ff. 234).
1. ff. 1-86. Correspondence, etc., relating to share holdings; 1915-1946.
2. ff. 87-176. Dividend counterfoils; 1938-1939.
3. ff. 177-193. Material relating to income tax returns; 1937-1942.
4. ff. 194-234. Miscellaneous receipts and invoices; 1898-1942.

63198 C. (ff. 12). Notebook, 'List of Securities', issued by the National Provincial and Union Bank of England for C. F. Shaw; 1900-1940.

63199. (ff. 91). Correspondence of Messrs. Burne and Wykes, Solicitors, with and on behalf of C. F. Shaw; 1909-1918, n.d.

63200. (ff. 142). Correspondence of Messrs. Burne and Wykes, afterwards Laurence, Graham, Solicitors, with and on behalf of C. F. Shaw; 1919-1928 and 1940-1942.

63201. (ff. i+101). Accounts submitted by Laurence, Graham & Co. to Mr. and Mrs. Shaw; 1931-1942.

63202 A-CC. Twenty-seven cheque-book stubs and some cancelled cheques of C. F. Shaw; 1916-1942. *Autograph* and *printed*. Arranged as 63202 A-O, 63202 P-AA, 63202 BB and 63202 CC.

63203. (ff. 6). Photographs of T. E. Lawrence and others; 1927, 1928, n.d. Folios 1v, 2v and 3v carry *autograph* notes by Lawrence; 1927, 1928.

63728. (ff. 49). Correspondence and papers formerly on display at Shaw's Corner, Ayot St. Lawrence, co. Hertf.; 1924-1946, n.d. Partly *printed*. Presented by the National Trust, 6 June 1984 and 1 Nov. 1989.

1. ff. 1-1v. Certificate confirming life membership of the Cremation Society; 28 April 1924. *Signed* by Shaw.
2. f. 2. Letter from George H. M. Twyman; 19 Feb. 1927. *Signed*. Includes a caricature.
3. ff. 3-4. Letter from J. Rothwell; 6 Jan. 1934. With a caricature on the envelope.
4. f. 5. Letter from E. S. Lennox Robinson on behalf of the Council of the Irish Academy of Letters; 26 May 1937. *Typewritten*.
5. ff. 6-6v. Letter to Siegfried Trebitsch; 18 Feb. 1942. *Shorthand*.
6. ff. 7-7v. Letter from the Cremation Society; 25 May 1943. *Signed*.
7. ff. 8-9. Two letters to — Studman; 8 July 1944 and 15 Dec. 1946.
8. ff. 10-10v. Letter from Marie Stopes; 24 July 1946.
9. f. 11. 'Lines for the Ninetieth Birthday of George Bernard Shaw', by John Masefield; for 26 July 1946. *Autograph*.
10. f. 12. Christmas card from Theodore and Eleanor Roosevelt; n.d.
11. ff. 13-49. 'The Censorship of the Stage in England', written for the 'North American Review'; 1899. *Autograph*.

65134. (ff. 12). 'Man kann nie wissen', incomplete translation by Walter Leigh of the opening scene of Shaw's 'You Never Can Tell'; 1926. With annotations in another hand. Volume XXX of the papers and musical compositions of Walter Leigh, presented by Mrs. Veronica Jacobs, Julian Leigh and Andrew Leigh, on behalf of Mrs. Marion Leigh in July and November 1987.

65156 Q-W. Prompt copies of Shaw plays produced by John E. Vedrenne and Harley Granville-Barker at The Royal Court Theatre, London; 1904-1907. Mainly *printed*, with annotations in various hands. Part of the collection of Vedrenne-Barker Plays, 65156 A-Z, purchased from Bertram Rota in September 1986.

Seven volumes.

65156 Q. (ff. 54). 'Candida'; 1904-1905. Prompt Book of E. F. Saxon, Stage Manager, with his pencilled notes.

65156 R. (ff. 94). 'Captain Brassbound's Conversion'; 1906. Stage directions in an unknown hand. The theatre's printed programme for the season from 16 April 1906 is at ff. 1-2.

65156 S. (ff. 86). 'Don Juan in Hell'; 1907? *Typewritten*, with a few stage directions in an unknown hand. This text contains all three scenes of what was to become Act III of 'Man and Superman', and is so titled here. R. Mander and J. Mitchenson, in *Theatrical Companion to Shaw* (1954), state that Vedrenne and Barker first presented Act III Scene 2 of 'Don Juan in Hell' in June 1907, with the subtitle 'A Dream from Man and Superman'.

65156 T, U. (ff. ii+105, i+104). 'Man and Superman'; 1905-1907? Two copies, without Act III, with stage directions in various hands; many annotations in 65156 U, e.g. at f. 4, are in the hand of C. F. Shaw.

65156 V, W. (ff. 86, 81). 'The Philanderer'; 1906-1907. Two copies, with stage directions in an unknown hand.

65534-68881. Playscripts from the Lord Chamberlain's office; 1900-1968. Including plays submitted for performing licence by Shaw himself, or by theatre managers on his behalf. For an earlier series, see 52929-53701. The plays by Shaw are listed in Section 7, Lord Chamberlain's Plays and Correspondence, below. Incorporated in 1988.

68892 B. Letter from Carl S. Mahler to Shaw concerning Siegfried Trebitsch, with Shaw's *autograph* reply on the same letter; 1943. At f. 6 of a volume of miscellaneous Departmental acquisitions. Presented by Mrs. Carol Kroch-Rhodes, granddaughter of C. S. Mahler, 1989.

71068. (ff. 198). Letters of Shaw to Ellen Terry; 1892-1918. Followed by cards to two other correspondents; 1916, 1928. Partly *signed*. Purchased from

Quaritch with a grant from the Shaw Fund, 1992. See also 43800-43802; 46172 G and the *rotographs* of 71068 in Facsimile 496; and a letter from Shaw to T. J. Wise concerning the correspondence in Ashley 4011.

71451-71455. Wood engraving blocks made by John Farleigh to illustrate G. B. Shaw's *Short Stories, Scraps and Shavings* (Constable, 1934). The blocks are lettered according to their published sequence. Blocks for three of the illustrations are missing: 71453 I is the frontispiece for an earlier publication, *The Adventures of the Black Girl in her search for God* (Constable, 1932). Presented by the Shaw Estate, July 1991. Arranged as follows:

71451 A-I.	**71454 A-G.**
71452 A-J.	**71455 A-G.**
71453 A-I.	

71615. (ff. 119). Correspondence and papers of Sir Roy Forbes Harrod relating to the will of G. B. Shaw; 1955-1957. In 1956 solicitors acting for the British Museum and the Royal Academy of Dramatic Art asked Harrod to depose to an affidavit on their behalf. The Public Trustee was seeking directions from the Chancery Division of the High Court of Justice regarding the disposition of trusts specified in the will, and Harrod prepared evidence on the economic viability or otherwise of introducing a phonetic alphabet for the English language. Volume VII of the Supplementary Harrod Papers, purchased from Lady Harrod in January 1992.

71658. (ff. ii+60). Visitors' book, with letters, photographs, etc., of the actor and producer Walter Hudd; 1926-1976, n.d. Including letters from G. B. Shaw and T. E. Lawrence, and newscuttings added after Hudd's death. Purchased from Mrs. Peggy Clarke, December 1993.

72712. Denis Mackail, *The Story of J. M. B. (Sir James Barrie, Bart., O.M.)* (1941). Author's copy, interleaved with *MS.* letters including, between pp. 680 and 681, three letters of G. B. Shaw to Sir Charles Blake Cochran, theatrical manager and producer; 1935. Partly *typewritten*. Presented by Lady Quayle, May, 1996.

73198. (ff. 1-120v). Correspondence of G. B. Shaw with G. K. Chesterton, together with related papers and letters; 1906-1942. Vol. XIII of the

G. K. Chesterton Papers, 73186-73484, purchased in 1990 from the Dorothy Collins Charitable Trust, with the aid of a grant from the Shaw Fund. Full details are to be found in the Index.

74734 O. Letters of G. B. Shaw to Mr. and Mrs. Max Hecht; 1896-1933. Part of a volume of miscellaneous Departmental acquisitions. Purchased at Christie's, May 2000.

74734 P. Letters to Dr. Raymond Streatfield from Blanche Patch, secretary of G. B. Shaw; 1942-1943. Part of the same volume of miscellaneous Departmental acquisitions as the preceding. Purchased at Bloomsbury Book Auctions, May 2000.

78907 Z. Two letters and two cards of G. B. Shaw to Robin Flower, of the Department of Manuscripts at the British Museum; 1934. Partly *typewritten* and *signed.* Part of a volume of miscellaneous Departmental acquisitions. Previously in the archives of the Department, and transferred in December 2003.

79492-79494 C. Correspondence between G. B. Shaw and Sir Isaac James Pitman, together with related correspondence, and papers concerning the implementation of the clauses in Shaw's will providing for the introduction and diffusion of a phonetic alphabet; *circa* 1933-1982. Some of the *printed* and *duplicate* items in this collection are published in *George Bernard Shaw on Language*, ed. A. Tauber (1963). Presented by His Honour Judge David Christian Pitman, son of Sir Isaac James Pitman, in March 2003, with a further supplement, 79494 C, presented in January 2004.

Three volumes; British Library arrangement, except for the first, which was bound before presentation. See also: 50554-50556; 71615.

> **79492.** (ff. 112).
> 1.   ff. 1-100.   Correspondence, etc., between G. B. Shaw, Sir I. J. Pitman and Daniel Jones; 1941-1950. Includes *printed* articles and open letters and one draft 'Teachers' Preface' by Shaw. Letters of Shaw are mainly *typewritten* and *signed*; Pitman and Jones letters are *copies.*
> 2.   ff. 101-112.   Correspondence between G. B. Shaw and Kingsley Read; 1942-1948. *Copies*, followed by a *fragmentary* Shaw letter and a letter of Vivian Elliot; n.d.
> *Some items in this volume have been bound out of chronological sequence.*

79493. (ff. 155). Papers relating to the phonetic alphabet campaign following Shaw's death. Mainly *duplicated, copy* and *printed*.

1. ff. 1-26v. Extract from Shaw's will, followed by legal opinions 1956?-1957 and the House of Commons Official Report on the Adjournment Debate on Shaw's Will Trust, 7 May 1957.
2. ff. 27-71. Materials for press release, etc., relating to Shaw's will and the competition to design a new alphabet; 1956-1959.
3. ff. 72-84. Miscellaneous material, including press cuttings on the publication of 'Androcles and the Lion' in the 'Shaw Alphabet'; 1959-1967.
4. ff. 85-155. Materials relating to Sir I. J. Pitman's apparently unpublished 'Memorandum of some considerations relevant to an appreciation of the proposals made in the will of George Bernard Shaw for a new British alphabet', and to his published books and articles relating to the phonetic alphabet; 1953-1969, n.d.

79494 A-C.

> **79494 A.** (pp. 32). *The Case for the Improvement of Spelling: Correspondence with the President of the Board of Education. Printed* by the Simplified Spelling Society; 1933?
>
> **79494 B.** (ff. 36). Specimen phonetic alphabets entered for the design competition; 1958.
>
> **79494 C.** (ff. 25). Notes, etc., of Sir James Pitman relating to Shaw's interest in spelling reform, together with *photocopies* of letters from Shaw to C. K. Ogden and Sydney Cockerell, of 1940 and 1944, the originals being held in American repositories; 1978, 1982, n.d.

79522. (ff. i+145). Chronology of the lives of G. B. Shaw and C. F. Shaw, compiled by Shaw's biographer Michael Holroyd. Presented by the compiler, with a covering letter, in February 1993. *Computer print-out*.

79532 MM. Correspondence between G. B. Shaw and Sunder Kabadi, Indian journalist, relating to the new Indian constitution; 1949-1950. Included is a questionnaire completed by Shaw for publication in the Indian press. Part of a volume of miscellaneous Departmental acquisitions. Presented in December 2004.

80801-80809. Vols. I-IX of the series 80801-80837, the papers of Sir Cedric Webster Hardwicke, actor; 1923-1949, n.d. Purchased through Quaritch in April 2002.

> **80801.** Correspondence of Sir Cedric Hardwicke and his wife, Helena, with G. B. and C. F. Shaw; 1929-1949, n.d.

> **80802.** 'Caesar and Cleopatra'. Published text (1920) with Hardwicke's *MS.* rehearsal notes; 1950?

> **80803.** 'Back to Methuselah'. Published text (1922) with Shaw's presentation inscription to Hardwicke, 1923.

> **80804.** 'St. Joan'. Published text (1924) with Hardwicke's *MS.* rehearsal notes; n.d.

> **80805.** 'The Apple Cart'. Rough proof, unpublished; 1929. With a note from Shaw to Hardwicke, 1929, on f. ii.

> **80806.** 'The Apple Cart'. Published text, 1930.

> **80807.** 'Immaturity'. Published text (no. 303 of a limited edition, 1930) with Shaw's dedicatory inscription to Hardwicke, 1930.

> **80808.** 'Too True to be Good'. Rough proof, unpublished; 1931, with Shaw's presentation inscription to Hardwicke, 1932.

> **80809.** 'Ellen Terry and Bernard Shaw. A Correspondence'. Published edition (1931) with Shaw's presentation inscription to Hardwicke, 1931.

ASHLEY MANUSCRIPTS

The following are manuscripts relating to Shaw in the Ashley Collection. The numeration of volumes in the Ashley Library follows the system of T. J. Wise, its creator; for further details, see the Preface to *The British Library Catalogue of the Ashley Manuscripts* (1999), pp. ix-xi. The abbreviation *ALC* in the following descriptions refers to the *Ashley Library Catalogue* by T. J. Wise, printed for private circulation in 11 volumes (1922-1936).

Ashley B1500, A4004, 5748. Letters (3) from G. B. Shaw to Clement Shorter; 5 Nov. 1904-16 Sept. 1925. In the letters Shaw sends 'my part of a "real conversation" between you and me' to Shorter, who had wished to interview him (B1500), declines to write a series of articles for *The Sphere* because he can make more money in the time by writing plays (5748), and expresses his views on ill-health and on Scotland (A4004). For a further letter from Shaw to Shorter see B5019. *ALC,* [v, p. 17]; ix, p. 124.

    5 Nov. 1904: B1500. Vol. B III, ff. 3, 3v.

    25 Dec. 1909: 5748. Octavo; ff. i+2.

    16 Sept. 1925: A4004. Vol. A IX, ff. 112, 112v.

Ashley B1506. Photograph of G. B. Shaw, with a note on verso 'Surly old dog I look now, don't I? G. B. S. 4/1/17.'; 1917. [*ALC*, ix, p. 124.]

    Vol. B III, f. 4.

Ashley B1509. Note from G. B. Shaw to [—], stating that he has just finished the first draft of a new play ['Getting Married'?]; 14 March 1908. [*ALC*, viii, p. 187.]

    Vol. B III, f. 5.

Ashley B1517, B1518, B1521, A1525, A4011. Two letters and two postcards from G. B. Shaw to T. J. Wise, and one letter to Wise from Blanche Patch, Shaw's secretary (B1521); 7 Nov. 1916-13 July 1933. The letters chiefly concern George Borrow (B1518), the bibliography of Shaw's *Heartbreak House* (published 1919. See F. E. Loewenstein, *The Rehearsal Copies of Bernard Shaw's Plays,* 1950) (B1517, B1521), bibliographies of Shaw's works (A1525), and the correspondence of Shaw with Ellen Terry (A4011) (for Ellen Terry's letters see 43800-43802). The letters also illustrate Wise's gifts of his publications to Shaw, and his efforts to secure rehearsal copies of Shaw's plays. For further letters from Shaw to Wise see B1529; B4019. *ALC,* v, pp. [21, 22], 208; [viii, p. 188]; xi, p. 106.

> 7 Nov. 1916: B1518. Vol. B III, f. 7.
> 18 Aug. 1918: B1517. Vol. B III, f. 6.
> 29 May 1924: B1521. Vol. B III, f. 8.
> 24 June 1924: A1525. Vol. A III, f. 118.
> 13 July 1933: A4011. Vol. A IX, ff. 113, 113v.

Ashley A1521. Sketches by G. B. Shaw, on the paper of the Great Southern Hôtel, Parknasilla, showing the intended arrangement of scenery and props in Acts I, II and III of *Heartbreak House*; 1917? Apparently this folio once formed part of a letter to Hugo Vallentin, Shaw's translator into Swedish (see *ALC,* v, p. 23). *ALC,* v, pp. 22-23.

> Vol. A III, f. 117.

Ashley 1525*. Letter from G. B. Shaw to Edmund Gosse, discussing a criticism of Shaw's *St. Joan* by Louis Gillet in the *Revue des Deux Mondes* for 1 Aug. 1924; 9 Aug. 1924. *ALC,* x, p. 182.

> Octavo; ff. ii+1.

Ashley B1529.
1. Two letters from Mrs. D. Thorne to T. J. Wise, sending him a copy of her father, Henry Arthur Jones's attack on G. B. Shaw, *Mr Mayor of Shakespeare's Town*, and discussing certain aspects of the book; 21 June, 12 Sept. 1929. [*ALC*, x, p. 183].
    Vol. B III, ff. 11-14.
2. Postcard, with a portrait of the writer, from G. B. Shaw to T. J. Wise, thanking him for 'a jolly book'; 9 Feb. 1930. [*ALC*, x, p. 183].
    Vol. B III, ff. 15, 15v.

Ashley A1968 (3).
b. Printed title-page from a copy of the revised proof of G. B. Shaw, *Too True to be Good*, 1932, bearing on the recto the *autograph* note by Shaw

'to T. J. Wise. This has all the changes made at rehearsal incorporated, and is pretty well as the play was performed. G. Bernard Shaw 20th July 1933', and on the verso the *autograph* note by Maurice Buxton Forman 'Mr. Wise subsequently ascertained that 'Juvenilia' was not by Swinburne, but by Antony Coningham Sterling — and apparently failed to enter it in his Catalogue under either name. M.B.F.'. f. 106.

Ashley B4019. Letters from various correspondents, chiefly concerning the sale to T. J. Wise by Floryan Sobieniowski, translator of G. B. Shaw's plays into Polish, of rehearsal copies of certain plays by Shaw. [*ALC*, xi, p. 109]. As follows:

1. Letter, with envelope (f. 112), and postcard (f. 113), from Shaw to Sobieniowski, the letter concerning the reception of Shaw's *The Adventures of The Black Girl In her Search for God* and its banning in the Irish Free State, the postcard elucidating various points in the text of *On The Rocks*; 24 July, 4 Oct. 1933. ff. 111-112, 113, 113v.
2. Two letters and a note (f. 116) from Shaw to Wise, the letters concerning the desire of Elizabeth Yeats to sell a complete set of Dun Emer and Cuala Press publications and, in the case of the later letter (f. 115), explaining the status of rehearsal copies of Shaw's plays, and the note acknowledging receipt of 'the bibliography'; 27, 29 Sept. (the letters), 20 July (the note) 1933. ff. 114, 115, 116.
3. Three fragments of brown paper cut from the wrappings of parcels, each bearing Wise's address in the hand of Shaw. ff. 117, 118, 119.
4. Three letters from Sobieniowski to Wise, the two earlier concerning the sale to Wise of a rehearsal copy of Shaw's *Too True to be Good*, the latest (ff. 122, 123) sending the postcard described under (1) and promising further material of that kind together with rehearsal copies of *The Political Madhouse* and other plays, in return for which Sobieniowski asks Wise for the loan of £15; 9, 11 July, 5 Oct. 1933. ff. 120, 121, 122, 123.
5. Envelope originally addressed to Mrs. Wise, bearing the note '"Black Girl" Letters' in Wise's hand. f. 124.
   Vol. B VII, ff. 111-124.

Ashley 5018. Letter from G. B. Shaw to Alma Murray [Mrs. Alfred Forman], concerning the casting of his 'The Devil's Disciple'; 8 April 1898. ff. 1, 1v. Also included is a letter (f. ii) from Alma Murray Forman to T. J. Wise, agreeing to sell this letter and [three?] others to him for £30; 30 July 1927. *ALC*, ix, p. 123.

Ashley A5019. Letter from G. B. Shaw to Hugo Vallentin, advising him not to send his articles to *The Statesman* as they are insufficiently serious, and describing a motor accident that he has had; 28 March 1913. *ALC*, v, p. 23.

Vol. A XII, ff. 62, 63, 63v.

Ashley B5019.
1. Letter from G. B. Shaw to Clement Shorter, concerning a booklet on the subject of the appeal and execution of Sir Roger Casement; 27 Jan. 1922. [*ALC*, v, p. 23].
    Vol. B XI, ff. 45, 46.
2. Letter from Clement Shorter to [—] Nicoll, concerning the execution of Sir Roger Casement and Irish politics; 4 Aug. 1916. [*ALC*, v, p. 23].
    Vol. B XI, ff. 47-48v.

Ashley 5768. Miscellaneous letters, etc.; 1721-1933. Including at ff. 97-98 a letter from G.B. Shaw to Edward Clodd, 1925; and at ff. 99-100 postcards from Shaw to Floryan Sobieniowski, 1933.

UNINCORPORATED MANUSCRIPTS

The following items do not have accession numbers within the series allocated to the rest of the manuscripts listed and indexed in the present catalogue. This is either because they are awaiting full incorporation into the Library's collections and catalogues, or because they are, for the present, held as loans.

Loan 103. Archive of Laurence Binyon, loaned by Mrs. N. Gray in October 1990. Volume 10 contains a portrait postcard of G. B. Shaw to Binyon of 1924, and a letter from C. F. Shaw of 1938.

Music Deposit 1999/10. Archive of Harriet Cohen. Bequeathed to the Music Collections, and reserved from use until 1998. At the time of going to press, may be seen on application to the Curator, Music Collections. The archive contains the following Shaw items:

3.xv.
1. Forty-two letters, cards, etc.; 1920-1949.
2. Nine items sent on Shaw's behalf; 1921-1948.
3. Invitation issued by Harriet Cohen to a private view of paintings by Gertrude Harvey, within which is printed a 'Note by Mr. Bernard Shaw'; 1929.

3.xxv. Two letter cards; 1922, 1924.

Deposit 9394 (part). Archive of the Cockerell Bindery, including a volume of correspondence of G. B. and C. F. Shaw and Blanche Patch with Douglas Cockerell, mostly relating to binding commissions; 1927-1946. Partly *signed*. Including a cover design for Shaw's *Intelligent Woman's Guide to Socialism*. Purchased from the Cockerell family in July 1994.

Paper; ff. 112. 311 x 246 mm. Quarter binding of green leather with marbled boards.

Deposit 10014.   2nd Supplementary Series of papers from the Lord Chamberlain's Office, presented by the Royal Archives at Windsor, June 2001. Contains the following Shaw item:

> File 104. 'Mrs. Warren's Profession': report of Advisory Board of 1911. Includes letters of Edward Carson, Squire Bancroft, Stanley Buckmaster and Prof. Walter Raleigh.
> Supplementing L.C.P. Corr. 1924/5632. See also: 50599; 50600; 53654 H; 66402 G.

Deposit 10270.   Working papers, correspondence, articles, manuscript and typescript drafts relating to Michael Holroyd's biography, *Bernard Shaw*, 3 vols. (London, Chatto & Windus, 1988-1992). Purchased in February 2005.

LORD CHAMBERLAIN'S PLAYS
AND
LORD CHAMBERLAIN'S CORRESPONDENCE

The series of Additional Manuscripts 42865-43038, 52929-53701 and 65534-68881 constitute the collection known as The Lord Chamberlain's Plays, playscripts received for licensing between 1824 and the abolition of censorship in 1968. They were presented by the Lord Chamberlain's Office and incorporated between 1932 and 1988. A further series of related Correspondence Files is listed under the heading L.C.P. Corr.

The two later series of plays contain Shaw items, which are listed below. They are also itemised in the Index, where all entries for individual plays are amalgamated under the heading 'Shaw: Dramatic Works', in alphabetical order of title; the cross-referencing in the following list is not intended to be exhaustive. It should be noted that the granting of a licence may postdate the completion and publication of a play, and that a Correspondence File may cover the submission of the same script at different dates.

The volumes in these series each consist of several plays of similar licence date, often bound together. They are mostly unfoliated, but the separate plays are lettered in sequence within the volumes.

I. PLAYSCRIPTS.

53513 K. 'Widowers' Houses'; 1892. *Typewritten.*

53546 O. 'Arms and the Man'; 1894. *Typewritten* with *autograph additions.*

53572 A. 'Candida'; 1895. *Typewritten* with Shaw's *autograph* amendments *passim.*

53628 D. 'The Devil's Disciple'; 1897. *Typewritten* with a few *autograph* amendments.

53633 K. 'The Man of Destiny'; 1897. *Typewritten.*

53654.
F. 'You Never Can Tell'; 1898. Undated *printed proof* of rehearsal copy.
G. 'The Philanderer'; 1898. Undated *printed proof* of rehearsal copy.
H. 'Mrs. Warren's Profession'; 1898. *Printed proof* (1897) of rehearsal copy. Cover states 'Expurgated version in 3 Acts'. Some pages have been pasted over with blank sheets, and some pasted together. Shaw's *autograph* additions to the text are on pp. 13, 14, 29, 32 and 36. See also: 50599; 50600; 66402 G and L.C.P. Corr 1924/5632.

53680 U. 'Caesar and Cleopatra'; 1899. *Typewritten.*

53693 C. 'Captain Brassbound's Conversion'; 1899. *Typewritten.*

65567 L. 'The Admirable Bashville'; 1901. *Printed proof,* with cover bearing Shaw's *autograph* note of 1901 that this is an adaptation of 'Cashel Byron's Profession', and the first page of the script his *autograph* note that this version of his novel is intended solely to secure the author's stage rights.

65659 J. 'Man and Superman'; 1903. Undated *printed proof.*

65697 H. 'How He Lied to her Husband'; 1904. *Typewritten.*

65701 H. 'John Bull's Other Island'; 1904. *Typewritten.*

65736 L. 'Major Barbara'; 1905. *Typewritten.*

65776 J. 'The Doctor's Dilemma'; 1906. *Typewritten.*

65826 J. 'Getting Married'; 1908. *Typewritten.*

65866 E. 'The Shewing-Up of Blanco Posnet'; 1909. *Printed* (1909). Censor's instruction on passages to be omitted at pp. 11 and 21. See also: 66125 O and L.C.P. Corr. 1909/122; 1916/91.

65879 I. 'Misalliance'; 1910. *Printed* (1909), with some *autograph* amendments by Shaw. See also L.C.P. Corr. 1910/223.

65905 Q. 'The Dark Lady of the Sonnets'; 1910. *Printed* (1910), with some *autograph* amendments by Shaw.

65920 C. 'Fanny's First Play'; 1911. *Printed* (1911), with a few of Shaw's *autograph* amendments. *Typewritten* insertion of 'Prologue to be substituted for the Induction when the play alone is performed'.

65987 F. 'Overruled'; 1912. *Printed* script under title 'Trespassers will be Prosecuted; one of three Plays by J. M. Barrie, Arthur Pinero and Bernard Shaw' (1912). Together with *MS.* and *typewritten* report and recommendation for licence by E. A. Bendall.

66026 I. 'Androcles and the Lion'; 1913. *Printed* (1913), together with *MS.* report and reluctant recommendation for licence by C. H. E. Brookfield. See also L.C.P. Corr. 1913/1827.

66042 A. 'Great Catherine'; 1913. *Typewritten,* together with *MS.* and *typewritten* report and recommendation for licence by E. A. Bendall. See also L.C.P. Corr. 1913/2148.

66052 E. 'The Music Cure'; 1914. *Typewritten,* with an alternative scene at the end of the text. Together with *MS.* and *typewritten* report and recommendation for licence by E. A. Bendall.

66056 F. 'Pygmalion'; 1914. *Printed* (1913), together with *MS.* and *typewritten* report and recommendation for licence by G. S. Street, and followed by two *typewritten* folios of dialogue from Act II taken from another published version. See also L.C.P. Corr. 1956/9245, report and recommendation for 'My Fair Lady'.

66118 F. 'The Inca of Perusalem'; 1915. *Typewritten,* together with *MS.* report and recommendation for licence by G. S. Street. See also L.C.P. Corr. 1915/3885.

66125 O. 'The Shewing-Up of Blanco Posnet'; 1916. *Printed* (1913). Script preceded by extended preface on the censorship system and on the history of the play's performing rights. See also 50643, ff. 145-150; 65866 E and L.C.P. Corr. 1909/122; 1916/91.

66183 G. 'Annajanska, the Wild Grand Duchess, from the Russian of Gregory Biessipoff'; 1918. *Printed* (1917), together with *MS.* and *typewritten* report and recommendation for licence by E. A. Bendall, December 1917.

66295 D. 'Heartbreak House'; 1921. *Printed* (1920). See also L.C.P. Corr. 1921/3794.

66322 N. 'O'Flaherty, V.C.'; 1922. Undated *printed* rehearsal copy. See also L.C.P. Corr. 1922/4288.

66356 A. 'Back to Methuselah'; 1923. *Printed* (1922), together with two *type-written* folios containing additional dialogue, and *MS.* and *typewritten* report and recommendation for licence by G. S. Street. See also L.C.P. Corr. 1923/4900.

66385 A. 'St. Joan'; 1924. *Printed* (1924). See also L.C.P. Corr. 1924/5376.

66395 P. 'Augustus does his Bit'; 1924. *Typewritten.*

66402 G. 'Mrs. Warren's Profession'; 1924. *Printed* (1924), with *MS.* amendments and additions in an unknown hand, as well as censorial interventions. See also 50599; 50600; 53654 H; Deposit 10014; L.C.P. Corr. 1924/5632.

66414 J. 'Jitta's Atonement'; 1924. Play by Siegfried Trebitsch translated by Shaw. *Typewritten.*

66656 I. 'The Apple Cart'; 1929. *Typewritten.* See also L.C.P. Corr. 1929/8971.

66759 O. 'The Fascinating Foundling'; 1931. *Printed*, n.d.

66811 M. 'Too True to be Good'; 1932. *Printed* (1931). See also L.C.P. Corr. 1932/11312.

66866 F. 'On the Rocks'; 1933. *Printed* (1933). See also L.C.P. Corr. 1933/12381.

66892 I. 'Village Wooing'; 1933. *Printed* (1933). See also L.C.P. Corr. 1934/12935.

66901 L. 'The Six of Calais'; 1934. *Printed* (1934). See also L.C.P. Corr. 1934/13107.

66926 O. 'The Simpleton of the Unexpected Isles'; 1935. *Printed* (1934). See also L.C.P. Corr. 1935/13605.

67019 C. 'The Millionairess'; 1936. *Printed* (1936). See also 67234 P; L.C.P. Corr. 1936/15352 and 1940/3437.

67084 L. 'Cymbeline Refinished'; 1937. *Typescript* of Act V. See also L.C.P. Corr. 1937/771.

67148 H. 'Geneva'; 1938. *Printed*, 'Second rehearsal copy, revised after Bombardone's conversion to anti-semitism'. Shaw's *autograph* revisions and additions are at pp. 31, 64-65, 71-72, 80. See also L.C.P. Corr. 1938/1624 and 1938/1857.

67204 H. 'In Good King Charles's Golden Days'; 1939. *Printed* (1939). See also L.C.P. Corr. 1939/2967.

67234 P. 'The Millionairess'; 1940. *Printed* (1940). See also 67019 C; L.C.P. Corr. 1936/15352 and 1940/3437.

67577 K. 'Buoyant Billions'; 1948. *Printed* (1948). See also L.C.P. Corr. 1948/9778.

67676 R. 'The Glimpse of Reality'; 1950. *Typewritten.* See also L.C.P. Corr. 1950/1641.

67714 F. 'Farfetched Fables'; 1950. *Duplicated typescript.* See also L.C.P. Corr. 1950/2375.

68725 E. 'Passion, Poison, and Petrifaction'; 1967. *Printed.* Submitted in an edition of *Translations and Tomfooleries* (1949) where it appears on pp. 189-203. See also L.C.P. Corr. 1967/1288.

II. CORRESPONDENCE.

L.C.P. Corr. 1909/80. 'Press Cuttings'. File includes 1909 reports and recommendations for licence by G. A. Redford and correspondence concerning press controversies with James Anning, together with a note of November 1913 from the Lord Chamberlain to the German Ambassador.

L.C.P. Corr. 1909/122. 'Blanco Posnet'. Includes correspondence of 1913 with Gertrude Kingston and Frederick Whelen, *typewritten* copies of passages to be excised, and *typed* extracts from 1909 press reviews. See also 65866 E; 66125 O; L.C.P. Corr. 1916/91.

L.C.P. Corr. 1910/223. 'Misalliance'. Includes report, etc., of G. A. Redford, and correspondence with James Vincent, 4th Baron de Saumarez. See also 65879 I.

L.C.P. Corr. 1913/1827. 'Androcles and the Lion'. Includes report by Sir Stanley Buckmaster and correspondence with Sir Walter Alexander Raleigh. See also 66026 I.

L.C.P. Corr. 1913/2148. 'Great Catherine'. Report by E. A. Bendall, and correspondence with the Russian diplomatist Nikolai Sebastianovich von Etter. See also 66042 A.

L.C.P. Corr. 1915/3885. 'The Inca of Perusalem'. Includes report by G. S. Street and correspondence with Gertrude Kingston. See also 66118 F.

L.C.P. Corr. 1916/91. 'The Shewing-Up of Blanco Posnet'. See also 65866 E; 66125 O; L.C.P. Corr. 1909/122.
> Includes G. A. Redford's report of September 1909 and *copies* of correspondence with Frederick Whelen specifying passages to be excised. Other correspondence from 1909 includes a *typed copy* of a letter from Shaw to the actor-manager Ben Iden Payne, and correspondence of the Office with Sir Herbert Beerbohm Tree, Sir William Patrick Byrne, and T. P. Le Fanu of the Irish Office.
> Correspondence of 1916 includes E. A. Bendall's report, a *typed copy* of a letter from Shaw to St. John Ervine, and correspondence of the Office with St. John Ervine, Gertrude Kingston, Frederick Whelen, Sir Owen Seaman, Sir Walter Alexander Raleigh and Squire Bancroft.

L.C.P. Corr. 1921/3794. 'Heartbreak House'. Report and recommendation by G. S. Street. See also 66295 D.

L.C.P. Corr. 1922/4288. 'O'Flaherty, V.C.' Report and recommendation by G. S. Street. See also 66322 N.

L.C.P. Corr. 1923/4900. 'Back to Methuselah'. Includes report and recommendation for licence by G. S. Street, and *typed copy* of a letter of the Lord Chamberlain to Shaw of September 1923. See also 66356 A.

L.C.P. Corr. 1924/5376. 'St. Joan'. Report and recommendation by G. S. Street, with *autograph* note of Lord Chamberlain. See also 66385 A.

L.C.P. Corr. 1924/5632. 'Mrs. Warren's Profession'. Includes extensive *signed* correspondence between Shaw and the Lord Chamberlain of October 1916, and two *autograph* letters of Shaw of February and March 1926, with a *copy* of the reply. See also: 50599; 50600; 53654 H; 66402 G; Deposit 10014.

L.C.P. Corr. 1929/8971. 'The Apple Cart'. Includes report and recommendation of G. S. Street, *copy* of letter from the Lord Chamberlain to Sir Barry Jackson, and *signed* letter of Baron Stamfordham to the Lord Chamberlain. See also 66656 I.

L.C.P. Corr. 1932/11312. 'Too True to be Good'. Report and recommendation by G. S. Street. See also 66811 M.

L.C.P. Corr. 1933/12381. 'On the Rocks'. Report and recommendation by G. S. Street. See also 66866 F.

L.C.P. Corr. 1934/12935. 'Village Wooing'. Report and recommendation by G. S. Street. See also 66892 I.

L.C.P. Corr. 1934/13107. 'The Six of Calais'. Report and recommendation by G. S. Street. See also 66901 L.

L.C.P. Corr. 1935/13605. 'The Simpleton of the Unexpected Isles'. *Autograph* opinions by Lord David Cecil and the Lord Chamberlain, together with report and recommendation by G. S. Street; December 1934. See also 66926 O.

L.C.P. Corr. 1936/15352. 'The Millionairess'. Report and recommendation by H. C. Game. See also 67019 C; 67234; L.C.P. Corr. 1940/3437.

L.C.P. Corr. 1937/771. 'Cymbeline Refinished'. Report and recommendation by G. Dearmer, together with *printed* letter to *The Times* of Laurence Housman. See also 67084 L.

L.C.P. Corr. 1938/1624. 'Geneva'. Report of G. Dearmer, June 1938, with *autograph* note of Lord Chamberlain. See also 67148 H; L.C.P. Corr. 1938/1857.

L.C.P. Corr. 1938/1857. 'Geneva'. Reports by G. Dearmer, C. L. Gordon and H. C. Game, September and October 1938, together with *typewritten* passages of revised text. Correspondence of 1938 and 1939 with Roy Limbert, A. N. Noble and F. K. Roberts of the Foreign Office, Sir Reginald Kennedy-Cox, and F. H. Burroughs.

L.C.P. Corr. 1939/2967. 'In Good King Charles's Golden Days'. Report and recommendation by G. Dearmer. See also 67204 H.

L.C.P. Corr. 1940/3437. 'The Millionairess'. Report and recommendation by H. C. Game. See also 67019 C; 67234 P; L.C.P. Corr. 1936/15352.

L.C.P. Corr. 1948/9778. 'Buoyant Billions'. Report and recommendation by C. D. Heriot. See also 67577 K.

L.C.P. Corr. 1950/1641. 'The Glimpse of Reality'. Report and recommendation by C. D. Heriot. See also 67676 R.

L.C.P. Corr. 1950/2375. 'Farfetched Fables'. Report and recommendation by C. D. Heriot. See also 67714 F.

L.C.P. Corr. 1967/1288. 'Passion, Poison and Petrifaction'. Report and recommendation by C. D. Heriot. See also 68725 E.

APPENDIX I

HANDLIST OF THE BRITISH LIBRARY'S RARE BOOKS COLLECTION OF WORKS OWNED BY G. B. SHAW

The vast majority of G. B. Shaw's published works, whether British or foreign publications, are held at the British Library and entered in the British Library's Integrated Catalogue which is available on the Internet at http://catalogue.bl.uk.

In addition, there is a special collection of works which were owned by Shaw. These include works privately printed by Shaw, such as the playscripts he used for rehearsals. A number of these are represented here in different states of revision. All items in this collection have the shelfmark prefix Shaw. They are also entered in their own right in the British Library's Integrated Catalogue. These editions are not included in the index to the present catalogue.

The George Bernard Shaw Collection.

Buoyant billions: a comedy of no manners. [Ayot St. Lawrence]: Privately published, 1949. Revised rehearsal copy. Shelfmark: Shaw 18

Buoyant billions: a comedy of no manners. [London]: [Privately printed by the author], 1949. Revised rehearsal copy. Shelfmark: Shaw 5

Cymbeline refinished: a variation. [Ayot St. Lawrence]: Privately printed, 1937. Shelfmark: Shaw 17

Farfetched fables, by a Fellow of the Royal Society of Literature [i.e. Bernard Shaw]. [Ayot St. Lawrence]: Private edition, [1949]. First rehearsal copy. Shelfmark: Shaw 14

Farfetched fables, by a Fellow of the Royal Society of Literature [i.e. Bernard Shaw]. [London]: [Privately printed for the author], [19--]. First rehearsal copy. Shelfmark: Shaw 4

Geneva: a fancied page of history, by a Fellow of the Royal Society of Literature [i.e. Bernard Shaw]. [Ayot St. Lawrence]: Privately printed, 1938. Charlotte Shaw's copy, with *MS.* amendments. Shelfmark: Shaw 15

Geneva: a fancied page of history, by a Fellow of the Royal Society of Literature [i.e. Bernard Shaw]. [Ayot St. Lawrence]: Privately printed, 1938. Second rehearsal copy, revised. Shelfmark: Shaw 16

Irish nationalism and Labour internationalism. London: Labour Party, [1920]. Bernard Shaw's own copy. Shelfmark: Shaw 22

Mr. Mallock's ideals: a letter by G. Bernard Shaw, printed in The Times of February 5th, 1909, and reprinted for the information of members. London: Fabian Society, 1909. Bernard Shaw's own copy. Shelfmark: Shaw 35

On the rocks: a political fantasy in two acts, by a Fellow of the Royal Society of Literature [i.e. Bernard Shaw]. [Ayot St. Lawrence]: Privately printed, 1933. Author's prompt copy. Shelfmark: Shaw 6

On the rocks: a political fantasy in two acts, by a Fellow of the Royal Society of Literature [i.e. Bernard Shaw]. [Ayot St. Lawrence]: Privately printed, 1933. First revision after rehearsal (unpublished). Shelfmark: Shaw 7

On the rocks: a political fantasy in two acts, by a Fellow of the Royal Society of Literature [i.e. Bernard Shaw]. [London]: [Privately printed by the author], 1933. First rough proof. Shelfmark: Shaw 3

On the rocks: a compendium of contemporary politics in two acts. [London]: [Privately printed by the author], 1933. First revision after rehearsal. Shelfmark: Shaw 2

Press cuttings: a topical sketch compiled from the editorial and correspondence columns of the daily papers, etc. London: Constable, 1909. Bernard Shaw's copy. Shelfmark: Shaw 20

Saint Joan: a chronicle play. London: Constable, 1924. Issued without the preface. Shelfmark: Shaw 19

Shakes versus Shav: a puppet play, by a Fellow of the Royal Society of Literature [i.e. Bernard Shaw]. [Ayot St. Lawrence]: Private edition, [1949]. First rehearsal copy. Shelfmark: Shaw 8

Shakes versus Shav: a puppet play, by a Fellow of the Royal Society of Literature [i.e. Bernard Shaw]. [London]: [Privately printed by the author], [19--]. First rehearsal copy. Shelfmark: Shaw 1

The Simpleton of the unexpected isles. [Ayot St. Lawrence]: [Privately printed], [1934]. Unbound sheets of which the first sheet is stamped 'second proof' and the others stamped 'third proof'. Shelfmark: Shaw 9

The Simpleton of the unexpected isles. [Ayot St. Lawrence]: [Privately printed], [1934]. [Indeterminate proof]. Shelfmark: Shaw 39

The Six of Calais: a medieval war story, told by Froissart and now retold with certain necessary improvements by a Fellow of the Royal Society of Literature [i.e. Bernard Shaw]. [Ayot St. Lawrence]: Privately printed, 1934. Second rough proof (unpublished). Shelfmark: Shaw 10

The Six of Calais: a medieval war story, told by Froissart and now retold with certain necessary improvements by a Fellow of the Royal Society of Literature [i.e. Bernard Shaw]. [Ayot St. Lawrence]: Privately printed, 1934. Second rough proof (unpublished). [Another copy]. Shelfmark: Shaw 11

The Six of Calais: a medieval war story, told by Froissart and now retold with certain necessary improvements by a Fellow of the Royal Society of Literature [i.e. Bernard Shaw]. [Ayot St. Lawrence]: Privately printed, 1934. First proof after rehearsal (unpublished). Shelfmark: Shaw 12

Village wooing: an unladylike corredieltina for two voices in three conversations, by a Fellow of the Royal Society of Literature [i.e. Bernard Shaw]. [Ayot St. Lawrence]: Privately printed, 1933. Shelfmark: Shaw 13

Other works with George Bernard Shaw associations.

Annie Besant, *The Socialist movement*. London: Freethought Publishing Company, 1887. Bernard Shaw's own copy. Shelfmark: Shaw 24

Erskine Childers, *Clause by clause: a comparison between "The Treaty" and Document no. 2*. Dublin: Irish Nation Committee, [1922]. Bernard Shaw's own copy. Shelfmark: Shaw 33

Joseph Deedy, *First aid to the unemployed and poor*. [London?]: The Poor Defence, [1907]. Presentation copy to Bernard Shaw by the author, 2 Dec. Shelfmark: Shaw 26

C. H. Denyer (ed.), *St. Pancras through the centuries. Being an historical survey of the Metropolitan Borough of St. Pancras*. Prepared by a sub-committee of the Survey Committee of the St. Pancras Rotary Club and the St. Pancras Council of Social Service, and edited C. H. Denyer, etc. [With plates and a map.]. London: Le Play House Press, 1935. Bernard Shaw's own copy, with an invoice from the Press. Shelfmark: Shaw 37

Eamon De Valera, *The Alternative to the "Treaty" ("Document no. 2")*. Dublin: Irish Nation Committee, [1922]. Bernard Shaw's own copy. Shelfmark: Shaw 21

Muriel Hilton, *Vagabond's prayer: and other poems*. Hastings: Denbigh Hilton, [192-?]. Bernard Shaw's own copy. Shelfmark: Shaw 30

T. E. Lawrence, *The Letters of T. E. Lawrence*. Edited by David Garnett. [With plates, including portraits, and maps.] London: Jonathan Cape, 1938. Bernard Shaw's own copy. Shelfmark: Shaw 34

T. E. Lawrence, *Revolt in the desert*. [With portraits and a map.] London: Jonathan Cape, 1927. Bernard Shaw's own copy. With dustwrapper. Shelfmark: Shaw 38

Erwin McCall (ed.), *The Martyrdom of Percy Whitcomb, socialist and agnostic*. London: Watts, [1897]. With extracts from Whitcomb's writings and a prefatory correspondence between Bernard Shaw and Erwin McCall. Bernard Shaw's own copy. Shelfmark: Shaw 31

H. M. Paull, *The Painter and the millionaire: a modern morality play in two acts*. London: Chapman and Hall, 1909. Bernard Shaw's own copy. Shelfmark: Shaw 23

Proceedings of International Conference on Speech Training: held in London from 8th November 1927 to 10th November 1927. London: Central School of Speech Training and Dramatic Art, [1928]. Bernard Shaw's own copy. Shelfmark: Shaw 32

Louis Segal, *Say it in Russian: English-Russian word & phrase book with pronunciation*. Southport: A. Zeltser, 1942. Shelfmark: Shaw 28

Niels Th. Thomsen, *Oscar Wilde: Literaturbilleder fra det moderne England.* Kobenhavn: Privattryk, 1920. Presentation copy from the author to Bernard Shaw. Shelfmark: Shaw 25

J. C. Wells, *Fifteen poems.* Blackpool: J. C. Wells, 1942. Presentation copy from the author to Bernard Shaw. Shelfmark: Shaw 27

Miscellaneous small collections with George Bernard Shaw associations.

Ancoats Brotherhood. [Programmes]. Manchester: Ancoats Brotherhood, [1878?]-[19--]. Holdings: 1897, 1914/15 only. Bernard Shaw's own copies. Shelfmark: Shaw 29

Fabian Society, [A collection of leaflets, forms, etc., collected by Bernard Shaw]. London: Fabian Society, 1887-1949. Fifty-nine leaflets which complement the Library's general collection of Fabian Society leaflets. Shelfmark: Shaw 36

Addenda.

G. B. Shaw, *Drei Dramen ... Candida, Ein Teufelskerl, Helden.* J. G. Cotta'sche, Stuttgart & Berlin, 1903. Presentation copy from the translator, Siegfried Trebitsch, to Shaw. Shelfmark: 11783.df.39.

G. B. Shaw, *Der Verlorene Vater.* Fischer, Berlin, 1906. Presentation copy from the translator, Siegfried Trebitsch, to Shaw. Shelfmark: 11783.de.2.

G. B. Shaw, *Amor de Artistas.* Minerva, Lisbon, 1946. Presentation (in 1948) copy from the translator, Manuel L. Rodrigues, to Shaw. Shelfmark: 012635.aa.45.

APPENDIX II

COLLECTIONS RELATING TO G. B. SHAW IN THE BRITISH LIBRARY SOUND ARCHIVE

The Sound Archive's holdings include recordings of Shaw himself, drawn from radio broadcasts and commercially issued discs, and of performances of his plays from 1931 to the present day. Many of these recordings originated with the BBC, to whose archival holdings the Sound Archive acts as a national point of access. The Sound Archive's catalogue is to be found on the British Library website, currently at http://www.bl.uk/collections/sound-archive/cat.html and new users are directed to 'Tips on Searching'. Any queries should be referred to the Curator of Drama and Literature at the Sound Archive.

APPENDIX III

COLLECTIONS OF MANUSCRIPTS OF GEORGE BERNARD SHAW HELD OUTSIDE THE BRITISH LIBRARY

It is impossible to give here an exhaustive list of repositories of Shaw correspondence and papers, bearing in mind that the final volume of Dan H. Laurence's edition of Shaw's letters cites no fewer than 132 sources. The following list is of the principal collections and omits repositories of largely printed materials. On these, see *Shaw: The Annual of Bernard Shaw Studies, Vol. 20* (Pennsylvania State University Press, 2000), pp. 129-176, which also contains further details on the institutions listed below. All email and url addresses are current at the time of going to press, but the reader will need to check them periodically. Like the British Library, the institutions named here do not own copyright in their Shaw holdings. Permissions for use in publication must be sought from the Society of Authors, 84 Drayton Gardens, London SW10 9SB; [0]208-7373-6642; http://www.societyofauthors.net

1. London School of Economics, Houghton Street, London WC2A 2AE, UK. The Archives Department of the British Library of Political and Economic Science at the L.S.E. holds 22 boxes of the business papers, 1872-1950, as mentioned in the Introduction to the present Catalogue; 18 volumes of diaries, 1885-1897 (microfilmed); and 29 boxes and 14 albums of photographs, *circa* 1895-1950, including many of theatrical productions. In addition, letters and papers of Shaw may be found in the L.S.E.'s holdings of archives of the Independent Labour Party and the Fabian Society (975 boxes), and in the personal papers of close friends and colleagues such as Sidney and Beatrice Webb. Inquiries may be addressed to: Document@lse.ac.uk

2. The National Library of Ireland, Kildare Street, Dublin 2, Eire. Shaw presented the manuscripts of his early novels to the N.L.I., which also holds original and copied manuscripts of correspondence and draft papers. http://www.nli.ie

3.   New York Public Library, 5th Ave. at 42nd St., New York, NY 10018-
      2788, U.S.A. The Berg Collection of literary manuscripts includes
      approximately 700 Shaw letters, 125 other manuscript items, 200 first
      edition publications, many rough proofs and rehearsal copies, pamphlets
      and broadsides, as well as photographs. Much of the correspondence is
      with Trebitsch and other translators. Inquiries: brgref@nypl.org Smaller
      holdings can be found in the Arents Collection – rbkref@nypl.org – and
      in the Manuscripts and Archives Division – mssref@nypl.org

4.   Cornell University, Ithaca, NY 14853-5302, U.S.A. The Bernard F.
      Burgunder Collections, part of the Rare and Manuscript Collections in the
      Carl A. Kroch Library, includes 900 letters and manuscripts of Shaw, over
      2,500 photographs, and, among 2,600 printed items, much rare theatrical
      and political ephemera. af33@cornel.edu

5.   Harry Ransom Humanities Research Center, University of Texas at
      Austin, TX 78712, U.S.A. The equivalent of 100 boxes of manuscript
      plays, essays, correspondence, financial and legal records, diaries and
      printed and manuscript ephemera. A very full inventory can be found at
      http://www.lib.utexas.edu

6.   Colgate University, Hamilton, NY 13346-1398, U.S.A. The Richard S.
      Weiner Collection, housed in the Case Library, Department of
      Special Collections, contains over 1,000 letters written by Shaw and
      many by Charlotte Shaw, together with manuscripts, books,
      photographs and art work. The collection covers topics related to the
      theatre, social reform, publication and literary translation. See
      http://exlibris.colgate.edu/services/departments/SpecColl

7.   University of North Carolina, Chapel Hill, NC 27514-8890, U.S.A. The
      Archibald Henderson Collection, housed in the Wilson Library,
      Department of Rare Books, contains both published and manuscript
      materials which derive from Henderson's correspondence and papers over
      the 46 years that he worked on biographical publications about Shaw.
      They include a Rare Book Archive which contains several thousand items
      by or about Shaw, including 55 proofs, rehearsal copies and Shaw's own
      corrected prompt copies of plays. There are also a large number of
      playbills, photographs, cartoons, news cuttings and other ephemera.
      Henderson's notes and correspondence with Shaw are to be found in the
      Southern Historical Collection's George Bernard Shaw papers, together
      with a number of Shaw's literary drafts and proofs as well as letters, and
      supplementary collections of Shaw's correspondence with publishers

and individuals in the world of politics and the theatre.
rbcref@email.unc.edu
http://www.lib.unc.edu/rbc
http://www.lib.unc.edu/mss

8. The University of Guelph, Guelph, Ontario NlG 2W1, Canada. The holdings of the Archival and Special Collections in the McLaughlin Library include Canadian theatre archives with a strong Shaw focus; the Shaw Festival archives date back to 1962, and are supplemented by smaller theatre collections such as the Shakespeare Memorial Committee Collection, and the Augustin Hamon Collection (supplemented by microfilms of the Hamon archive at the University of Brest). An outstanding acquisition is the collection of Dan H. Laurence, which includes very rare printed or duplicated items by Shaw, most of the published works in first editions, rough-proof copies of the plays, and the largest extant collection of works about Shaw. This is completed by the archive of Laurence himself, containing all the materials used in preparation of the *Collected Letters* and the *Bibliography*.

INDEX

A

Abbott (Bill), *hairdresser, of Ealing.*
Letter to G. B. Shaw, 1938. 50522,
f. 119.

Abbott (W. D.), *of Birmingham.*
Letter to G. B. Shaw, 1913. 50516,
f. 350.

Abdullah (Mahmoud), *former Stage
Manager, Anglo-Egyptian Amateur
Dramatic Society.* Letter, with
Sergeant J. E. Jones, Sergeant J.
Stout and Sergeant J. L. Price, to
Consul General at Alexandria,
1916. *Signed.* 56627, f. 185.

Abdy-Williams *afterw.* **Whishaw**
(Ellen Mary); *editor of 'Time'.*
Letters to G. B. Shaw, 1884, 1885.
Partly *shorthand draft.* 50510, ff.
307, 323; 50511, ff. 45, 48-51v,
104.

Aberconway, *Baroness.*
v. McLaren *née* Macnaghten
(Christabel Mary Melville).

**Aberdaron Co-operative Housing
Society.** Letter of C. S. Jones to
G. B. Shaw concerning, 1908.
Signed. 50515, f. 140.

Academy of Dramatic Art. Letter to
G. B. Shaw of Sir S. B. Bancroft
concerning, 1908. *Signed* and
mainly *printed.* 50515, f. 102.

Acheson (Sinead), *of London.* Letter
to G. B. Shaw, n.d. *Imperf.* 50527,
f. 1.

Achurch (Janet), *actress; wife of C.
Charrington.* Letters of G. B. Shaw
to C. Charrington and J. Achurch,
1889-1924, n.d. *Typewritten copies.*
50532; 50561 *passim.*
— Letter of G. B. Shaw to J. Achurch,
1911. *Typewritten copy.* 50562,
f. 72.

Acland (*Sir* Francis Dyke), *M.P.,
P.C.; 14th Bart.* Letter of
Vandercom & Co., solicitors, to Sir
F. D. Acland as Under-Secretary at
the Foreign Office, 1912. *Copy.*
50516, f. 204.

'Aclet', *pseudonym.* 'The New
Democratic Freedom and the
Democratic Freedomain', 1940.
Printed. 50742, ff. 149-162v.

**'A Constitution for World Govern-
ment'.** Letter, etc., to G. B. Shaw of
S. Chaudhuri, 1949. *Signed.* 63186,
f. 224.

Adam (Ronald), *director of the
Embassy Theatre.* Letter to G. B.
Shaw, 1937. *Signed.* 50521, f. 323.

Adams (Bessie), *of Rathmines,
Dublin.* Letter, etc., to G. B. Shaw,
1946. 50525, f. 331.

Adams (E. H.), *[widow?] of F. W. L.
Adams.* Letter to G. B. Shaw, 1893.
50513, f. 29.

Adamson (Ethel McClintock), *wife of
Robert Adamson, of New York.*
Letter to G. B. Shaw, 1915. *Signed.*
50517, f. 230.

Adkins (D. A.), *Director of public
relations, Max Parrish and Co.*
Letter to G. B. Shaw, 1950. *Signed.*
50526 B, f. 491.

1944. *Typewritten copies.* 50524, ff. 123-127.

— 'The State's Responsibility': Memorandum rel. to residential homes for children, 1944. *Copy.* 50524, ff. 128-132v.

Allen (Percy), *author and spiritualist.* Letter to G. B. Shaw, 1946. 50525, f. 346.

Allen (Reginald Clifford), *Baron Allen of Hurtwood.* 'Manifesto on Fabian Policy', 1911. *Printed,* with pencil marginalia. 50681, ff. 110-111.

— Correspondence with G. B. Shaw, 1912-1915. Partly *signed, copy* and *dictated.* 50516, ff. 123, 124, 131; 50557, f. 234.

— Manifesto in reply to that of the German Social Democratic Party, 1915. *Typewritten draft.* 50557, ff. 235-236.

Allen (Richard), *teacher at Alberni Residential School, Vancouver Island.* Letter to G. B. Shaw, 1944. *Signed.* 50555, f. 144.

Allerton (W. E.), *bookmaker, of Wallasey, Cheshire.* Letter to G. B. Shaw, 1944. 50524, f. 207.

Alma-Tadema (Laurence), *author; daughter of Sir L. Alma-Tadema.* Letters to G. B. Shaw, 1895-1924. Partly *typewritten copy.* 50513, f. 89; 50514, ff. 18, 55; 50519, f. 166.

Aloe (Francisco), *of Buenos Aires, Argentina.* Letter to G. B. Shaw, 1946. Partly *Span.* 50525, f. 57.

Alston (Madeline), *of Stellenbosch.* Letter to C. F. Shaw, 1932. 56493, f. 20.

Alviella (*Comte* — Goblet d'), *Belgian senator.* Introductory statement on behalf of 'Potentia Organization', signed with Sir V. H. P. Caillard, Sir G. H. Darwin, Sir M. Foster, J. Claretie, F. W. Foerster, J. Le Jeune and Dr. C. Richet, 1930? Partly *printed,* with *duplicated* signatures. 50742, f. 140.

American Offset Printers, *of Los Angeles.* Prospectus, 1937. *Printed.* 50521, f. 321v.

American Shaw Society. Note of G. B. Shaw rel. to, 1950. *Typewritten draft.* 50679, f. 387.

Ames (Percy Willoughby), *LL.D.; F.S.A; Secretary of the Royal Society of Literature.* Letter to G. B. Shaw, 1911. *Signed.* 50516, f. 55.

Andersen (Johannes C.), *of the Alexander Turnbull Library, Wellington, New Zealand.* Letter, etc., to G. B. Shaw, 1934. Partly *printed.* 50520, f. 235.

Anderson (*Mrs.* C.), *of Goodmayes, co. Essex.* Letter, etc., to G. B. Shaw, 1938. 50582, ff. 121-123.

Anderson (Elizabeth Garrett), *M.D.* Letter to C. F. Payne-Townshend, 1896. 56490, f. 145.

Anderson (*Mrs.* G.), *of Goodmayes, co. Essex.* Letter with pastel portrait of G. B. Shaw, 1938. 50582, ff. 121-123.

Anderson (R. Wherry), *Fabian.* Cartoon sketch of G. B. Shaw, E. B. Bax and the Prince of Wales, 1893. 50680, f. 125.

Anderson (S.), *of Carnarvon.* Letter to G. B. Shaw, 1888. 50512, f. 46.

Aravinda Gosha, *Indian guru.* Letter to Dilipa-Kumara Raya, n.d. *Copy.* 50527, f. 117.

Arbuthnot (Malcolm), *photographer, of New Bond Street, London.* Portrait photographs of G. B. Shaw, 1930? 50582, ff. 31, 32, 46.

Archer *née* **Trickett** (Frances Elizabeth), *wife of William Archer.* Letter of G. B. Shaw to, 1915. *Signed.* 45296, f. 230.

Archer (William), *drama critic and author.* Portrait photograph of, *circa* 1880-1890. 50584, f. 1.

— Letter to, of C. R. Morley, 1885. 50528, f. 34.

— Correspondence with G. B. Shaw of and concerning, 1885-1924. Partly *shorthand* and *typewritten draft.* Partly *signed.* 45296; 50528, ff. 29-83; 50660, f. 2; 50682, ff. 41v-27v (vol. rev.); 73484, f. 30.

— Letter to, of E. Yates, 1886. 50528, f. 40.

— 'Masks and Faces', annotated by G. B. Shaw, 1888. *Printed* proofs *(fragm.).* 45296, ff. 14v-17.

— Letters to, of C. F. Shaw, 1902-1919, n.d. 45296, ff. 102-104v, 178, 225, 229, 249, 278.

— Letter to, of F. Humphreys, 1903. 45296, f. 125.

— Letter to the editor of 'The Tribune', 1907. *Printed,* with *autogr.* amendments. 45296, f. 186.

— Letter to, of G. B. Shaw, concerning stage construction, *circa* 1907. *Draft.* 50682, ff. 41v-27v.

— Letter to W. Archer, H. G. Granville-Barker and G. B. Shaw of Dame E. S. Lyttelton concerning Shakespeare Memorial National Theatre, 1909. *Typewritten copy.* 50539, f. 175.

— Group portrait in cowboy costume with T. E. Scott-Ellis, Sir J. M. Barrie, G. K. Chesterton and G. B. Shaw, 1914. 50582, f. 39.

Argyll, *Duke of.* v. Campbell (Niall Diarmid).

Aristotelian Society. Programme of meetings, 1916. *Printed.* 50701, f. 241.

Arliss (George), *actor.* Letters to G. B. Shaw, 1940, 1941. 50522, ff. 310, 311, 429.

Armagh, *Archbishop of.* v. Gregg (John Allen Fitzgerald).

Armitage (John), *of 'The Fortnightly'.* Letter to G. B. Shaw, 1940. *Signed.* 50522, f. 262.

Armstrong (A. Q.), *of Vancouver, British Columbia.* Letter to G. B. Shaw, 1946. 50526 B, f. 360.

Armstrong (Gertrude), *of North Western Polytechnic, London.* Letter to Dr. F. E. Loewenstein, 1949. 56632, f. 127.

Arncliffe (Thomas), *of Wakefield; spelling reformer.* Letter, etc., to G. B. Shaw, 1941. *Signed, typewritten* and *printed.* 50554, ff. 144-182.

Arnold (Mary), *of Ramsgate.* Letter, etc., to G. B. Shaw, *circa* 1923. Partly *typewritten.* 50527, f. 3.

— 'What After Death', *circa* 1923. *Typewritten.* 50527, f. 5.

Arnold-Forster (Hugh Oakeley), *P.C.; M.P.* Correspondence with G. B. Shaw, 1888. Partly *signed* and *shorthand draft.* 50512, ff. 22v, 57v.

Shavings' by J. Farleigh, 1932, 1934. 71451-71455.

— Model of memorial to 'Mark Twain' by W. Russell, 1935. *Photogr. Signed.* 50521, ff. 104-105.

— Sketch of B. Patch by Mrs. B. Ward, *circa* 1936. *Newsprint.* 50741, ff. 70, 245.

— Pencil portrait of T. G. Masaryk, 1937. 50742, f. 170.

— Self-portrait of J. J. Muller, *circa* 1938. 50522, f. 128.

— Painting by C. Atwood of Edith Craig and friends, 1939. *Photogr.* 50522, f. 317v.

— Drawing of E. de Valera by S. O'Sullivan, *circa* 1940?-1947? *Reproduction.* 50584, f. 45.

— Portrait of a French prisoner of war by Kurt Reuter, 1941. *Copy.* 50526 B, f. 426.

— Portrait of [Lord Alfred Douglas?] in childhood, 1941? *Photographic copy. Signed.* 50584, f. 47.

— Self-portrait of Andrew MacLaren, 1943. 50523, f. 183.

— Portrait of Albert Einstein by J. Plesch, 1944. *Photogr.* 50524, f. 265v.

— Greetings cards of S. Brett, n.d. 50563, ff. 11, 12.

v. also Shaw (G. B.). PHOTOGRAPHS, PORTRAITS AND CARICATURES.
Shaw, *family.*
Names of individual subjects and artists.

Ashley (*Rev.* Frederick J.), *Methodist minister.* Letters to G. B. Shaw and C. F. Shaw, 1935. 50521, f. 53; 56493, f. 129.

Ashton (Winifred), *al.* '*Clemence Dane'; author.* Letter of G. B. Shaw to, 1922. *Copy.* 50518, f. 299.

Ashwell (Lena), *O.B.E.; actress and director.* Correspondence with G. B. Shaw, 1898-1915, n.d. Partly *typewritten copy.* 50528, ff. 84-98; 50561, f. 119; 50562, ff. 67, 69, 98.

— Letters to C. F. Shaw, *circa* 1912. 56491, f. 87; 63186, f. 227.

— 'Considerations', [issued by?], 1938. *Duplicated.* 56494, f. 12.

Askew and Company Ltd., *tailors.* Letter to G. B. Shaw, 1940. 50522, f. 272.

Aspinall (*Mrs.* E. M. G.), *of London.* Letter to G. B. Shaw, 1940? *Fragm.* 50522, f. 319.

Asquith *afterw.* **Bibesco** (Elizabeth). *v.* Bibesco *née* Asquith.

Asquith *née* **Tennant** (Emma Alice Margaret *called* Margot), *2nd wife of 1st Earl of Oxford and Asquith.* Correspondence with C. F. Shaw, 1900, 1905. 56491, ff. 19, 42.

Asquith (Herbert Henry), *1st Earl of Oxford and Asquith; Prime Minister.* Letter to, from G. B. Shaw, 1908. 80801.

— Invitation to the wedding of his daughter Elizabeth, 1919. Mainly *printed.* 50518, f. 142.

Association of Teachers of Speech and Drama. Programme of course, 1936. *Printed.* 50521, ff. 200-201.

Astbury (J. B.), *of Camden Town.* Letter to G. B. Shaw, 1903. 50514, f. 128.

Astor (John Jacob), *1st Baron Astor of Hever; younger son of William,*

B

Bab (Julius), *German theatre scholar and critic.* Correspondence with G. B. Shaw, 1909-1946. Partly *signed.* Partly *Germ.* and *copy.* 50515, ff. 307, 384, 386, 390; 50525, f. 28; 50562, f. 70.

Bab-Loos (Elisabeth), *wife of Julius Bab.* Letter to G. B. Shaw, 1910. 50515, f. 387.

Backer-Grondahl (Agathe), *pianist and composer.* Letter to G. B. Shaw, 1890. 50512, f. 218.

Bagley (Richard), *of the United Telephone Company.* Letters to G. B. Shaw, 1880, 1881. 50508, f. 282; 50509, ff. 44, 47.

Bahr (Hermann), *German dramatist and critic.* Photographs of Hermann Bahr, 1910. 50584, ff. 3, 4.

— Postcard, with S. J. Loeb, to G. B. Shaw, 1911. 50516, f. 71.

Bahr-Mildenburg (Anna).
v. Mildenburg.

Bailey (David Algar), *author.* Letter, etc., [to B. Patch?], 1935. *Signed.* 50521, f. 81.

— Letter to G. B. Shaw, 1935. *Copy.* 50521, f. 82.

Bailey (Francis A.), *waiter, in Brisbane, Queensland.* Letter to G. B. Shaw, 1946. 50525, f. 298.

Bailey (Iris), *of Canterbury, co. Kent.* Letters to G. B. Shaw, 1943. 50523, ff. 90, 148.

Bailey (William Frederick), *P.C.; Irish Land Commissioner.* Letter to G. B. Shaw, 1915. 50517, f. 322.

— Letter to W. B. Yeats, 1915. 50553, f. 156.

Baird Smith (Ellen M.), *wife of A. M. Baird Smith, rector of Wheathampstead.* Letter to G. B. Shaw, 1944. 50524, f. 270.

Baker (Edwin D.), *student at McGill University, Montreal.* Letter, with B. R. Woodburn-Heron and M. Giri, to G. B. Shaw, 1946. *Signed.* 50526 B, f. 326.

Baker (Ernest S.), *agent for Norton, Lilly and Company in Balboa, Canal Zone.* Letter, etc., to C. F. Shaw, 1936. *Signed* and partly *printed.* 56493, f. 159.

Baker (F. A.), *of Johannesburg, South Africa.* Letter to G. B. Shaw, 1946. 50525, f. 48.

Baker (Frederick C.), *of Whittier, California.* Letter, etc., to G. B. Shaw, 1946. *Signed.* Partly *printed.* 50526 B, f. 280.

Baker (George), **& Co.**, *pharmacists at Rome.* Medical prescriptions, 1894. Partly *printed.* 56490, ff. 105-109.

Bakker (C.), *secretary to the International Society of Sculptors, Painters and Gravers.* Letter to G. B. Shaw, 1908. *Signed.* 50515, f. 105.

Baldwin (Stanley), *1st Earl Baldwin of Bewdley; Prime Minister.* Letter of G. B. Shaw to, annotated by D. G. Hogarth, 1923. *Typewritten draft.* 50540, f. 10.

— Letter of G. B. Shaw and others to, 1937. *Typewritten draft.* 50543, f. 199.

Bale (Owen T.), *formerly engineer on the R.M.M.V. 'Winchester Castle'.* Letter to G. B. Shaw, 1944. 50524, f. 66.

Bales (E. R.), *member of Royal Canadian Institute.* Letter, etc., to G. B. Shaw, 1930. 50520, f. 21.

Balfour (Arthur James), *1st Earl of Balfour; Prime Minister.* Letter of G. B. Shaw to, concerning Ashton Ellis, 1905. *Draft.* 50514, f. 241.

Balfour-Browne (John Hutton). *v.* Browne.

Bancroft (George E.), *[actor?].* Photograph of G. E. Bancroft, T. Mowbray and G. S. Wray, 1926? 50584, f. 7.

Bancroft *formerly* **Butterfield** (*Sir* Squire Bancroft), *actor-manager.* Letter to G. B. Shaw concerning Academy of Dramatic Art, 1908. *Signed* and mainly *printed.* 50515, f. 102.

— Correspondence with G. B. Shaw, 1908-1917. Partly *signed* and *shorthand draft.* 50515, ff. 102, 162; 50516, ff. 101, 146-147v; 50518, f. 52.

— Letters, etc., to the Lord Chamberlain, 1911-1922. *L.C.P. Corr.* 1916/91; *L.C.P. Corr.* 1924/5632, f. 95; *Deposit* 10014/104.

Bandmann (Maurice E.), *of the Empire Theatre, Calcutta.* Letters to G. H. Thring, 1912. *Signed.* 56627, ff. 78, 80.

Bank (Alma von), *German translator, in London.* Letters to G. B. Shaw, 1936, 1937. 50521, ff. 185, 280.

Banning (L.), *graphologist, of Shoreham-by-Sea.* Letter to G. B. Shaw, 1932. *Signed.* 50520, f. 178.

Bannister (Albert H.), *of Highbury.* Letter to G. B. Shaw, 1943. 50523, f. 126.

Bannister *afterw.* **Parry** (Gertrude), *cousin of Sir Roger Casement.* Letters, etc., to C. F. Shaw, 1916-1941, n.d. 56491, ff. 215, 230; 56494, ff. 102, 166; 63197, f. 92.

— Letters to G. B. Shaw, 1916, 1944. 50517, f. 427; 50524, f. 20.

Banthiya & Co., *publishers, of Ajmer, India.* Letters to G. B. Shaw, 1944. Partly *copy.* 63186, ff. 191, 192.

Barber (Mary Elizabeth), *barrister; of the Society of Authors.* Letter, etc., to G. B. Shaw, 1944, 1945. *Signed.* 50524, f. 332; 50555, f. 100.

Barbera (*Monsignor* M.), *S.J.* Letter concerning the film version of 'St. Joan', 1935. *Typewritten copy.* 50633, f. 48.

Barbour (William), *of the American Foundation for the Blind.* Letter, etc., to G. B. Shaw, 1942. *Signed.* 50522, f. 459.

Barbusse (Hélyonne), *widow of Henri Barbusse.* Letter to G. B. Shaw, 1937. *Fr.* 50521, f. 247.

Barclay (*Sir* Thomas), *barrister.* Letter to G. B. Shaw, 1918. 50518, f. 99.

Bárdos (*Dr.* Artur), *Director of the City Theatre, Budapest.* Correspondence with G. B. Shaw, 1935, 1936. *Signed.* Partly *shorthand draft.* 50521, ff. 121, 121v, 163.

— Photographs of production of 'St. Joan' at Budapest staged by Dr. A. Bárdos, 1936. 50591.

Baring (*Hon.* Maurice), *writer.* Letters to G. B. Shaw, 1911-1934. Partly *typewritten.* 50516, f. 4;

50518, f. 103; 50520, f. 232; 63186, f. 38.

Baring (Rowland Thomas), *2nd Earl of Cromer.* Correspondence, as Lord Chamberlain, with G. B. Shaw, 1923, 1926. Partly *copy. L.C.P. Corr.* 1923/4900; *L.C.P. Corr.* 1924/5632.

Baring-Gould (E. S.), *Managing Director, The Oatine Co.* Letter to A. C. Smith, 1911. *Signed.* 50549, f. 181.

Barker (Harley Granville Granville-). *v.* Granville-Barker.

Barker (Henry A.), *secretary of the Socialist League.* Correspondence with G. B. Shaw, 1886-1889. Partly *draft.* 50511, ff. 157, 272v, 281v-283; 50512, f. 90v.

Barker (*Sir* Herbert Atkinson), *manipulative surgeon.* Letters to G. B. Shaw, 1939, 1946. 50522, f. 192; 50526 A, f. 80.

Barker (John), *secretary of the Lester-Jones Tribute.* Letter to G. B. Shaw, 1946. *Signed.* 50525, f. 192.

Barlow (E. G.), *secretary of the National Society for the Abolition of Cruel Sports.* Letter to G. B. Shaw, 1946. 50525, f. 190.

Barlow (George), *author.* Letter to G. B. Shaw, 1936. *Typewritten.* 50521, f. 219.

Barnard (Egbert), *of New York.* Telegram to G. B. Shaw, 1946. 50526 B, f. 351.

Barnes (*Sir* Kenneth Ralph), *Principal of R.A.D.A.* Letters, etc., to G. B. Shaw, 1912-1914. *Signed.* 50516, ff. 274, 324, 326; 50517, f. 120.

— Letter to, of Sir J. Hare, 1913. *Copy.* 50516, f. 327.

— R.A.D.A. termly report, signed by E. G. H. Williams and Sir K. R. Barnes, 1938. 50742, f. 166.

Barnes (Laurence), *of Haslingden, co. Lancs.* Letter to G. B. Shaw, 1938. 50522, f. 123.

Barnes (Michael), *son of Kenneth Barnes.* Photograph of, 1944? 50584, f. 2.

Barnett (A.), *chairman of Bracknell Labour Party.* Letter to G. B. Shaw, 1946. 50526 A, f. 209.

Barnett (M.), *of Chelsea.* Letter to G. B. Shaw, 1941. 50522, f. 350.

Barnsley British Co-operative Society. Poster advertising Fabian lectures, 1890. *Printed.* 50701, f. 80.

Barr (W. F.), *of Durban, South Africa.* Letter to G. B. Shaw, n.d. 50527, f. 9.

Barrett (Horace), *member of the executive committee of the Shakespeare Memorial Theatre.* Letter to G. B. Shaw, 1937. *Signed.* 50521, f. 262.

Barrett (R.), *socialist, of Pretoria, South Africa.* Letter to G. B. Shaw, n.d. 50527, f. 12.

Barrett (Rowland), *socialist, of Devon.* Letter, etc., to G. B. Shaw, 1944. Partly *printed.* 50555, f. 118.

Barrett (Wilson), *actor-manager.* Letter to G. B. Shaw, 1900. *Signed.* 50513, f. 213.

Barrie (*Sir* James Matthew), *Bart., author.* Letters to G. B. Shaw, 1901-1913, n.d. Partly *typewritten copy.* 50529, ff. 1-14.

— Group portrait in cowboy costume of T. E. Scott-Ellis, W. Archer, Sir J. M. Barrie, G. K. Chesterton and G. B. Shaw, 1914. 50582, f. 39.

— Sketches, 1914. *Typewritten carbons.* 50643, ff. 182-185.

Barrington (Christina), *wife of Sir B. E. E. Barrington.* Letters to G. B. Shaw, 1904, 1905. 50548, ff. 30, 41.

Barrows (Winifred), *of the Lawnside Girls' School, Great Malvern.* Letter to G. B. Shaw, 1946. 50525, f. 193.

Barry (Arthur Hugh Smith), *P.C.; Baron Barrymore.* Letter to C. F. Shaw, 1907. 56491, f. 50.

Barrymore (John), *Jr.; actor.* Letter to G. B. Shaw, 1933. 50520, f. 198.

Barshay (A. E.), *at the Office of Military Government for Germany (U.S.).* Letter, etc., to G. B. Shaw, 1948. *Signed.* 50526 B, f. 403.

Barthas (*Dr.* Thérèse), *of Alexandria.* Letter to G. B. Shaw, 1946. 50526 A, f. 123.

Bartholomew (*Gen. Sir* William Henry), *G.C.B.* Chalk drawing of, by C. U. Gill, 1922. *Photographic copy.* 56499, f. 52.

Bartlett (Walter W.), *Fabian.* Letter to G. B. Shaw, 1888. 50512, f. 68.

Bartlett Dixon and Company Ltd, *travel agents.* Letters to C. F. Shaw, 1935-1936. *Typewritten* and *signed.* 56493, ff. 135-153 *passim.*

Barton (James Kingston), *M.R.C.S.* Correspondence with G. B. Shaw, 1879-1891. 50508 *passim*; 50509 *passim*; 50510, ff. 42, 57, 67; 50522, f. 435; 60391, f. 158.

— Letter to, of R. G. Hill, 1880. 50508, f. 237.

— Letter to Sir J. Paget, 1880. 50508, f. 258.

— Letter to, of C. B. Lockwood, 1881? 50509, f. 75.

— Letter, on behalf of G. B. Shaw, to F. Schneider, 1883. 50510, f. 59.

Barton (William), *brother of Dr. J. K. Barton.* Letter to G. B. Shaw, 1881. 50509, f. 21.

Baschet (René), *editor, 'L'Illustration', Paris.* Letter to A. F. A. Hamon, 1914. *Signed. Fr.* 50517, f. 33.

Bassett (Catherine), *ratepayer, of Tottenham.* Letter to G. B. Shaw, *circa* 1910. 50527, f. 14.

Bassett-Lowke (Wenman Joseph). *v.* Lowke.

Bastard (*Mme.* J.), *President of the Ligue de Protection des Animaux.* Circular letter, 1931. *Printed.* 50520, f. 50.

Bastheim (Louis), *of Pittsburgh, Pennsylvania.* Letter to G. B. Shaw, 1946. *Signed.* 50526 A, f. 145.

Basu (Tarapada), *of the 'Hindusthan Standard'.* Letter to G. B. Shaw, 1945. *Signed.* 50524, f. 299.

Bates (Peggy), *patient in St. Mary Islington Hospital, Highgate.* Letter to G. B. Shaw, 1944. 50524, f. 195.

Bathurst (Benjamin Ludlow), *Q.C.; 2nd Viscount Bledisloe.* Joint opinion concerning the will of G. B. Shaw of B. L. Bathurst and J. Brunyate, 1957. *Typewritten copy.* 79493, f. 19.

Batson (Eric J.), *library assistant, of St. Pancras.* Letter to G. B. Shaw, 1943. 50523, f. 109.

Batthyany (Hester M.), *daughter of Ernest and Dolly Radford*. Letter to G. B. Shaw, 1944. 50524, f. 21.

Baulkwill (*Sir* Reginal Pridham), *Public Trustee*. Letter to Sir I. J. Pitman, 1957. *Copy*. 79493, f. 20.

— Letter to press, 1958. *Copy*. 79493, f. 45.

Bax (Ernest Belford), *socialist writer*. Letters to G. B. Shaw, 1884. 50510, ff. 223, 253, 265.

— Cartoon sketch by R. W. Anderson of G. B. Shaw, E. B. Bax and the Prince of Wales, 1893. 50680, f. 125.

Bayon (Henry Peter), *medical writer*. Letter to G. B. Shaw, 1941. *Signed*. 50522, f. 375.

Beach (Sylvia), *bookseller and publisher*. Letter to, from G. B. Shaw, 1921. *Copy*. 57346, f. 64.

Beacon Hill School, *near Bath*. Play by pupils, 1940. *Typewritten*. 50579.

Beadle (M. Ethel), *Fabian*. Letter to F. E. Loewenstein, 1948. *Signed*. 50565, f. 191.

Beagin (Alfred Henry). Portrait photograph of A. H. Beagin, 1910?-1920? *Signed*. 50584, f. 9.

Beal (Arthur), *of Cambria, California*. Letter to G. B. Shaw, 1946. 50526 B, f. 352.

Beasley (F.), *of Luton*. Letter to G. B. Shaw, 1946. 50525, f. 107.

Beattie (*Lt.* Hugh), *20th N.Z. Armoured Regiment*. Letter to G. B. Shaw, 1944. 50555, f. 117.

Beatty (Octavius Holmes), *barrister; brother of P. T. Beatty*. Notice of meeting in support of candidature of O. H. Beatty, 1895. *Printed*. 50701, f. 153.

Beatty (Pakenham Thomas), *friend of G. B. Shaw*. Correspondence with G. B. Shaw, 1878-1889, n.d. Partly *draft* and *printed*. 50530, ff. 1-224.

— 'Songs for the People No. 2: Today', *circa* 1885. *Printed*. 50530, f. 224.

Beatty (Pakenham William Albert Hengist Mazzini), *son of P. T. Beatty*. Correspondence with G. B. Shaw, 1899, 1911. Partly *signed* and *typewritten copy*. 50530, ff. 225-228v; 50561, f. 134.

Beaumont (Hugh), *managing director, H. M. Tennent Ltd*. Letter to G. B. Shaw, 1941. *Signed*. 50522, f. 418.

Beaumont (Mabel Edith), *wife of Sir J. W. F. Beaumont*. Letter to C. F. Shaw, 1933. 56493, f. 57.

Beavan (John), *editor of the 'Manchester Evening News'*. Letter, etc., to G. B. Shaw, 1946. *Signed*. Partly *printed*. 50525, f. 171.

Bebb (John), *of Wilmington, California*. Letter to G. B. Shaw, 1947. 50526 B, f. 377.

Becher (C.), *music shop owner, of Breslau*. Letter to G. B. Shaw, 1911. *Germ*. 50516, f. 80.

Beck (W. J.), *of Bournemouth*. Letter to G. B. Shaw, 1946. 50525, f. 54.

Becker (Harry), *regional publicity organiser, National Savings Committee*. Letter to G. B. Shaw, 1943. *Signed*. 50523, f. 175.

Beckett (Edmund), *1st Baron Grimthorpe*. Letters to A. R.

Wallace and F. T. Bond, 1902. *Printed.* 50514, ff. 69, 69v.

Beckett (Tom), *of the Connolly Association, Slough, co. Bucks.* Letter to G. B. Shaw, 1943. 50523, f. 161.

Bedendo (*Dr.* Piero), *director of the Banca d'Italia, Savona.* Letter to G. B. Shaw, 1936. *Signed. Ital.* 50521, f. 131.

Bedford Debating Society. Annual reports, and notices of meetings, 1884-1888. *Printed.* 50701, ff. 9, 24; 50702, ff. 158-159, 191-194.

Beeby (George Stephenson), *K.B.E. (1939); New South Wales politician.* Letter to G. B. Shaw, 1912. *Signed.* 50516, f. 263.

Beech (Patrick), *son of Stella Beech.* Letters, etc., to G. B. Shaw, 1943, 1949. Partly *signed* and *copy.* 50531, f. 51; 63186, f. 185.

Beech (*Mrs.* Stella Mervyn), *daughter of Mrs. Patrick Campbell.* Letter to G. B. Shaw, 1942. 50522, f. 467.

Beecher (Robert), *American journalist, in Vienna.* Letter to G. B. Shaw, 1922. 50518, f. 316.

Beerbohm (*Sir* Max), *author and cartoonist.* Letters, etc., to G. B. Shaw, 1898-1935. Partly *copy.* 50529, ff. 15-58.

— Cartoon, 'Man and Superman', 1903. 50529, f. 31.

— Letter to G. B. Shaw with cartoon [of Rebecca West?], 1918. *Copy.* 50529, ff. 57, 58.

— Assignation of copyright to Sir M. Beerbohm in memorial essay, by G. B. Shaw, 1920. 50743 B, f. 347.

— Letter to C. F. Shaw, 1935. 56493, f. 145.

Beeton (Bessie), *[wife of H. R. Beeton?].* Letter to G. B. Shaw, 1912. 50516, f. 260.

Belfield (Jane), *of Germantown, Pennsylvania.* Letter to 'Metropolitan', New York, 1913? *Copy.* 50517, ff. 8-16.

— Letter, etc., to G. B. Shaw, 1914. Partly *printed* and *copy.* 50517, f. 7.

'Belgravia Magazine'. Note to G. B. Shaw, 1882. Mainly *printed.* 50509, f. 188.

Bell (Aileen), *sister of C. A. Bell and S. C. Horne.* Letters to G. B. Shaw, 1883, 1885, n.d. 50510, ff. 12, 36, 72; 50511, ff. 19, 81; 50527, f. 17.

Bell (Charles James), *brother of Chichester Bell.* Letter to S. C. Horne, 1881. 50509, f. 107.

— Letters to G. B. Shaw, 1881, 1882. Partly *signed.* 50509, ff. 100, 197.

Bell (Chichester Alexander), *M.B.; cousin of Alexander Graham Bell.* Letters to G. B. Shaw, 1879-1881. 50508, ff. 128, 153, 155, 186; 50509, f. 106.

Bell (George) **and Sons,** *publishers.* Letter to G. B. Shaw, 1884. 50510, f. 199.

Bell (George Kennedy Allen), *Bishop of Chichester.* Letter to G. B. Shaw, 1941. *Signed.* 50522, f. 363.

Bell (*Sir* Harold Idris), *Keeper of Manuscripts, British Museum.* Letter to, from C. F. Shaw, 1940. 59530, f. 191.

— Receipt for C. F. Shaw's deposit of letters of T. E. Lawrence, 1940. 63197, f. 43.

concerning G. B. and C. F. Shaw to E. Rumbold, 1951. 52752, f. 321.

— Letter to G. B. Shaw, n.d. 50527, f. 25.

Bentley (George), *of Richard Bentley and Son, publishers.* Correspondence with G. B. Shaw, 1879-1883. Partly *shorthand draft.* 50508, ff. 183, 202-203v; 50509, f. 114; 50510, ff. 69, 142.

Bentley (Richard) **and Son** *formerly* **Henry Colburn and Richard Bentley** *formerly* **Richard Bentley, publishers, of London.** Correspondence with G. B. Shaw, 1880-1884. Partly *copy* and *shorthand draft.* 50508, f. 187; 50509, ff. 39, 40-41v, 130-131, 137; 50510, ff. 49, 62-66, 320.

'Bereaved Mother', *of Dublin; pseudonym.* Letter to G. B. Shaw, 1916. *Typewrittem.* 50517, f. 386.

Berendse (Adri), *of Scherpenzeel, Holland.* Letter to G. B. Shaw, 1946. 50525, f. 83.

Berlin (Horst), *schoolboy, of Hamburg.* Letter to G. B. Shaw, 1950. 50526 B, f. 488.

Bermondsey Gladstone Club. Programme of lectures, 1889. *Printed,* with *MS.* notes by G. B. Shaw. 50701, f. 46.

Bernard Shaw Branch of the Irish Labour Party. Photographs of the Chairman, P. J. O'Reilly, 1946, 1949. 50585, ff. 6, 7; 50586, ff. 46, 49, 50.

Bernstein (B.), *theatrical impresario, of Berlin.* Letter to C. T. H. Helmsley, 1894. 50513, f. 56.

— Letter to G. B. Shaw, 1894. 50513, f. 57v.

Bernstein (Eduard), *German socialist.* Letter, 1896. *Typewritten copy.* 50557, f. 45.

Bernstein (Henri Léon Gustave Charles), *dramatist.* Notes concerning, sent by J. Painlevé, 1925? *Typewritten copy. Fr.* 50740, f. 176.

Berry (B.), *of Bournemouth; member of the Women's Social and Political Union.* Letter to M. Cunningham, 1914. *Copy.* 50517, f. 150.

Bertram (Julius), *solicitor.* Letter to C. F. Shaw, 1923. 56492, f. 68.

— Letters, etc., to G. B. Shaw, 1923, 1924. Partly *printed.* 50519, ff. 36, 63, 125v.

Besant (Annie), *theosophist.* Letters to G. B. Shaw, 1885-1919. 50529, ff. 59-67.

— Telegram of Sir Rabindranath Tagore concerning, 1917. *Copy.* 50529, f. 66.

Better Citizenship Association, *Portland, Oregon.* Message of G. B. Shaw to, 1910. *Typewritten.* 50703, ff. 200-202.

Bevin (R. H.), *chief agronomist, Department of Agriculture, Tasmania.* Letter, etc., to F. C. Shaw, 1935. *Signed;* partly *copy.* 50521, f. 94.

Bevington (*Lt.* Robert J.), *R.F.C.* Letter to G. B. Shaw, *circa* 1915-1918. *Copy.* 50518, f. 121.

Bibesco (*Prince* Antoine), *First Sec., Rumanian Legation.* Invitation to his marriage to Elizabeth Asquith, 1919. Mainly *printed.* 50518, f. 142.

Bloom (*Maj.* Edward L.), *5th Battalion, U.S. Army*. Letter to G. B. Shaw, 1943. 50523, f. 49.

Bloom (Leslie), *of the Gallery First Nighters' Club, London*. Letter to G. B. Shaw, 1946. 50525, f. 310.

Bloomsbury Socialist Society. Notice of Lecture, printed by T. Bolas, 1888. *Printed*. 50701, f. 32.

— Programme of lectures, 1889. *Printed*. 50701, f. 51.

Blumenfeld (Ralph David), *Editor, 'Daily Express'*. Letter to G. B. Shaw, 1917. *Signed*. 50518, f. 80.

Blumenfeld (Simon), *author*. Letter to G. B. Shaw, n.d. 50527, f. 30.

Blunt (Wilfrid Scawen), *poet*. Letter to G. B. Shaw, 1907. 50515, f. 5.

Blunt-Lytton (Judith Anne Dorothea) *v*. Lytton.

Bluntschli (*Lt.-Col* .G.). Correspondence with G. B. Shaw, 1922. Partly *printed* and *shorthand draft*. 50518, ff. 310, 311, 313.

Bodkin (*Sir* Archibald Henry), *Director of Public Prosecutions*. Letter to Messrs. Rubenstein, Nash and Co., 1928. *Copy*. 50519, f. 362.

Bodkin (*Professor* Thomas Patrick), *art historian*. Letter to G. B. Shaw, 1944. 50524, f. 27.

Bolas (Thomas), *of the Leaflet Press, Cursitor Street; Sec., Hammersmith Fabian Society*. Notice of Lecture, printed by, 1888. 50701, f. 32.

— Circular letter to clergymen, signed on behalf of Hammersmith branch, 1895. *Printed*. 50680, f. 136.

Bond (Acton), *treasurer of the British Empire Shakespeare Society*. Correspondence between A. Bond

and P. Carr, 1909. *Copies*. 50515, ff. 341-344.

— Letter to S. R. Littlewood, 1910. *Copy*. 50515, f. 339.

Bond (*Sir* Edward Augustus), *K.C.B.; Principal Librarian, British Museum*. Application of G. B. Shaw to Sir E. A. Bond for admission to the Reading Room of the British Museum, countersigned by G. J. V. Lee, 1879. Partly *printed*. 48341, ff. 231-232.

Bond (Francis Thomas), *M.D*. Letters to A. R. Wallace and F. T. Bond of E. Beckett, 1902. *Printed*. 50514, ff. 69, 69v.

Bondfield (Margaret Grace), *P.C.; M.P*. Letter to G. B. Shaw, 1910. 50515, f. 360.

— 'War Against Poverty' issued by Independent Labour Party, contributions by J. R. MacDonald, W. C. Anderson, M. G. Bondfield, G. Lansbury, M. MacArthur, G. B. Shaw, S. J. Webb and M. B. Webb, *circa* 1912. *Printed pamphlet*. 50686, ff. 121-130v.

Bone (*Sir* Muirhead), *artist*. Letter, copied to G. B. Shaw, to Viscount Peel, 1925. *Copy*. 50519, f. 264.

Bonner (Charles Bradlaugh), *son of Hypatia Bradlaugh Bonner*. Letter to G. B. Shaw, 1938. 50522, f. 96.

Bonner (Hypatia Bradlaugh), *daughter of Charles Bradlaugh*. Letter to G. B. Shaw, 1933. 50520, f. 215.

Book Emporium Ltd., *Bengali publishers, of Calcutta*. Letter to G. B. Shaw, 1945. 63186, f. 195.

Bontine (*Hon*. Anne Elizabeth), *mother of R. B. Cunninghame*

Graham. Letters to G. B. Shaw, 1892-1897. 50512, f. 279; 50513, ff. 98, 144.

Boole *afterw.* **Voynich** (Ethel Lilian). *v.* Voynich *née* Boole.

Borough of Chelsea Liberal Association. Notice of meetings, 1889. *Printed.* 50701, f. 47.

Borough Polytechnic Institute. Programmes of lectures for Economic Club, 1894, 1896. *Printed.* 50701, ff. 154, 171.

Borrow (George), *writer.* Postcard of G. B. Shaw to T. J. Wise rel. to, 1916. *Ashley* B1518, f. 7.

Bose (*Sir* Jagadis Chunder), *Indian naturalist.* Letter to G. B. Shaw, 1927. 50519, f. 318.

Bostock (Elizabeth A.), *of the Kyrle Society.* Letters to G. B. Shaw, 1883, 1886. 50510, f. 30; 50511, ff. 197, 206.

Bostock (John Stuart Louis Wynne), *al. 'Lewis Wynne'; literary forger.* Letter to of G. B. Shaw, 1928. 71068, f. 198.

Bottomley (Arthur G.), *mayor of Walthamstow.* Letter to G. B. Shaw, 1946. *Signed.* 50525, f. 187.

Bótzaris (Sava), *Yugoslav sculptor.* Letter to G. B. Shaw, 1937. 50521, f. 249.

— Photographs of busts by, *circa* 1938. *Newsprint.* 50741, f. 120.

Boucicault (Dionysius George), *called 'Dion Boucicault the younger'; actor-manager; 2nd son of D. L. Boucicault.* Letters to G. B. Shaw, 1912. Partly *signed.* 50516, ff. 217, 233, 234, 250.

Boucicault (Nina), *daughter of D. L. Boucicault; actress.* Letter to G. B. Shaw, n.d. 50527, f. 31.

Boughton *formerly* **Davis** (Kathleen). *v.* Davis *afterw.* Boughton.

Boughton (Rutland), *composer.* Correspondence with G. B. Shaw, 1912-1949. Partly *draft.* 50524, f. 38; 50529, ff. 68-87v; 52365 *passim*; 63186, ff. 89, 91, 189, 197.

— Letter to — Clark drafted by G. B. Shaw, in the name of R. Boughton, 1934. 52365, f. 47.

— Letter to A. N. Chamberlain concerning civil list pension for, drafted by Sir J. S. Wilson, signed by G. B. Shaw, 1937. *Draft.* 50529, f. 78.

— Letter to, from C. F. Shaw, 1938. 52365, f. 63.

— Philosophical notes, 1940? *Typewritten.* 50742, ff. 145-148.

— 'A Note regarding the Completed Cycle of Arthurian Music-Dramas', 1945? Mainly *printed.* 50529, f. 86.

— Memorandum addressed to the Prime Minister, 1946. *Draft.* 52365, f. 73.

— Advertisement for 'Bethlehem: a Choral Drama', performed by Wilderness Opera Group and Orchestra, 1946. *Printed.* 52365, f. 80.

— Note concerning G. B. Shaw's letters from Constable and Company, annotated by R. Boughton, 1951. *Typewritten.* 52365, f. 89.

Boult (*Sir* Adrian Cedric), *C.H.; conductor.* Letter of G. B. Shaw to, 1931. 60499, f. 96.

'**Bounder**', *pseudonym*.

v. Fay (Edward Francis).

Bourchier (Arthur), *actor-manager*. Letters to G. B. Shaw, 1904. *Signed*. 50514, ff. 199, 201, 217.

Bourdariat (Roland), *of J. B. Janin, Editeur*. Letter to Constable and Co., 1946. *Signed. Fr.* 50526 A, f. 213.

Bourne (Adeline), *of the Actors' Benevolent Fund*. Letter to G. B. Shaw, 1946. *Signed*. 50525, f. 177.

Bourne (John), *editor of the 'Amateur Theatre'*. Letter to G. B. Shaw, 1936. *Signed*. 50521, f. 168.

Boutell (M.). Entry in alphabet design competition, 1958. 79494 B, ff. 22-24.

Bovill (W. B. Forster), *Secretary, the Authors' Producing Society*. Letter to C. F. Shaw, 1914. 56491, f. 137.

Bowen-Jones (*Sir* John Bowen), *1st Bart*. Correspondence between G. Davison and Sir J. B. Bowen-Jones, 1909. Partly *copy* and *signed*. 50513, f. 230; 50515, f. 293.

Bower (Frank W.), *of the Bower Family Laboratories, California*. Letter to G. B. Shaw, 1946. *Signed*. 50526 A, f. 49.

Bowerman (Elsie Edith), *barrister*. Letters to M. Cunningham concerning the suffrage campaign, 1914. *Copies*. 50517, ff. 154, 155.

Bowker (G. H.), *organising secretary of the National Anti-Vivisection Society*. Letters to G. B. Shaw, 1947, 1950. *Signed*. 50526 B, ff. 390, 501.

Bow Liberal Club. Programme of lectures, 1889. *Printed*. 50701, f. 60.

[Boya?] (Eley), *composer*. Letter to G. B. Shaw, n.d. *Signed*. 50527, f. 33.

Boyd (Elizabeth), *of Birkenhead*. Letter to G. B. Shaw, *circa* 1949. 50526 B, f. 476.

Boyd (H. A. K.), *of Chelsea*. Letter to G. B. Shaw, 1946. 50525, f. 231.

Brace (Donald), *of Harcourt, Brace, publishers*. Correspondence with G. B. Shaw, 1922. *Signed* and *shorthand draft*. 50565, f. 117.

Bradbury (Joseph), *of Sheffield*. Photograph of J. Bradbury [with his brother?], 1940. 50584, f. 15.

Bradley (Julius), *retired civil servant*. Letter to G. B. Shaw, 1939. 50522, f. 250.

Bradley-Birt (Francis Bradley), *author*. Letter to G. B. Shaw, *circa* 1941-1943. 50523, f. 52.

Brady (Edward), *formerly R.I.C. constable*. Letters, etc., to G. B. Shaw, 1946. 50525, f. 131; 50526 A, f. 218.

— Letter to E. Brady of G. T. H. Morris, 1946. *Signed*. 50525, f. 133.

Brady (William A.), *American stage manager*. Photograph of W. A. Brady and son, 1915? 50588, f. 119.

Brækstad (Hans Lien), *Norwegian writer*. Letter to G. B. Shaw, 1894. 50513, f. 53.

Brandes (George), *author*. Letter to G. B. Shaw, 1913. 50516, f. 361.

Brandon (Harry), *of the R.A.F.* Letter to G. B. Shaw, 1944. 50524, f. 240.

Branford (Margaret G.), *[wife of Frederick Branford, poet ?]*. Letter to B. Patch, 1940. 63186, f. 156.

Letter to G. B. Shaw, 1937. *Signed.* 50521, f. 306.

Briggs (William H.), *of Harper & Brothers, New York.* Correspondence with G. B. Shaw, 1919. Partly *signed, typewritten copy* and *shorthand draft.* 50565, ff. 99-101v.

Brightwell (Daniel Barron), *of the 'Birmingham Daily Post'.* Letter to G. B. Shaw, 1884. 50510, f. 192.

Brise (*Sir* Evelyn John Ruggles-). *v.* Ruggles-Brise.

Brisman (Irving), *of Long Beach, California.* Letter, etc., to G. B. Shaw, 1931. Partly *typewritten.* 50520, f. 84.

Bristol Sunday Society. Programmes of lectures, 1889, 1890. *Printed.* 50701, ff. 65-67v, 91, 92.

British-American Home for Governesses and Lady Teachers in Budapest. Letter to G. B. Shaw concerning, 1910. *Signed.* 50515, f. 334.

British and International Addressing Limited, *of London.* Letter to G. B. Shaw, 1947. 50526 B, f. 384.

British Anti-Vivisection Society. Notice of meeting, 1912. *Printed.* 50701, f. 220.

British Broadcasting Corporation. Papers of Advisory Committee on Spoken English, 1931, 1936. *Typewritten.* 50679, ff. 319v-324.

— Letter to Director of B.B.C. from G. B. Shaw, 1949. *Typewritten.* 61891, f. 33.

British Council. Letter, etc., to Mrs. G. Gillmore, 1946. 50527, f. 34.

British Drama League. Programme of Ibsen Centenary Lectures, 1928. *Printed.* 50701, f. 254.

British Empire. Papers and Reports of the Empire Reconstruction Committee of Fabian Society, 1917. *Typewritten.* 50681, ff. 168-200.

British Federation of University Women. Programme of lectures, in aid of Crosby Hall Endowment Fund, 1923. *Printed.* 50701, f. 251.

British Film Producers Association. Agreement with Screenwriters Association, 1943. *Printed.* 50523, ff. 144-145.

— Letter to G. B. Shaw of J. A. Rank, on behalf of, 1946. 50525, f. 128.

British Interplanetary Society. Certificate of membership issued to G. B. Shaw, 1947. *Signed* and partly *printed.* 50711 A, f. 131.

British Music Society. *Draft* prospectus by G. B. Shaw for British Music Society, 1918. *Shorthand.* 50679, ff. 388-399.

British Nationality Act, 1948. Home Office memorandum regarding the British citizenship of G. B. Shaw, 1949. *Signed.* 63186, f. 221.

British Sexological Society. Letter to G. B. Shaw of L. Housman concerning, 1931. 50520, f. 72.

British Socialist Party. Statement on War Aims, 1917. *Printed.* 50681, ff. 207-208.

Brittain (William James), *chairman, Brittain Publishing.* Letter to G. B. Shaw, 1944. *Signed.* 50524, f. 219.

Britton (Lionel Erskine), *author.* Letters, etc., to G. B. Shaw of and concerning, 1934-1943. Partly *printed.* 50520, f. 249; 50529, ff. 146-178.

Broadbent (Benjamin), *J.P.; woollen merchant, of Huddersfield.* Letter to G. B. Shaw, 1915. 50517, f. 286.

Broadley ([May?]). Letter of G. B. Shaw to [M.?] Broadley, 1918. *Typewritten copy.* 50562, f. 178.

Brockman (H. T.), *cereals broker.* Letter to J. C. Shaw, 1909. 50515, f. 257.

Brockway (*Baron* Archibald Fenner), *socialist and pacifist politician.* Letters to G. B. Shaw, 1921, 1943. *Signed.* 50711 A, f. 141; 63186, f. 34.

Bronta *al.* **Brout** (Julius).
v. Brout (Julio).

Brooke (Emma Frances), *novelist and Fabian.* Letters to G. B. Shaw, 1884-1888. 50510, f. 282; 50511, ff. 129, 135, 143, 149, 300, 308; 50512, ff. 25, 29, 30, 35, 61.

Brooke *afterw.* **Throckmorton** (*Lady* Lilian).
v. Throckmorton *née* Brooke.

Brooke (Sarah), *actress.* Letter to G. B. Shaw of A. M. Hayward concerning S. Brooke, 1907. *Signed.* 50515, f. 21.

Brooke (*Rev.* Stopford Augustus), *author.* Letters to G. B. Shaw, 1885, 1886. 50511, f. 145; 50723, f. 12.

Brooke *née* **Brett** (*Lady* Sylvia Leonora).
v. Brett *afterw.* Brooke.

Brookfield (Charles Hallam Elton), *actor, dramatist, and Examiner of Plays.* Licensing report on 'Androcles and the Lion', 1913. 66026 I.

Brooks (David), *town clerk of Richmond, co. York.* Letter, etc., to G. B. Shaw, 1946. *Signed.* 50525, f. 160.

Brooks (Joseph Barlow), *Methodist minister, of Stalybridge.* Letters to G. B. Shaw, 1934, 1935. 50520, f. 246; 50521, f. 102.

Brough (Fanny), *actress.* Letters to G. B. Shaw rel. to 'Mrs. Warren's Profession', 1901. 50514, ff. 37, 39.

Brout *al.* **Bronta** (*Dr.* Julio), *Spanish translator of G. B. Shaw.* Letters of G. B. Shaw concerning, 1915, 1924. *Partly signed* and *copy.* 50520, f. 43;. 56627, f. 150.

— Letter and postcard to G. B. Shaw, 1920-1931. *Partly Fr.* and *Spanish.* 50518, f. 243v; 50520, ff. 39, 40; 63186, f. 42.

— Photograph of J. Bronta, 1931. *Newsprint.* 50741, f. 1.

Brown (F. Lucy Rudston), *Sec., The Royal Society of Literature.* Letter to G. B. Shaw, 1944. 50524, f. 154.

Brown (Horace W. Cowley-).
v. Cowley-Brown.

Brown (Ivor John Carnegie), *writer and theatre critic.* Correspondence with G. B. Shaw, 1934-1949. Partly *signed* and *draft.* 50520, f. 248; 50523, f. 179; 50525, f. 103; 50526 B, f. 461.

Brown (Susan Lyon), *[secretary of W. Cooper, osteopath?].* Letter to C. F. Shaw, 1940. *Signed.* 63197, f. 53.

Browne (Alice), *of Isipingo Beach, Natal.* Letter to C. F. Shaw, 1935. 56493, f. 134.

Browne (John Hutton Balfour-), *K.C.* Letter to R. G. A. Allanson-Winn, 1917. *Printed.* 50518, f. 261.

Browne (Maurice), *actor-manager and dramatist.* Letter of G. B. Shaw to M. Browne, 1915. *Typewritten copy.* 50562, ff. 88, 90.

Browning Society. Subscription receipt to G. B. Shaw, 1887. Mainly *printed.* 50511, f. 265.

— Monthly Abstract of Proceedings, 1889. *Printed.* 50702, ff. 266-271.

Bruce *afterw.* **Scott** *afterw.* **Young** (Kathleen)
v. Young.

Brumwell (Charles E.), *bookseller.* Letter, etc., to G. B. Shaw concerning 'The Seven Pillars of Wisdom', 1935. *Typewritten* and *signed.* 50540, f. 61.

Brunel (Adrian), *dramatist and screen-writer.* Letter to G. B. Shaw, annotated by Shaw, 1950. *Signed.* 56633, f. 7.

Brunius (Jacques B.), *English correspondent of the 'Revue Fontaine'.* Correspondence with G. B. Shaw, 1943, 1945. Partly *signed* and on Shaw's behalf. 50523, ff. 127, 156; 61893, f. 74.

Brunner (*Dr.* Roland), *chemical engineer, of Spiez, Switzerland.* Letter to G. B. Shaw, 1946. *Signed.* 50525, f. 374.

Brunton (*Sir* Thomas Lauder), *1st Bart.; physician.* Prescription for C. F. Payne-Townshend made out by Sir T. L. Brunton, 1896. 56490, f. 144.

Brunyate (John), *barrister, of Lincoln's Inn.* Joint opinion of B. L. Bathurst and J. Brunyate concerning the will of G. B. Shaw, 1957. *Typewritten copy.* 79493, f. 19.

Bryan (Charles), *private detective.* Letter to G. B. Shaw, 1908. 50515, f. 197v.

Bryant (*Mrs.* Sophie), *D.Sc.; Headmistress of North London Collegiate School.* Postcard to G. B. Shaw, 1882. 50509, f. 125.

Buchanan (Robert Williams), *poet and novelist.* Letters to G. B. Shaw, 1891-1896. 50529, ff. 179-212.

Buckingham (Dorothy Page), *author.* Letter to G. B. Shaw, 1935. *Signed.* 50521, f. 126.

Buckmaster (John), *actor.* Photographs of R. Forbes, J. Buckmaster and A. Treacher in 'Caesar and Cleopatra', 1950. 50588, ff. 41, 45.

Buckmaster (Stanley Owen), *Baron Buckmaster of Cheddington; 1st Viscount Buckmaster 1933.* Comments on 'Mrs. Warren's Profession', 1911-1922. *L.C.P. Corr.* 1924/5632, ff. 62, 91; *Deposit* 10014/104.

— Licensing report on 'Androcles and the Lion', 1913. *L.C.P. Corr.* 1913/1827.

Bucovich (Mario), *photographer.* Letter, etc., to G. B. Shaw, 1936. *Signed.* Partly *printed.* 50521, f. 158.

— Advertising leaflet, *circa* 1936. *Printed.* 50521, ff. 159-160.

Bughi (Erasmo Giocondo), *of Turin; spelling reformer.* Letters, etc., to G. B. Shaw, 1946. 50525, f. 13; 50526 A, f. 42; 50556, ff. 45-90.

Bullard (Alfred), *director of Ouse Parklands Estates.* Letter, etc., to G. B. Shaw, n.d. *Imperf.* 50527, f. 37.

Byard (Herbert), *organist and choirmaster, St. Paul's Church, Clifton, Bristol.* Letter to G. B. Shaw, 1946. *Signed.* 50525, f. 309.

Byles (Rennie B.), *business manager of 'New Statesman'.* Annotated, 1915. 50483, f. 91.

Byrne (Anne), *of Coalisland, co. Tyrone.* Letter to G. B. Shaw, 1946. 50525, f. 304.

Byrne (Terence), *of Coventry.* Letter, on behalf of the inmates of the Whoberley Hostel, to G. B. Shaw, 1946. 50525, f. 306.

Byrne (*Sir* William Patrick), *K.C.V.O.* Correspondence with the Lord Chamberlain's Office, 1909. *Signed. L.C.P. Corr.* 1916/91.

C

Caillard (*Sir* Vincent Henry Penalver). Introductory statement on behalf of 'Potentia Organization', signed by Sir V. H. P. Caillard, Sir G. H. Darwin, Sir M. Foster, J. Claretie, F. W. Foerster, Comte G. d' Alviella, J. Le Jeune and Dr. C. Richet, 1930? Partly *printed,* with *duplicated* signatures. 50742, f. 140.

Caine (*Sir* Thomas Henry Hall), *K.B.E.; novelist.* Correspondence with G. B. Shaw, 1904-1928. Partly *signed.* Partly *copy* and *typewritten draft.* 50531, ff. 1-41.

Caine (William Sproston), *M.P.* Letter to E. R. Pease, 1892. *Copy.* 50557, f. 18.

Calcutta, *Bishop of.*
  v. Johnson (Edward Ralph).

Call (W. A.), *architectural and archaeological photographer.* Letter to G. B. Shaw, 1936. 50521, f. 206.

Calleja (F.), *of the Berlitz School of Languages, Nottingham.* Letter, etc., to G. B. Shaw, 1940. Mainly *typewritten.* 50555, ff. 27-40.

Calmour (Alfred Cecil), *playwright.* Letter to G. B. Shaw, 1912. 50516, f. 189.

Calvert (Louis), *actor.* Letter to G. B. Shaw, 1904. 50514, f. 218.

Cameron (Donald Andreas), *British Consulate, Port Said.* Letter to D. A. Cameron as Consul General at Alexandria of Sergeant J. E. Jones, M. Abdullah, Sergeant J. Stout and Sergeant J. L. Price, 1916. *Signed.* 56627, f. 185.

— Letter as Consul General at Alexandria to G. H. Thring, 1916. *Signed.* 56627, f. 187.

Cameron (H. H. Hay), *photographer.* Letter to G. B. Shaw, 1890. 50512, f. 228.

Campbell (Beatrice Moss), *wife of Sir C. H. G. Campbell.* Letters, etc., to C. F. Shaw, 1898-1929, n.d. Partly *photogr.* 56491, f. 4; 56492, f. 70; 56494, ff. 170-174v.

Campbell *afterw.* **Cornwallis-West** (Beatrice Stella), *actress.* Letters, etc., to G. B. Shaw of and concerning, 1901-1949. Partly *signed.* 50531, ff. 42-53v; 63186, f. 66.

— Correspondence between B. S. Campbell and A. E. F. Horniman, 1909. *Copy.* 50534, ff. 174-175.

— Portrait postcard of, 1933? 63186, f. 66v.

Chang (Hsueh-liang), *Marshal; son of Marshal Hsiao-liang Chang.* Note to G. B. and C. F. Shaw, 1933. Partly *printed.* 56493, f. 90.

Chant (*Mrs.* Laura Ormiston), *author and social reformer.* Letters to G. B. Shaw, 1894. 50513, ff. 60, 69.

Chaplin (H.), *maker of keyboard instruments, of Letchworth.* Letter to G. B. Shaw, 1938. 50522, f. 57.

Chapman ([J. C. H?]), *widow of J. Chapman of the 'Westminster Review'.* Letters of and concerning, 1914. Partly *copy.* 50517, ff. 99, 103, 113, 118, 119.

Chapman (Joseph A.), *of the Music Club, Gateshead, co. Durh.* Letter, etc., to G. B. Shaw, 1946. *Signed.* Partly *copy.* 50525, f. 313.

Chapman and Hall, *publishers.* Letters to G. B. Shaw, 1884. 50510, ff. 194, 222.

Chappell (Mattie), *of Oberlin, Louisiana.* Letter to G. B. Shaw, 1946. 50525, f. 217.

Chappelow (Eric Barry Wilfred), *author; conscientious objector.* Letters, etc., to G. B. Shaw, 1916. Partly *copy.* 50517, ff. 372, 378, 381.

Charles (A. Aloysius), *of British Guiana.* Letter to G. B. Shaw, 1946. 50525, f. 197.

Charles-Dean (B.), *managing director of the Moviegram Company Ltd.* Letter to G. B. Shaw, 1946. *Signed.* 50526 A, f. 149.

Charlier (P. L.), *French teacher and writer.* Letter to G. B. Shaw, 1903. 50514, f. 165.

Charlton Liberal Club. Programme of lectures, 1889. *Printed.* 50701, f. 44.

Charrington *al.* **Martin** (Charles), *actor.* Letters of G. B. Shaw to C. Charrington and J. Achurch, 1889-1924, n.d. *Typewritten copies.* 50532, 50561 *passim.*

— Letters to G. B. Shaw, 1895-1912. 50513, f. 35; 50515, ff. 420, 434; 50516, f. 239.

— Letters, etc., of G. B. Shaw to A. Dukes concerning C. Charrington, 1929. *Typewritten copies.* 50532, ff. 312-338.

Chartres (*Mrs.* Annie) *al.* 'Anita Vivanti'; *author.* Letter to G. B. Shaw, 1896. 50513, f. 102v.

Chase (William D.), *secretary-treasurer of the Shaw Society of America.* Letter to G. B. Shaw, 1950. *Signed.* 50526 B, f. 504.

— Letter to, of C. P. Freshel, 1950. *Copy.* 50534, f. 85.

Chateau (Henriette), *of Paris.* Letter to G. B. Shaw on behalf of Dr. Epstein-Estienne, 1905. 50514, f. 249.

Chatteris (*Mrs.* Fanny), *of the Park Lane Musical Society.* Letters to G. B. Shaw, 1883, n.d. 50510, ff. 151, 174; 50527, f. 45.

Chatto and Windus, *publishers, of London.* Letters to G. B. Shaw, 1879-1892. 50508, f. 180; 50509, f. 32; 50510, f. 334; 50512, ff. 267, 304.

Chaudhuri (B. B. Ray), *secretary, Tagore Society.* Letter to G. B. Shaw, 1944. *Signed.* 50524, f. 109.

Chaudhuri (Sanjib), *lawyer, of Calcutta.* Letter, etc., to G. B. Shaw, 1949. *Signed.* 63186, f. 224.

Cheale (Laurence Michael), *17/21 Lancers.* Letter to G. B. Shaw, 1946. 50526 A, f. 87.

Chen (Shi-hsiang), *teacher and translator; Chinese exile in California.* Letter, etc., to G. B. Shaw, 1944. 50524, f. 144.

Chen (Shixiang)
v. Chen (Shi-hisiang).

Chenhalls (A. T.), *F.C.A.* Letter, etc., to G. B. Shaw, 1942. *Signed.* 50522, f. 448.

Cherry-Garrard (Angela), *wife of A. G. B. Cherry-Garrard.* Postcard to G. B. Shaw, 1946. 50525, f. 218.

Cherry-Garrard (Apsley George Benet), *polar explorer.* Photographs of Apsley Cherry-Garrard, 1925? 50584, ff. 26-34.

— Postcard to C. F. Shaw, 1927. 56492, f. 101.

— Postcard to G. B. Shaw of A. G. B. Cherry-Garrard and A. Cherry-Garrard, 1946. 50525, f. 218.

— Letters to G. B. Shaw, 1947, 1949. 50526 B, f. 454; 63186, f. 205.

Chesshire (L. Kathleen), *secretary to G. K. Chesterton.* Letter to, from B. Patch, 1926. *Signed.* 73198, f. 95.

Chester (Jerome), *of Odhams Press Ltd.* Letter to G. B. Shaw, 1946. *Dictated.* 50525, f. 144.

Chesterton *née* **Jones** (Ada Elizabeth), *al. 'J. Keith Prothero'; journalist and author; wife of Cecil Chesterton.* Letter to G. B. Shaw, 1941. *Signed.* 50522, f. 420.

Chesterton (Cecil Edward), *brother of G. K. Chesterton; journalist.* Letters to G. B. Shaw, 1903, 1914. Partly *signed.* 50514, f. 108; 50517, f. 189; 73198, f. 61.

— Obituary notice by G. B. Shaw, 1919. *Typewritten draft.* 50696, ff. 265-268.

Chesterton *née* **Blogg** (Frances Alice), *wife of G. K. Chesterton.* Correspondence with G. B. Shaw, 1911-1938. 73198, ff. 35-42, 67-69, 83-86, 92, 99, 101, 104, 113-118.

Chesterton (Gilbert Keith), *author.* Correspondence with G. B. Shaw, 1906-1935. *Copies,* partly *imperf.* 50515, f. 111; 50518, f. 152; 50522, ff. 472-474; 50695, f. 178; 73198, ff. 1-112 *passim.*

— Articles by G. B. Shaw on, 1908-1919. Partly *typewritten draft* and *printed.* 50695, ff. 7-20, 25-30, 34; 50696, ff. 255-263.

— Scenario proposed by G. B. Shaw for, 1909, 1938. Partly *typewritten.* 50643, ff. 162-180; 73198, ff. 15-29.

— Report of a debate on democracy and socialism with G. B. Shaw, chaired by Hilaire Belloc, 1911. *Typewritten.* 50686, ff. 16-105.

— Group portrait in cowboy costume of T. E. Scott-Ellis, W. Archer, Sir J. M. Barrie, G. K. Chesterton and G. B. Shaw, 1914. 50582, f. 39.

— Notice of debate with Lady Rhondda, 1927. 50701, f. 253.

— Painting of G. B. Shaw as Don Quixote with G. K. Chesterton as Sancho Panza, by Charles

W. Hopper, 1934. *Photographic copy.* 50582, f. 91.

— Agreement with H. Robinson annotated by G. B. Shaw, 1938. *Autogr.* 73231 A, f. 14.

Chesterton (Maurice), *architect; cousin of G. K. Chesterton.* Letter to G. B. Shaw, 1944. 50524, f. 174.

Cheston *afterw.* **Bennett** (Dorothy). *v.* Bennett (Dorothy Cheston).

Chevreau (Cécile), *actress.* Letter, etc., to G. B. Shaw, *circa* 1945. Partly *photogr.* 50524, f. 379.

— Photographs of C. Chevreau, *circa* 1945. 50524, ff. 380-381.

Cheyney (Edward Ralph), *American poet.* Letter of G. B. Shaw to, 1913. *Copy.* 50516, f. 370.

Chichester, *Bishop of.* *v.* Bell (George Kennedy Allen).

'China Weekly Review, The'. Issue for January 1933, 1933. 50741, f. 11.

Chiswick Liberal Club. 'Sunday Evenings for the People', 1887. *Printed poster.* 50701, f. 5.

Chiswick Press, The. Handbill printed for Independent Labour Party, 1906. *Printed.* 50701, f. 209.

Cholmondeley (*Brig.-Gen.* Hugh Cecil), *brother-in-law of Mrs. C. F. Shaw.* Photograph of Brig.-Gen. H. C. Cholmondeley, 1930? 50584, f. 35.

— Letter to G. B. Shaw, 1936. 50521, f. 221.

Cholmondeley (*Mrs.* Mary Stewart al. 'Sissy'), *sister of Mrs. C. F. Shaw.* Photograph of M. S. Cholmondeley and 'Jack Straw', 1890?-1900? 56524 B, f. 132.

— Letter to G. B. Shaw, 1924? 50519, f. 363.

— Correspondence with C. F. Shaw, 1926. Partly *draft.* 56492, ff. 80-86.

Cholmondeley (Violet Maud), *2nd wife of Brig-Gen. H. C. Cholmondeley.* Letter to C. F. Shaw, 1942. 56494, f. 156.

Chrismer (Leslie), *journalist, of Pennsylvania.* Letter to G. B. Shaw, 1935. *Signed.* 50521, f. 93.

Christiani (M.), *musician.* Letter to G. B. Shaw, 1878. 50508, f. 119.

Christiansen ([Thora?]), *of Copenhagen.* Letter to G. B. Shaw, 1915. 50517, f. 261.

Christian Social Union. Notice of meeting, 1900. *Printed.* 50701, f. 180.

Christie (John), *founder of the Glyndebourne opera.* Letter to G. B. Shaw, 1945. 50524, f. 329.

Christy (Eva), *teacher of riding.* Letter to, from G. B. Shaw, *circa* 1900. *Draft.* 50527, f. 47.

Christy (Gerald), *of 'The Lecture Agency Ltd'.* Letter to G. B. Shaw, 1900. *Signed,* and partly *printed.* 50513, f. 220.

Chu (Hsiang), *Chinese poet.* Sonnet 'To George Bernard Shaw', *circa* 1932. *Copy. Engl. transl.* 50524, f. 146.

Chugerman (Samuel), *counselor at law and author, of New York.* Letter to G. B. Shaw, 1944. *Signed.* 50524, f. 79.

Church (Hayden), *journalist.* Letters, etc., to G. B. Shaw, 1945, 1946. *Signed.* 50524, f. 303; 50526 A, f. 125.

Church and Stage Guild. Lecture by G. B. Shaw for, 1889. *Draft.* 50702, ff. 256-265.

— Notice of meetings, 1890. *Printed.* 50701, f. 86.

Church of All Saints, Inverary. Letter, etc., to G. B. Shaw of 10th Duke of Argyll concerning peal of bells, 1925. Mainly *printed.* 50519, ff. 211-220.

Churchward (*Col.* James), *writer on Latin American civilisations.* Letter to G. B. Shaw, 1928. *Signed.* 63186, f. 49.

Chwalibog (Felix), *translator, of Cracow.* Letter to G. B. Shaw, 1906. 50514, f. 319.

Citrine (Walter MacLennan), *1st Baron Citrine.* Letter to G. B. Shaw, 1934. *Signed.* 63186, f. 73.

City Socialist Circle. Notice of meeting, 1900. *Printed.* 50701, f. 178.

City Temple Literary Society. Programme of meetings, 1913. *Printed.* 50701, f. 224.

— Lecture, etc., on 'Christian Economics' to City Temple Literary Society of G. B. Shaw, 1913. Speaking notes, *typewritten* transcript and *printed* report. 50704, ff. 23-27, 29-90.

Civic Playhouse Committee, Cheltenham. Letter to G. B. Shaw of F. D. Littlewood, on behalf of, 1946. *Signed.* 50525, f. 137.

Claflin (W. M.), *of Boston.* Letter, etc., to G. B. Shaw, 1936. Partly *printed.* 50521, f. 223.

— Letter to the 'Boston Herald', 1936. *Printed.* 50521, f. 235.

Clairmonte *afterw.* **Bright** (Mary Chavelita), *al.* '*George Egerton*'; *author; wife of R. Golding Bright.* Letter to C. F. Shaw, 1902. 56491, f. 32.

— Letter to G. B. Shaw, 1904. 50514, f. 211.

'Clam (Ernest)', *pseudonym.* *v.* Czech-Jochberg (Erich).

Clann (Elva), *of Oakland, California.* Letter to G. B. Shaw, 1946. *Signed.* 50526 B, f. 276.

Claremont (Arthur), *[actor?].* Photograph of A. Claremont and V. Richards, 1926? 50584, f. 39.

Clarendon, *Earl of.* *v.* Villiers (George Herbert Hyde).

Claretie (Jules), *Administrateur général de la Comédie Française.* Introductory statement on behalf of 'Potentia Organization', signed by Sir V. H. P. Caillard, Sir G. H. Darwin, Sir M. Foster, J. Claretie, F. W. Foerster, Comte G. d' Alviella, J. Le Jeune and Dr. C. Richet, 1930? Partly *printed,* with *duplicated* signatures. 50742, f. 140.

Clark (Alice), *historian and company director.* Letter to C. F. Shaw, 1914. 56491, f. 183.

Clark (Arthur Scarlett), *dramatist.* Letter of G. B. Shaw to A. S. Clark, 1895. *Typewritten copy.* 50561, f. 80.

Clark (C. F.), *Librarian, Fox Photos Ltd.* Letter to F. E. Loewenstein, 1947. *Signed.* 50565, f. 131.

Clark (C. W.), *great-niece of Sir Edward Thomas Holden.* Letter to G. B. Shaw, 1946. 50525, f. 136.

Coates (William Peyton), *Secretary, Anglo-Russian Parliamentary Committee.* Letter to G. B. Shaw, 1934. *Signed.* 50520, f. 256.

Cobbe (Frances Power), *writer.* 'Why women desire the Franchise', 1869? *Printed.* 50721 B, f. 65.

Cobden *afterw.* **Unwin** (Emma Jane Catherine).

v. Unwin *née* Cobden.

Coburn (Alvin Langdon), *American photographer.* Christmas greetings to G. B. Shaw with S. L. Clemens and A. Henderson, 1908. 50515, f. 199.

— Announcement of his marriage to E. W. Clement, 1912. *Printed.* 50516, f. 247.

— Letter to G. B. Shaw, 1946. 50525, f. 285.

— Photographs of Mr. and Mrs. A. L. Coburn, 1950. 50584, ff. 40, 41.

Coburn (Edith W.), *wife of A. L. Coburn.* Letter to G. B. and C. F. Shaw, 1940. 63186, f. 114.

— Letters to G. B. Shaw, 1944, 1946. 50524, ff. 28, 256; 50525, f. 308.

— Photographs of Mr. and Mrs. A. L. Coburn, 1950. 50584, ff. 40, 41.

Cochran (*Sir* Charles Blake), *theatrical manager and producer.* Letters to, of G. B. Shaw, 1935. Partly *typewritten.* 72712.

Cockburn (*Sir* John Alexander), *Premier of South Australia.* Letter to C. F. Shaw, 1903. 56491, f. 33.

Cockerell (Douglas Bennett), *bookbinder.* Correspondence with C. F. Shaw, 1927-1940. 56492, f. 102; *Deposit* 9394.

— Correspondence with G. B. Shaw, 1927-1946. 63186, f. 60; *Deposit* 9394.

Cockerell *née* **Kingsford** (Florence Kate).

v. Kingsford *afterw.* Cockerell.

Cockerell (*Sir* Sydney Carlyle), *Director, Fitzwilliam Museum, Cambridge.* Correspondence with G. B. Shaw, 1895-1950. Partly *printed* and *copy.* 42577, f. 148; 50531, ff. 59-104v; 50563, f. 17; 59892, f. 132; 63186, ff. 52, 103; 79494 C, f. 7.

—Correspondence with C. F. Shaw, 1907-1943, n.d. 52752, ff. 212-297; 56491, ff. 100, 122.

— Christmas cards of C. F. Shaw to Sir S. C. Cockerell and his wife, 1913-1940. 52752, ff. 222, 282, 296.

Coffin (Adeline Hayden), *wife of C. Hayden Coffin.* Letter to G. B. Shaw, 1906. 50514, f. 320.

Cogman (John Keymer), *of Croydon, co. Surr.* Letter, etc., to G. B. Shaw, 1943. *Signed.* 50523, f. 73.

— 'Religion and its Reason', etc., *circa* 1943. Mainly *typewritten.* 50523, ff. 74-87.

Cohen (Harriet), *C.B.E.; pianist.* Correspondence with G. B. Shaw, 1920-1949. 50527, f. 51; *Music Deposit* 1999/10, 3.xv, 3xxv.

Colbourne (Maurice), *author.* Letter to G. B. Shaw, 1946. 50526 A, f. 191.

Colburn (Henry) **and Bentley** (Richard) *afterw.* **Bentley** (Richard) *afterw.* **Bentley** (Richard) **and Son,** *publishers.*

v. Bentley (Richard) and Son.

Cole (*Miss* F. Winifred), *descendant of Bishop Henchman.* Letter to G. B. Shaw, 1938. 50522, f. 166.

Cole (George Douglas Howard), *Professor of Social and Political Theory, Oxford University.* Circular letters relating to the Fabian Society, 1917. *Typewritten.* 50681, ff. 141, 223.

Cole (Kathleen Mary), *of Ewell, co. Surr.* Letter to G. B. Shaw, 1937. 50521, f. 298.

Colefax *née* **Halsey** (Sibyl), *wife of Sir A. Colefax, K.B.E.* Postcard to G. B. Shaw, 1927. 63186, f. 44.

Coleman (Alfred), *stage hand at the Royal Court Theatre.* Letter to G. B. Shaw, n.d. 50527, f. 52.

Coleridge (*Hon.* Stephen William Buchanan), *anti-vivisectionist.* Letter [to 'The Times?'] of G. B. Shaw concerning, 1905. *Draft.* 50743 B, f. 359.

Coll (John), *of Letterkenny, co. Donegal.* Letter to G. B. Shaw, 1946. 50526 A, f. 150.

Collet (Antonia May), *author.* Letter, etc., to C. F. Shaw, 1919. 56492, ff. 11, 16, 17v.

— Postcard to A. M. Collet from E. M. [Reed?], 1919. 56492, f. 17.

Collier (Bernard), *[musician?]; of Brompton Square, London.* Letters to G. B. Shaw, 1882. 50509, ff. 111, 115.

Collier (*Miss* D. M. B.), *journalist.* Letter, etc., to G. B. Shaw, 1938. *Signed.* 50522, f. 45.

Collier (*Mrs.* E. A.), *of Brompton Square, London.* Letter, etc., to G. B. Shaw, 1878. 50508, ff. 116-118.

Collier *née* **Huxley** (Ethel Gladys), *2nd wife of John Collier, painter.*

Letters to C. F. Shaw, 1940. 56494, ff. 61, 66.

Collins (Arthur Jefferies), *Keeper of Manuscripts, British Museum.* Letter to G. B. Shaw, 1948. *Signed.* 50526 B, f. 419.

Collins (Dorothy Edith), *secretary to G. K. Chesterton.* Correspondence with G. B. Shaw, 1942. 50522, f. 471; 73198, ff. 119, 120.

Collins (Helen), *of Media, Pennsylvania.* Letter to G. B. Shaw, n.d. 50527, f. 53.

Collins (Kerree), *of Twickenham.* Letters to G. B. Shaw, 1938, 1940. *Signed.* 50522, ff. 50, 297.

Collins (William Job), *F.R.C.S.* Letter to G. B. Shaw, n.d. 50527, f. 55v.

Collison (Francis), *bookseller, of Woking.* Letters of G. B. Shaw to F. Collison, 1902, 1903. *Typewritten copies.* 50562, ff. 11, 28.

Collison (Francis Algernon), *schoolmaster; associate of R. J. G. Dutton.* Letters, etc., to G. B. Shaw, 1912, 1940. *Signed;* partly *printed.* 50516, f. 173; 50554, f. 110.

Colthurst (Cecily Charlotte), *niece of C. F. Shaw.* Letters to C. F. Shaw, 1940?-1943? 56494, ff. 182-192v.

— Letters to G. B. Shaw, 1944, 1945. 50524, ff. 104, 310.

Combe (Shournagh Dorothy), *daughter of Sir R. Colthurst, 8th Bart.; great-niece of C. F. Shaw.* Letter to C. F. Shaw, *circa* 1940. 56494, f. 193.

Comité du Défense du Théâtre. Circular letter from P. Nivoix, on behalf of, 1946. *Duplicated* signature. 50525, f. 106.

Common (Thomas), *translator of Nietzsche.* Correspondence on topics related to the writings of Nietzsche, 1900? Partly *duplicated.* 50742, ff. 15-30.

— Letters, etc., to G. B. Shaw, 1900-1911. Partly *duplicated* and *printed.* 50514, ff. 58, 78, 121; 50515, ff. 25, 83; 50516, f. 102; 50742, ff. 16-22, 27-32v.

— Letters to, of Dr. W. A. Haussmann, 1911. *Copies.* 50516, ff. 91, 92.

'Common Sense'. 'Wagner and Germany' addressed to 'Common Sense' by T. Mann, 1939? *Typewritten.* 50741, ff. 140-147.

Communist Club, *Tottenham Street, London.* Notice of lecture, 1888. *Printed.* 50701, f. 29.

Communist Party of Great Britain. *Draft* protest against official prosecution of communists, 1925. *Typewritten* with *autogr. amendments* by G. B. Shaw. 50697, ff. 209-218.

Conant (Wallace B.), *spelling reformer, of Concord, Massachusetts.* Letter to G. B. Shaw, 1949. *Signed.* 50556, f. 167.

Cond (Eileen M.), *of Droitwich, co. Chest.* Letter to G. B. Shaw, 1946. 50526 A, f. 48.

Conference of Repertory Theatres. Telegram to G. B. Shaw on behalf of, 1946. 50525, f. 277.

Conference on the Abolition of Destitution and Unemployment. Invitation card and agenda, 1910. *Printed.* 50681, ff. 69-70.

— Programme, 1910. *Printed.* 50681, ff. 71-72.

'Conference Record, The'. First of eight-issue newspaper, July 1896. *Printed.* 50680, ff. 165-166v.

Coniglio (Sirio Bruno), *of Tampa, Florida.* Letter, etc., to G. B. Shaw, 1946. *Signed.* Partly *printed.* 50526 B, f. 355.

Conley (William), *of Edmondson-Sweeney, Inc., motor dealers, of Detroit, Michigan.* Letter, etc., to G. B. Shaw, 1946. *Signed.* Partly *printed.* 50526 B, f. 308.

Conlin (William), *Professor of Latin at Grey University College, Bloemfontein.* Letter, etc., to G. B. Shaw, 1919. Mainly *printed.* 50518, ff. 162-183.

'Connell (F. Norreys)', *pseudonym.* v. O'Riordan (Conal Holmes O'Connell).

Connell (James *called* Jim), *socialist and journalist.* Letter to H. Quelch, 1892. *Copy.* 50512, f. 291.

— Correspondence with G. B. Shaw, 1892, 1896. Partly *typewritten copy.* 50512, f. 289; 50561, f. 103.

Connell (Lena), *photographer.* Portrait photographs of G. B. Shaw, 1910? 50582, ff. 48-61.

— Portrait of W. B. Yeats, 1915? 50585, f. 93.

Connolly (*Mrs.* —), *widow of J. Connolly, Irish nationalist.* List of subscribers to fund collected for Mrs. J. Connolly, 1917? Mainly *typewritten.* 50548, f. 190.

Conolly (Daniel), *farmer, of Derry, co. Cork.* Memorandum of Agreement with Rev. H. Townsend, witnessed by [C. C.?] Townsend and J. Driscoll, 1822. 56526, f. 1.

Constable and Company, *publishers, of London.* Telegram concerning 'Peace Conference Hints' to, from Saarbach Company, 1919. 50518, f. 143.

— Letter concerning translations of G. B. Shaw to, from The Hindustani Academy, Allahabad, 1929. *Signed.* 50519, f. 393.

— Letter to, of Y. Polech, 1945. 50524, f. 351.

— Note concerning G. B. Shaw's letters, annotated by R. Boughton, 1951. *Typewritten.* 52365, f. 89.

Constance (Arthur), *of Cheltenham.* Letter to G. B. Shaw, 1946. *Signed.* 50525, f. 391.

Cook (*Sir* Edward Tyas), *K.B.E.* Letter, etc., to G. B. Shaw, 1911. Partly *printed.* 50516, f. 108.

Cooke (Alice), *secretary of 'The Three Arts Club'.* Letter to G. B. Shaw, 1917. *Signed.* 50518, f. 2.

Cooper (John Paul), *gold and silversmith.* Letter to G. B. Shaw, 1931. 50520, f. 52.

Cooper (William), *osteopath.* Letter to C. F. Shaw, 1940. 63197, f. 55.

Corkran (Florence Caroline Seymour), *C.B.E.* Letter to M. Ponsonby concerning Countess F. Gleichen, 1912. 50516, f. 287.

Cornell (Katharine), *American actress and director.* Photographs of K. Cornell in 'The Barretts of Wimpole Street', 1931? 50584, ff. 42, 43.

'Cornhill Magazine'. Communications to G. B. Shaw, 1879, 1880. *Printed.* 50508, ff. 163, 230.

Cornwallis-West *formerly* **Campbell** (*Mrs.* Beatrice Stella).

v. Campbell *afterw.* Cornwallis-West.

Cornwallis-West (*Maj.* George Frederick Myddleton). Correspondence with G. B. Shaw, 1914-1941. Partly *copy* and *signed.* 50517, f. 164; 50522, f. 97; 58433, ff. 1-21v.

— Play, 'The Woman who stopped War', with *autogr.* annotations by G. B. Shaw, 1933. *Copy.* 58432.

Corry (Raymond H.), *of the Franklin D. Roosevelt Library, New York.* Letter to, of J. J. Tunney, 1948. *Copy.* 50526 B, f. 430.

Cosmopolitan Dramatic Centre, *London.* Bulletin, 1940. *Duplicated.* 50742, f. 173.

Costello (Catherine Elizabeth Conn). *v.* Stephen *née* Costello.

Coster (Howard), *photographer.* Letter, etc., to F. E. Loewenstein, 1947. *Signed* and partly *printed.* 50565, ff. 152, 153.

Couch (Ernest Ambrose), *vicar of Stogumber, co. Som.* Letter and postcard to G. B. Shaw, 1924. 50519, ff. 115, 119.

Coulson (Frederick Raymond), *author and journalist.* Letter to G. B. Shaw, 1896. 50513, f. 105.

Coultar (H. G.), *of Palm Springs, California.* Letter, etc., to G. B. Shaw, 1946. Partly *printed.* 50526 B, f. 303.

Coulter (Leonard J.), *editor of 'News Review'.* Letter to G. B. Shaw, 1941. *Signed.* 50522, f. 430.

Council of Austrians in Great Britain. *Draft* Manifesto by G. B. Shaw, 1941. Mainly *typewritten.* 50698, ff. 180-183.

Courcy-Wheeler (Robert Cecil de).
v. Wheeler.

Courtney (T.), *of Kenmare, co. Kerry.* Letter to G. B. Shaw, 1919. 50518, f. 156.

Covici (Pascal), *of Doubleday, Doran & Co., New York.* Letter to A. L. Ross, 1937. *Copy.* 50538, f. 40.

Coward McCann Inc., *of New York.* Letter to, of Incorporated Society of Authors, Playwrights & Composers, 1934. *Copy.* 63197, f. 21.

Cowley-Brown (Horace W.), *al. 'Horace Wyndham'; author.* Letter, etc., to G. B. Shaw, 1899. Partly *printed.* 50513, f. 202.

Cox (William Drought), *American author.* Correspondence with G. B. Shaw, 1934. Partly *signed* and *shorthand draft.* 50520, ff. 242, 242v.

Cragg (Alliston), *American author.* Letter to G. B. Shaw, 1941. *Signed.* 50522, f. 385.

Craig (*Miss* Edith), *daughter of Ellen Terry; Hon. Stage Director, Pioneer Players.* Pen-and-ink caricature of G. B. Shaw, 1896. 43800, f. 126.

— Letters to C. F. Shaw, 1902. 56491, ff. 25, 26.

— Correspondence with G. B. Shaw, 1929, 1940. Partly *copy.* 43800, f. 1; 50522, ff. 299, 302, 317.

— Painting of Edith Craig and friends by C. Atwood, 1939. *Photogr.* 50522, f. 317v.

Craig (Edward Henry Gordon), *son of Ellen Terry; stage designer.* Pen-and-ink caricature of G. B. Shaw, 1898. 43801, f. 226.

— Letters to G. B. Shaw, 1929, 1930. Partly *copy.* 50519, f. 388; 50526 B, f. 389.

Craig (Edy).
v. Craig (Edith).

Craig (James), *1st Viscount Craigavon.* Photograph of, 1940. *Newsprint.* 50584, f. 44.

Craigavon, *Viscount.*
v. Craig (James).

Crampin (W.), *[motor engineer?].* Letter to C. A. McEvoy, 1907. *Typewritten copy.* 50543, f. 11.

Crane (Walter), *artist.* Letters to G. B. Shaw, 1885-1904. 50531, ff. 105-125v.

— Delegate's card made out to G. B. Shaw designed by W. Crane, 1896. Mainly *printed.* 50680, f. 168.

Crapsey (Algernon), *of Brotherhood House, Rochester, New York.* Letter to G. B. Shaw, 1911. 50516, f. 72.

Craske (H. Marian), *of Belgravia.* Letter to G. B. Shaw, 1937. 50521, f. 310.

Creasy (Patricia), *cousin of G. B. Shaw.* Letters to C. F. Shaw, 1940. Partly *imperf.* 50527, f. 57; 56494, ff. 67, 73.

Creasy (Rhoda), *cousin of G. B. Shaw.* Letter to C. F. Shaw, 1940. 56494, f. 76.

Crees (*Mrs.* J. R.), *of Brisbane, Australia.* Letter, etc., to G. B. Shaw, 1946. *Signed.* 50525, f. 17.

— Speech on G. B. Shaw, 1946. *Copy.* 50525, ff. 18-19.

Cremation Society. Certificate and letter to G. B. Shaw, 1924, 1943. *Signed.* 63728, ff. 1-1v, 7.

— 'Why Cremation?', *circa* 1945. *Printed.* 63186, ff. 245-251.

Cresswell (Frederic Hugh Page), *D.S.O.; South African politician.* Letters to C. F. Shaw, 1932. 56493, ff. 9, 10.

Cristoid Ltd., *manufacturers of films and plate.* Letter, etc., to G. B. Shaw of L. Smith concerning Cristoid Ltd., 1907. Partly *copies.* 50515, ff. 72-80v.

Critchett (Richard Claude), *al. 'R. C. Carton'; dramatist.* Letter to G. B. Shaw, 1917. 50517, f. 301.

'Critic, The'. Letter to G. B. Shaw of W. Mankowitz, on behalf of editorial board, 1946. *Signed.* 50526 A, f. 144.

Cromer, *Earl of.*
v. Baring (Rowland Thomas).

Cromwell (John), *American actor.* Photographs of C. O. Skinner's production of 'Candida', 1939. 50588, ff. 81-83.

Crosby Hall Endowment Fund. Programme of lectures in aid of, 1923. *Printed.* 50701, f. 251.

Cross (*Professor* W.), *phrenologist.* 'Phrenological Chart', 1892, 1902. *Printed,* with *autogr.* insertions of 1902. 50711 A, ff. 5-23v.

— Phrenological assessment of G. B. Shaw, 1902. 50711 A, ff. 6-7.

Crottet (Robert A.), *French writer on Lapland.* Letter to G. B. Shaw, n.d. 50527, f. 58.

Crowley (Alister), *occultist.* Letter to G. B. Shaw, 1936. *Signed.* 63186, f. 87.

Crowther (Godfrey D.), *of the Civic Guild, Plymouth.* Letter to G. B. Shaw, 1913. 50516, f. 306.

Crozier (*Brig.-Gen.* Frank Percy). Letter to G. B. Shaw, 1931. 50520, f. 74.

Cruikshank (Alfred Byron), *American author.* Letter, etc., to G. B. Shaw, 1925. 50519, f. 231.

Cudlip (F. W.), *indexer.* Letter to C. F. Shaw, 1931. 56492, f. 168.

Cullum (R. L.), *manager of the Midland Bank, Basingstoke.* Correspondence with G. B. Shaw, 1943. *Signed.* 50523, f. 170; 50527, f. 226.

Cumellas (Juan), *of the Teatre Català de la Comèdia, Barcelona.* Letter, etc., to G. B. Shaw, 1938. *Signed. Fr.* 50522, f. 71.

Cummins (Charles), *amateur musician.* Group photograph taken at Dalkey, co. Dublin by R. Pigott, *circa* 1865. *Copies.* 50583, ff. 6, 7; 50587, f. 10.

Cunningham (Margaret), *suffragist, at Lincoln's Inn House, Kingsway.* Letters to, concerning Women's Social and Political Union, 1914. *Copies.* 50517, ff. 141-155.

Cunninghame Graham (Robert Bontine).
v. Graham.

Cureton (Edward), *of Bootle.* Letter to G. B. Shaw, 1931. 50520, f. 125.

Curkulakis (T. D.), *translator, of Athens.* Letter to G. B. Shaw, 1935. 63186, f. 83.

Currall (Ivo L.), *solicitor.* Letters to G. B. Shaw, 1930-1946. 50520, f. 161; 50526 A, f. 182; 50704, f. 228; 63186, f. 196.

— Letter to, of J. T. Kirk, 1947. *Signed.* 50565, f. 146.

Curran (Aileen), *actress.* Letter to G. B. Shaw, 1935. 50521, f. 38.

Cutter (Charles Forrest), *of Low Fell.* Letter to G. B. Shaw, 1934. *Signed.* 63186, f. 77.

Czech Academy of Sciences and Art. Letter to G. B. Shaw, 1930. *Signed.* 50520, f. 19.

Czech-Jochberg (Erich) *al. 'Ernest Clam'; author.* Letter to G. B. Shaw, 1946. *Signed.* 50525, f. 219.

D

Dadourian (Armen), *Armenian, of Cairo.* Letter to G. B. Shaw, 1950. *Signed.* 50526 B, f. 503.

Dags Expres, *Sweden.* Telegram to G. B. Shaw, 1946. 50525, f. 86.

Dahlbender (Grover C.), *of 'The Seekers', San Quentin Penitentiary, California.* 'The Seekers', 1946. *Printed.* 50526 A, ff. 92-105.

— Letter to, of Professor L. E. Hinsie, 1946. *Printed.* 50526 A, f. 106.

'Daily Mirror' Studios. Portrait of G. B. Shaw during rehearsals for 'Pygmalion', 1913? 50582, f. 38.

Dakin (William Radford), *F.R.C.P.; obstetrician.* Letter to G. B. Shaw, 1881. 50509, f. 26.

Dallas (Duncan C.), *printer; formerly of the Socialist Co-operative Society.* Letters, etc., to G. B. Shaw, 1906. Partly *printed.* 50514, ff. 307-373v *passim.*

Dallmeyer (J. H.) **Ltd.,** *opticians and lens manufacturers.* Letter to G. B. Shaw, 1900. 50513, f. 233.

Dal Mar (James), *writer on Dartmoor prison.* Letter to G. B. Shaw, 1937. *Signed.* 50521, f. 287.

Daly (Peter Christopher *al.* Arnold), *actor.* Correspondence with G. B. Shaw, 1903-1911. Partly *signed* and *draft.* 50514, ff. 174-178v, 213, 227-240; 50516, ff. 54, 58; 50527, f. 59 (n.d.).

'Dane (Clemence)', *pseudonym.* *v.* Ashton (Winifred).

Daniell (Madeline M.), *companion of Constance Naden.* Letters to G. B. Shaw, 1889. 50512, ff. 97, 118.

D'Annunzio (Gabriele). *v.* Annunzio.

Dansie (*Dr.* M.), *of Welwyn.* Letter to C. F. Shaw, 1940. 63197, f. 46.

D'Arcy Power (*Dr.* H.), *at Freiburg.* Letter, etc., to G. B. Shaw, 1931. *Signed* and *typewritten.* 50554, ff. 86-95.

Dark (Sidney), *singer, writer and journalist.* Letter to G. B. Shaw, circa 1899-1902. 50527, f. 60.

[Darras?] (George), *actor.* Portrait photograph of George [Darras?], circa 1910-1920. *Signed.* 50584, f. 8.

Darwin (Charles Robert), *naturalist.* Unpublished lecture materials of G. B. Shaw on Darwin, 1906, n.d. *Typewritten* with *autogr.* corrections. 50661, ff. 45-99.

Darwin (*Sir* George Howard), *K.C.B.; astronomer.* Introductory statement on behalf of 'Potentia Organization', signed by Sir V. H. P. Caillard, Sir G. H. Darwin, Sir M. Foster, J. Claretie, F. W. Foerster, Comte G. d' Alviella, J. Le Jeune and Dr. C. Richet, 1930? Partly *printed,* with *duplicated* signatures. 50742, f. 140.

Dearmer (Geoffrey), *Examiner of Plays.* Licensing reports on plays by G. B. Shaw, 1937-1939. *L.C.P. Corr.* 1937/771; *L.C.P. Corr.* 1938/1624; *LCP. Corr.* 1938/1857; *L.C.P. Corr.* 1939/2967.

Dearmer (Jessie Mabel), *author; wife of Canon Percy Dearmer.* Letter to G. B. Shaw, 1911. *Signed.* 50516, f. 104.

De Chair *née* **Struben** (Enid), *wife of Adm. Sir D. R. S. de Chair.* Letter, etc., to C. F. Shaw, 1931. 56492, f. 221.

— Letter to C. Struben, 1931. 56492, f. 222.

— Letter to [E.?] Struben, 1931. 56492, f. 224.

Deck (Richard), *singer.* Letters to G. B. Shaw, 1881. *Fr.* 50509, ff. 27, 34.

Deedy (Joseph), *of Bromley, co. Kent.* Letters to G. B. Shaw, 1907. 50515, ff. 63, 64.

Defries (Violet), *journalist.* 'Mr. Bernard Shaw on things promiscuous', 1906? Mainly *typewritten.* 50694, ff. 205-210.

Deghy (Guy Stephen), *author.* Letter to G. B. Shaw, 1943. 50523, f. 157.

Degnan (J.), *of the Nonos Printinghouse Ltd., Ennis, co. Clare.* Letter to G. B. Shaw, 1946. 50526 A, f. 74.

Deighton-Patmore (J.), *of the Deighton-Patmore Society of Colour Ltd.* Letter, etc., to B. Patch, 1938. *Signed* and partly *printed.* 50522, f. 161.

— 'Can Colour Cure?', *circa* 1938. *Printed.* 50522, f. 162.

De la Bere (*Capt. — *), *English master, R.A.F. Cadet College.* Review of 'The Seven Pillars of Wisdom', 1927. *Printed.* 45903, ff. 123v-126v.

Delahaye (*Col.* Joseph Viner), *D.S.O.; M.C.* Letter, etc., to G. B. Shaw, 1936. *Signed.* Partly *printed.* 50521, f. 213.

de Lara (Adelina), *pianist and composer.* Letter to G. B. Shaw, 1946. 50526 A, f. 81.

Del Giudice (F.), *Managing Director, Scenario Institute Ltd.* Memorandum rel. to Scenario Institute Ltd., 1943. *Typewritten draft.* 50523, ff. 35-39.

Dell (Robert Edward), *journalist.* Letter to E. R. Pease, 1912. *Copy.* 50557, f. 202.

Delle Sedie (Enrico), *Italian baritone.* Letter, etc., to G. B. Shaw, 1893. *Printed.* 50513, f. 13v.

Delme-Radcliffe (*Brig.-Gen. Sir* Charles). Letter of G. B. Shaw to, 1917. *Copy.* 50518, f. 27.

De Mattos (William S.), *Fabian.* Correspondence with G. B. Shaw, 1891. Partly *copy.* 50557, ff. 18, 19.

De Mille (Anna Angela George), *daughter of Henry George.* Letter to G. B. Shaw, *circa* 1929. 63186, f. 53.

Democratic Club. Programme of lectures, 1893. *Printed.* 50701, f. 130.

Deptford Liberal Club. Programmes of lectures, 1889, 1891. *Printed.* 50701, ff. 49, 102.

Derby, *Earl of.*
v. Stanley (Edward George Villiers).

Deroche (Mathieu), *photographer, of Paris.* Portrait of J-L. Janvier, 1902. 50584, f. 98.

De Sa' (J.), *at Gray's Inn.* Letter to G. B. Shaw concerning Indian nationalism, 1917. 50518, f. 73.

De Saumarez, *Baron.*
  v. Saumarez (James St. Vincent).

De Smet (Léon), *Belgian artist.* Letters to G. B. Shaw, 1924, 1925. 50519, ff. 173, 275.

Desmond (G. G.), *of 'The Daily News'.* Letter to E. R. Pease, 1896. 50680, f. 144.
— Letter, on behalf of the editor, to G. B. Shaw, 1908. *Signed.* 50695, f. 3.
— Letter to 'The Author', 1945? *Copy.* 50556, f. 223.

De Sola (Katherine).
  v. Samuel *afterw.* De Sola.

Deutsch (Elise), *of Tel Aviv.* Letter to G. B. Shaw, 1946. 50525, f. 129.

De Valera (Eamon), *President of the Republic of Ireland. Draft* articles on Ireland and the War by G. B. Shaw, 1940. Mainly *typewritten.* 50698, ff. 155-156, 158-162.
— Drawing of E. de Valera by S. O'Sullivan, *circa* 1940-1947. *Reproduction.* 50584, f. 45.
— Correspondence with G. B. Shaw, 1946-1947. Partly *signed* and *draft.* 50526 A, f. 201; 50526 B, f. 399; 50527, f. 272.

de Veer (Willem).
  v. Veer.

De Villiers (Adelheid), *wife of 2nd Baron De Villiers.* Letters to C. F. Shaw, 1932, 1935. 56493, ff. 22, 132.

Devine (Alexander), *of Clayesmore School, Pangbourne.* Letter to G. B. Shaw, 1907. 50515, f. 38.

Devine (Patricia), *tenant of 33 Synge Street, Dublin.* Correspondence with G. B. Shaw, 1944. Partly *shorthand draft.* 50524, ff. 47-47v.

De Vleeschouwer (G. E.), *writing from Camberwell.* Correspondence with G. B. Shaw, 1883. Partly *shorthand draft.* 50510, ff. 123-123v.

Dewer (William J.), *of Ayr, Scotland.* Letter to, from G. B. Shaw, n.d. *Dictated.* 50527, f. 227.

Dibdin (Edward Rimbault Vere), *art critic.* Letters to G. B. Shaw, 1912. 50516, ff. 165, 206.

Dick (Oliver Lawson), *editor of Aubrey's 'Brief Lives'.* Letter to G. B. Shaw, 1946. 50526 A, f. 58.

Dickinson (Goldsworthy Lowes), *Fellow of King's College, Cambridge.* Order of service following the death of G. L. Dickinson, 1932. *Printed; annotated* by G. B. Shaw in 1940. 63183, f. 32.

Dickison (*Capt.* Joyce M.), *of the Salvation Army.* Letter, etc., to G. B. Shaw, 1946. Partly *printed.* 50526 B, f. 323.

Diehl (George W.), *of Illinois.* Note to G. B. Shaw, *circa* 1946-1948. Partly *typewritten.* 50563, f. 41.

'Die Zeit', *Austria.* Correspondence with G. B. Shaw, 1911. Partly *duplicated* and *typewritten draft.* 50695, ff. 125-129.

Dilipa-Kumara Raya, *Indian author.* Letter, etc., to G. B. Shaw, n.d. *Signed.* 50527, f. 116.

Dilke (*Sir* Charles Wentworth), *2nd Bart.; P.C.; M.P.* Correspondence

G. B. Shaw, 1946. *Signed.* 50526 A, f. 167.

Dowson *née* **Filippi** (Rosina).
v. Filippi *afterw.* Dowson.

Doyle (*Sir* Arthur Conan), *writer.* Letter to G. B. Shaw, n.d. 50527, f. 63.

Drabig (Paul), *German language teacher and translator.* Letters to G. B. Shaw, 1894-1900. Partly *Germ.* 50513, ff. 55, 78, 216.

Dramatists' Club. Correspondence and papers of G. B. Shaw rel. to, 1909-1918, n.d. Partly *printed;* partly *shorthand* and *typewritten draft.* 50679, ff. 126-164; 56628, ff. 9-12.

Drawbell (James Wedgwood), *Editor, 'Sunday Chronicle'.* Letter to C. F. Shaw, 1935. 56493, f. 126.

Dreher (Felix), *of Mannheim, Germany.* Letter to G. B. Shaw, 1946. 50526 A, f. 14.

Dreiser (Theodore), *American novelist.* Letter, etc., to G. B. Shaw, 1942. *Signed* and partly *printed.* 50522, f. 463.
— Report of speech, 1942. *Printed.* 50522, f. 464.

Drew (Henry Thomas Bertie), *of the New Zealand Government Offices in London.* Letters to G. B. Shaw, 1934, 1946. 50520, f. 230v; 50525, f. 307.

Drew (Margaret), *[of the Tagore Society?].* Letter to G. B. Shaw, 1943. 50523, f. 40.

Drew (W. H.), *President of Bradford and District Labour Union.* Letter to E. R. Pease, 1892. *Copy.* 50557, f. 21.

Drexel (Conrad), *of Hampton, Virginia.* Letter to G. B. Shaw, 1946. *Signed.* 50526 A, f. 61.

Dring (H. G.), *of the Canadian Pacific Railway Company.* Note to G. B. Shaw, 1933. *Signed.* 50741, f. 31.

Drinkwater (John), *playwright and theatre manager.* Letter, etc., to G. B. Shaw, 1916, 1924. 50519, f. 154; 50549, f. 36.
— Photograph of J. Drinkwater, 1929. *Signed.* 50584, f. 49.

Driscoll (John). Memorandum of Agreement between Rev. H. Townsend and D. Conolly, witnessed by [C. C.?] Townsend and J. Driscoll, 1822. 56526, f. 1.

Drummond (*Mrs.* Flora), *of the Women's Guild of Empire, Glasgow.* Circular letter, 1938. *Copy* with *printed* signature. 50522, f. 1.

Drury (Arthur), *M.B., C.M.* Letter to 'The Daily News', 1906. *Printed.* 50514, f. 304.

Družstevni pracé, *publishers, of Prague.* Letter to Dr. F. E. Loewenstein, 1946. *Typewritten.* 50526 B, f. 273.

Dryhurst (Alfred Robert), *Assistant Secretary, British Museum; Fabian.* Postcard to G. B. Shaw, 1889. 50512, f. 96.

Dublin, *Archbishop of.*
v. Gregg (John Allen Fitzgerald).

Dublin, *Department of Posts and Telegraphs.* Letter to A. L. Shaw on behalf of Controller, 1931. *Signed.* 50520, f. 61.

Duddington (John Nightingale), *rector of Ayot St. Lawrence.*

Correspondence with C. F. Shaw, 1912. Partly *draft*. 50516, f. 179; 56491, ff. 77-79v; 56494, f. 177.

— Letter of G. B. Shaw to, 1912. *Draft*. 50516, f. 185.

Duddington (Lily Nightingale), *theosophist and poet*. Letters, etc., to G. B. Shaw, 1912, n.d. 50516, ff. 152, 169, 251; 50742, ff. 130-135.

Duerden (D. G.), *of Wheathampstead, co. Herts*. Letter to G. B. Shaw, 1943. 50523, f. 158.

Duffin (Henry Charles), *author*. Letter of G. B. Shaw to H. C. Duffin, 1920. *Copy*. 50518, f. 195.

Dugdale *afterw*. **Hardy** (Florence). *v*. Hardy *née* Dugdale.

Dukes (Ashley), *author and dramatist*. Letters of Shaw selected for publication by, *circa* 1924-1928. *Typewritten copies*. 50561, 50562.

— Correspondence with G. B. Shaw, 1929, 1930. Partly *typewritten copy*. 50532, ff. 312-338; 50561, f. 2; 50562, f. 235.

Dukes (Cuthbert Esquire), *O.B.E.; M.B., Ch.B., M.D.* Correspondence, etc., with G. B. and C. F. Shaw of A. G. Evans, J. S. Hensman, C. E. Dukes and R. Roche, 1938-1943. Partly *signed, copy* and *printed*. 56494, ff. 1-63 *passim*, 101, 163; 63197, f. 47.

Dulac (Edmund), *artist*. Letter, etc., to G. B. Shaw, 1912. Partly *printed*. 50516, f. 248v.

Dulwich Working Men's Liberal and Radical Club. Programme of lectures, 1894. *Printed*. 50701, f. 139.

Dunbar *afterw*. **Webb** (Janet). *v*. Webb *née* Dunbar.

Duncan (*Sir* Patrick), *G.C.M.G* (1937); *Governor-General of Union of South Africa*. Letter to, of P. H. Kerr, 1931. *Signed*. 56492, f. 229.

Dunn (Edward), *clerk, of Stoke-on-Trent*. Letter, etc., to G. B. Shaw, 1910. 50515, f. 397.

Dunn (Frank), *of Redhill, co. Surr*. Letter to G. B. Shaw, 1878. 50508, f. 111.

Dunny (James J.), *priest, of Carlow*. Letter to G. B. Shaw, 1938. 50522, f. 132.

Dunsany, *Baron*. *v*. Plunkett (Edward John Moreton Drax).

Dupernex (W. E.), *of Hove*. Letter to G. B. Shaw, 1924. 50519, f. 116.

Durham (Mary Edith), *artist and writer*. Correspondence with G. B. Shaw concerning Serbia, 1914. Partly *signed* and *shorthand draft*. 50517, f. 219.

Durkin (Jimmie), *of the United Securities Indemnity Company, Spokane, Washington*. Letter to G. B. Shaw, 1909. *Signed*. 50515, f. 228.

Durran (William), *writer on law*. Letter to G. B. Shaw, 1912. *Signed*. 50516, f. 284.

Dussauze (Henri), *writer on philosophy*. Letter to G. B. Shaw, concerning the translation of the works of Sir W. Petty, from M. Pasquier and H. Dussauze, 1902. *Signed. Fr.* 50514, f. 53.

Dutton (Hugh Thompson), *local historian, of Ellesmere Port*. Letter to G. B. Shaw, 1939. 50522, f. 210.

Dutton (Reginald J. G.), *journalist and inventor of Dutton Shorthand.* Letter, etc., to G. B. Shaw, 1940. Partly *printed.* 50554, f. 114; 63186, f. 153.

Dye (John Homer), *of Phillips Academy, Andover, U.S.A.* Letter to G. B. Shaw, 1929. *Signed.* 50519, f. 370.

Dyer (Sidney Reginald), *M.R.C.S.* Letter as Senior Medical Officer, H.M. Prison, Brixton, to G. B. Shaw, 1912. 50516, f. 142.

Dyke (— Van)
v. Van Dyke.

Dyke (Tom A.), *of Newport, co. Salop.* Letter to G. B. Shaw, 1932. 50520, f. 160.

E

Earp (Oswald), *Hon. Sec., The Health League.* Letter to G. B. Shaw, 1944. 50524, f. 162.

East (C.), *syndicalist.* Letter to G. B. Shaw, 1937. 50521, f. 341.

'East and West', *monthly magazine.* Letter, etc., to G. B. Shaw of T. R. Macquoid concerning, 1889. Partly *printed.* 50512, ff. 152-155v.

East Finsbury Radical Club. Programme of Fabian lectures, 1889. *Printed.* 50701, f. 62.

Easthaugh (J.), *architectural sculptor, of Windlesham, Surrey.* Letter to G. B. Shaw, 1948. *Signed.* 50526 B, f. 440.

East London Federation of Suffragettes. Lecture, 'The Nation's Vitality' of G. B. Shaw, arranged by East London Federation of Suffragettes, 1915. Speaker's notes and *printed* reports. 50704, ff. 122-126.

Eaton (*Sir* Frederick Alexis), *Sec., Royal Academy.* Letter to G. B. Shaw, 1906. *Signed.* 50514, f. 339.

Eaton (Horace Ainsworth), *American biographer.* Letter to G. B. Shaw, 1936. *Signed.* 50521, f. 217.

Ebert (Elsbeth), *music student, of Stein bei Nürnberg.* Letter, etc., to G. B. Shaw, 1948. *Germ.* 50526 B, f. 420.

Ebner (*Dr.* Anton), *of the South Tyrolese People's Party.* Letter to G. B. Shaw of Dr. O. von Guggenberg and Dr. A. Ebner, 1946. *Signed.* 50525, f. 102.

Ede (*Very Rev.* William Moore), *Dean of Worcester.* Letter to G. B. Shaw, 1932. 50520, f. 163.

Edward VII, VIII, *of England.*
v. England.

Edwards (Alfred Cecil Wall), *housemaster at Christ's Hospital.* Letter of G. B. Shaw to, 1923. *Copy.* 50519, f. 20.

Edwards (Hamilton), *of the Amalgamated Press.* Correspondence, as managing editor of the 'Penny Pictorial', with G. B. Shaw, 1909. Partly *signed* and *copy.* 50515, ff. 263, 264.

Edwards (Henry Sutherland), *writer.* Correspondence with G. B. Shaw, 1883. Partly *shorthand draft.* 50510, ff. 10, 125.

Edwards (John), *Fabian, of Liverpool.* Letter to G. B. Shaw, 1908. 50685, f. 114.

Edwards (Norman), *of the Amal-gamated Press Ltd.* Letter to G. B. Shaw, 1945. *Signed.* 50524, f. 324.

Egan (Peggy), *of Cork.* Letter to G. B. Shaw, 1928. 50519, f. 350.

'Egerton (George)', *pseudonym.*
v. Clairmonte *afterw.* Bright (Mary Chavelita).

Eight Hours' League. Leaflets, etc., of campaign for eight hour day, 1887-1894. *Printed.* 50701, ff. 6, 93, 94, 120, 121, 133.

— Speech to open-air demonstration by G. B. Shaw, 1890. *Typewritten draft.* 50702, ff. 278-280.

Einstein (Albert), *physicist.* Address of G. B. Shaw in honour of, under auspices of Joint British Committee Ort-Oze, 1930. Partly *typewritten* transcript and *printed* report. 50704, ff. 229-236.

— Letter to Upton Sinclair, 1938. *Typewritten copy.* 63183, f. 64.

— Portrait of, by J. Plesch, 1944. *Photogr.* 50524, f. 265v.

Elder *afterw.* **Jackson** (Ann M.), *secretary to G. B. Shaw.* Lists of permissions granted 1897-1925 to perform plays, 1915. 50649.

Elder *afterw.* **Mackay** (Eleanor), *author; sister of Ann Elder.* Letters to G. B. Shaw, 1941, 1944. 50522, f. 380; 50524, f. 24.

Elder (Una), *sister of Ann Elder.* Letter to G. B. Shaw, 1920. *Draft.* 63186, f. 23.

Elek (Paul), *publishers.* Letter to G. B. Shaw, 1949. *Signed.* 63186, f. 217.

Eleusis Club, *Chelsea.* Programme of lectures, 1893. *Printed.* 50701, f. 129.

Elgar (*Sir* Edward William), *Bart.; O.M.; composer.* Letters to G. B. Shaw, 1926-1933. 50519, f. 282; 50520, f. 227; 63186, f. 64.

— Postcard to C. F. Shaw, 1929. *Printed.* 63197, f. 13.

'Elliot (Gertrude)', *pseudonym.*
v. Forbes-Robertson (May Gertrude).

Elliott and Fry, *photographers.* Letter to G. B. Shaw, 1889. *Type-written.* 50512, f. 194.

Ellis (Alec R.), *of Liverpool.* Letter to G. B. Shaw, 1938. *Signed.* 50522, f. 34.

Ellis (Ashton).
v. Ellis (William Ashton).

Ellis (Henry Havelock), *sociologist.* Correspondence with G. B. Shaw, 1888, 1889. Partly *shorthand draft.* 50533, ff. 84-102; 61891, ff. 80-87.

— Letter to H. H. Ellis of H. M. G. Wilson, 1932. *Draft.* 78939, f. 18.

Ellis (J.), *Ph.D.; of the University of Hull.* Entry in alphabet design competition by J. Ellis and P. J. Burnhill, 1958. 79494 B, ff. 25-36.

Ellis (Jake), *of the Oxford Playhouse Company.* Letter to G. B. Shaw, 1923. 50519, f. 35.

Ellis (Oliver Coligny de Champfleur), *author and dramatist.* Letter to G. B. Shaw, 1946. 63186, f. 204.

Ellis (Thomas Evelyn Scott-).
v. Scott-Ellis.

Ellis (William Ashton), *translator of Wagner.* Letters to G. B. Shaw, 1903-1908. 50514, ff. 118, 221-226v; 50515, f. 123.

— Correspondence of G. B. Shaw relating to a Civil List pension on behalf of W. A. Ellis, 1905-1908.

Partly *signed* and *draft.* 50514, f. 241; 50515, ff. 66, 70, 81, 120.

Ellmann (Richard), *literary biographer.* Letter to G. B. Shaw, 1946. *Signed.* 50553, f. 168.

Elmy (Elizabeth C. Wolstenholme), *suffragist.* Letter to G. B. Shaw, 1903. *Signed.* 50514, f. 167.

El Wakif (Mokhtar), *of Cairo, Egypt; translator of G. B. Shaw into Arabic.* Letter to G. B. Shaw, 1936. 50521, f. 132.

Ely (Robert Erskine), *director of the Civic Forum, New York.* Letter to G. B. Shaw, 1908. *Signed.* 50515, f. 126.

Embleton (Leslie), *of Hendon.* Letter to G. B. Shaw, 1940. 50522, f. 266.

Emery *née* **Farr** (Florence), *actress.* Letters, etc., to G. B. Shaw of and concerning, 1905-1948. Partly *printed* and *signed.* 50533, ff. 103-116.

— Biographical essay on, by G. B. Shaw, 1941. 50664, ff. 143-145.

Emery *afterw.* **Maude** (Isabel Winifred Maud).

v. Maude *née* Emery.

Employers' Liability Bill. Official programme of demonstration, 1894. *Printed.* 50701, f. 132.

Encyclopaedia Britannica. 'Socialism' by G. B. Shaw, reprinted from Encyclopaedia Britannica, 1930. *Printed.* 50690, ff. 239-243v.

Engert (C. George). Letter to G. B. Shaw, 1941. 50522, f. 398.

ENGLAND. Sovereigns of, *and transactions in particular reigns. EDWARD VII.* Cartoon sketch by R. W. Anderson of G. B. Shaw, E. B. Bax and the Prince of Wales, 1893. 50680, f. 125.

— *EDWARD VIII.* Article on Abdication Crisis by G. B. Shaw, critical of H. W. Steed, 1937. Mainly *typewritten.* 50698, ff. 55-59.

English (Henry W.), *master in chancery, of Jacksonville, Illinois.* Letter, etc., to G. B. Shaw, 1944. *Signed.* Partly *printed.* 50524, f. 239.

English Land Restoration League. Notices of public meetings, etc., 1887, n.d. *Printed.* 50701, f. 2; 50721 B, ff. 33v, 34v, 67.

'English Review'. Letter drafted by W. B. Yeats and T. S. Moore, on behalf of 'English Review', 1911. *Copy.* 50538, f. 61.

Enns (Henry), *of Calgary.* Entry in alphabet design competion, 1958. 79494 B, ff. 1-6.

Enthoven (Augusta Gabrielle Eden), *O.B.E.* Letter to B. and H. White Publications Ltd., 1947. *Signed.* 50565, f. 137.

Epstein (*Sir* Jacob), *sculptor.* Correspondence concerning Sir J. Epstein's monument to O. Wilde at Père Lachaise, Paris, 1912. Partly *copy.* 50516, ff. 203-205, 277.

— Description, with photograph, of Sir J. Epstein's sculpture of a lion, 1912. 50516, ff. 277-279v.

— Letters, etc., to G. B. Shaw, 1912, 1925. 50516, f. 203; 50519, f. 206.

Epstein (Margaret), *wife of Jacob Epstein.* Correspondence with G. B. Shaw, 1916, 1937. Partly *copy.* 50517, f. 419; 50521, ff. 353, 365.

Epstein-Estienne (*Dr.* Stéphane), *French author and translator.*

Letter to G. B. Shaw of H. Chateau on behalf of, 1905. 50514, f. 249.

Ernst (Clara), *of Pittsburgh, Pennsylvania.* Letter to G. B. Shaw, 1946. 50526 A, f. 45.

Ernst *afterw.* **Ernest** (Maurice), *LL.D.; biologist.* Correspondence, etc., with G. B. Shaw, 1945, 1946. Partly *copy* and *signed.* 50524, f. 320; 50526 A, f. 152; 50711 A, f. 132.

Eroignoux (L.), *schoolteacher, of Corrèze.* Letter to G. B. Shaw, 1946. 50525, f. 98.

Ervine (St. John Greer), *author.* Correspondence with the Lord Chamberlain's Office, 1916. *L.C.P. Corr.* 1916/91.

— Correspondence with G. B. Shaw, 1916-1948. Partly *signed* and *copy.* 50533, ff. 117-169v; 63186, f. 92; *L.C.P. Corr.* 1916/91.

— Letters to C. F. Shaw, 1920, 1938. Partly *signed.* 56492, f. 26; 56494, f. 17.

Esclasans Folch (Agusti), *Spanish author.* Broadcast talk, 'Le Théâtre de Bernard Shaw', 1938. *Signed. Fr. transl.* 50522, ff. 72-75.

Escott (Thomas Hay Sweet), *journalist.* Letter of G. B. Shaw to, 1900? *Draft.* 50557, f. 306.

Esdaile (Ernest), *author.* Letter to G. B. Shaw, 1935. 50521, f. 55.

Essipoff (Annette), *pianist.* Letter to —, 1876. *Fr.* 56364, f. 1.

— Memorandum on, by G. B. Shaw, 1940. 56364, f. 3.

Etchells (Frederick), *F.R.I.B.A.; architect and artist.* Letter of P. W. Lewis, E. A. Wadsworth, F. Etchells and C. Hamilton concerning Omega Workshops, 1913. *Signed.* 50534, f. 93.

Etlin (Jeanne), *of Paris.* Letter to G. B. Shaw, 1946. *Fr.* 50526 A, f. 23.

Etter (Nikolai Sebastianovich von), *Russian diplomatist.* Correspondence with the Lord Chamberlain's Office, 1913. *L.C.P. Corr.* 1913/2148.

Ettlinger (L. M.), *[graphologist?], of Charlottenburg, Germany.* Letter, etc., to G. B. Shaw, 1927. *Signed.* Partly *Germ.* 50565, ff. 172-175.

Eulenspiegel (Till). Postcards to G. B. Shaw of G. Schmidt concerning, *circa* 1950. 50526 B, ff. 494, 495.

Evans (Arthur Geoffrey) *M.R.C.S.; M.D.* Correspondence, etc., with G. B. and C. F. Shaw of A. G. Evans, J. S. Hensman, C. E. Dukes and R. Roche, 1938-1943. Partly *signed, copy* and *printed.* 56494, ff. 1-63 *passim,* 101, 163; 63197, f. 47.

Evans *afterw.* **Booth** (Edith Mary), *D.B.E.; actress.* Letter to G. B. Shaw, 1923. 50519, f. 50.

Evans (Frederick Henry), *photographer.* Photographs of Frederick Evans, 1895?, 1915. 50584, ff. 50, 51.

— Portrait photographs of G. B. Shaw, 1896-1905, n.d. 50582, ff. 2-6, 14-16, 18, 20, 27.

— Correspondence with G. B. Shaw, 1903-1941. Partly *typewritten copy.* 50514, f. 112; 50515, ff. 284, 287; 50517, ff. 104, 106, 339; 50519, ff. 58, 108, 113, 127, 149; 50522, f. 379; 50562, f. 18.

— 'Evans — an Appreciation!' by G. B. Shaw. 1903 publication in *typescript* of 1945. 50694, ff. 68-74.

— Letter to C. F. Shaw, 1913. 56491, f. 121.

Evans (Luther Harris), *librarian of the Library of Congress.* Letter to G. B. Shaw, 1946. *Signed.* Mainly *printed.* 50526 B, f. 272.

Evans (Madeline), *of Dun Laoghaire.* Letter to G. B. Shaw, 1946. 50525, f. 280.

Evans (Maurice), *actor and theatrical producer.* Photographs of New York production of 'Man and Superman', directed by M. Evans, 1947-1948. 50589, ff. 64-126, 129-148.

— Photographs of American production of 'The Devil's Disciple', produced by M. Webster, 1950. 50589, ff. 1-10.

Evans (*Dr.* Raymond A.), *of Huntingdon Park, California.* Letter to G. B. Shaw, 1946. *Signed.* 50526 A, f. 56.

Everyman Theatre, *Hampstead.* Correspondence of and concerning Everyman Theatre, 1923-1942. Partly *signed* and *copy.* 56628, ff. 73, 118, 120, 122-125, 132-134, 173-177, 180-182; 56630, ff. 185, 191.

Ewen-Munden (*Mrs.* M. L. C.), *of the British Phrenological Society.* Letter to G. B. Shaw, 1943. *Signed.* 50523, f. 128.

Ewing (Alfred Washington), *son of Sir J. A. Ewing, F.R.S.* Letter to G. B. Shaw, 1941. 50522, f. 431.

Eyles (F. A. H.), *of 'The Observer'.* Letter of G. B. Shaw to F. A. H. Eyles, 1910. *Copy.* 50515, f. 323.

F

Fabes (Gilbert H.), *bookseller.* Letter to G. B. Shaw, 1945. *Typewritten.* 56364, f. 13.

— Letter to — Breslauer, 1945. *Typewritten.* 56364, f. 14.

Fabian Reform Committee. 'Manifesto on Fabian Policy', 1911. *Printed,* with *pencil* marginalia. 50681, ff. 110-111.

Fabian Research Department. Circular letters, 1913-1917. *Printed* and *draft.* 50557, f. 218, 224; 50681, ff. 155-159.

— Papers regarding a proposed Year Book of Fabian Research Department and Labour Party, 1914. *Typewritten.* 50681, ff. 114-122.

— Papers and reports of the Trade Union Survey, 1917. *Printed.* 50681, ff. 141-149, 162-167, 223.

— Accounts, 1917. *Typewritten.* 50681, ff. 150-151.

— Annual Reports, 1917. *Printed.* 50681, ff. 160-161, 217-222.

— Membership form, 1917. *Printed.* 50681, f. 164.

— Report on Women in Trade Unions of Fabian Women's Group and Fabian Research Department, 1918. *Typewritten.* 50681, ff. 234-237.

— Papers relating to a conference on the legal position of trade unions, 1918. *Typewritten.* 50681, ff. 238-242.

'Faith', *Superior of the Society of the Sacred Heart, Belgrave Road.* Letter to G. B. Shaw, 1937. 50521, f. 317.

Falkenberg (Derek), *schoolboy, of East London, South Africa.* Letter, with three other schoolboys, to G. B. Shaw, 1946. *Signed.* 50526 A, f. 195.

Fane *afterw.* Rumbold (Etheldred). *v.* Rumbold *née* Fane.

Farleigh (John), *C.B.E.; painter and engraver.* Letters of G. B. Shaw to J. Farleigh, 1932. *Printed* 1937. 50658, ff. 155-163v.

— Wood engraving blocks for 'Short Stories, Scraps and Shavings', 1932, 1934. 71451-71455.

— Letters to G. B. Shaw, 1933-1938. 50534, ff. 1-21.

— Letter to F. E. Loewenstein, 1947. 50565, f. 161.

Farmer (E. Howard), *director of the Polytechnic School of Photography.* Letter, enclosing prospectus, to G. B. Shaw, 1900. Partly *printed.* 50513, ff. 221-223v.

Farnsworth (Seth), *of Chicago.* Letter, etc., to G. B. Shaw, 1907. Mainly *duplicated.* 50515, f. 29.

Farrell (Vincent), *of the 'Chicago Daily News'.* Letter to G. B. Shaw, 1916. 50517, f. 428.

Farren (William), *actor; b. 1853.* Letter of G. B. Shaw to, 1908. *Typewritten copy.* 50562, f. 52.

Fassett *al.* Watts-Phillips (Dorothea), *managing director of the London Play Company.* Letter to the Council of the Society of Authors, Playwrights and Composers, 1935. *Signed.* 50521, f. 25.

Fay (Edward Francis), *socialist writer.* Portrait photograph on New Year's greeting signed by J. K. Hardie, 1896. *Printed.* 50584, f. 142.

Fay (William), *actor and director.* Letter to W. B. Yeats, 1904. 50553, f. 146.

Fazan (William), *actor.* Letter to G. B. Shaw, 1935. 50521, f. 37.

Feeney (*Miss —*), *amateur musician.* Group photograph taken at Dalkey, co. Dublin by R. Pigott, *circa* 1865. Two *copies.* 50583, ff. 6, 7; 50587, f. 10.

Feipel (Louis Nicholas), *American bibliographer.* Letter to G. B. Shaw, 1924. *Signed.* 50519, f. 150.

Feisal I, *King of Iraq.* Portraits of King Feisal by A. E. John, 1927? *Photographic copies.* 56499, ff. 35, 36.

Fellowship of the Way. 'Considerations', [issued by?] L. Ashwell, 1938. *Duplicated.* 56494, f. 12.

Fells (John Manger), *secretary of the Zetetical Society.* Letter from G. B. Shaw to J. M. Fells, 1880. *Shorthand draft.* 50508, f. 269v.

Fenn (Frederick), *dramatist.* Letter to G. B. Shaw, 1909. 50515, f. 221.

Fenton (Reginald), *of Coronado, California.* Letter to 'Metropolitan', New York, 1913. *Signed* and *annotated typescript.* 50516, f. 409.

Fernald (Chester Bailey), *playwright.* Letter to G. B. Shaw, 1911. *Signed.* 50516, f. 24.

FitzGerald *née* **McConnell** (Mabel W.), *Irish nationalist; wife of Desmond FitzGerald.* Letters, etc., to G. B. Shaw, *circa* 1914-1916. Mainly *signed.* 50517, ff. 195, 210, 252, 396, 398; 50527, f. 66.

— Letter to Nationalist M.P.s, 1916. *Copy.* 50517, f. 399.

FitzGerald (Mary G.), *of Dublin.* Letter to G. B. Shaw, n.d. 50527, f. 67.

Fitzgibbon (Dene), *of Chelsea.* Letter to G. B. Shaw, 1944. *Signed.* 50524, f. 92.

Fitzmaurice (Henry Charles Keith Petty-).

v. Petty-Fitzmaurice.

Fitzmaurice (W.), *[land agent?], of Carlow, co. Leinster.* Letter to G. B. Shaw, 1902. 50514, f. 66.

Fixsen (Theo F. G.), *W.E.A. member, of Henley-on-Thames.* Letter, etc., to G. B. Shaw, n.d. Partly *printed.* 50527, f. 69.

— 'Britain', n.d. *Printed.* 50527, ff. 71-73.

Flanagan (Frank C.), *of Crumlin, co. Dublin.* Letter, etc., to G. B. Shaw, 1942, n.d. 50582, ff. 130, 131.

Flatter (Richard), *Austrian author.* Letter to G. B. Shaw, 1944. *Signed.* 50524, f. 268.

Flecker (Herman James Elroy), *poet and dramatist.* Letter of G. B. Shaw to J. E. Flecker, 1911. *Copy.* 50516, f. 12.

Fleming Shepherd (H. Le), *of the Albermarle Club.* Letters to C. F. Shaw, 1940. Partly *signed* and *printed.* 63197, ff. 50-52v, 67, 69.

Flower (*Sir* Archibald Dennis), *High Steward, Borough of Stratford-upon-Avon.* Letters to G. B. Shaw, 1928, 1932. *Signed.* 50519, f. 331; 50520, f. 165.

Flower (Robin Ernest William), *Deputy Keeper, Dept. of Manuscripts, British Museum.* Letters to, of G. B. Shaw, 1934. Partly *typewritten* and *signed.* 78907 Z.

'Foemina', *pseudonym.* Article on G. B. Shaw, 1907. *Printed. Fr.* 45296, f. 188.

Foerster (Friedrich Wilhelm), *German philosopher and educationist.* Introductory statement on behalf of 'Potentia Organization', signed by Sir V. H. P. Caillard, Sir G. H. Darwin, Sir M. Foster, J. Claretie, F. W. Foerster, Comte G. d'Alviella, J. Le Jeune and Dr. C. Richet, 1930? Partly *printed,* with *duplicated* signatures. 50742, f. 140.

Fogerty (Elsie), *Principal, The Central School of Speech Training and Dramatic Art.* Letters, etc., to G. B. Shaw, 1936-1944. Partly *signed* and *printed.* 50521, f. 198; 50523, f. 131; 50524, f. 1.

Folkard (Henry), *of Ipswich.* Letter to G. B. Shaw, 1946. 50525, f. 127.

Follick (*Dr.* Mont), *M.P.* Letter to G. B. Shaw, 1945. *Signed.* 50555, f. 129.

— Letter, etc., to, from K. G. Mashruwala, 1946. Mainly *typewritten copy.* 50556, ff. 98-100v.

'Fontaine', *French literary monthly published in Algiers.* Correspondence with G. B. Shaw of J. B.

Brunius, 1943, 1945. Partly *signed* and *on Shaw's behalf.* 50523, ff. 127, 156; 61893, f. 74.

Foote (George William), *editor of 'The Freethinker'.* Correspondence with G. B. Shaw, 1908, 1909. Partly *typewritten copy.* 50515, ff. 176, 188; 50562, f. 63.

Forbes (Ralph), *actor.* Photographs of R. Forbes, J. Buckmaster and A. Treacher in 'Caesar and Cleopatra', 1950. 50588, ff. 41, 45.

Forbes-Robertson (Ian), *actor.* Letters of G. B. Shaw to, 1899-1901. Partly *signed.* 62700, ff. 135-153.

Forbes-Robertson (Jean), *daughter of Sir J. Forbes-Robertson.* Letter of G. B. Shaw to, 1934. 61998, f. 30.

Forbes-Robertson (*Sir* Johnston), *actor.* Correspondence with G. B. Shaw, 1897-1935. Partly *draft.* 50534, ff. 22-69; 61998, ff. 7, 12-17, 22, 27-29.

— Financial statement for 'Mr. Forbes Robertson's Farewell', 1912. Partly *printed.* 50742, f. 163.

Forbes-Robertson (May Gertrude), *al. 'Gertrude Elliot'; actress; wife of Sir J. Forbes-Robertson.* Correspondence with G. B. Shaw, 1903-1946. 50534, f. 31; 61998, ff. 1-6v, 11, 18, 23-26, 31.

Ford (E. J.), *conscientious objector.* Memorandum concerning his treatment in Wandsworth Prison, 1919. *Copy.* 50518, f. 139.

Ford (Frederick Walter), *curate of Holy Trinity, Hoxton.* Letters to G. B. Shaw, 1887. 50512, ff. 274, 279.

Forman *née* **Murray** (Alma), *actress; wife of Alfred Forman.* Correspondence with G. B. Shaw, 1886-1904. Partly *typewritten copy.* 50511, ff. 180, 223, 226; 50512, ff. 13, 100v, 264; 50562, f. 34; *Ashley* 5018, f. 1.

— Letter to T. J. Wise, 1927. *Ashley* 5018, f. ii.

— Press notice concerning, 1944. 50524, f. 226.

— Biographical notices by G. B. Shaw, 1944, 1946? *Typewritten.* 50699, ff. 85, 144-145.

Forrester (*Mrs.* H.), *of San Bernardino, California.* Letter, with her husband, to G. B. Shaw, 1946. *Dictated.* 50526 B, f. 289.

Forrester (H.), *of San Bernardino, California.* Letter, with his wife, to G. B. Shaw, 1946. 50526 B, f. 289.

Forsdyke (*Sir* Edgar John), *K.C.B.; Director of the British Museum.* Letters to G. B. Shaw, 1945, 1948. *Signed.* Mainly *printed.* 50524, f. 318; 50526 B, f. 413.

Forster (Edward Morgan), *novelist.* Letters to C. F. Shaw, 1924, 1927. 56492, ff. 77, 97, 100.

Forster (Henry A.), *of New York.* Letter to, from G. B. Shaw, aft. 1918. *Copy.* 50527, f. 74.

Forster (Hugh Oakeley Arnold-). *v.* Arnold-Forster.

Forster-Bovill (W. B.), *secretary of the Authors' Producing Society.* Letter to G. B. Shaw, 1914. 50517, f. 36.

Förster-Nietzsche (Elisabeth), *sister of F. W. Nietzsche.* Letter and note to G. B. Shaw, 1906, 1914. Partly *printed. Germ.* 50514, f. 329; 50517, f. 121.

Fortnum (M. G.), *of Harrow; member of the Women's Social and Political Union.* Letter to M. Cunningham, 1914. *Copy.* 50517, f. 147.

Foster (George Sherwood), *painter.* Correspondence with G. B. Shaw, 1911-1912. Partly *draft* and *signed.* 50516, ff. 110, 133-137.

Foster (*Sir* Michael), *K.C.B.; F.R.S.* Introductory statement on behalf of 'Potentia Organization', signed by Sir V. H. P. Caillard, Sir G. H. Darwin, Sir M. Foster, J. Claretie, F. W. Foerster, Comte G. d' Alviella, J. Le Jeune and Dr. C. Richet, 1930? Partly *printed,* with *duplicated* signatures. 50742, f. 140.

Foster (*Sir* Thomas Gregory), *Provost of University College, London.* Letter to G. B. Shaw, 1920. *Signed.* 50518, f. 197.

Fottrell (Edward), *of London.* Letter to G. B. Shaw concerning S. Carr, 1948. 50526 B, f. 434.

Foulds (John Herbert), *composer.* Letter to G. B. Shaw, 1925. 50519, f. 224.

Foulger and Co., *publishers, of London.* Postcard to, of L. Gronlund, 1884. 50510, f. 276.

Fox (Edward), *socialist; electrical engineer.* Letter to G. B. Shaw, 1932. 50520, f. 157.

Foxwell (Herbert Somerton), *economist.* Letters to G. B. Shaw, 1886, 1888. 50511, f. 227; 50512, f. 11.

Foyster (W. H.), *of Altrincham.* Letter to G. B. Shaw, 1937. 50521, f. 315.

Fradelle and Young, *photographers.* Letter to G. B. Shaw, 1901. 50514, f. 9.

FRANCE. SOVEREIGNS OF, *and transactions in particular reigns. THIRD REPUBLIC.* Correspondence and papers rel. to the National Defence Loan of the Government of the French Republic, 1915-1932. Mainly *printed.* 63198 B, ff. 1-64.

— Ministère de l'Instruction Publique et des Beaux-Arts. Letter to G. B. Shaw concerning Bibliothèque et Musée de la Guerre (Paris), 1919. *Signed.* 50518, f. 148.

— *Decree of 9 April 1940.* Correspondence with G. B. Shaw and others of R. de Margerie, 1940. *Copies.* Partly *Fr.* 50522, ff. 276-289.

'France (Anatole)', *pseudonym.* v. Thibault (Jacques Anatole).

Frances (Juanita), *Chairman, Married Women's Association.* Letter to G. B. Shaw, 1944. *Signed.* 50524, f. 12.

Francis (Edith), *of Wallasey; member of the Women's Social and Political Union.* Letter to M. Cunningham, 1914. *Copy.* 50517, f. 152.

Franckenstein (*Baron* George), *Austrian diplomatist.* Letters to G. B. Shaw, 1935, 1937. *Signed.* 50521, f. 334; 52635, f. 56.

Frankau (Julia), *writer on art.* Letter to G. B. Shaw, 1887. 50511, f. 297.

'Free Life, The'. Issue for June 1901. *Printed.* 50740, f. 36.

Free Speech Defence Association. Tickets to demonstration, 1912. *Printed.* 50701, ff. 218, 219.

Freestone (F. S.), *engineer, of Burton-on-Trent.* Letter to G. B. Shaw, 1924. *Signed.* 50519, f. 120.

Freiberg (J. G.), *of Washington State.* Letter to G. B. Shaw, 1946. 50526 B, f. 315.

Fremlin (R.), *of the Association of Scientific Workers.* Letter to G. B. Shaw, 1944. *Signed.* 50555, f. 84.

Freshel (Curtis P.), *of New York.* Letters to G. B. Shaw, 1937-1950. Partly *signed.* 50534, ff. 70-85.

— Letter to W. D. Chase, 1950. *Copy.* 50534, f. 85.

Friars (Austin). Letter from G. B. Shaw to A. Friars, 1928. 59892, f. 133.

Fridberg (Maurice), *publisher, of Dublin.* Letter to G. B. Shaw, 1946. *Signed.* 50525, f. 66.

Friedrich Wilhelm Viktor Albert, *Emperor of Germany.*

v. Germany.

Friends' Ambulance Unit. Report, 1941. *Printed.* 56494, ff. 116-133.

Frohman (Charles), *theatrical manager.* Correspondence with G. B. Shaw, 1904, 1912. Partly *draft* and *dictated.* 50514, f. 191; 50516, f. 194.

Frood (Dorothea).

v. Hyams (Dorothea Frood).

Frost (Caroline).

v. Blacker *née* Frost.

Frost (Horace Crawshay), *of Maldon, co. Essex.* Letter, etc., to G. B. Shaw, 1944. Partly *printed.* 50524, f. 88.

Frost (Robert Percival Bodley), *M.B.E.; secretary of the Land Reform Union.* Letter to G. B. Shaw, 1883. 50510, f. 103.

Fry (Margery).

v. Fry (Sara Margery).

Fry (Roger Eliot), *painter and critic.* Letters to G. B. Shaw, 1912-1926. Partly *signed.* 50534, ff. 86-100.

— Letter to C. F. Shaw, 1914. 56491, f. 158.

Fry (Sara Margery), *Principal of Somerville College, Oxford.* Letter, on behalf of the China Campaign Committee, to G. B. Shaw, 1938. *Signed.* 50522, f. 44.

Fulda (Boris), *of Brussels; former concentration camp inmate.* Letter to G. B. Shaw, 1947. *Signed.* 50526 B, f. 385.

Fuller (Harry H.), *deputy U.S. manager, Zurich General Accident and Liability Insurance Company, Limited, of Chicago.* Letter to G. B. Shaw, 1936. *Signed.* 50521, f. 207.

Fülöp-Miller (Réné), *Austrian author.* Correspondence with G. B. Shaw, 1923. Partly *signed, shorthand draft* and *copy.* 50519, ff. 21-25.

Fulton (Alexander Strathern), *C.B.E.; D. Litt.; Keeper of Oriental Printed Books and Manuscripts in the British Museum.* Letter to G. B. Shaw, 1947. *Signed.* Mainly *printed.* 50526 B, f. 394.

Funck (Edith C.), *of Surrey.* Letter to G. B. Shaw, 1944. 50524, f. 275.

Furlong (George), *director of the National Gallery of Ireland.* Letter to G. B. Shaw, 1944. *Signed.* 50524, ff. 81, 242.

Furness (Christopher), *M.P.; 1st Baron Furness 1910.* Letter to G. B. Shaw, 1908. *Signed.* 50515, f. 193.

— 'Industrial Peace and Industrial Efficiency', 1908. *Printed,* with annotations by G. B. Shaw. 50681, ff. 37-56.

— Letter to 'The Morning Leader' concerning, 1908. *Typewritten draft* with *MS.* amendments. 50695, f. 21.

Furniss (Harry), *artist.* Letter and card to G. B. Shaw, 1888, 1895. 50512, f. 31; 63183, f. 1.

— Sketch of G. B. Shaw, 1895. With *signed* message. 63183, f. 1.

— Pen and ink wash illustrations for 'Passion, Poison and Petrifaction', 1905. 50643, ff. 72-76v.

Furnivall (Frederick James), *D. Litt.; scholar and editor.* Letters to, of A. Smith, 1884. 50510, ff. 172, 179, 235.

— Letter to, of Miss E. Worth, 1884. 50510, f. 292.

— Correspondence with G. B. Shaw, 1884-1887. 50510, f. 189; 50511, ff. 91, 107, 159, 179, 182, 356.

Fursland (A. J.), *of Swansea.* Letters to G. B. Shaw, 1938. 50522, ff. 129, 131.

Fyfe (Henry Hamilton), *author and journalist.* Letters, etc., to G. B. Shaw, 1902, 1946. Partly *signed* and *printed.* 50525, f. 371; 50694, f. 8.

— Verses on G. B. Shaw, 1946. *Printed.* 50525, f. 373.

Fyfe (*Sir* William Hamilton), *classicist.* Correspondence with G. B. Shaw, 1923. Partly *copy.* 50519, ff. 18, 26.

G

Gaiger (E. A.), *of Herne Hill, co. Kent.* Letter to G. B. Shaw, 1943. 50523, f. 181.

Galaviz (Luis C.), *of Houston, Texas.* Letter to G. B. Shaw, 1946. 50526 B, f. 340.

[Gallifant ?] (C. O.), *of Llanelly, co. Carmarthen.* Letter to G. B. Shaw, 1939. 50522, f. 243.

Galsworthy (John), *O.M.; author and dramatist.* Letter to C. F. Shaw, 1909. 56491, f. 62.

— Correspondence with G. B. Shaw, 1914, 1919. Partly *signed, copy* and *shorthand draft.* 50517, f. 115; 50518, ff. 152, 155.

Galt (Tom), *of Annisquam, Massachusetts.* Letter, etc., to G. B. Shaw concerning spelling reform, 1931. Mainly *typewritten.* 50554, ff. 36-86.

Galton (Frank Wallis), *Fabian author.* 'Notes on hours of work in Naval establishments', *circa* 1893. 50553, ff. 107-108.

— Correspondence with G. B. Shaw, 1924-1931. *Copies.* 50557, ff. 268, 271-278, 293.

—Correspondence with B. Patch, 1929. *Copies.* 50557, ff. 273-274.

Galway (R. McB.), *manager, Stratstone Ltd. car showrooms.* Letter to G. B. Shaw, 1938. *Signed.* 50522, f. 4.

Game (Henry Clement), *C.V.O.; Examiner of Plays.* Licensing reports on plays of G. B. Shaw, 1936-1940. *L.C.P. Corr.* 1936/15352;

Gillespie (Percy J.), *manager of 'The Irish Homestead'*. Appeal for financial support, 1922. *Printed.* 56492, f. 40.

Gillis (*Mrs.* Georgiana), *of New York.* Letter to G. B. Shaw, 1938. 50522, f. 133.

Gillmore (Georgina *called* Judy). *v.* Musters *née* Gillmore.

Gilmore (Albert F.), *of Boston, Massachusetts.* Letter to N. W. Astor, 1942. *Signed.* 50528, f. 101.

Girdlestone (Edward Deacon), *Fabian.* Correspondence with G. B. Shaw, 1890, 1891. Partly *typewritten copies.* 50561, ff. 20, 23; 50660, f. 3.

— Proposed amendments to Report on Fabian Policy, 1896. Partly *printed* proof with *MS.* corrections. 50680, ff. 151-159.

Gladstone Radical Working Men's Club & Institute. Programme of Fabian lectures, 1889. *Printed.* 50701, f. 52.

Glasgow (E.), *of Charlbury, co. Oxon.; friend of Emily Carroll.* Letter to G. B. Shaw, 1945. 50524, f. 298.

Glasgow Clarion Scouts. Programme of meetings, 1892?-1903? *Printed.* 50701, f. 264.

Glasgow Playgoers' League. Correspondence etc., rel. to production of 'Mrs. Warren's Profession', 1913. *L.C.P. Corr.* 1924/5632, ff. 1-13.

Glasier (John Bruce), *socialist.* Letter from G. B. Shaw to, 1892. 59892, f. 125.

Glazer (*Dr.* W. H.), *optometrist, of Philadelphia.* Letter to G. B. Shaw, 1938. *Signed.* 50522, f. 142.

Gleichen (*Countess* Feodora), *sculptor.* Letter, etc., to G. B. Shaw concerning Sir A. Gilbert, 1906. Partly *printed.* 50514, ff. 312-317v.

— Letter to M. Ponsonby of F. C. S. Corkran concerning Countess F. Gleichen, 1912. 50516, f. 287.

Glen (James B.), *of Busby, co. Lanark.* Letter to G. B. Shaw, 1946. 50526 B, f. 316.

Glennie (John Stuart Stuart-), *author.* Correspondence, etc., with G. B. Shaw, 1889-1903. Partly *draft, printed* and *typewritten.* 50512, ff. 190, 193; 50513, ff. 208, 244; 50514, ff. 1, 2, 10, 15, 47, 100; 50742, ff. 1-15.

— 'The Desirability of Treating History as a Science of Origins', 1890, 1891. *Printed* proof with *MS.* additions. 50742, ff. 1-8v.

— 'A Plea for the Endowment of History as a Science', 1901. *Typewritten* with *MS.* amendments. 50742, ff. 10-15.

Gloss (George), *secretary of the editorial committee, Workers Socialist Party, Boston, U.S.A.* Letter to G. B. Shaw, 1944. *Dictated.* 50524, f. 40.

Glossop (George Henry Pownall), *honorary Canon of St. Albans Cathedral.* Letter to G. B. Shaw, 1924. 50519, f. 145.

Glover (Ernest Augustus), *D.D.; vicar of East Marden and rector of North Marden, co. Suss.* Letter to G. B. Shaw, 1907. 50515, f. 54.

Glover (James Mackey), *author; d. 1931.* Letter to G. B. Shaw, n.d. 50527, f. 83.

Glyn *née* **Sutherland** (Elinor), *novelist.* Letters to G. B. Shaw, 1919. 50518, ff. 184, 186.

Glynne (Maurice E.), *at the Government Training Centre, Letchworth.* Letter to G. B. Shaw, n.d. 50527, f. 80.

Gobat (*Dr.* Charles-Albert), *Swiss statesman; Nobel Laureate.* Building appeal addressed to G. B. Shaw on behalf of Bureau International Permanent de la Paix, 1908. *Signed.* 50515, f. 108.

Goblet d'Alviella (*Comte* —).
v. Alviella.

Godard (John George), *solicitor to G. B. Shaw.* Letters, etc., to G. B. Shaw, 1901-1915. Partly *signed.* 50514, ff. 19, 77, 300v, 365; 50515, ff. 7v, 161, 268v; 50516, f. 211v; 50517, f. 275.

Godwin (John S.), *schoolboy, of East London, South Africa.* Letter, with three other schoolboys, to G. B. Shaw, 1946. *Signed.* 50526 A, f. 195.

Gogh (Otto Wichers von), *Swiss author.* Postcard to G. B. Shaw, 1896. 50513, f. 97.

Goldberger (Fanny), *of Nitra, Czechoslovakia.* Letters to G. B. Shaw, 1938. *Germ.* 50522, ff. 69, 86.

Golding Bright *formerly* **Clairmonte** (Mary Chavelita).
v. Clairmonte *afterw.* Bright.

Goldmann (*Dr.* Karl), *teacher of English in Germany.* Letter to G. B. Shaw, 1946. 50525, f. 96.

Gollancz (*Sir* Israel), *F.B.A.* Letter to G. B. Shaw, 1913. *Dictated.* 50516, f. 346.

Goodchild (William H.), *metallurgist.* Letter to G. B. Shaw, 1925. *Signed.* 50519, f. 208.

Goodman (Margaret G.), *of Cape Town.* Letter to C. F. Shaw, 1932. 56493, f. 21.

Goodwin (C. F.), *agent of the London Guarantee and Accident Company, Ltd.* Letter, etc., to G. B. Shaw, 1873. Partly *printed.* 50508, ff. 39-41.

Gordon (*Maj.* Colin Lindsay), *Assistant Comptroller, Lord Chamberlain's Office; Extra Equerry to the King.* Licensing report on 'Geneva', 1938. *L.C.P. Corr.* 1938/1857.

Gordon (D.), *manager of Walter Scott, publisher.* Letters to G. B. Shaw, 1889-1894. 50512, ff. 81-83v, 86, 93-95v, 182, 185, 222, 231, 233, 234, 248, 259; 50513, ff. 43, 44.

Gordon (Newton R.), *of the Edison Telephone Company.* Letters to G. B. Shaw, 1880. 50508, ff. 209, 294.

Gordon-Howley *al.* **Lawrence** (Gertrude).
v. Lawrence.

Gore (Charles), *Bishop successively of Worcester, Birmingham and Oxford.* Letter to G. B. Shaw, 1924. 50519, f. 129.

Gorky (Maxim).
v. Pyeshkoff (Alexei Maximovich).

Gosse (*Sir* Edmund William), *writer.* Letter to Lord Chamberlain, 1917. *L.C.P. Corr.* 1924/5632, f. 76.
— Letter of G. B. Shaw to, 1924. *Ashley* 1525*.

Gott (Barbara), *actress.* Letter to G. B. Shaw, 1939. 50522, f. 254.

Gottlieb (Wolfram), *London correspondent of official Latvian newspaper.* Letter to G. B. Shaw, 1938. *Signed.* 50522, f. 98.

Gottschalk (Ferdinand), *actor and dramatist.* Letter to St.J. E. C. Hankin, 1908. 50515, f. 190.

Gough (Lionel), *senior English master, Marlborough College.* Letter to G. B. Shaw, 1941. *Signed.* 50522, f. 378.

Gould (*Lt. Commander* Rupert T.), *R.N.* Letter to G. B. Shaw, 1944. *Signed.* 50524, f. 237.

Gour (*Sir* Hari Singh), *Vice Chancellor, University of Saugar, India.* Letter to G. B. Shaw, 1949. *Signed.* 63186, f. 222.

Gower (*Sir* George Granville Leveson-).

v. Leveson-Gower.

Graham (James), *translator.* Letters to G. B. Shaw, 1896. 50513, ff. 128, 132.

Graham (Robert Bontine Cunninghame), *author.* Letters to G. B. Shaw, 1888-1913. 50531, ff. 126-166v.

Graham (W. F.), *of Simpkin, Marshall.* Letter to G. B. Shaw, 1889. 50512, f. 143v.

'Grand (Sarah)', *pseudonym.*

v. MacFall (Frances Elizabeth).

Granville-Barker (Harley Granville), *actor, theatrical critic and manager.* Prompt copies of plays by G. B. Shaw produced at The Royal Court Theatre by H. Granville-Barker and J. E. Vedrenne, 1904-

1907. *Printed,* with *MS.* annotations. 65156 Q-W.

— Correspondence with G. B. Shaw, 1905-1943. Partly *signed* and *typewritten copy.* 50534, ff. 101-167; 50562, f. 38.

— Letter to W. Archer, H. G. Granville-Barker and G. B. Shaw of Dame E. S. Lyttelton concerning Shakespeare Memorial National Theatre, 1909. *Typewritten copy.* 50539, f. 175.

— Letter to the 'Daily Mail', 1912. *Copy.* 50516, f. 229.

— Letter, etc., to, of A. C. Smith, 1913. 50549, ff. 193-203.

— Play, 'Vote by Ballot', 1914. *Typewritten,* with *MS.* notes. 50568.

— Photographs of, 1914, n.d. 50584, ff. 56-58.

— Letter to, of C. D. Medley, 1917. Mainly *typewritten.* 50534, f. 151.

Granville Hall Literary Society. Notice of lecture, 1919. *Printed.* 50701, f. 245.

Grappe (Georges), *Curator of the Musée Rodin, Paris.* Letter to G. B. Shaw, 1931. *Signed. Fr.* 50520, f. 51.

Graucob (F.), *director of the Nuswift Engineering Co. Ltd.* Letter to G. B. Shaw, 1945. *Signed.* 50524, f. 317.

Graves (Arnold J.), *Secretary, Commissioners of Charitable Donations and Bequests for Ireland.* Letter of recommendation, on behalf of J. Shaw, 1911. *Copy.* 50516, f. 23.

Graves (Ernest), *ex-serviceman.* Letter to G. B. Shaw, 1940. 50522, f. 290.

Graves (Robert Ranke), *author.* Letter to T. E. Lawrence, annotated by T. E. Lawrence, 1927. *Fragm.* 45903, f. 169.

— Letter to C. F. Shaw, annotated by C. F. Shaw, 1927. 45903, f. 170.

Graveson (S.), *of the Society of Friends in Hertford.* Letter to G. B. Shaw, 1922. 50518, f. 314.

Gravestock (Alice E.), *alchemist.* Letter to G. B. Shaw, 1909. 50515, f. 220.

Gray (Cecil William Turpie), *music critic.* Letters of G. B. Shaw to, 1916-1946. 57786, ff. 39-46.

Gray (John), *author and pacifist, of Lingfield, co. Surrey.* Letter to G. B. Shaw, 1943. *Signed.* 50523, f. 163.

Gray (*Miss* Marie), *of Louis Meier, print dealers.* Letter to G. B. Shaw, 1944. 50524, f. 5.

Greb (N. P.), *of Detroit, Michigan.* Letter to G. B. Shaw, 1946. 50526 B, f. 317.

Green *née* **Stopford** (Alice Sophia Amelia), *Irish nationalist and historian; widow of J. R. Green.* Letter to G. B. Shaw, 1916. *Signed.* 50517, f. 417.

[Green?] ([F. E.?]), *Fabian.* Letter, 1896. 50557, f. 41.

Green (Sidney G.), *secretary of the South Place Ethical Society.* Letter to G. B. Shaw, 1943. *Signed.* 50523, f. 3.

Greene (F.), *secretary, Irish Anti-Vaccination League.* Letter to G. B. Shaw, 1913. *Copy.* 50516, f. 329.

Greene (Marc T.), *journalist, of Providence, R.I.* Letter to G. B. Shaw, 1944. *Signed.* 50524, f. 216.

Greening (Walter M.), *of Hammersmith.* Letter to G. B. Shaw, 1937. 50521, f. 318.

Greenwood (Frederick), *editor of 'The Pall Mall Gazette'.* Letter to G. B. Shaw, 1884. 50510, f. 269.

Greenwood (Reginald), *lance-corporal, 2nd North and Lancaster Regiment.* Letter to G. B. Shaw, 1907. 50515, f. 58.

Gregg (John Allen Fitzgerald), *Anglican Archbishop of Dublin; afterw. Archbishop of Armagh.* Letter to G. B. Shaw, 1935. 50521, f. 28.

Gregg (John Robert), *American inventor of a shorthand system.* Letter, etc., to G. B. Shaw, 1925. *Signed* and partly *printed.* 50519, f. 202.

Gregory *née* **Persse** (Isabella Augusta), *author; wife of Sir W. H. Gregory.* Photograph of Lady Gregory, 1900? 50585, f. 56.

— Correspondence with A. E. F. Horniman, 1909. *Copy.* 50534, f. 173.

— Correspondence with G. B. Shaw, 1909-1925, n.d. Partly *copy, signed* and *draft.* 50534, ff. 171-216v; 63186, ff. 27, 30, 229.

— Notes of G. B. Shaw concerning, 1910. Partly *shorthand* and *type-written.* 50703, ff. 193-199.

— Account of attempt to suppress performance of 'The Playboy of the Western World' in Philadelphia, 1912. *Typewritten.* 50534, ff. 194-207.

— Letter to C. F. Shaw, 1912. 56491, f. 104.

Grenfell (Harold), *Commander, R.N.; at H. M. Embassy, Petrograd.* Letter to G. B. Shaw, 1915. 50517, f. 273.

Gresham Press.
v. Unwin Brothers.

Greville (Frances Evelyn), *Countess of Warwick.* Letter to G. B. Shaw, *circa* 1926. 50527, f. 274.

Greville (Ursula), *Editor, 'The Sackbut'.* Letter to G. B. Shaw, n.d. 50527, f. 82.

Griffin (Gerald), *journalist.* Letter to G. B. Shaw, 1937. 50521, f. 290.

Griffiths (*Maj.* Arthur George Frederick), *inspector of prisons and author.* Correspondence, as editor of 'The World', with G. B. Shaw, 1894. Partly *shorthand draft.* 50513, ff. 49, 51; 50596 F, f. 48v.

Grigsby (B. J.), *editor of 'The Spoon River Journal'.* Letter, etc., to G. B. Shaw, 1946. *Signed.* Partly *printed.* 50526 A, f. 70; 50556, ff. 91-93.

— 'The Tower of Babel', 1946. *Copy.* 50526 A, ff. 71-72.

Grimthorpe, *Baron.*
v. Beckett (Edmund).

Grindea (Miron), *secretary of the International Arts Guild.* Letter to G. B. Shaw, 1946. *Signed.* 50525, f. 229.

Grinling (Charles Harry), *Fabian; Sec., Woolwich Council of Social Services.* Letter to G. B. Shaw, 1943. *Signed.* 50557, f. 303.

Grogan (Elmira), *of New York.* Letter to G. B. Shaw, 1944. *Signed.* 50524, f. 50.

Gronlund (Laurence), *American socialist.* Postcard to Foulger and Co., 1884. 50510, f. 276.

— Letter and postcard to H. H. Champion, 1884, 1885. 50510, f. 281; 50511, f. 67.

— Sketch with message to Shaw [by L. Gronlund?], 1885. 50743 B, f. 340.

Gross (Elliot B.), *of Montreal.* Letter to G. B. Shaw, 1938. 50522, f. 37.

Groth (*Dr.* Ernst), *of Leipzig.* Letter [to S. Trebitsch?], 1908. *Type-written copy. Germ.* 45296, f. 197.

Grove (*Sir* George), *musicologist.* Letters to G. B. Shaw, *circa* 1883-1896. 45345, f. 243; 50513, f. 119.

Grover (Kate), *of Teddington, co. Midd.* Letter to, of A. M. Field, 1946. *Signed.* 50526 A, f. 173.

— Letter, etc., to G. B. Shaw, 1946. 50526 A, f. 197.

Groves (Robert S.), *of Holland Park, London.* Letter to G. B. Shaw, 1946. 50526 A, f. 172.

'Guardians of the Life Force', *music group.* Letter of E. A. M. Langton to G. B. Shaw, 1939. 50522, f. 241.

Guedalla (F. B.), *solicitor.* Letter to G. B. Shaw, 1949. *Signed.* 50531, f. 53.

Guest (*Miss* Emily), *of West Hampstead.* Letter to, from G. B. Shaw, 1902. *Draft,* partly *type-written.* 50519, f. 69.

Guest (*Dr.* Leslie Haden-).
v. Haden-Guest.

Guggenberg (*Dr.* Otto von), *of the South Tyrolese People's Party.* Letter to G. B. Shaw of Dr. O. von Guggenberg and Dr. A. Ebner, 1946. *Signed.* 50525, f. 102.

Guilbert (Yvette), *actress.* Letters to G. B. Shaw, 1907, n.d. Partly *copy.* Partly *Fr.* 50515, f. 13v; 50527, ff. 84, 86, 87.

Haden-Guest (*Dr.* Leslie), *M.P.; Baron Haden-Guest (1950)*. Correspondence on topics related to the writings of Nietzsche, 1900? Partly *duplicated*. 50742, ff. 15-30.
— Letters, etc., to G. B. Shaw, 1906-1914? Partly *printed*. 50514, ff. 306, 311, 342, 349; 50515, f. 306; 50742, f. 171.

Haessler (George), *student at the University of Michigan*. Letter to G. B. Shaw, 1947. *Signed*. 50526 B, f. 397.

Hahn (*Prof.* E. Adelaide), *chairman of the Department of Classics, Hunter College, New York*. Letter to G. B. Shaw, 1946. *Signed*. 50526 A, f. 194.

Haig (Florence E.), *of Chelsea; member of the Women's Social and Political Union*. Letter to M. Cunningham, 1914. *Copy*. 50517, f. 148.

Haines (Clara), *widow of Rev. W. Haines*. Letters to G. B. Shaw, 1907, 1909. 50515, ff. 42, 44, 51, 53, 56, 230.

Hake (*Sir* Henry Mendelssohn), *Director, National Portrait Gallery*. Letter to G. B. Shaw, 1945. *Signed*. Partly *printed*. 50524, f. 307.

Haldane (John Burdon Sanderson), *F.R.S.; geneticist*. Letter to C. F. Shaw, 1940. *Signed*. 56494, f. 81.
— Letter to G. B. Shaw, 1941. 63186, f. 172.

Haldane (Richard Burdon), *Viscount Haldane*. Letters to G. B. Shaw, 1900-1919. 50517, ff. 282; 50538, ff. 1-7.
— Views on peace, 1915. *Press cuttings*. 50687, ff. 205-208.

— Letter to Lord Chamberlain, 1918. *L.C.P. Corr.* 1924/5632, f. 78.
— Letter to Beatrice Webb rel. to 'Mrs. Warren's Profession', 1918. *Signed. L.C.P. Corr.* 1924/5632, f. 79.

Hale (Ralph T.), *of Small, Maynard & Company, publishers, of Boston, Massachusetts*. Letter to Prof. T. D. O'Bolger, 1919. *Copy*. 50565, f. 111.

'Hall (Anmer)', *pseudonym*.
v. Horne (Alderson Burrell).

Hall (Charles H.), *of the Old Guard, of Summit, New Jersey*. Letter, etc., to G. B. Shaw, 1946. *Signed*. Partly *printed*. 50525, f. 51.

Hall (Evelyn), *actress*. Letter to G. B. Shaw, 1940. *Signed*. 50522, f. 263.
— Photographs of Evelyn Hall, 1940? *Signed*. 50584, ff. 60-62.

Hall (Fernau), *dancer and ballet critic*. Letter to G. B. Shaw, on behalf of the Marxist Writers' Group, 1946. *Signed*. 50525, f. 75.

Hall (G. R. B.), *of 'The Times of India'*. Statement of Account regarding 'St. Joan', 1934. *Signed*. 63186, f. 78.

Hall (H. Duncan), *of the League of Nations Secretariat, Geneva*. Summary of the Case For and Against Imperial Federation, 1917. *Typewritten*. 50681, ff. 185-197.

Hall (Marguerite Radclyffe), *author*. Letters to G. B. Shaw, 1928. Partly *signed*. 50519, ff. 359, 361.
— Letter to Messrs. Rubenstein, Nash and Co. of Sir A. H. Bodkin rel. to 'The Well of Loneliness', 1928. *Copy*. 50519, f. 362.

Hall (S.), *spelling reformer, of West Worthing, co. Suss.* Letter, etc., to G. B. Shaw, 1944. Mainly *typewritten.* 50555, ff. 90-99.

Hall (William Stephen Richard King), *Baron King-Hall.*
v. King-Hall.

Hall Caine (*Sir* Thomas Henry).
v. Caine.

Hallett (Ronald V.), *of H.M.S. 'Bermuda'.* Letter to G. B. Shaw, 1943. 50523, f. 96.

Hallward (Reginald Francis), *artist.* Letter to G. B. Shaw, 1889. 50512, f. 205.

Halsey *afterw.* **Colefax** (Sibyl).
v. Colefax *née* Halsey.

Halstan (Margaret), *actress.* Letters of G. B. Shaw to, 1901, 1911. *Typewritten copies.* 50562, ff. 1, 76.
— Speech introducing H. M. Walbrook, by G. B. Shaw, written for M. Halstan, 1911. *Typewritten copy.* 50562, f. 78.
— Photograph of, 1920-1940? *Signed.* 50584, f. 63.
— Letter to G. B. Shaw, 1944. 50524, f. 205.

Halstead (Constance Beatrice), *of Burnley, co. Lanc.* Letter to G. B. Shaw, 1946. 50526 A, f. 90.

Hambros Bank Limited. Letter to G. B. Shaw, 1926. 50519, f. 289.

Hamer (Gladys), *actress.* Letter to G. B. Shaw, 1943. 50523, f. 166.

Hamer (Leslie Pryce), *actor.* Photographs of the Hamer-Pearson 'Candida' Company, 1908. 50588, ff. 49-52.
— Letters to G. B. Shaw, 1909-1915. Partly *printed.* 50515, f. 235;

50516, ff. 26, 76; 50517, f. 279; 50588, f. 49v.

Hamilton (Albert Douglas), *cousin of G. B. Shaw.* Letter to G. B. Shaw, 1943. V-Mail *copy.* 50523, f. 99.

Hamilton (Cicely Mary), *author.* Letter to G. B. Shaw, 1937. 50521, f. 254.

Hamilton (Cuthbert), *artist.* Letter of P. W. Lewis, E. A. Wadsworth, F. Etchells and C. Hamilton concerning Omega Workshops, 1913. *Signed.* 50534, f. 93.

Hamilton and Brandon, *Duchess of.*
v. Douglas-Hamilton.

Hamilton-Gordon (A. H.), *of 'Simpli-Spelt', Paris.* Letter to G. B. Shaw, 1936. *Signed.* 50554, f. 96.

Hammell (Agnes), *Canadian teacher.* Letter to Dr. G. Meisner of D. McIntyre, on behalf of A. Hammell, 1931. *Signed.* 50520, f. 28.
— Letter, etc., to G. B. Shaw, 1931. 50520, f. 29.

Hammersmith Club. Programme, 'Sunday Evenings for the People', 1889. *Printed.* 50701, f. 55.

Hammersmith Socialist Society. Programmes of lectures, etc., 1891, 1895. *Printed.* 50701, ff. 96, 157, 160.

Hammon (H. J.), *of Solihull.* Letter, etc., to G. B. Shaw, 1940. Mainly *typewritten.* 50554, ff. 100-107.

Hammond (Bertha M.), *hairdresser, of Bond St.* Letters to Mr. and Mrs. G. B. Shaw, 1940, 1944. Partly *printed.* 50524, f. 71; 63198 B, ff. 201, 202.

Hamon (Augustin Frédéric Adolphe), *French author; translator of G. B.*

— Affidavit in respect of the will of G. B. Shaw, amended by J. H. A. Sparrow, 1956. *Typewritten draft* with *MS.* amendments. 71615, ff. 78-104.

Hart (Alexander Ethan Tudor), *M.R.C.S.; L.R.C.P.; of the International Brigade Association, Tyneside Branch.* Letter to G. B. Shaw, 1946. 50525, f. 47.

Hart (Denis), *of Trinity College, Dublin.* Letter to G. B. Shaw, 1946. 50525, f. 81.

Hart (Gerda), *of Long Beach, California.* Letter to G. B. Shaw, 1946. 50525, f. 361.

Hart (Margaret Anne), *schoolgirl of Perth, Australia.* Letter, etc., to G. B. Shaw, 1937. 50521, f. 367.

— Photographs of M. A. Hart, *circa* 1937. 50521, ff. 370, 371.

Hartley (*Miss* Caroline), *anti-vivisectionist, of West Worthing.* Letter to G. B. Shaw, 1937. 50521, f. 308.

Harvey (A. R.), *of Waterloo Place, London.* Letter to C. F. Shaw, 1914. *Signed.* 56491, f. 180.

Harvey (Edmund), *of Grange, co. Waterford.* Correspondence with G. B. Shaw, 1885, 1886. Partly *shorthand draft.* 50511, ff. 10, 14, 166.

Harvey (Gertrude), *painter.* 'Note by Mr. Bernard Shaw' introducing a private view, 1929. *Printed. Music Deposit* 1999/10, 3xv.

[Harvey?] (Nell Martin), *of East Sheen, co. Surrey.* Letter to G. B. Shaw, 1944. 50524, f. 173.

Hasdell (P.), *of Weston-super-Mare.* Letter to G. B. Shaw, 1941. 50522, f. 434.

Hasegawa (S.), *magazine editor, of Japan.* Letter to G. B. Shaw, 1911. 50549, f. 226.

Haslam (Ethel), *of Ilford; member of the Women's Social and Political Union.* Letter to M. Cunningham, 1914. *Copy.* 50517, f. 151.

Hassall (Gordon), *New Zealand farmer.* Letter to G. B. Shaw, 1934. 50520, f. 233.

Hassall (S. J.), *of Auckland, New Zealand.* Letter to G. B. and C. F. Shaw, 1934. 63186, f. 75.

Hassenally (Adamally), *of Morvi, India.* Letter to G. B. Shaw, 1938. 50522, f. 137.

— 'Love O' Mine, O Stay', 1938. *Autogr.* 50522, f. 138.

Hastings (*Dr.* Somerville), *M.P.* Letter, etc., to G. B. Shaw, 1938. *Dictated.* Partly *copy.* 50522, f. 32.

Hatcham Liberal Club. Lecture programmes, 1887, 1890. *Printed.* 50701, ff. 19, 73.

Hatton (Joshua), *editor, 'Colburn's New Monthly Magazine'.* Correspondence with G. B. Shaw, 1882, 1883. Partly *shorthand draft.* 50509, ff. 221-222v; 50510, ff. 7, 19.

Hauptmann (Gerhart), *author.* Photographs of G. Hauptmann, 1936? 50585, ff. 65, 68.

Haussmann (*Dr.* William A.), *American translator of Nietzsche; anti-semite.* Letters to T. Common, 1911. 50516, ff. 91, 92.

Hauxhurst (Edith). Note to C. F. Shaw, 1936. 56493, f. 162.

Havers (W. H.), *of Hopeman, co. Moray.* Letters, etc., to G. B. Shaw, 1938. *Signed.* 50522, ff. 65, 99.

Henry (Nancy), *author.* Letter to B. Patch, 1939. 50522, f. 205.

Henry (Théodore), *French playwright.* Letter of G. B. Shaw to T. Henry, 1908. *Draft.* 50515, f. 143.

Henry and Company, *publishers.* Letters to G. B. Shaw, 1893. 50513, ff. 1, 8, 11.

Hensman (James Stuart), *M.R.C.S.; L.R.C.P.* Correspondence, etc., with G. B. and C. F. Shaw of A. G. Evans, J. S. Hensman, C. E. Dukes and R. Roche, 1938-1943. Partly *signed, copy* and *printed.* 56494, ff. 1-63 *passim,* 101, 163; 63197, f. 47.

Hentschel (Carl), *photo-engraver.* Letter to C. F. Shaw, 1902. 56491, f. 28.

Hepburn *née* **Harper** (Edith Alice Mary), *al. 'Anna Wickham'; poet.* Note of G. B. Shaw to, 1929. *Copy.* 71894, f. 14.

Hepburn (Richard Houghton), *American playwright.* Letter to G. B. Shaw, 1936. *Signed.* 50521, f. 147.

Herbert (*Hon.* Auberon Edward William Molyneux), *M.P.* Letters to G. B. Shaw, 1900. 50513, ff. 226, 232.

Herbert (Ethel), *actress.* Letters to G. B. Shaw, 1886. 50511, ff. 250, 255.

Herczeg (Ferencz), *Hungarian author.* Article on G. B. Shaw, 1936. *Engl. transl.* 50521, ff. 142-145.

Hereford (Eula Shaw), *of Lorreta, Texas.* Letter to G. B. Shaw, 1946. 50525, f. 31.

Heretics, *Cambridge University society.* Notice, speaker's notes, reports, etc., of address to, by G. B. Shaw, 1911. Partly *printed.* 50703, ff. 203-214.

Heriot (C. D.), *Examiner of Plays.* Licensing reports on plays of G. B. Shaw, 1948-1967. *L.C.P. Corr.* 1948/9778; *L.C.P. Corr.* 1950/1641; *L.C.P. Corr.* 1950/2375; *L.C.P. Corr.* 1967/1288.

Hermes (Gertrude Anna Bertha), *O.B.E.; R.A.; sculptor and engraver.* Woodblock engraving, *circa* 1926-1932. 56494, f. 178.

— Christmas card to C. F. Shaw with B. R. Hughes-Stanton, *circa* 1926-1932. 56494, f. 178.

Hernon (P. J.), *City Manager and Town Clerk of Dublin.* Letter, concerning the freedom of the city, to G. B. Shaw, 1946. *Signed.* 50525, f. 7.

— Letter to G. B. Shaw, 1946. *Signed.* 50526 A, f. 215.

Heron (A.), *son-in-law of James Connolly.* Letter to G. B. Shaw, 1944. 50524, f. 191.

Heron (David), *D.Sc.; eugenist.* Letter, etc., to G. B. Shaw, 1933. 50520, f. 208.

Herringham (Wilmot Parker), *M.R.C.S.; M.R.C.P.* Letters to C. F. Shaw, 1913-1914. 56491, ff. 123, 149.

Hertz (H. A.), *founder of the German Theatre in London.* Letter of G. B. Shaw to, 1902. *Typewritten copy.* 50562, f. 9.

Hertz (Robert), *socialist.* Letter to E. R. Pease, 1912. *Copy.* 50557, f. 206.

Correspondence with G. B. Shaw, 1931. Partly *shorthand draft.* 50520, f. 44.

— Letter to Rt. Rev. Monseigneur de la Villerabel, 1931. *Signed copy.* 50520, f. 45.

Holiday (Catherine), *suffragist, of Hawkshead.* Letter, with W. Holiday, to G. B. Shaw, 1912. 50516, f. 227.

Holiday (Henry), *R.A.* Letter to G. B. Shaw, 1907. 50515, f. 85.

Holiday (Winifred), *musician and suffragist.* Letters to G. B. Shaw, 1912, 1913. 50516, ff. 227, 322.

Holland (J. Leslie), *of Birmingham.* Letter to G. B. Shaw, 1947. 50526 B, f. 374.

Holland (Sydney George), *2nd Viscount Knutsford.* Letter to G. B. Shaw, n.d. 50527, f. 102.

Hollingshead (John), *author.* Letter to G. B. Shaw, 1897. 50513, f. 141.

Holloway (Baliol), *actor.* Letter to G. B. Shaw, 1938. 50522, f. 164.

Holman (Rosaleen), *President of the L.S.E. Students' Union.* Letter to C. F. Shaw, 1940. 63197, f. 71.

Holmes (Margot A.), *at Grosvenor House, Park Lane.* Letter to G. B. Shaw, 1941. 50522, f. 348.

Holroyd (Michael), *biographer.* Papers rel. to biography of Shaw, *circa* 1988-1992. *Deposit* 10270.

— Biographical chronology, bef. 1993. *Computer print-out.* 79522.

Holst (Elsie G.), *of West Roxburg, Massachusetts.* Postcard to G. B. Shaw of F. J. Morris, A. Koltoff, S. E. Richard and E. G. Holst, 1946. 50526 B, f. 325.

Holtby (Winifred), *author.* Letter to G. B. Shaw, 1929. *Signed.* 50519, f. 395.

Holtzmann (Fanny E.), *Counsellor at Law, New York.* Correspondence of and concerning F. E. Holtzmann, 1947, 1948. Partly *typewritten.* 56631, f. 206; 56632, f. 113.

Home Colonization Society. Notice of aims, 1884? *Printed,* with *annotation* by G. B. Shaw. 50721 B, f. 50v.

Hone (Joseph Maunsell), *President, Irish Academy of Letters.* Letter to G. B. Shaw, 1944. *Signed.* 50524, f. 170.

Hood (Agnes M.), *of Edinburgh.* Letter to G. B. Shaw, 1946. 50525, f. 99.

Hood (Sam), *journalist, of Harrisburg, Pennsylvania.* Letter to G. B. Shaw, 1944. 50524, f. 156.

Hope (Francis), *actor.* Letter to G. B. Shaw, 1935. 50521, f. 39.

Hope (Richard), *M.R.C.S.; L.R.C.P.* Letter to G. B. Shaw, 1937. 50521, f. 312.

Hopkins (Edwin), *literary agent, of New York.* Letter to G. B. Shaw, 1940. *Signed.* 50522, f. 267.

Hopkins (Tighe), *journalist and novelist.* Letters to G. B. Shaw, 1886, 1887. 50511, ff. 189, 295.

Hoppé (Alfred John), *Director, J. M. Dent & Sons.* Letters to G. B. Shaw, 1941, 1947. *Signed.* 50554, f. 126; 50556, f. 157.

Hoppé (E. O.), *author and photographer.* Portrait of A. Henderson, 1905? *Signed* by E. O. Hoppé. 50584, f. 66.

— Portrait photographs of G. B. Shaw, 1910? 50582, ff. 44, 63.

Hopper (Charles W.), *of Barnet Labour Party; artist.* Letter to G. B. Shaw, 1919. *Signed.* 50518, f. 190.

— Painting of G. B. Shaw as Don Quixote with G. K. Chesterton as Sancho Panza, 1934. *Photographic copy.* 50582, f. 91.

— Letter, etc., to B. Patch, 1934. 50582, ff. 91, 92.

Horn (George), *of Montreal.* Letter, etc., to G. B. Shaw, 1944. Partly *typewritten copy.* 50524, f. 8.

Horne (Agneta), *Chairman of the Albermarle Club.* Circular letter, 1941. 63197, f. 79.

Horne (Alderson Burrell), *al. 'Anmer Hall'; actor-manager.* Letter to G. B. Shaw, 1941. 63186, f. 171.

Horne (*Rev.* Charles Silvester), *M.P.* Letter to G. B. Shaw, 1904. 50514, f. 179.

Horne (*Capt.* Richard Hare). Letter to L. E. Shaw, 1878. 50508, f. 126.

— Correspondence with G. B. Shaw, 1880-1885. Partly *shorthand draft.* 50508, f. 252; 50509, ff. 215, 218-220, 224, 226-228, 231, 262-263v, 268; 50510, ff. 128, 131; 50511, ff. 115, 116, 118, 119, 121.

Horne (Sophie C.), *wife of Capt. R. H. Horne.* Correspondence with G. B. Shaw, 1880-1914. 50508, ff. 206, 234, 247; 50509, ff. 6, 7, 14, 29, 88, 92, 108, 120, 140, 152; 50510, ff. 138, 247, 239; 50517, ff. 191, 193.

— Letter to S. C. Horne of C. J. Bell, 1881. 50509, f. 107.

Horniman (Annie Elizabeth Fredericka), *C.H.; theatrical impresario.* Letters to G. B. Shaw, 1907-1912. 50538, ff. 75-87v.

— Correspondence with Lady Gregory, 1909. *Copy.* 50534, f. 173.

— Correspondence with B. S. Campbell, 1909. *Copy.* 50534, ff. 174-175.

Hornsby (*Capt.* F. Noel), *Managing Director, Whitehall Court Ltd.* Letters to Mr. and Mrs. G. B. Shaw, 1940-1942. Partly *signed.* 63187, ff. 22, 92, 112, 119.

Hornsey Socialist Society. Programme of meetings, 1896. *Printed.* 50701, f. 170.

Hornung (Ernest William), *novelist.* Letter to G. B. Shaw, 1908. 50515, f. 103.

Horsbrugh-Porter (*Sir* John Scott). *v.* Porter.

Horvat (*Dr.* Mladen), *editor of the 'Pantheon', Zagreb.* Letter to G. B. Shaw, 1929. *Signed.* 50519, f. 369.

Hoskyn (Donald Templeton), *M.R.C.S.* Letters to G. B. Shaw, 1880. 50508, ff. 276, 285.

Hotung (*Sir* Robert), *industrialist and philanthropist, of Hong Kong.* Photograph with G. B. Shaw, 1933. 50582, f. 90.

— Letter and telegram to G. B. Shaw, 1939, 1945. Partly *signed.* 50522, f. 256; 50524, f. 376.

Houghton (William Stanley), *playwright.* Letter to G. B. Shaw, 1912. 50516, f. 216.

Houlgate (Alexander), *actor.* Letter to G. B. Shaw, 1946. 50526 A, f. 133.

Housman (Laurence), *author and art critic.* Letters to G. B. Shaw, 1910, 1931. 50515, f. 351; 50520, f. 72.

Houston (Robert), *schoolboy, of East London, South Africa.* Letter, with three other schoolboys, to G. B. Shaw, 1946. *Signed.* 50526 A, f. 195.

Howard (Francis), *art collector; Hon. Sec., International Society of Sculptors, Painters and Gravers.* Letter to G. B. Shaw, 1909. Partly *printed.* 50515, f. 233.

Howard (Henry Newman), *poet and dramatist.* Letters to G. B. Shaw, 1906. 50514, ff. 367, 379.

Howard *afterw.* **Murray** (*Lady* Mary Henrietta), *wife (1889) of Gilbert Murray.* Letters to G. B. Shaw, 1933, 1947. 50542, ff. 89, 90.

Howard de Walden, *Baron.*
v. Scott-Ellis (Thomas Evelyn).

Howdill (Charles B.), *architect, of Leeds.* Letter, etc., to G. B. Shaw, 1912. *Signed; partly printed.* 50516, f. 158.

Howells (William Dean), *American author.* Letter to G. B. Shaw, 1913. 50516, f. 344.

Howet (Marie), *Belgian artist.* Letter to C. F. Shaw, 1936. *Fr.* 56493, f. 181.

Howie (John MacFarlane), *of Bing-hamton, New York.* Letter to the 'New York Times', 1946. *Copy.* 50526 B, f. 314.

Hoy (H. A.), *of Dallas, Texas.* Letter to V. Korenchevsky, 1949. *Type-written.* 50526 B, f. 450.

Hoyland (William Henry), *of Sheffield.* Letter to G. B. Shaw, 1937. *Signed.* 50521, f. 291.

Hronek (Rozhlas), *editor-in-chief, Czechoslovak Radio.* Telegram to G. B. Shaw, 1946. 50525, f. 176.

Hsiung (Shih I), *author.* 'Some Conventions of the Chinese Stage', 1933?-1950? *Typewritten.* 50742, f. 142.

— Letters to G. B. Shaw, 1941, 1943. 50522, f. 357; 50523, f. 42.

Huan (Oong Chao).
v. Oong Chao Huan.

Hubbard (Elbert), *author; founder of the Roycroft Printing Shop, New York.* Letter to G. B. Shaw, 1896. 50513, f. 106.

Hubbard (*Mrs.* P.), *nurse, of Highgate Rd., London.* Letter to G. B. Shaw, 1944. 50524, f. 189.

Hudd (Walter), *actor and producer.* Inscribed photograph to, of F. Sobieniowski, [1926-1939?]. 71658, f. 59.

— Letter to, of G. B. Shaw, revising 'Too True to be Good' 1932. *Signed.* 71658, f. 53.

— Letter to, of T. E. Lawrence, concerning 'To True to be Good', 1932. 71658, f. 55.

— Visitors' Book, 1932-1976, n.d. 71658.

Huddart (Elinor L.), *al.* 'Elinor Hume'; *al.* 'Louisa Rouile'; *novelist.* Letters to G. B. Shaw, 1878-1894. 50535-50537.

Hueffer (Francis *formerly* Franz), *music critic.* Correspondence with G. B. Shaw, 1883. Partly *shorthand draft.* 50510, ff. 3, 5; 50721 A, f. 84v; 50722, f. 8.

Hughes (*Mrs.* C. A.), *of Laurens, South Carolina.* Letter to G. B. Shaw, 1946. 50526 A, f. 67.

Hughes (Gillian Marjorie), *schoolgirl, of Nottingham.* Letter to G. B. Shaw, 1946. 50525, f. 184.

Hughes (John), *of Youth of All Nations, Inc., New York.* Letter, on behalf of his organisation, to G. B. Shaw, 1946. *Signed.* 50525, f. 256.

Hughes (Richard Vincent), *of Rosebery Ave., London.* Bequeathed, in 1978, 59892, ff. 125-147.

Hughes (W. R.), *of Welwyn Garden City Regional Survey Committee.* Notice of archaelogical meeting, 1938. *Copy.* 50522, f. 5.

Hughes-Stanton (Blair Rowlands), *painter and engraver.* Christmas card with G. A. B. Hermes to C. F. Shaw, *circa* 1926-1932 56494, f. 178.

Hughes Massie & Co., *literary and dramatic agents.* Correspondence with G. B. Shaw, 1919. Partly *shorthand draft.* 50518, ff. 144, 144v.

Hugh-Jones (Edward Maurice), *economist.* Letter to G. B. Shaw, n.d. 50527, f. 104.

Huish (Marcus Bourne), *editor of 'The Art Journal'.* Letter to G. B. Shaw, 1889. 50512, f. 163.

Hull (Carl William), *librarian, of Dubois, Pennsylvania.* Letter to G. B. Shaw, 1938. *Signed.* 50522, f. 77.

Hull (Richard Francis Carrington), *translator from German.* Letter to G. B. Shaw, 1946. 50526 A, f. 188.

Hulsebosch (Harry A.), *of Haarlem.* Letter to G. B. Shaw, 1946. Mainly *Germ.* 50525, f. 244.

Human *formerly* **Black** (Grace). *v.* Black *afterw.* Human.

Humanitarian League. Annual Report, etc., 1895, 1904. *Printed.* 50701, ff. 156, 190-195v.

'Hume (Elinor)', *pseudonym.* *v.* Huddart (Elinor L.)

Humphreys (Frank), *of Birmingham.* Letter to W. Archer, 1903. 45296, f. 125.

Humphreys (T.), *of the Social Democratic Federation.* Letter of G. B. Shaw to, concerning E. B. Aveling, 1885. *Draft.* 50511, f. 126.

Humphries (Hubert). Photograph of H. Humphries, 1940. 50584, f. 75.

Huneker (James Gibbons), *American author and critic.* Letter from G. B. Shaw to J. G. Huneker, 1905? *Draft.* 50514, f. 281.

Hungerford (Henry Jones), *of Cahirmore, co. Cork.* Letter to C. F. Payne-Townshend, 1891. 50512, f. 245.

Hunt (A. Leigh), *of the Dominion Farmers' Institute.* Letter to G. B. Shaw, 1934. *Signed.* 50520, f. 244.

Hunt (James), *secretary of the Labour Party, Sligo.* Letter to G. B. Shaw, n.d. *Imperf.* 50527, f. 106.

Hunt (Marsha), *actress.* Photographs of American production of 'The Devil's Disciple', produced by M. Webster, 1950. 50589, ff. 1-10.

Hunter (Henry E.), *manager, Cromwell Road branch, National Provincial and Union Bank.* Letter to C. F. Shaw, 1921. 56492, f. 37.

Hurl (Michael), *writer of verse.* Letter to G. B. Shaw, 1944. 50524, f. 116.

Hurley (Timothy), *of Dublin.* Letters to G. B. Shaw, 1946. 50525, ff. 10, 20.

I

Ibrahim (M. Mohammed), *Beg, of Saharanpur, India.* Letter to G. B. Shaw, 1946. 50525, f. 55.

Ibsen (Henrik), *dramatist.* G. B. Shaw, 'From Dickens to Ibsen', 1889? 50693, ff. 201-222.

— Papers rel. to Shaw's *Quintessence of Ibsenism*; 1890-1913. Partly *printed* and *typewritten* 50659; 50660, ff. 25-182; 50661, ff. 1-44.

— Letters to G. B. Shaw concerning, 1890-1897. 50660, ff. 2-22v.

— Photographs of H. Ibsen, 1895, n.d. 50584, ff. 77-85.

— Letter to G. B. Shaw of I. M. Pagan concerning production of 'Peer Gynt', 1912. 50516, f. 119.

— Photograph of Japanese production of 'A Doll's House', *circa* 1912. 50548, f. 64v.

— Programme of Ibsen Centenary Lectures, 1928. *Printed.* 50701, f. 254.

— Correspondence with G. B. Shaw of H. Olav concerning, 1938. *Signed.* Partly *shorthand draft* and *copy.* 50522, ff. 55, 63.

— Introduction to B.B.C. radio production of 'Ghosts', 1944. *Printed.* 50524, f. 293.

'Ich Dien', *at the Carmel Nursing Home, Chalfont St. Peter, co. Bucks.* Letter to G. B. Shaw, 1946. 50525, f. 311.

Ievers (Mary Shinkwin), *of Mount Ievers, co. Clare.* Correspondence with G. B. Shaw, 1886. Partly *shorthand draft.* 50511, f. 168.

Ikeda (Hiroshi), *director, Tokyo Institute for Municipal Research.* Letter to G. B. Shaw, 1932. *Signed.* 50520, f. 145.

Illing (Meta), *German actress.* Letter to G. B. Shaw, 1908. 50549, f. 222.

Ince (*Sir* Godfrey Herbert), *civil servant.* Letter to G. B. Shaw, 1944. *Signed.* 50555, f. 83.

Incorporated Society of Authors, Playwrights & Composers. Correspondence, etc., with C. F. Shaw regarding E. Brieux, 1933-1940. Partly *copy* and *signed.* 63197, ff. 15-33, 42, 58.

— Letter to Coward McCann Inc., 1934. *Copy.* 63197, f. 21.

Independent Labour Party. Notices of meetings, etc., 1888-1926. *Printed.* 50701, ff. 36, 124-259 *passim*; 50703, f. 79.

— Conference delegate's admission card made out to G. B. Shaw, 1893. Mainly *printed.* 50680, f. 12.

— 'War Against Poverty' issued by Independent Labour Party, contributions by J. R. MacDonald, W. C. Anderson, M. G. Bondfield, G. Lansbury, M. MacArthur, G. B. Shaw, S. J. Webb and M. B. Webb, *circa* 1912. *Printed pamphlet.* 50686, ff. 121-130v.

— Note on war issues, 1917. *Printed.* 50681, ff. 205-206.

— Speech for gramophone recording of G. B. Shaw, on behalf of Independent Labour Party, 1929. Partly *shorthand draft;* partly *fragm. typewritten* transcript. 50704, ff. 207-210.

— Platform ticket for Demonstration in favour of Universal Peace annotated by G. B. Shaw, 1896. Mainly *printed*. 50680, f. 164.

— 'The Conference Record', 1896. *Printed*. 50680, ff. 165-166v.

— Delegate's card made out to G. B. Shaw designed by W. Crane, 1896. Mainly *printed*. 50680, f. 168.

International Transport Workers' Federation. Papers relating to trial of Black Sea seamen, 1915. Mainly *copies*. 50517, ff. 231-234.

Irish Academy of Letters. Letter to G. B. Shaw from Lennox Robinson on behalf of, 1937. *Typewritten*. 63728, f. 5.

Irish Dominion League. Notice of meeting, 1919? *Printed*. 50701, f. 261.

'Irish Homestead, The'. Letters, etc., to C. F. Shaw concerning, 1915, 1922. Partly *printed*. 56491, ff. 202, 203; 56492, ff. 39-46.

Irish Protestant Home Rule Committee. Letters, etc., to G. B. Shaw of S. L. Gwynn concerning, 1912. Partly *copy*. 50516, ff. 264-270.

Irish Republican Democrats. Letter to G. B. Shaw of M. King, n.d. 50527, f. 114.

Irving (Dorothea), *wife of H. B. Irving*. Letter of G. B. Shaw to D. Irving, 1917. *Copy*. 50538, f. 213.

Irving (*Lady* Florence), *wife of Sir H. Irving*. Letter to G. B. Shaw, 1905. Partly *copy*. 50538, f. 211.

Irving (*Sir* Henry), *actor*. Photographs of Sir Henry Irving, 1879, n.d. 50584, ff. 86, 87.

— Letters to G. B. Shaw, 1896, 1897. Partly *copy*. 43801, f. 91; 50538, f. 216.

Irving (Laurence), *grandson of Sir H. Irving*. Letter to G. B. Shaw, 1946. *Signed*. 50538, f. 215.

Irving (Laurence Sydney Brodribb), *actor*. Letter to C. F. Shaw, *circa* 1900-1908. 56494, f. 180.

— Letters to G. B. Shaw, 1900-1913. 50538, ff. 200-209.

Irwin (George), *of Belfast*. Letter to G. B. Shaw, 1946. *Signed*. 50525, f. 343.

Isserlis (Leon), *D.Sc.; statistician to the Chamber of Shipping of the United Kingdom*. Letter to G. B. Shaw, 1944. 50524, f. 75.

ITALY. SOVEREIGNS OF, *and transactions in particular reigns. VICTOR EMMANUEL III.* Correspondence of G. B. Shaw concerning Italian fascism, published in 'International Information', 1927. *Duplicated*. 50697, ff. 237*-245.

Iversen (Herbert), *Danish philosopher and socialist*. Letter to G. B. Shaw, 1917. 50518, f. 14.

J

Jackman (George) **and Son**, *landscape gardeners*. Letter to C. F. Shaw, 1930. 63186, f. 61.

Jacks (Lawrence Pearsall), *principal of Manchester College, Oxford*. Letter to G. B. Shaw, 1907. 50515, f. 22.

Jackson (*Sir* Barry Vincent), *dramatist and theatre director*.

Letter of Lord Chamberlain to, 1929. *Copy. L.C.P. Corr.* 1929/8971.

— Letters to C. F. Shaw, 1940-1941. *Typewritten* and partly *signed.* 56494, ff. 100, 105; 63186, f. 130.

— Letters to G. B. Shaw, *circa* 1940, 1944. *Dictated.* 50524, ff. 231, 377; 50527, f. 107.

Jackson (*Mrs.* F.), *al. 'Lisa Jacsone', of New Malden, co. Surr.* Letter, etc., to G. B. Shaw, 1946. *Signed.* 50526 A, f. 109.

— 'Dust Under the Almond Trees', 1946. *Copy.* 50526 A, ff. 110-122.

Jackson (Frederick), *al. 'Vox Clamans'; solicitor.* Correspondence with G. B. Shaw, 1910-1914. Partly *signed* and *copy.* 50539, ff. 1-27v.

— Letter to C. F. Shaw, 1912. *Signed.* 56491, f. 82.

Jackson (Holbrook), *author.* Correspondence with G. B. Shaw, 1906-1907. Partly *signed* and *printed.* 50515, f. 62; 62992, ff. 1, 11-12.

Jackson (Janet), *secretary of the Theatre Section of the Society for Cultural Relations between the Peoples of the British Commonwealth and the U.S.S.R.* Letter to G. B. Shaw, 1948. *Signed.* 50526 B, f. 439.

Jacobs (Aaron Jonah), *author, of Wynberg, Cape Province.* Letter to G. B. Shaw, 1943. 50523, f. 95.

Jacquin (Noel), *chirognomist.* Letter with reading of G. B. Shaw's hand, 1928. *Signed.* 50519, f. 338.

'Jacsone (Lisa)'.
v. Jackson (*Mrs.* F.).

James (Henry), *novelist.* Letters to G. B. Shaw, 1909. *Signed.* 50515, ff. 208, 214.

James (Norah Cordner), *author.* Letter to G. B. Shaw, 1937. *Signed.* 50521, f. 325.

James (R. Edwards), *solicitor, of Birmingham.* Letter, etc., to G. B. Shaw, 1941. *Signed.* 50522, f. 408.

— Report of interview with Sir Rabindranath Tagore, 1941. *Typewritten.* 50522, ff. 410-417.

James (*Prof.* William), *of Harvard University; philosopher.* Letter and postcard to G. B. Shaw, 1907. 50515, ff. 16, 20.

Janiewski (A. M.), *Polish actor.* Portrait photograph, 1900. *Signed.* 50584, f. 88.

Janus (Oscar), *M.B., Ch.B.; resident medical officer, Manchester Royal Infirmary.* Letter to H. Walker, 1946. *Signed.* 50525, f. 330.

Janvier (Jean-Louis), *French actor.* Portrait photograph of Jean-Louis Janvier, 1902. *Inscribed.* 50584, f. 98.

Jarman (Fred), *of Exeter.* Correspondence with the Lord Chamberlain's Office, 1917. Partly *copy. L.C.P. Corr.* 1924/5632, ff. 37, 38.

Jarvis (H.), *spelling reformer, of Balham, London.* Letter, etc., to G. B. Shaw, 1944. Partly *typewritten.* 50555, f. 104.

Javeri (Hirachand Kasturchand), *of Bombay.* Letters to G. B. Shaw, 1926-1927. 50519, ff. 294, 295.

Jayne (Henry La Barre), *Counsellor at Law; Secretary, Drama League* *of Philadelphia.* Letter to G. H. Thring, 1916. *Signed.* 56627, f. 178.

Jeakes (*Rev.* James Malcolm), *Vicar of Grayshott, co. Hants.* Letter to G. B. Shaw, 1902. 50514, f. 72.

Jeffery (F.), *manager, London Joint City and Midland Bank Ltd., Paddington branch,* Letter to G. B. Shaw, 1923. *Signed.* 50519, f. 44.

Jeffreys (W. Rees), *chairman, Roads Improvement Association, Inc.* Letter to G. B. Shaw, 1943. *Signed.* 50523, f. 44.

Jenkins (*Cdr.* T. H.), *naval air attaché at the American Embassy.* Letter to G. B. Shaw, 1946. *Signed.* 50526 A, f. 228.

Jennings (Herbert H.), *Secretary, Chelsea Hospital for Women.* Correspondence with G. Kingston, 1914. *Copies.* 50539, ff. 64, 66.

Jennison (Florence Tye), *former secretary of the League of Nations Non-Partisan Association of Illinois.* Letter, etc., to G. B. Shaw, 1943. *Signed.* Partly *copy.* 50523, f. 115.

—Notes rel. to international law, *circa* 1943. *Copy.* 50523, ff. 116-119.

Jensen (Christine), *of Los Angeles.* Letter to G. B. Shaw, 1946. 50525, f. 182.

Jerome (Helen), *playwright.* Letter to G. B. Shaw, 1943. 50523, f. 7.

Jerome (Jerome Klapka), *author.* Letter to G. B. Shaw, 1915. 50517, f. 299.

Jevers (*Capt.* Robert H.), *of the Army Medical Services, Eire.* Letter to G. B. Shaw, 1943. 50523, f. 124.

Jhaveri (Vithal-Bhai K.), *of Bombay, author.* Letter to G. B. Shaw of

V.-B. K. Jhaveri and D. G. Tenulkar, 1946. *Signed.* 50525, f. 282.

Joad (Cyril Edwin Mitchinson), *philosopher.* Postcard to G. B. Shaw, 1946. 50526 B, f. 275.

Joan of Arc Statue Committee, *New York.* Letter to G. B. Shaw, 1923. 50519, f. 71.

Jochberg (Erich Czech-). *v.* Czech-Jochberg.

John (Augustus Edwin), *painter.* Letters to G. B. Shaw, 1915-1944. 50539, ff. 28-38.

—Portrait drawings of T. E. Lawrence, 1927? *Photographic copies.* 56499, ff. 34, 41.

— Portraits of King Feisal, 1927? *Photographic copies.* 56499, ff. 35, 36.

— Letter to 'T. E. Shaw', 1929. 45904, f. 83.

Johnson (Edward Ralph), *Bishop of Calcutta.* Invitation to C. F. Shaw, 1893. Mainly *printed.* 63197, f. 4.

Johnson (Hewlett), *Dean of Canterbury.* Letter to G. B. Shaw, 1940. *Signed.* 50522, f. 260.

Johnston (Charlotte Jane), *sister of G. C. Shaw.* Letter to L. E. Shaw, 1857. 50508, f. 38.

Johnston (Denis), *Irish dramatist and author.* Letter to G. B. Shaw, 1938. 50522, f. 59.

Johnston (J. Dudley), *secretary of the Royal Photographic Society.* Letter to G. B. Shaw, 1944. *Signed.* 50524, f. 204.

Joint Committee of English Socialists. 'Manifesto of English Socialists', 1893. *Printed.* 50690, ff. 118-123.

Joyce (James Augustine Aloysius), *author*. Letter to G. B. Shaw, 1926. 50519, f. 284.

Joynes (James Leigh), *of the Social Democratic Federation*. Letters, etc., to G. B. Shaw, 1883-1891. 50510, ff. 81, 93, 162, 176, 181-183; 50512, ff. 212, 215, 252.

— Letter to, of E. Mathews, 1891. 50512, f. 255.

Junosza-Stepowski (Kazimierz). *v.* Stepowski.

K

Kabadi (Sunder), *Indian journalist*. Correspondence with G. B. Shaw, 1949-1950. 79532 MM.

Kafka (František), *of Prague*. Letter to G. B. Shaw, 1946. *Signed*. 50526 A, f. 83.

Kahn (David E.), *of New York*. Letter to G. B. Shaw, 1946. *Signed*. 50525, f. 385.

Kalich (Bertha), *actress in Yiddish and English*. Portrait photograph of Bertha Kalich, *circa* 1920. *Signed*. 50584, f. 99.

Kalman (*Dr.* Eugene), *of Berkeley, California*. Letter to G. B. Shaw, 1946. *Signed*. 50556, f. 29.

Kamrad (S.), *Editor of 'Smena', Moscow*. Letter to G. B. Shaw, 1931. *Signed*. 50520, f. 115.

Kapelovitch (I.), *secretary of King's College Socialist Society*. Letter to G. B. Shaw, 1919. 50518, f. 150.

Kapur (*Dr.* P. D.), *secretary of the India Society for the Protection of Animals*. Letter to G. B. Shaw,

1946. *Signed*. 50526 A, f. 187.

Karavaev (Boris Ivanovich), *Russian diplomat*. Letter, etc., to G. B. Shaw, 1944. *Signed*. 50524, f. 175.

— Letter to F. E. Loewenstein, 1947. *Signed*. 50565, f. 164.

Karsh (Yousuf), *photographer, of Ottawa*. Portrait photograph of G. B. Shaw, 1940? *Printed reproduction*. 50582, ff. 142, 164.

Kashner (Jesse M.), *of New York*. Letter to G. B. Shaw, 1946. *Signed*. 50526 B, f. 363.

Kassin (Arthur R.), *conscientious objector, of Brooklyn, New York*. Letter to G. B. Shaw, 1946. *Signed*. 50525, f. 375.

Katzin (Olga) *al. 'Sagittarius'*. Verses written on the re-opening of the Theatre Royal, Richmond, 1943. *Copy*. 50525, f. 161.

Kavanagh (*Mrs.* S. M.), *of Rosslare, co. Wexford*. Letter to G. B. Shaw, 1946. 50526 A, f. 146.

Kaysser-Spezial, *alternative health institute, in Berlin*. Letter to G. B. Shaw, 1946. *Signed. Germ*. 50526 A, f. 256.

Kazantzakes (Nikos), *Greek novelist*. Script of radio talk on G. B. Shaw, 1946. *Signed copy*. 50527, f. 35.

Kean (Charles John), *actor*. Letter, 1844. *Typewritten copy*. 63183, f. 62.

Keane *al.* **Deane** (Clifford). *v.* Deane *al.* Keane.

Kearney (Chalmers), *F.R.E.S.* Letter to G. B. Shaw, 1943. *Signed*. 50523, f. 129.

Keaveney (Patrick), *of the Shaw Society, Dublin*. Letters to G. B. Shaw, 1944. *Signed*. 50524, ff. 82, 187.

Keddell (Frederick), *Fabian; translator of Lassalle.* Letter to G. B. Shaw, 1885. 50511, f. 125.

Keeble (*Sir* Frederick William), *botanist, civil servant and industrial adviser.* Letter to C. F. Shaw, 1942. 56494, f. 161.

Keeling (—), *at Lanbedr.* Photograph of — Keeling, 1910 annotated by G. B. Shaw, 'killed in the Great War 1914-18', 50584, f. 100.

Keen (Gordon Alan), *antiquarian bookseller.* Letters, etc., to G. B. Shaw, 1929-1943. Partly *signed* and *copy.* 50522, ff. 301, 325, 366; 50563, f. 21; 63186, f. 182.

— Letter to, of G. S. Royds, 1941. *Copy.* 50522, f. 367.

Keene (Violet), *photographer.* Portrait photograph of G. B. Shaw, 1940? 50582, f. 145.

Kegan Paul, Trench and Co., *publishers, of London.* Correspondence with G. B. Shaw, 1879-1884. Partly *typewritten* and *shorthand draft.* 50508, f. 176; 50509, ff. 243, 246-247v; 50510, ff. 23, 24, 27, 158-160, 166.

Keith (D. B.). *of Thurso.* Letter to G. B. Shaw, 1946. 50525, f. 1.

Keith-Johnston (Colin), *M.C.; actor.* Letter to G. B. Shaw, 1945. 50524, f. 306.

Kellegher (Elizabeth), *of Dublin.* Letter to G. B. Shaw, 1946. 50525, f. 60.

Kellison (Charles), *attorney, of Plymouth, Indiana.* Letter to G. B. Shaw, 1914. *Signed.* 50517, f. 30.

Kellner (*Prof. Dr.* Leon). Articles on G. B. Shaw, 1908? *Printed. Germ.* 45296, ff. 199-200v.

Kellogg (*Dr.* John Harvey), *American entrepreneur and health reformer.* Photograph of, 1942. 50584, f. 101.

Kelly (Edmond), *socialist, of New York.* Report on socialism in New York, *circa* 1906. *Typewritten.* 50681, ff. 320-326.

Kelly (Francis J.), *of Dublin.* Report of speech by G. B. Shaw, n.d. *Imperf.* 50527, f. 108.

Kelly (Harold), *of Stapleford Abbots, co. Essex.* Letter to G. B. Shaw, 1946. *Signed.* 50525, f. 283.

Kelly (K.), *Irish nationalist.* Correspondence with G. B. Shaw, 1916. Partly *shorthand draft.* 50517, ff. 429-430v.

Kelly (Richard John), *K.C., of Dublin.* Letter to G. B. Shaw, 1909. 50515, f. 252.

Kelly (*Air Vice-Marshall* Thomas James), *C.B.E.; M.C.* Letter to G. B. Shaw, 1944. *Signed.* 50524, f. 184.

Kemeny (*Baron* Jànos), *Rumanian poet.* Letter on behalf of, 1925. 50519, f. 221.

Kempner *afterw.* **Kerr** (Alfred). *v.* Kerr *formerly* Kempner.

Kempston (Ernest), *of Dublin.* Correspondence with G. B. Shaw, 1917, 1918? Partly *signed* and *copy.* 50518, ff. 38, 123.

Kendal *née* **Robertson** (*Dame* Margaret Shafto *called* Madge), *actress; wife of W. H. Kendal.* Letters to G. B. Shaw, 1896-1901. 50513, ff. 113, 116, 227; 50514, f. 7.

Kidd (Jean) *al. 'J. F. Hutton'; of Glasgow.* Letter to G. B. Shaw, 1945. *Signed.* 50524, f. 279.

Kilham Roberts (Denys), *Sec.-Gen., Society of Authors.* Correspondence with G. B. Shaw, 1935-1940. Partly *signed* and *copy.* 50521, f. 23; 56630, ff. 12, 15-18, 123-130.

Killfeather (Gertrude), *of Spokane, Washington.* Letter to G. B. Shaw, 1946. 50526 B, f. 291.

Kindersley [(Ann Molesworth)?], *at 4, St. James' Square.* Letters to G. B. Shaw concerning travel arrangements, 1931. *Signed.* 50520, ff. 82, 105.

Kindersley (Robert Molesworth), *1st Baron Kindersley.* Letter to G. B. Shaw, 1944. *Signed.* 50524, f. 39.

King (Charles Richard), *author.* Letter to G. B. Shaw, n.d. 50527, f. 112.

King (Dennis), *actor.* Photographs of American production of 'The Devil's Disciple', produced by M. Webster, 1950. 50589, ff. 1-10.

King (George S.), *theatre manager, Plymouth.* Appeal for licence to perform 'Mrs. Warren's Profession', 1916. *L.C.P. Corr.* 1924/5632, ff. 14, 20.

King (*Mrs.* Helena G.), *Hon. Sec. of the Dolmetsch Foundation.* Letter to G. B. Shaw, 1940. *Signed.* 50522, f. 274.

King (Margaret), *of Dublin.* Letter to G. B. Shaw, n.d. 50527, f. 114.

King-Hall (William Stephen Richard), *Baron King-Hall.* Letter to G. B. Shaw, aft. 1936. 50521, f. 236.

Kingsford *afterw.* **Cockerell** (Florence Kate), *scribe and illuminator; wife of Sir S. C. Cockerell.* Christmas cards of C. F. Shaw to Sir S. C. Cockerell and his wife, 1913-1940. 52752, ff. 222, 282, 296.

Kingsford (Reginald John Lethbridge), *President of the Publishers' Association; fellow of Clare College, Cambridge.* Letter to G. B. Shaw, 1944. *Signed.* 50524, f. 166.

Kingsley Read (R.), *spelling reformer.* Correspondence, etc., with B. Wrenick, 1942, 1946. Partly *signed, copy* and *printed.* 50554, ff. 219, 226-232v; 50556, f. 102.

— Correspondence, etc., with G. B. Shaw, 1942-1948. Mainly *printed* and *copy.* 50554, ff. 196-232v; 50555, ff. 1, 13-20; 50556, ff. 24-28, 101-102; 79492, ff. 101-109.

— Correspondence, etc., with Sir I. J. Pitman, 1943-1966. Mainly *printed* and *copies.* 50555, ff. 22-26; 79493, ff. 81-83, 138-143, 149.

Kingsmill (Hugh), *author.* Letter to G. B. Shaw, 1932. 50538, f. 50.

Kingston (Gertrude), *actress.* Correspondence with the Lord Chamberlain's Office, 1909-1916. *L.C.P. Corr.* 1909/122; *L.C.P. Corr.* 1915/3885; *L.C.P. Corr.* 1916/91.

— Letters to G. B. Shaw, 1912-1916. Partly *signed.* 50539, ff. 39-102v.

— Portrait photographs of, 1912?, 1929. *Inscribed.* 50584, ff. 102, 103.

— Correspondence with J. L. Palmer, 1913. *Copies.* 50539, ff. 56, 57.

Kropotkin (*Prince* Petr Alekseevich), *Russian revolutionary.* Letters to G. B. Shaw, 1903, 1913. 50514, f. 113; 50516, f. 298.

Krutch (Joseph Wood), *American writer on drama.* Open letter of G. B. Shaw to, 1935. *Printed* proof with *autogr.* corrections. 50637, ff. 48-55.

Kumar Roy (Dilip).
v. Dilipa-Kumara Raya.

Kunz (George Frederick), *President of the Joan of Arc Statue Committee, New York.* Letter to G. B. Shaw, 1923. *Signed.* 50519, f. 71.

Kupfer-Koberwitz (Edgar), *German author.* Letter to G. B. Shaw, 1946. *Signed.* 50526 B, f. 274.

Kyllmann (Otto), *of Constable, Archibald & Co., publishers.* Letters to G. B. Shaw, 1910, 1938. *Signed.* 50515, f. 374; 50522, f. 24.
— Letter to C. F. Shaw, 1931. *Signed.* 56492, f. 190.

L

'L', *of Croydon.* Letter to G. B. Shaw concerning public lavatory provision, 1898. 50513, f. 183.

Labour Emancipation League. Lecture programme, 1887. *Printed.* 50701, f. 7.

Labour League. Notices of meetings, 1890, 1892. *Printed.* 50701, ff. 76, 79, 122.

Labour Party. Notice of meeting in support of candidature of W. S. Sanders, 1906. *Printed.* 50701, f. 206.

— Notices of meetings and demonstrations, 1909-1922. *Printed.* 50701, ff. 215, 216, 246, 250, 263.

— Papers of Fabian Research Department and Labour Party regarding a proposed Year Book, 1914. *Typewritten.* 50681, ff. 114-122.

— Agreement on future co-operation between Labour Party and Fabian Research Department, 1918. *Typewritten.* 50681, f. 251.

— Statement of the National Executive Committee on G. B. Shaw's ninetieth birthday, 1946. *Typewritten.* 50525, f. 228.

Labour Party Publicity Department. Memorandum, with Fabian Research Department, on a Labour News Service, 1918. *Typewritten.* 50681, ff. 299-301.

Labour Research Department. Minutes of Executive Committee, 1918. *Typewritten.* 50681, ff. 252-253.

— Report on Ireland, drafted by G. B. Shaw, *circa* 1920. *Typewritten* with *autogr.* amendments. 50681, ff. 254-275.

Laden (*Mrs.* Alice), *housekeeper to G. B. Shaw.* Correspondence with M. C. C. Stopes, 1949, 1950. Partly *draft.* 58493, ff. 103, 105-107.

Laffan (William M.), *London agent for Harper and Brothers.* Correspondence with G. B. Shaw, 1883. Partly *shorthand draft.* 50510, ff. 29, 68, 108.

[Lailler?] (Hélène), *writer on theatre, in Brussels.* Letter to G. B. Shaw, n.d. *Fr.* 50527, f. 121.

Laker (Ann), *[actress?]*. Letter to G. B. Shaw, *circa* 1935. 50527, f. 123.

Lamb (Adam).

v. Lamb (Francis Adam Johnstone).

Lamb (David C.), *Commissioner of the Salvation Army*. Letter to G. B. Shaw, 1941. *Signed*. 50522, f. 393.

Lamb (Francis Adam Johnstone), *incumbent of Julianstown with Colpe, co. Meath*. Letter to G. B. Shaw, 1946. 50525, f. 6.

Lamb (J. B.), *of The Queen's Laundry, North Kensington*. Letter concerning wartime conditions, 1941. 63198 B, f. 224.

Lamb (Joseph Percy), *City Librarian, Sheffield*. Letter to G. B. Shaw, 1949. 63186, f. 223.

Lambart (*Field-Marshal Sir* Frederick Rudolph), *10th Earl of Cavan*. Letters to G. B. Shaw, *circa* 1916-1919, n.d. 50518, ff. 122, 187; 50527, f. 43.

Lambert (Ambrose), *of 'The Sun', New York*. Letter to G. B. Shaw, 1915. *Signed*. 50553, f. 164.

Lancaster Trades and Labour Council. Notice of meeting, 1905. *Printed*. 50701, f. 197.

Landau (Rom), *author*. Letters of C. F. Shaw to, 1936. 56494, ff. 183-189v, 192, 193.

— Letter to G. B. Shaw, 1946. *Signed*. 56494, f. 165.

Landless-Turner (E.), *treasurer of Oldham Repertory Theatre Club*. Letter to G. B. Shaw, 1946. *Signed*. 50525, f. 274.

Land Nationalisation Society. Notice of meeting addressed by H. George, 1882. *Printed*. 50655 A, f. 27v.

Land Reform Union.

v. English Land Restoration League.

Lane (Alfred Church), *American scientific author*. Letter to G. B. Shaw, 1907. 50515, f. 94.

Lane (*Sir* Hugh Percy), *art collector*. Correspondence of G. B. Shaw with and concerning, 1907-1912. Partly *copy* and *printed*. 50515, ff. 40, 158, 159; 52752, f. 218.

Lane (John), *publisher*. Letter to Sir M. L. Macnaghten, 1910. *Copy*. 50515, f. 441.

— Letter to G. P. Taylor, 1910. *Copy*. 50515, f. 443.

— Letter to, of T. Hardy, 1910. *Copy*. 50515, f. 456.

— Correspondence with G. B. Shaw, 1910, 1913. Partly *copy* and *signed*. 50515, ff. 350, 439, 451-455; 50516, f. 331.

Lane (Vera Perin), *acting secretary, Family Welfare Foundation, Boston, Massachussetts*. Correspondence with G. B. Shaw, 1919. Partly *copy* and *signed*. 50518, ff. 159-161.

Lane-Claypon (Edward William).

v. Claypon.

Lang (Margaret M.). 'A New Heaven and A New Earth', 1935-1936. *Typewritten*. *Signed*. 50521, ff. 137-140.

Langdon-Davies (Bernard Noel), *publisher and politician*. Letters, etc., to G. B. Shaw, 1916. *Signed; partly printed*. 50517, ff. 384, 413.

Langford (Joseph M.), *London manager of William Blackwood and Sons*. Correspondence with G. B.

Shaw, 1880. Partly *shorthand draft.*
50508, ff. 263-264v.

Langner (Lawrence), *of the Theatre
Guild of New York.* Correspondence with G. B. Shaw, 1921-1943.
Mainly *typewritten copies.* 50539,
ff. 103-139, 142, 143, 146.

— Play, 'St. Bernard and St. Joan',
1924. *Typewritten.* 50578.

— Photograph of G. B. and C. F.
Shaw taken by, n.d. 50582, f.
136.

Langton (E. A. May), *leader of the
'Guardians of the Life Force' music
group.* Letter to G. B. Shaw, 1939.
50522, f. 241.

Lansbury (George), *P.C.; M.P.* 'War
Against Poverty' issued by
Independent Labour Party, contri-
butions by J. R. MacDonald, W. C.
Anderson, M. G. Bondfield, G.
Lansbury, M. MacArthur, G. B.
Shaw, S. J. Webb and M. B. Webb,
circa 1912. *Printed pamphlet.*
50686, ff. 121-130v.

— Letter to G. B. Shaw, 1914. *Signed.*
50517, f. 167.

Lansdowne, *Marquess of.*
v. Petty-Fitzmaurice (Henry Charles
Keith).

Lanyi (Adorné), *of Budapest.* Letter
to G. B. Shaw, 1936. 50521, f. 133.

Lara (Adelina de).
v. de Lara.

Larkin (James), *general secretary of
the Workers' Union of Ireland.*
Letters, etc., to G. B. Shaw, 1946.
Signed. Partly *printed.* 50525, ff. 3,
8.

— Letter, etc., to, of P. Meehan, 1946.
Partly *copy.* 50525, f. 4.

Lascelles (Ernita), *[actress?], of New
York.* Portrait photograph of Ernita
Lascelles, 1921. 50584, f. 106.

Lassalle (Ferdinand), *German
socialist.* Photograph of tomb of
F. Lassalle by F. Krapp, 1893?
50586, f. 91.

Latey (John), *Jr.; editor of the 'Penny
Illustrated Paper'.* Letters to G. B.
Shaw, 1889. 50512, ff. 138v, 140v,
145.

Latham (Charles), *1st Baron Latham,
1942.* Correspondence with G. B.
Shaw, 1943. Partly *signed, imperf.*
and *shorthand draft.* 50523, ff. 101,
101v, 113.

Latham (Grace), *actress.* Letters to
G. B. Shaw, 1884. 50510, ff. 195,
198.

— Lecture on 'Troilus and Cressida' to
New Shakespeare Society by G. B.
Shaw, read by G. Latham, 1884.
Draft. 50702, ff. 41-124v.

Launder (Frank), *secretary, the
Screenwriter's Association.* Letters,
etc., to G. B. Shaw, 1943. *Signed.*
Partly *printed* and *copy.* 50523, ff.
142-147.

— Correspondence with R. A.
Habbijam, 1943. *Copies.* 50523, ff.
146, 147.

Laurie (T. Werner), *publisher.*
Letters, etc., to C. F. Shaw, 1941,
1942. *Signed* and partly *printed.*
56494, ff. 111, 160.

Lautenburg (Sigmund), *manager of
the Neues Theater, Berlin.* Letter to
G. B. Shaw, 1894. *Signed.* 50513,
f. 45v.

[Lautre?] (Gladys), *[of Cape
Province?].* Letter to C. F. Shaw,
1932. 56493, f. 12.

Lavery *née* **Martyn** (Hazel), *2nd wife of Sir John Lavery.* Letter from G. B. Shaw to, 1924. *Copy.* 50519, f. 186.

— Portrait of G. B. Shaw, 1925. *Signed photogr.* 50582, f. 43.

Lawless (Anne), *of Freeport, Illinois.* Letter to G. B. Shaw, 1946. *Signed.* 50525, f. 243.

Lawrence (— Pethick-). *v.* Pethick-Lawrence.

Lawrence (A.), *of the Golden Syndicate Publishing Company, Los Angeles.* Letter, etc., to G. B. Shaw, 1931. Partly *signed* and *printed copy.* 50520, f. 103.

Lawrence (Amy), *Fabian.* Letter to G. B. Shaw, 1896. 50557, f. 40.

Lawrence (Arnold Walter), *brother of T. E. Lawrence.* Notes to C. F. Shaw, 1935? 56499, ff. 11, 12.

Lawrence (Gerald Leslie), *actor.* Letter to G. B. Shaw, 1935. 50521, f. 35.

Lawrence *née* **Klasen** *afterw.* **Gordon-Howley** *afterw.* **Aldrich** (Gertrude), *actress.* Letter to, from G. B. Shaw, *circa* 1941. [*Draft?*]. 50527, f. 124.

Lawrence (Marjory R.), *[relative of T. E. Lawrence?].* Letters to C. F. Shaw, 1929, n.d. 56492, ff. 121, 122, 125; 56494, f. 195.

Lawrence (P.), *of Bradford, co. York.* Letter, etc., to G. B. Shaw, n.d. *Signed.* 50527, f. 125.

Lawrence (Sarah), *mother of T. E. Lawrence.* Letters to C. F. Shaw, 1928-1940. 56492, ff. 108, 117, 120, 123, 124, 128, 129; 63186, f. 122.

Lawrence *afterw.* **Shaw** (Thomas Edward), *called 'Lawrence of Arabia'.* Wartime photographs of, 1916?-1918? 50584, ff. 108-118.

— Letter to V. W. Richards, 1918. *Autogr. copy.* 45903, f. 129v.

— Notes of C. F. Shaw suggesting amendments to 'The Seven Pillars of Wisdom', *circa* 1921. 56498.

— Correspondence, etc., with C. F. Shaw, *circa* 1921-1935, n.d. Partly *typewritten, copy* and *draft.* 45903, 45904; 45922; 56495-56498; 56514, f. 30; 63203, ff. 1v-3v.

— Miscellaneous papers of and concerning T. E. Lawrence, *circa* 1921-1938. Partly *printed.* 56498, 56499; 63203.

— Correspondence with G. B. Shaw, 1922-1935. Partly *copies.* 45904, ff. 2, 17, 80, 228; 50540, ff. 1-59, 91; 56496, ff. 137, 301; 56497, ff. 67-96.

— Introduction to R. Garnett, 'The Twilight of the Gods', 1924. *Printed* with *autogr.* notes. 56499, ff. 1-4v.

— Note to, of Maj. H. W. Young, 1926. 56499, f. 13.

— Letter to, of R. R. Graves, annotated by T. E. Lawrence, 1927. *Fragm.* 45903, f. 169.

— Portrait drawings of, by A. E. John, 1927? *Photographic copies.* 56499, ff. 34, 41.

— Bust of, by E. H. Kennington, 1927? *Photogr.* 56499, f. 42.

— Notes on verso of photographs, 1927, 1928. 63203, ff. 1-3v.

— Letter to 'T. E. Shaw' of A. E. John, 1929. 45904, f. 83.

— Telegrams to 'T. E. Shaw' of N. W. Astor, 1930. Partly *copy*. 45904, ff. 127, 128.

— Notes on 'Too True to be Good', 1932. 45904, ff. 164, 165.

— Letter to W. Hudd concerning 'To True to be Good', 1932. 71658, f. 55.

— Letter to T. E. Lawrence of M. L. Bennington, 1935. 50540, f. 66.

— Note on photograph of memorial to, by R. V. Buxton, aft. 1935? 63203, f. 4v.

Laws (E. C.), *secretary of the Paddington and Bayswater branch, Social Democratic Federation.* Letter, etc., to G. B. Shaw, 1884. Partly *printed*. 50510, ff. 277-279.

Laws (Ernest Eugene), *author.* Letter to G. B. Shaw, 1937. 50521, f. 252.

Lawson (Dora), *schoolteacher.* Postcard and letter to G. B. Shaw, 1946, n.d. 50526 B, f. 339; 50527, f. 127.

Lawson (Elizabeth), *wife of William Lawson, artist.* Correspondence with G. B. Shaw, 1880. Partly *draft*. 50508, ff. 189-191v.

Lawson (Sylvia), *of Arlington, Massachussetts.* Letter to G. B. Shaw, 1946. 50526 A, f. 62.

Layton (T. A.), *caterer.* Letter to G. B. Shaw, 1946. *Signed*. 50526 A, f. 54.

Layton *formerly* **Fransky** (Valerie), *shorthand typist.* Letter to G. B. Shaw, 1944. 50524, f. 243.

Lazarus [(Robert Stephen), *Q.C?*]. Opinion on the will of G. B. Shaw, 1957. *Copy*. 79493, ff. 21-22.

Leach (William), *M.P.* Letter to Beatrice Webb, 1914. 50517, f. 40.

League of Nations Society. Circular letter, 1917. *Printed*. 50688, f. 3v.

Leahy (Eugene), *actor.* Letter to G. B. Shaw, 1935. 50521, f. 83.

Leahy (Maurice), *Secretary, University of London Catholic Society.* Letter of G. B. Shaw to, 1927. *Printed*. 50697, f. 247.

Leake (Henry Dashwood Stucley), *C.B.; Chief Charity Commissioner.* Letter to G. B. Shaw, 1944. *Signed*. 50555, f. 72.

Leao (Manuel), *of Oporto, Portugal.* Letter to G. B. Shaw, 1949. *Portug.* 50526 B, f. 473.

Leathes (*Sir* Stanley Mordaunt), *K.C.B.* Letter to G. B. Shaw, 1914. 50517, f. 228.

Lebedev *née* **Kropotkin** (Alexandra Pyotrovna).
v. Kropotkin *afterw.* Lebedev.

Lebedev (Boris F.), *Russian journalist and translator; husband of Sasha Kropotkin.* Letters and postcard to G. B. Shaw, 1916-1939. 50517, f. 358; 50518, ff. 269, 271; 50519, f. 191; 50522, f. 177.

Lebenstein (Walter O.), *of Pix Publishing Inc.* Letter to J. W. R. Scott, 1937. *Signed*. 50521, f. 330.

Lecky (James), *of the Exchequer and Audit Department.* Correspondence with G. B. Shaw, 1879-1884. 50508 *passim*; 50509, ff. 45, 250, 256-261; 50510, ff. 32, 41, 291.

Lecky (S.), *[sister of J. Lecky?].* Letters to G. B. Shaw, 1882, 1883. 50509, f. 217; 50510, f. 120.

Lee (George John Vandeleur), *musician*. Group photograph taken at Dalkey, co. Dublin by R. Pigott, *circa* 1865. Two *copies*. 50583, ff. 6, 7; 50587, f. 10.

— Correspondence with Capt. D. Shaw, 1877. 50508, ff. 48-107v *passim*.

— Correspondence with G. B. Shaw, 1877-1886. Partly *shorthand draft*. 50508, ff. 57v, 67v, 72v, 74v, 80v, 192; 50509, ff. 49, 51, 72, 171, 174, 178, 189, 232, 242, 277; 50510 *passim*; 50511, f. 213.

— Application of G. B. Shaw for admission to the Reading Room of the British Museum countersigned by, 1879. Partly *printed*. 48341, ff. 231-232.

Lee (Gerald Stanley), *author*. Letter, etc., to G. B. Shaw, 1911. *Signed; partly printed*. 50516, f. 84.

Lee (Marian), *of Finchley*. Letter to G. B. Shaw, 1944. 50524, f. 114.

Lee (Susie), *lecturer on dance history*. Photograph, n.d. 50527, f. 128.

— Postcard to G. B. Shaw, n.d. 50527, f. 128.

'Lee (Vernon)', *pseudonym*. *v*. Paget (Violet).

Leeds Arts Club. Programme of meetings, etc., 1905. *Printed*. 50701, ff. 203-205.

— Notes for a lecture to, by G. B. Shaw, 1905. Partly *typewritten*. 50703, ff. 106-109.

Lees-Milne (James), *writer*. Letter to G. B. Shaw, on behalf of National Trust, 1944. *Signed*. 50524, f. 42.

Le Fanu (T. P.), *of the Irish Office*. Correspondence with the Lord Chamberlain's Office, 1909. *Signed*. *L.C.P. Corr*. 1916/91.

Le Gallienne (Richard), *author*. Letter to G. B. Shaw, 1920. 50518, f. 214.

Legge (Robin Humphrey), *music editor of 'The Daily Telegraph'*. Letter to 'The World', 1893. 50527, f. 129.

Légrády (*Dr*. Ottó), *editor of the 'Pesti Hirlap', Budapest*. Letter, etc., to G. B. Shaw, 1936. *Signed*. 50521, f. 141.

Leigh (Vivien), *actress*. Photographs of Vivien Leigh as Cleopatra, 1944. 50588, ff. 36-39.

Leigh (Walter), *composer*. Incomplete German translation of G. B. Shaw's 'You Never Can Tell', 1926. 65134.

Leigh-Taylor (N. H.), *of Los Angeles*. Letter to G. B. Shaw, 1939. *Signed*. 50522, f. 252.

Leipoldt (Oskar), *schoolteacher, of Plauen, Saxony*. Letter to G. B. Shaw, 1905. *Imperf. Germ*. 50514, f. 255.

Leiser (Clara), *executive director of Youth of All Nations, Inc*. Letter, etc., to G. B. Shaw, 1946. *Signed*. Partly *printed*. 50525, ff. 255-258.

Leithead (Queenie B.), *of Sacramento, California*. Letter to G. B. Shaw, 1946. 50526 B, f. 292.

Le Jeune (Jules), *Ministre d'Etat, Belgium*. Introductory statement on behalf of 'Potentia Organization', signed by Sir V. H. P. Caillard, Sir G. H. Darwin, Sir M. Foster, J. Claretie, F. W. Foerster, Comte G. d' Alviella, J. Le Jeune and Dr. C. Richet, 1930? Partly *printed*, with *duplicated* signatures. 50742, f. 140.

Lenanton, *Lady.*
v. Oman (Carola Mary Anima).

Lenihan (Winifred), *American actress.* Telegram to G. B. Shaw, 1923. *Copy.* 50539, f. 134.

Lennon (M.), *photographer, of Dublin.* Letter to — , 1947. 50565, f. 160.

Léon (Marie), *photographer.* Letter to G. B. Shaw, 1908. 50515, f. 139.

Leonard (*Father* Joseph S.), *C.M.; of St. Mary's Training College, Hammersmith.* Letters to G. B. Shaw, 1920-1925. 50518, ff. 334, 339; 50519, ff. 56, 123, 168, 201, 237.

— Letter to C. F. Shaw, 1925. 56492, f. 78.

— Photographs of, with G. B. Shaw, 1930? 50582, ff. 110-112.

Leschetitzsky (Annette Essipoff).
v. Essipoff.

Leslie *afterw.* **Schütze** (Henrietta), *novelist.* Receipt, on behalf of the Hermon Ould Fund, to G. B. Shaw, 1945. 50524, f. 335.

— Letter, etc., to G. B. Shaw, 1945. *Signed.* 50524, f. 336.

Leslie (Samuel Clement), *Head of the Information Division of the Treasury.* Postcard to G. B. Shaw, 1943. *Signed.* 50523, f. 51.

Lester (Katie), *daughter of Scott Alexander, actor and producer.* Letter to G. B. Shaw, n.d. *Signed.* 50527, f. 131.

Lethaby (*Prof.* William Richard), *architect.* Letter to G. B. Shaw, 1900. 50513, f. 231.

Lett (Amelia Elizabeth *called* Muffie), *cousin of G. B. Shaw.* Letter to G. B. Shaw, *circa* 1913. 50527, f. 224.

Leveson-Gower (*Sir* George Granville), *K.B.E.* Correspondence with G. B. Shaw, 1899. Partly *draft.* 50513, ff. 210-210v.

Levi (Jean O.), *of Wilmslow, co. Chest.* Letter to G. B. Shaw, 1946. 50526 A, f. 148.

Levine (Isaac Don), *American writer on Russian affairs.* Telegram to C. I. Andrews, 1925. 50519, f. 229.

Levinskaya *afterw.* **Antonoff** (Maria).
v. Antonoff *formerly* Levinskaya.

Levinson (Jesse), *American lawyer.* Letter of G. B. Shaw to, 1927. *Draft.* 50738, f. 16.

Levy (Arnold), *of Tottenham.* Letter to G. B. Shaw, 1950. 50526 B, f. 508.

Levy (Joe), *of the Glasgow Zionist Organisation.* Letter to G. B. Shaw, 1944. 63186, f. 188.

Levy (Joseph Hiam), *of the Board of Education; editor of 'Personal Rights'.* Announcement of death of J. H. Levy by L. Garreau, 1913. *Signed.* 50516, f. 354.

Levy (S.), *of Stamford Hill.* Letter to G. B. Shaw, 1944. 50524, f. 23.

Lewin (W. Henry), *author.* Letter to G. B. Shaw, 1943. *Signed.* 63186, f. 183.

Lewin (William Charles James), *al. 'William Terriss'; actor.* Letter to G. B. Shaw, 1897. 50513, f. 147.

Lewis (Cecil Arthur), *M.C.; author and film director.* Film scenario, 'Golgotha', 1935. *Typewritten.* 50521, ff. 68-75.

— Letters, etc., to G. B. Shaw, 1935-1943. *Signed.* 50521, ff. 67, 204; 50523, f. 155.

— Letter to C. F. Shaw, 1942. *Signed.* 56494, f. 147.

Lewis (E.), *of the 'Architect's Journal'.* Letter to G. B. Shaw, 1944. *Signed.* 50524, f. 65.

Lewis (Evan), *of Builth, co. Brecon.* Letter to G. B. Shaw, 1946. 50526 A, f. 160.

Lewis (*Sir* George Henry), *1st Bart.* Letter to G. B. Shaw, 1909. *Signed.* 50515, f. 217.

Lewis (Joseph), *of the Memorial Committee to Thomas Paine.* Postcard to G. B. Shaw, 1949. 63186, f. 215.

Lewis (*Pte.* Owen), *3rd Rhondda Welsh Regiment; anti-vaccinationist.* Letters to G. B. Shaw, 1916. Partly *copy.* 50517, ff. 367-371, 376, 390.

Lewis (Percy Wyndham), *artist and writer.* Letter of P. W. Lewis, E. A. Wadsworth, F. Etchells and C. Hamilton concerning Omega Workshops, 1913. *Signed.* 50534, f. 93.

Lewis-Crosby (*Very Rev.* Ernest Henry), *Dean of Christ Church Cathedral, Dublin.* Letter to G. B. Shaw, 1946. 50526 A, f. 204.

Lewisham and Lee Liberal and Radical Club. Programme of lectures, 1893. *Printed.* 50701, f. 126.

Leyel (Carl Frederick), *theatrical agent.* Letter to G. B. Shaw, 1912. *Signed.* 50516, f. 196.

Liberal Press Ltd., *publishers.* Letter to E. R. Pease, 1910. 50557, f. 97.

Licence (F. H.), *journalist.* Letter to G. B. Shaw, 1944. Mainly *shorthand.* 50742, f. 168.

Light (Henry), *captain of the Vegetarian Cycling Club.* Letter to G. B. Shaw, 1898. 50513, f. 198v.

Lilien (Ignace), *Dutch composer and pianist.* Letter to G. B. Shaw, 1932. *Engl. transl.* 50520, f. 147.

Lilley (Kate), *of Clacton; member of the Women's Social and Political Union.* Letter to M. Cunningham, 1914. *Copy.* 50517, f. 153.

Limard (Marie-Louise), *sculptor, of Paris.* Bronzes of Shaw as Don Quixote, 1931. *Photogr.* 50582, ff. 78, 79.

— Note to G. B. Shaw, 1931. 50582, f. 80.

Limbert (Roy), *co-founder and director of the Malvern Festival.* Correspondence with the Lord Chamberlain's Office, 1938, 1939. *Signed. L.C.P. Corr.* 1938/1857.

— Letters to G. B. Shaw, 1938-1949. *Signed.* 50539, ff. 147-164.

— Letters to F. E. Loewenstein, 1947. *Signed.* 50565, ff. 125, 153, 167, 168.

— Correspondence with the Society of Authors, 1947-1949. *Signed.* 56635, 56636 *passim.*

Limerick *afterw.* **Payne** (Mona). *v.* Payne *née* Limerick.

Limosin (Febo de), *of Havana, Cuba.* Letter to G. B. Shaw, 1935. *Signed. Span.* 50521, f. 119.

Lind-af-Hageby (Emelie Augusta Louise), *of the Animal Defence and Anti-Vivisection Society.* Letter,

Portrait photograph of Jane Lockett, 1881. 50584, f. 120.

— Letter to G. B. Shaw, 1882. 50509, f. 183.

Lockhart (Leonora W.), *of the Orthological Institute.* Letter to G. B. Shaw, 1940. 50554, f. 109.

Lockwood (*Maj.* A. F.), *secretary of the London College of Osteopathy.* Letter to G. B. Shaw, 1946. *Signed.* 50525, f. 148.

Lockwood (Charles Barrett), *F.R.C.S.* Letter to J. K. Barton, 1881? 50509, f. 75.

Lodge (*Sir* Oliver Joseph), *F.R.S.* Letters to C. F. Shaw, 1912, 1914. 56491, ff. 106, 160-162.

— Photograph of, 1926. 50584, f. 123.

Lodge (Thomas), *author.* Index slips for an edition of T. Lodge's works by G. B. Shaw, 1885. Partly *shorthand.* 50511, ff. 92-94v.

Loeb (Mathilde H.).
v. Richter *afterw.* Loeb.

Loeb (Sydney John), *son-in-law of Hans Richter.* Postcards and letters to G. B. Shaw, *circa* 1911-1944. 50516, ff. 57, 71, 98, 100, 435; 50524, f. 177; 50527, f. 132; 50584, f. 122.

Loeb (Sylvia), *daughter of S. J. Loeb; granddaughter of H. Richter.* Portrait photographs of, 1913?, 1920? 50516, f. 435; 50584, f. 122.

Loewenstein (*Dr.* Fritz Erwin), *of the Shaw Society.* Notes to G. B. Shaw, 1945-1947. 50524, f. 341; 50526 A, f. 25; 50526 B, f. 395.

— Correspondence with Wilfred Partington, 1945-1949. Partly

copies. 59620 C, ff. 274-298; 59620 D, f. 12; 59621 A, f. 25.

— Correspondence relating to photographs of Shaw and Shaw productions, 1947-1948. Partly *signed.* 50565, ff. 120-285.

— Letter to Dr. F. E. Loewenstein of G. Armstrong, 1949. 56632, f. 127.

Logier (Johann Bernhard), *musician.* Reminiscences of, by L. E. Shaw, 1894. 50513, ff. 33, 39-41v.

Lombroso (*Professor* Cesare). Introductory statement on behalf of 'Potentia Organization', signed by Sir V. H. P. Caillard, Sir G. H. Darwin, Sir M. Foster, J. Claretie, F. W. Foerster, Comte G. d' Alviella, J. Le Jeune and Dr. C. Richet, 1930? Partly *printed,* with *duplicated* signatures. 50742, f. 140.

LONDON. CITY AND COUNTY. London School Board election leaflets, 1894. *Printed.* 50701, ff. 134, 137.

— Freedom of the city granted to G. B. Shaw, 1935. Partly *printed.* 50711 A, ff. 133, 134.

— Letters concerning wartime conditions in London, 1940-1942. Partly *signed.* 63187, ff. 53, 63, 92, 101-102v, 111-112v, 117, 144-154v; 63198 B, ff. 209, 224.

London County Council. Notes on results at London County Council elections by G. B. Shaw, 1892. Partly *printed.* 50680, ff. 6-9.

— List of lantern slides of Fabian Society, depicting aspects of the work of London County Council *circa* 1894. 50680, ff. 130-135.

— Notice of meeting in support of candidature of Dr. E. Bentham, 1910. *Printed.* 50701, f. 216.

Londonderry, *Marchioness of.*
v. Vane-Tempest-Stewart (Edith Helen).

London Dialectical Society. Notice of meetings, 1889. *Printed.* 50701, f. 42.

London Lancashire Life Assurance Company, Limited. Letter of G. B. Shaw to, concerning A. M. Lockett, 1919. *Copy.* 50517, f. 447.

London Patriotic Club. 'Coercion in London'; notice of demonstration, 1887. *Printed.* 50701, f. 22.

London Reform Union. Notices of meetings, 1894. *Printed.* 50701, ff. 136, 145.

London School of Economics and Political Science. 'At Home' card of C. F. Shaw, 1896. *Printed.* 56490, f. 169.

— Note of subscriptions to, by C. F. Shaw, 1896-1902. 56491, f. 30.

— Correspondence relating to, 1899-1910. Partly *copy.* 56491, ff. 6-75 *passim.*

— Note of C. F. Shaw on recipients of Shaw scholarships, 1910. 56491, f. 75.

London Socialist Forum. Programme of lectures, 1926. *Printed.* 50701, f. 252.

London Vegetarian Society. Notice of meeting, 1895. *Printed.* 50701, f. 158.

Lones (W. T. N.), *of Johannesburg.* Letter, with F. Potter, to G. B. Shaw, 1937. *Signed.* 50521, f. 302.

Long (Ethel), [*daughter of E. Longsden Long, R.A.?*]. Letters to G. B. Shaw, 1881. 50509, ff. 58, 66.

Longmans, Green and Co., *publishers.* Letter to G. B. Shaw, 1881. 50509, f. 60v.

Loomis (Roger Sherman), *Professor at Columbia University.* Letter to G. B. Shaw, 1930. 50520, f. 2.

Loraine (Robert), *M.C.; actor and aviator.* Letter to C. F. Shaw, *circa* 1900. 56494, f. 167.

— Correspondence with G. B. Shaw, 1906?, 1914. Partly *draft.* 50517, f. 2; 50732, ff. 36-37.

— Portrait photographs of Robert Loraine, 1912, 1915. Partly *inscribed.* 50584, ff. 124, 125.

Lord (Miriam), *O.B.E.; nursery school teacher.* Letters of G. B. Shaw to, 1950. 74767, ff. 43, 44.

Lothian, *Marquess of.*
v. Kerr (Philip Henry).

Loveday (R. W.), *of Southampton.* Letter to G. B. Shaw, 1946. 50525, f. 67.

Lovegrove (W. F.), *of Wonersh, co. Surr.* Letter to G. B. Shaw, 1949. *Signed.* 50526 B, f. 465.

Lovejoy (*Prof.* Arthur Oncken), *of Johns Hopkins University.* Letter to G. B. Shaw, 1921. *Signed.* 50518, f. 263.

Loveless (*Lt.* Owen R.), *in Okinawa.* Letter to G. B. Shaw, 1946. *Signed.* 50556, f. 19.

Lovibond (J. Locke), *of Salisbury.* Letter to B. Patch, 1946. *Signed.* 50526 A, f. 12.

Low (*Lady* Ebba Cecilia), *widow of Sir Sidney James Low.* Letter to

G. B. Shaw, 1946. *Signed.* 50525, f. 196.

Lowe (Trevor), *actor.* Letter to G. B. Shaw, 1909. 50515, f. 202.

Lowenfeld (Henry), *manager of the Prince of Wales Theatre.* Correspondence with G. B. Shaw, 1897. Partly *signed* and *copy.* 50513, ff. 153-155.

Lowke (Wenman Joseph Bassett-), *author.* Letter and postcard to G. B. Shaw, 1941. *Signed.* 50522, f. 356; 63186, f. 175.

Lowne (Charles M.), *actor.* Letter, as administrator of the Academy of Dramatic Art, to G. B. Shaw, 1915. *Signed.* 50517, f. 327.

Lowry (A.), *of Bolsover St., London.* Letter to B. Patch, 1937. 50521, f. 350.

Loyson (Paul Hyacinthe), *French author.* Letter to G. B. Shaw, 1910. *Fr.* 50515, f. 437.

Lucas (Edward Verrall), *of Methuen and Co.; author and publisher.* 'A Talk with Edward Verrall Lucas', by C. C. Clemens, *circa* 1938. *Printed.* 50522, ff. 180-181.

Ludovici (Albert), *artist.* Letter to G. B. Shaw, 1889. 50512, f. 176.

Ludowyk (Evelyn Frederick Charles), *formerly in Ceylon.* Letter to G. B. Shaw, 1947. *Signed.* 50526 B, f. 396.

Ludwig (Elga), *wife of Emil Ludwig.* Letters to G. B. Shaw, 1932-1941. 50539, ff. 165, 167, 172.

Ludwig (Emil), *Swiss author.* Letters to G. B. Shaw, 1932-1948, n.d. 50539, ff. 165, 166, 169-171v, 173, 174.

Lugné *al.* **Lugné-Poë** (Aurélien-François), *director of the Théâtre des Oeuvres, Paris.* Letters to G. B. Shaw, 1896-1914. *Fr.* 50513, f. 125; 50515, f. 135v; 50517, f. 117.

— Letter to C. F. Shaw, 1903. *Fr.* 56491, f. 37.

— Photographs of Paris production of 'The Doctor's Dilemma', directed by A.-F. Lugné, 1922. 50589, ff. 11-17.

Lundholm (N.), *of C. A. V. Lundholm, publishers, Stockholm.* Letter to G. B. Shaw, 1914. *Signed.* 50517, f. 202.

Lunn (Hugh Kingsmill).
  v. Kingsmill.

Lygon *afterw.* **Romanovsky-Pavlovsky** (Mary), *daughter of the 7th Earl of Beauchamp.* Letter to G. B. Shaw, n.d. 50527, f. 133.

Lyndon (Charlotte), *wife of Dr. Arnold Lyndon.* Letter of G. B. Shaw to C. Lyndon, 1902. *Draft.* 50527, f. 134.

Lynn-Clayton (H.), *of Salcombe, co. Devon.* Letter to G. B. Shaw, 1949. 50526 B, f. 472.

Lyth (Jisbella), *postmistress, Ayot St. Lawrence.* Photographs of Mrs. J. Lyth, 1938, 1939. 50582, ff. 124v, 127.

Lyttelton (*Dame* Edith Sophy), *G.B.E.; wife of A. Lyttelton.* Letter to W. Archer, H. G. Granville-Barker and G. B. Shaw concerning Shakespeare Memorial National Theatre, 1909. *Typewritten copy.* 50539, f. 175.

— Letters to G. B. Shaw, 1909-1913, n.d. Partly *copy* and *signed.* 50539, ff. 175-208v.

— Letter, as 'D. D', to G. B. Shaw, 1946. 50525, f. 195.

Lyttleton (Raymond Arthur), *professor of theoretical astronomy at Cambridge University*. Letters to G. B. Shaw, 1944, 1946. *Signed.* 50524, f. 181; 50525, f. 12.

Lytton, *Earl of.*
v. Bulwer-Lytton (Victor Alexander George Robert).

Lytton (*Lady* Constance Georgina Bulwer-).
v. Bulwer-Lytton.

Lytton (Judith Anne Dorothea Blunt), *16th Baroness Wentworth; wife of Neville, 3rd Earl of Lytton.* Letter, etc., to G. B. Shaw, 1906, 1908. Partly *printed.* 50515, f. 200; 54155, f. 208.

— Correspondence with C. F. Shaw, 1920, 1926. Partly *draft.* 54155, f. 209; 56492, ff. 32, 33.

Lytton (Neville Stephen), *3rd Earl of Lytton; artist.* Letters and postcard to G. B. Shaw, 1906-1928. 50514, f. 330; 50515, f. 163; 50516, f. 277; 50519, f. 330.

— Postcard to C. F. Shaw, 1923. 63197, f. 10.

Lytton-Hall (S.), *disciple of Robert Owen.* Letter to G. B. Shaw, 1900. Partly *printed.* 50513, f. 215.

M

Macadam (*Sir* Ivison Stevenson), *K.C.V.O.* Postcard to G. B. Shaw, 1945. 63186, f. 194.

McAlister (Deane J.), *of Greenville, Illinois.* Letter to G. B. Shaw, 1946. *Signed.* 50526 B, f. 318.

McAllister (Gilbert), *M.P.* Letter to C. F. Shaw, 1925. 50519, f. 241.

— Letter to G. B. Shaw, 1937. *Signed.* 50521, f. 320.

MacArthur (Mary), *socialist.* 'War Against Poverty' issued by Independent Labour Party, contributions by J. R. MacDonald, W. C. Anderson, M. G. Bondfield, G. Lansbury, M. MacArthur, G. B. Shaw, S. J. Webb and M. B. Webb, *circa* 1912. *Printed pamphlet.* 50686, ff. 121-130v.

McCabe (E.), *spelling reformer, of Brighton.* Letter, etc., to G. B. Shaw, 1942. 50554, ff. 233-257.

McCall (Erwin), [*of the Nietzsche Society?*]. Correspondence on topics related to the writings of Nietzsche, 1900? Partly *duplicated.* 50742, ff. 15-30.

MacCarthy (*Sir* Desmond), *author.* Correspondence with G. B. Shaw, 1944-1945. Partly *fragm.* and *drafts.* 50524, ff. 271, 278, 288.

McCarthy (Lillah), *O.B.E.; actress; first wife of H. G. Granville-Barker.* Letters to G. B. Shaw, 1909-1937. 50534, ff. 168-170v.

— Photograph of L. McCarthy and O. P. Heggie in 'Androcles and the Lion', 1915? 50588, f. 1.

McCarthy (Michael John Fitzgerald), *barrister and author.* Letter from G. B. Shaw to, 1917. *Copy.* 50518, f. 30.

Mac Carvill (Mary), *of Dundalk, co. Louth.* Letter to G. B. Shaw, 1946. 50526 A, f. 127.

MacClamroch (James), *American attorney and counselor at law.*

Letter to H. G. Wells, 1943. *Copy.* 50555, f. 63.

McCleary (George Frederick), *M.D.; D.P.H.; Medical Officer of Health, Battersea Borough Council.* Letter to C. F. Shaw, 1902. 56491, f. 31.

McCleary (Hilda), *sister of Harold Cox.* Letters, etc., to G. B. Shaw, 1948. 50526 B, ff. 433, 435.

MacClure (Victor), *author.* Letter to G. B. Shaw, 1925. 50519, f. 235.

MacColl (Dugald Sutherland), *Trustee of the Tate Gallery.* Letter, as Keeper of the Wallace Collection, to G. B. Shaw, 1916. 50517, f. 402.

McConnell *afterw.* **FitzGerald** (Mabel W.).
v. FitzGerald *née* McConnell.

McConnell (*Dr.* W. S.), *anaesthetist.* Receipt, 1940. 63197, f. 61.

McCorkle (G. P.), *of Hollywood, California.* Letter to G. B. Shaw, 1946. *Signed.* 50526 B, f. 313.

Mccormack (John), *Irish tenor.* Letter to G. B. Shaw, 1944. 50524, f. 85.

McCotter (Charles T.), *manager of The Ball Publishing Company.* Letter to G. B. Shaw, 1909. *Signed.* 50557, f. 84.

McCrea *al.* **Campbell** (Ellen), *governess.* Letters to G. B. Shaw, 1910. 50515, ff. 375, 377.

MacCunn (Hamish), *composer.* Letter to G. B. Shaw, 1889. 50512, f. 136.

MacDermot (Robert), *Head of Television Drama, B.B.C.* Letter to G. B. Shaw, annotated by Shaw, 1949. *Signed.* 56632, f. 166.

Macdermott (Norman), *dramatic producer.* Correspondence with the Lord Chamberlain's Office, 1922. Partly *signed* and *copy. L.C.P. Corr.* 1924/5632, ff. 103, 107, 108.

Macdona (Charles), *theatre manager.* Correspondence with the Lord Chamberlain's Office, 1924. Partly *signed* and *copy. L.C.P. Corr.* 1924/5632, ff. 109, 117, 118.

— Letters, etc., to G. B. Shaw, 1933, 1944. Partly *signed.* 50520, f. 225; 50524, f. 102v.

Macdonald (A. R. H.), *of the Indian Civil Service.* Letter, etc., to G. B. Shaw, 1946. 50556, ff. 20-44.

McDonald (Chester), *of Boston, Massachusetts.* Letter to G. B. Shaw, 1946. 50526 A, f. 37.

Macdonald (Edward J.), *journalist.* Letter to G. B. Shaw, 1938. 50522, f. 103.

Macdonald (Elizabeth), *housekeeper, Whitehall Court.* Letters to C. F. Shaw, 1940-1942. Partly *signed.* 63187, ff. 23, 53, 101-102v, 111, 117.

MacDonald (*Capt.* F. J.*), of Glenco.* Letter, etc., to G. B. Shaw, 1945. *Signed.* Partly *printed.* 50524, ff. 344, 345.

MacDonald (James Ramsay), *Prime Minister.* Letters to G. B. Shaw, 1897, 1929. 50513, f. 156; 50519, f. 394.

— Proposed referendum on the Boer War, 1899. *Draft.* 50680, f. 202.

— 'War Against Poverty' issued by Independent Labour Party, contributions by J. R. MacDonald, W. C. Anderson, M. G. Bondfield, G.

copies. 50561, ff. 22, 27, 31; 59892, f. 126.

Mahaffy (*Sir* John Pentland), *Provost of Trinity College, Dublin.* Letter to C. F. Shaw, 1908? 56491, f. 55.

Mahl (William), *American playwright.* Letter to G. B. Shaw, 1938. *Signed.* 50522, f. 90.

Mahler (Carl S.), *of Warrington.* Correspondence with G. B. Shaw rel. to S. Trebitsch, 1943. 68892, f. 6.

Mahler (Martha), *of Staten Island, U.S.A.* Letter to G. B. Shaw, 1946. 50525, f. 35.

Mahon (John Lincoln), *secretary of the Socialist League.* Letter to G. B. Shaw, 1885. 50511, f. 62.

Mair (Alexander), *Professor of Philosophy, University of Liverpool.* Letter to 'Liverpool Evening Express' of G. B. Shaw concerning, 1916. *Printed.* 50696, f. 16.

Maisky (Ivan Mikhailovich), *Soviet diplomatist.* Photograph of Mr. and Mrs. I. Maisky, 1935? 50584, f. 134.

Majumdar (B.), *proprietor, Sreeguru Library, Calcutta.* Letter to G. B. Shaw, 1937. *Signed.* 50521, f. 286.

Malicka (Maria), *Polish actress.* Portrait photographs of Maria Malicka as 'Candida', 1938. *Signed.* 50588, ff. 72, 79.

Mallock (William Hurrell), *author.* Letters, etc., of, and letters of G. B. Shaw and others concerning, 1909, 1910. *Printed.* 50690, ff. 211-225; 50695, ff. 40-42, 47v-48.

Mallon (James Joseph), *C.H.; Warden of Toynbee Hall.* Letter to G. B. Shaw, 1924. 50519, f. 112.

Maly Theatre, *Moscow.* Photographs of Moscow production of 'Pygmalion', 1932? 50590, ff. 13-27.

Mankowitz (Wolf), *writer.* Letter to G. B. Shaw, on behalf of editorial board of 'The Critic', 1946. *Signed.* 50526 A, f. 144.

Mann (Thomas), *novelist.* 'Wagner and Germany' addressed to 'Common Sense', 1939? *Typewritten.* 50741, ff. 140-147.

Manns (*Sir* August), *conductor.* Letter to G. B. Shaw, 1888. 50512, f. 69v.

Mansel (*Lt.-Col.* John Delalynde), *J.P., of Smedmore, co. Dors.* Letters to C. F. Payne-Townshend, 1882?-1886. 56490, ff. 14, 48-56, 65.

Mansfield *née* **Cameron** (Beatrice), *actress; wife of Richard Mansfield.* Letter to G. B. Shaw, 1895. 50513, f. 80.

— Letter to C. F. Shaw, 1901. 56491, f. 21.

— Photograph of, 1920?-1930? *Signed.* 50584, f. 135.

Mansfield (Richard), *American actor and producer.* Correspondence with G. B. Shaw, 1895-1898. Partly typewritten copy. 50543, ff. 55-87v.

Mansfield (William), *Viscount Sandhurst.* Correspondence, as Lord Chamberlain, with G. B. Shaw, 1916. *Signed* and *copy. L.C.P. Corr.* 1924/5632.

Mara (William P.), *Hon. Lay Secretary, Catholic Federation of the Archdiocese of Westminster.* Letter to the Lord Chamberlain, 1917. *Signed. L.C.P. Corr.* 1924/5632, f. 45.

Marbury (Elisabeth), *American author and agent.* Correspondence with G. B. Shaw, 1897, n.d. Partly *signed* and *draft.* 50513, f. 149; 50527, f. 145.

Marchesi (*Mme.* Blanche), *soprano.* Photograph of, 1924. *Signed.* 50584, f. 136.

Margerie (Roland de), *C.V.O.; French diplomatist.* Correspondence with G. B. Shaw and others, 1940. *Copies.* Partly *Fr.* 50522, ff. 276-289.

Margrie (William), *author; founder of the London Explorers' Club.* Letter to G. B. Shaw, 1946. 50525, f. 400.

Maril (*Dr.* Konrad), *literary and theatrical agent, of Berlin.* Correspondence with G. B. Shaw, 1936. Partly *signed* and *shorthand draft.* 50521, ff. 202, 202v.

Markovitch (Wéssa), *solicitor and author, of Belgrade.* Letters to G. B. Shaw of and concerning, 1926-1927. *Signed.* Partly *Fr.* 56628, ff. 126, 152, 167, 170.

'Marlow (Louis)', *pseudonym.*
v. Wilkinson (Louis Umfreville).

Mármol (F. Tarrida del).
v. Tarrida del Mármol.

Marriott (Alfred John), *socialist, author and furniture dealer.* Letters to G. B. Shaw, 1892. 50512, ff. 305, 308.

Marriott (R. B.), *author of 'The Blazing Tower'.* Letter to G. B. Shaw, 1949. 63186, f. 213.

Marsh (A.), *writing from St. James's, London.* Letter to G. B. Shaw, 1883. 50510, f. 18v.

Marshak (Samuil Yokovlevich), *Soviet writer.* Telegrams to G. B. Shaw of A. N. Tolstoy, K. M. Simonov and S. Y. Marshak, 1944. 50524, ff. 138, 147.

Marshall (Catherine E.), *suffragist and pacifist.* Letter, etc., to G. B. Shaw, 1916. 50517, f. 408.

Marshall (*Miss* Christabel), *al. 'Christopher St. John'.* Letter, with E. Craig, to G. B. Shaw, 1940. 50522, f. 299.

— Letter to G. B. Shaw, 1947. 50526 B, f. 387.

Marshall (Ernest), *American journalist.* Correspondence with G. B. Shaw, 1915, 1923. Partly *signed* and *shorthand draft.* 50517, f. 318; 50519, f. 17.

Marshall (John David), *of McKenzie, Tennessee.* Letter to G. B. Shaw, 1944. 50524, f. 135.

Martin *al.* **Charrington** (Charles).
v. Charrington *al.* Martin.

Martin (John William), *editor of 'The American Fabian'.* Letter to G. B. Shaw, 1945. *Signed.* 50524, f. 342.

Martlew (W. E.), *of Liverpool.* Letter to G. B. Shaw, 1945. *Signed.* 50524, f. 349.

Martyn (Carrie), *socialist.* Portrait photograph on New Year's greeting signed by J. K. Hardie, 1896. *Printed.* 50584, f. 142.

Martyn *afterw.* **Lavery** (Hazel).
v. Lavery *née* Martyn.

Martyn (Laurence D.). Letter to G. B. Shaw, 1946. *Signed.* 50526 A, f. 177.

Marx (Eleanor), *socialist; daughter of Karl Marx.* Letters to G. B. Shaw, 1885, 1887. 50511, ff. 88, 361.

Minchin (James Humphrey Cotton), *author and publisher.* Letter to B. Patch, 1926. *Signed.* 50519, f. 279.

Mindlin (Michael), *of New York.* Letter to G. B. Shaw, 1944. *Signed.* 50524, f. 206.

Minns (Sidney), *of Stoke Newington.* Letter to G. B. Shaw, 1937. *Signed.* 50521, f. 326.

Minter (Bruce), *of Alhambra, California.* Letter to G. B. Shaw, 1946. *Signed.* 50526 B, f. 293.

Mirenik (Johanna), *of Cernauti.* Letter to G. B. Shaw, 1937. *Copy.* 50521, f. 283.

Mitchell (Langdon), *adapter for the stage.* Letter to G. B. Shaw, 1912. 50516, f. 187.

Mitchell (*Miss* M. L.), *of the Women's International League.* Letter to C. F. Shaw, 1917. 63186, f. 14.

Mitchell (*Sir* Peter Chalmers), *secretary to the Zoological Society.* Letter to G. B. Shaw, 1915. *Signed.* 50517, f. 353.

Mitra (Souren), *proprietor of 'The Readers' Corner', Calcutta.* Letter to G. B. Shaw, 1946. *Signed.* 50526 A, f. 219.

[Mock?] (Louise), *friend of C. F. Shaw.* Letters to C. F. Shaw, *circa* 1940. 56494, f. 205; 63186, ff. 123, 124.

Modder (H. Jan), *of Kurunegala, Ceylon.* Letter to G. B. Shaw, 1937. 50521, f. 328.

Modlens (Joseph), *of Washington D.C.* Letter to G. B. Shaw, 1946. *Signed.* 50526 B, f. 294.

Mohamed (A. Abdou), *dragoman, of Luxor.* Letter, etc., to G. B. Shaw, 1935. Partly *printed.* 50521, f. 111.

— Card of Abdou Mohamed, 1935. *Printed.* 50521, f. 113.

— Photograph of Abdou Mohamed, *circa* 1935. 50521, f. 112.

Mohammed (Feroze L.), *steno-typist, of Port of Spain, Trinidad.* Letter, etc., to G. B. Shaw, 1946. *Signed.* 50526 A, f. 161.

Mohn (F. V.), *M.D., of Eagle Rock, California.* Letter to G. B. Shaw, 1939. 50522, f. 206.

Moissi (Alexander), *German actor.* Correspondence of S. H. Hobhouse with the Prisoners of War Information Bureau concerning, 1915. 50517, f. 290.

Mokhtar El Wakif.
  v. El Wakif (Mokhtar).

Moloney (Anne Mary), *of Windsor, Australia.* Letter to G. B. Shaw, 1944. 50524, f. 259.

Monck (Walter Nugent), *playwright.* Correspondence with G. B. Shaw, 1945. 50524, ff. 359-359v.

Mond (Amy Gwen), *wife of 2nd Baron Melchett.* Postcard to C. F. Shaw, 1942. 56494, f. 148.

Money (*Sir* Leo George Chiozza), *author and public servant.* Letter to G. B. Shaw, 1941. 50522, f. 362.

Monk's House, *co. Suss.; home of Leonard and Virginia Woolf.* Photograph of, 1940. 50522, f. 318v.

Monnier (Auguste Jacques), *French playwright and translator.* Letters to G. B. Shaw, 1902, 1903. *Fr.* 50514, ff. 70, 93.

Monot (*Mlle.* —), *of Belle Ile, Brittany.* Letter to G. B. Shaw, 1946. *Fr.* 50526 A, f. 31.

'**Morning Post, The**'. Letter of G. B. Shaw to the Editor, 1911. *Copy.* 50564, f. 107.

Morozov (*Professor* Mikhail Mikhailovich), *of Moscow University.* Letter to G. B. Shaw, 1944. *Signed.* 50524, f. 176.

Morrell *née* **Cavendish-Bentinck** (Ottoline Violet Anne), *half-sister of William, 6th Duke of Portland.* Portrait photograph of R. S. Bridges, taken by Ottoline Morrell, engraved by Sir E. Walker, 1924. 50529, f. 136.

Morris (F. J.), *of West Roxburg, Massachusetts.* Postcard to G. B. Shaw of F. J. Morris, A. Koltoff, S. E. Richard and E. G. Holst, 1946. 50526 B, f. 325.

Morris (G. T. H.), *senior administrative assistant at the Home Office.* Letter to E. Brady, 1946. *Signed.* 50525, f. 133.

Morris (Gwladys Evan), *actress.* Letter to G. B. Shaw, 1944. 50524, f. 246.

Morris (Margaret), *of Glasgow; founder of School of Dancing.* Letter to G. B. Shaw, 1944. 50524, f. 261.

Morris (Mary *al.* May), *daughter of William Morris.* Correspondence, etc., with G. B. Shaw, 1885-1936. 45346, f. 13; 45347, f. 82; 45348, ff. 45, 84; 50541, ff. 31-99; 50665, ff. 268-286 *passim.*

— Portrait photograph of, 1889. 50584, f. 141.

— Marginal notes on G. B. Shaw's 'Morris as I Knew Him', 1936. 50665, ff. 268-286 *passim.*

Morris (Richard), *M.P.* Letter to G. B. Shaw, 1925. 50519, f. 243.

— 'British Municipalities and Mutual Insurance', 1925. *Typewritten* and *signed.* 50519, ff. 244-253.

Morris (William), *poet and artist.* Correspondence with G. B. Shaw of and concerning W. Morris, 1884-1934. Partly *printed.* 45345, f. 138v; 50541, ff. 1-30.

— Portrait photograph on New Year's greeting signed by J. K. Hardie, 1896. *Printed.* 50584, f. 142.

Morris (William), *of Knightsbridge.* Letter to G. B. Shaw, 1938. *Signed.* 50522, f. 93.

Morteo (Francsico y Luis), *of Buenos Aires.* Letter to G. B. Shaw, 1946. *Span.* 50526 A, f. 214.

Mortlake (Harold), *bookseller.* Letter to G. B. Shaw, 1941. *Signed.* 50538, f. 55.

Moscheles (*Mrs.* A.), *widow of Felix Moscheles.* Letter to G. B. Shaw, 1918. 50518, f. 97.

Moscheles (Felix), *artist; son of I. Moscheles.* Letter to G. B. Shaw, 1889. 50512, f. 134.

Mosharrafa (M. M.), *Egyptian writer.* Letter to G. B. Shaw, n.d. 50527, f. 159.

Mosley (*Sir* Oswald Ernald), *6th Bart.; fascist politician.* Letters to G. B. Shaw, 1934, 1946. Partly *signed.* 50520, f. 228; 50525, f. 398.

Mosscrop (Elspeth C.), *fixtures secretary of Youth House, London.* Letter to G. B. Shaw, 1946. 50526 A, f. 89.

Motler (L. A.), *of Johannesburg.* Letter to, of Sir I. J. Pitman, 1958. *Copy.* 79493, f. 60.

Mouillot (*Miss M.*), *secretary of the Amateur Players' Association.* Letter to, from G. B. Shaw, 1906. *Draft.* 50527, f. 160.

Mowbray (Tom), [*actor?*]. Photograph of G. E. Bancroft, T. Mowbray and G. S. Wray, 1926? 50584, f. 7.

Moxon (Thomas Bouchier), *banker, of Manchester.* Correspondence with C. Rowley, 1906. Partly *signed* and *copy.* 50514, ff. 377-378.

Moye (*Mrs.* Pattie), *of the Dialectical Society.* Letters to G. B. Shaw, 1881. 50509, ff. 62, 101.

Moykopf (Charles) **Ltd.,** *shoemakers, of Burlington Arcade.* Letter concerning bombardment, 1940. *Printed.* 63198 B, f. 209.

Moylan (Thomas King), *secretary of the Irish Playwrights' Association.* Letter to G. B. Shaw, 1918. *Signed.* 50518, f. 145.

Mrozewski (Stefan), *engraver.* Woodcut, 'Bernard Shaw', 1935. *Printed.* 56098, f. 36.

Mudie-Smith (Richard).
v. Smith.

Muir (W. L.), *inventor.* Letter to G. B. Shaw, 1907. 50515, f. 28.

Muirhead (James Fullarton), *travel writer.* Correspondence with G. B. Shaw, 1915. Partly *draft.* 50517, ff. 236, 238, 247.

Muirhead (R. E.), *secretary of the Scottish Home Rule Association.* Letter to G. B. Shaw, 1920. *Signed.* 50518, f. 245.

Mulgan (Alan E.), *author.* 'Maori and Pakeha' by A. W. Shrimpton and A. E. Mulgan, 1934? *Typewritten extract.* 63186, ff. 79-81.

Muller (Frederick), *publisher.* Letter to G. B. Shaw, 1949. *Signed.* 63186, f. 218.

Muller (J. J.), *artist, of New York.* Letter, etc., to G. B. Shaw, 1938. 50522, f. 126.

— Self-portrait, *circa* 1938. 50522, f. 128.

Müller (R. O.), *of Zurich.* Letter to G. B. Shaw, 1946. *Signed. Germ.* 50525, f. 112.

Mullett (E. J.), *acting Sec., the Society of Authors.* Letter to C. F. Shaw, 1931? *Signed. Fragm.* 50520, f. 140.

Mumford (Kit), *wife of T. Mumford.* Postcard to G. B. Shaw from T. and K. Mumford, 1946. 50525, f. 74.

Mumford (Tom), *labourer, of Fulham.* Postcard to G. B. Shaw from T. and K. Mumford, 1946. 50525, f. 74.

Municipal Council of Mölln, Germany. Letter to G. B. Shaw, 1950. *Signed.* 50526 B, f. 492.

Municipal Mutual Insurance Company. 'British Municipalities and Mutual Insurance' by R. Morris, 1925. *Typewritten* and *signed.* 50519, ff. 244-253.

Munro (John James), *literary scholar.* Letter to G. B. Shaw, 1910. *Signed.* 50515, f. 396.

Munsell (Warren P.), *business manager, the Theatre Guild, Inc., New York.* Letter to G. B. Shaw, 1941. *Signed.* 50522, f. 388.

Munson (J. John), *of New York.* Postcard and letter to G. B. Shaw, 1935, 1936. 50521, ff. 36, 149.

Munthe (*Dr.* Axel Martin Fredrik), *author.* Medical prescriptions for C. F. Payne-Townshend made out by A. M. F. Munthe, 1894. 56490, ff. 105-108.

— Letters, etc., to C. F. Payne-Townshend, 1894. 56490, ff. 110-134.

Muray (Nickolas), *photographer, of New York.* Portrait photograph of G. B. Shaw, 1926. 50582, f. 143.

Murchison (Hector), *photographer.* Portrait photograph of G. B. Shaw, 1900? 50582, f. 42.

Murdoch (James Barclay), *of the Hunterian Club, Glasgow.* Correspondence with G. B. Shaw, 1885. Partly *shorthand draft.* 50511, ff. 21, 54, 61, 105, 108-111v, 138.

Murphy (F.), *engineer, of Wigan.* Letter to G. B. Shaw, 1944. 50524, f. 2.

Murray *afterw.* **Forman** (Alma).
v. Forman *née* Murray.

Murray (George Gilbert Aimé), *O.M.; classical scholar.* Letters to G. B. Shaw, 1900-1950. Mainly *typewritten.* 50542, ff. 1-88v; 63186, ff. 139, 140.

— Letter to C. F. Shaw, 1912. 56491, f. 98.

— Letter to, of T. B. Sanders, 1941. *Signed.* 50542, f. 62.

— Letter, with G. B. Shaw, on bombardment of cities, 1941. *Typewritten drafts.* 50698, ff. 169-174.

Murray (Kathleen), *of Cape Province.* Letter and card to C. F. Shaw, 1932. 56493, ff. 6, 32.

Murray (Margaret Alice), *archaeologist.* Letter to G. B. Shaw, 1924. 50519, f. 189.

Murray *formerly* **Howard** (*Lady* Mary Henrietta).
v. Howard *afterw.* Murray.

Murry (John Middleton), *literary critic.* Letter to G. B. Shaw, 1944. 50524, f. 110.

Murty (James John), *priest of St. Wilfreds, Blyth.* Letter to G. B. Shaw, 1946. 50525, f. 272.

Musical Association. Notice of meeting, 1910. *Printed.* 50701, f. 217.

Mussolini (Benito), *Italian dictator.* Correspondence of G. B. Shaw concerning Italian fascism, published in 'International Information', 1927. *Duplicated.* 50697, ff. 237*-245.

— Correspondence, etc., rel. to his representation in 'Geneva', 1938, 1939. 50643, ff. 194-199; 67148 H; *L.C.P. Corr.* 1938/1624; 1938/1857.

Musters *née* **Gillmore** (Georgina called Judy), *cousin of G. B. Shaw.* Letter to G. Musters of W. C. Heaton, 1908. 50515, f. 175.

— Letter to C. F. Shaw, 1940. 56494, f. 86.

— Letters to G. B. Shaw, 1941-1946. Partly *signed.* 50522, f. 377; 50524, f. 169; 50525, ff. 120, 356; 50526 A, f. 9.

— Letters to S. C. Cockerell, rel. to G. B. Shaw, 1960-1961. 52741, ff. 111-162.

Muyden (Arnold Fidor van), *of Barcelona.* Letter to G. B. Shaw, 1946. 50525, f. 340.

— Account of her friendship with G. B. Shaw, 1930? *Typewritten copy.* 50532, f. 310.

Newington Reform Club. Programmes of lectures, 1890, 1891. *Printed.* 50701, ff. 89, 116.

Newman (Douglas), *secretary, The Barradas League.* Letter to G. B. Shaw, 1939. *Signed.* 50522, f. 239.

Newman and Company, *publishers, of London.* Letter, etc., to G. B. Shaw, 1880. 50508, ff. 278, 280v.

New Shakespeare Society. Lecture on 'Troilus and Cressida' to New Shakespeare Society by G. B. Shaw, read by G. Latham, 1884. *Draft.* 50702, ff. 41-124v.

Newson (*Cpl.* Gerald E.), *R.A.F.* Letter to G. B. Shaw, 1941. *Signed.* 50522, f. 359.

Newton (Beatrice), *of Claremont, Cape Province.* Letter to C. F. Shaw, 1932. 56493, f. 44.

Newton (Edward), *of the Musical Association.* Letter to G. B. Shaw, 1882. 50509, f. 168.

Newton (Janet Foster), *editor of 'Child Life', Boston, Massachussetts.* Letter to G. B. Shaw, 1946. *Signed.* 50526 A, f. 84.

Nichols (C[laude?] A[ndrew?]), *associate editor, 'Biographical Encyclopedia of the World'.* Letter, etc., to G. B. Shaw, 1944. *Signed.* Partly *printed.* 50524, f. 13.

Nicol (Alexander M.), *Commissioner of the Salvation Army.* Letter to G. B. Shaw, 1906. *Dictated.* 50514, f. 318.

Nietzsche (Friedrich Wilhelm), *philosopher.* Correspondence on

topics related to the writings of Nietzsche, 1900? Partly *duplicated.* 50742, ff. 15-30.

Nieuwenhuis (Ferdinand Domela), *Dutch socialist.* Postcard to G. B. Shaw, 1896. 50513, f. 112.

Nikolaiev-Shevirev (A. D.), *of Petrograd.* Letter to G. B. Shaw, 1924. *Russ.* with *Engl. transl.* 50519, f. 80.

Nivoix (Paul), *French playwright.* Circular letter, on behalf of Comité du Défense du Théâtre, 1946. *Duplicated* signature. 50525, f. 106.

Noble (*Sir* Andrew Napier), *2nd Bart.* Correspondence with the Lord Chamberlain's Office, 1939. *Signed.* *L.C.P. Corr.* 1938/1857.

Noble (Charles James), *dentist.* Letter to G. B. Shaw, 1883. 50510, f. 146.

Noble *formerly* **Breguzzi** (*Mrs.* Diana), *of Camberwell.* Letter to G. B. Shaw, 1944. 50524, f. 164.

[Noble?] (Eileen), *in Knysna, Cape Province.* Letter to C. F. Shaw, 1932. 56493, f. 17.

Noble (George Alfred), *of the London Crematorium Co.* Letter, etc., to G. B. Shaw, 1924. 50519, f. 109.

Noble *afterw.* **Newman** (Vera), *housekeeper to C. F. Shaw.* Letters and notes of Charlotte Shaw to, 1930-1934. 74222 A.

Noel (Conrad le Despenser Roden), *Vicar of Thaxted; writer.* Letters, etc., to G. B. Shaw, 1941. *Signed.* 50522, ff. 320-322, 343-344.

— Letter, etc., to B. Patch, 1941. *Signed.* 50522, ff. 343-344.

Owen (Robert), *socialist and philanthropist.* Photograph of Robert Owen's Labour Note of 1833, n.d. 50527, f. 205v.

Owens (J. R. Penly), *of Newark, New Jersey.* Letter of G. B. Shaw to, 1908. *Signed.* 50515, f. 136.

Oxford, *Bishop of.*
v. Gore (Charles).

Oxford. *University of. Magdalen College.* Letters, etc., rel. to visit of G. B. Shaw, 1892. 50512, ff. 269-274v.

Oxford (Arnold Whitaker), *vicar of St. Philip, Regent Street.* Letter to G. B. Shaw, 1903. 50514, f. 127.

Oxford and Asquith, *Earl and Countess of.*
v. Asquith

Oxford Communist Club. Notes for address of G. B. Shaw to Oxford Communist Club, 1932. 50704, ff. 243-248v.

Oxford Reform Club. Notice of lecture, 1892. *Printed.* 50701, f. 118.

Oxley (Michael), *pupil of Hereford Cathedral School.* Letter, etc., to G. B. Shaw, 1942. 50522, f. 465.

P

Pabst (Charles F.), *M.D., of New York.* Letter to G. B. Shaw, 1943. *Signed.* 50523, f. 100.

Pack (Charles Lloyd), *actor.* Letter to G. B. Shaw, 1943. 50523, f. 45.

Paddington Radical Club. Programme of Fabian lectures, 1890. *Printed.* 50701, f. 88.

Pagan (Isabelle Mary), *teacher and adapter for the stage.* Letter to G. B. Shaw concerning production of 'Peer Gynt', 1912. 50516, f. 119.

— 'The Seven Ages of Man', *circa* 1914. 56491, ff. 164-166.

— Horoscope for C. F. Shaw, *circa* 1914. Partly *printed.* 56491, ff. 168, 170-177.

— Horoscope for G. B. Shaw, *circa* 1914. 56491, f. 169.

— Letters, etc., to C. F. Shaw, 1914, 1929. 56491, ff. 162-177; 56492, ff. 130-135v.

Page Arnot (Robin), *secretary to the Fabian Research Department.* Circular letter, 1915. *Typewritten.* 50681, f. 123.

Paget (Henrietta), *sister of Florence Farr.* Letter to G. B. Shaw, 1917? 50533, f. 114.

Paget (*Sir* James), *1st Bart.; surgeon.* Letter to, of J. K. Barton, 1880. 50508, f. 258.

Paget (Violet), *called 'Vernon Lee'; author.* Letter to G. B. Shaw, 1920. 50518, f. 225.

Pagliardini (Tito), *music teacher.* Letter to G. B. Shaw, 1890. 50512, f. 223.

Painlevé (Jean). Notes concerning H. L. G. C. Bernstein, sent by, 1925? *Typewritten copy. Fr.* 50740, f. 176.

Pallen (Conde B.), *of New York.* Correspondence with G. B. Shaw, 1919. *Printed.* 50696, f. 254.

Palmer (Edwin Paget), *editor of 'The Dramatic Review'.* Correspondence with G. B. Shaw, 1885. Partly *shorthand draft.* 50511, ff. 27, 33v, 40v.

Palmer (Frank), *manager of the New Age Press*. Letter, etc., to E. J. Read, 1909. *Signed* and partly *printed*. 50515, f. 203.

Palmer (Herbert Edward), *poet*. Letter, enclosing 'The Birth of the Irish Race', to G. B. Shaw, 1924. Partly *copy*. 50519, ff. 155-165.

Palmer (John Leslie), *writer; League of Nations official*. Letters to G. B. Shaw, *circa* 1910-1941. 50516, f. 353; 50519, f. 323; 50522, ff. 76, 424; 50527, ff. 177, 178v.

— Correspondence with G. Kingston, 1913. *Copies*. 50539, ff. 56, 57.

Palmer (Lilli), *actress*. Photographs of Cedric Harwicke and Lilli Palmer in 'Caesar and Cleopatra', 1950. 50588, ff. 40-48.

Palmstierna (*Baron* Erik Kule), *Swedish diplomatist*. Correspondence with G. B. Shaw, 1927, n.d. *Signed* and *draft*. 50519, ff. 290-292.

Pankhurst (Christabel Harriette), *D.B.E.; suffragette*. Letter, etc., to G. B. Shaw, 1910. *Signed*. 50515, f. 317.

Pankhurst (Estelle Sylvia), *suffragette and author*. Letter to C. F. Shaw, 1914-1918. 56494, f. 200.

— Letters to G. B. Shaw, 1935, n.d. *Signed*. 50521, f. 58; 50527, f. 180.

Papini (Giovanni), *Italian author*. Letter to G. B. Shaw, 1947. 50526 B, f. 398.

Parke (Ernest), *proprietor, 'North London Press'*. Letter of G. B. Shaw on behalf of, 1889?, 1890? *Draft*. 50693, ff. 223-227.

— Letters to G. B. Shaw, 1889, 1901. 50512, f. 195v; 50514, f. 11.

Parker (John), *M.P.; General Secretary of the Fabian Society*. Letters, etc., to G. B. Shaw, 1939, 1940. *Signed*. 50557, ff. 297, 301.

Parker (Lindsay E.), *of the Guards Club*. Letter to G. B. Shaw, 1935. 50521, f. 46.

Parker (Louis Napoleon), *author and composer*. Letter from G. B. Shaw to, 1932. 59892, f. 134.

Parker (Owen R. G.), *of Johannesburg, South Africa*. Letter to G. B. Shaw, 1946. *Signed*. 50525, f. 39.

Parker (Stanley), *artist*. Drawing of G. B. Shaw and Frances Day, 1946?-1949? *Printed*. 50563, f. 35.

Park Lane Musical Society. Correspondence etc., with G. B. Shaw, 1883, 1884. Partly *printed*. 50510, ff. 25, 79v, 97, 143, 187.

Parks *née* **Robins** (Elizabeth).
v. Robins.

Parnis (Alexander E. L.), *assistant principal at the Treasury*. Letters, etc., to C. F. Shaw, 1940-1941. Partly *printed*. 56494, ff. 89-99v, 115; 63197, f. 90.

—Letter to (?) from C. F. Shaw, 1941? *Imperf. draft*. 63197, f. 91.

Parris (—), [*associate of William Morris*?]. Letter to G. B. Shaw of J. Tochatti concerning — Parris, 1907. 50515, f. 27.

Parsons (Henry), *of the Subscriptions Dept. of the 'Daily Worker'*. Letter to C. F. Shaw, 1940. *Dictated*. 56494, f. 71.

Parsons *formerly* **Tree** (Viola).
v. Tree *afterw.* Parsons.

Correspondence with G. B. Shaw, 1909, 1915. Partly *copy* and *draft*. 50515, f. 236; 50517, ff. 277, 292-297, 310, 316, 324.

Pawsey (Clarice N.), *of Amwell Place farm, co. Herts*. Letter to G. B. Shaw, 1946. 50526 A, f. 86.

Pawsey (Thomas), *author, of Frinton, co. Essex*. Letter to G. B. Shaw, 1939. 50522, f. 229.

Payne (Ben Iden), *actor-manager*. Letter of G. B. Shaw to, 1909. *Typewritten copy. L.C.P. Corr.* 1916/91.

Payne *née* **Limerick** (Mona), *actress*. Letters to G. B. Shaw, 1909? 50512, f. 201; 50515, f. 299.

Payne-Townsend, *family*. Correspondence and miscellaneous papers rel. to the family and estates of C. F. Shaw, 1822-1936, n.d. 56525, 56526; 63198 A; 63199, ff. 1-3, 18-38v.

— Household inventories of the family of C. F. Shaw, 1865-1901. Partly *typewritten*. 63198 A, ff. 23-146 *passim*.

Payne-Townshend.
   v. Payne-Townsend, *family*.

Payne-Townshend *afterw.* **Shaw** (Charlotte Frances).
   v. Shaw *née* Payne-Townshend.

Payne-Townshend *afterw.* **Cholmondeley** (Mary Stewart *al.* 'Sissy').
   v. Cholmondeley.

Pchellas (V. A.), *M.D., of Buffalo, New York*. Letter to G. B. Shaw, 1946. 50526 B, f. 296.

Peacock (N.), *researcher*. Letter, etc., to C. F. Shaw, 1935. 56493, f. 147.

Pearce (*Mrs*. Phyllis M. C.). Owned, 1920-1960, 50483, ff. 78-91.

Peard (Bertha Selina), *of Sydney, New South Wales*. Letter to G. B. Shaw, 1947. 50526 B, f. 375.

Pearsall (Fanny B.), *widow of William Booth Pearsall*. Letter to G. B. Shaw, 1931. 50520, f. 108.

Pearson (Edward Hesketh Gibbons), *actor and biographer*. Photographs of the Hamer-Pearson 'Candida' Company, 1908. 50588, ff. 49-52.

— Correspondence with G. B. Shaw, 1918-1948. *Signed;* partly *fragm.* and *typewritten copy*. 50547, ff. 1-13; 50562, f. 192; 56632, f. 56; 63186, f. 174.

Pearson (Florence Eleanora F.), *of Belle, Missouri*. Letter to G. B. Shaw, 1946. 50526 B, f. 320.

Pearson (*Dr*. John Oliver), *of Ealing*. Letter to G. B. Shaw, 1945. 50524, f. 347.

Pearson (Karl), *F.R.S.* Letters to G. B. Shaw, 1893-1921. 50513, ff. 22, 196; 50514, ff. 33, 163; 50518, f. 265.

— Pencil drawing by Miss F. A. de Biden Footner of, 1927?-1933? *Photogr.* 50520, f. 210.

Pearson (Lorene), *in Caracas, Venezuela*. Letter to G. B. Shaw, 1944. *Signed*. 50555, f. 125.

Pearson (Norman), *young communist, of Stanley, co. Durh*. Letter to G. B. Shaw, 1946. 50526 B, f. 350.

Pearson (R. Meynell), *dentist and author*. Letter to G. B. Shaw, 1929. 50519, f. 385.

Pease (Edward Reynolds), *Sec., Fabian Society*. Correspondence with G. B. Shaw, 1886-1940. Mainly *copies*. 50557, ff. 9-262 *passim*; 50680, f. 238; 59784; 63186, f. 164.

— Circular letters to members of the Fabian Society, 1890-1913. *Typewritten draft* and *printed* proof. 50557, ff. 214, 218; 50680, ff. 4, 13; 50681, ff. 168, 170.

—Note on the Fabian Society and Imperial and Foreign Affairs, *circa* 1899. *Typewritten*. 50680, f. 203.

—Letter to H. Jackson, 1906. *Circular*. 62992, f. 2.

—Letters to, from the editor of 'The Liberal', 1910. Partly *signed*. 50515, ff. 313-315.

— Letter to C. F. Shaw, 1912. 56491, f. 83.

Pease *formerly* **Davidson** (Marjory). *v.* Davidson *afterw.* Pease.

Peckham and Dulwich Radical Club. Programme of lectures, 1887. *Printed*. 50701, f. 17.

Peddie (Robert Alexander), *bibliographer*. Proposed amendments to Report on Fabian Policy, 1896. *Printed* proof with *MS.* corrections. 50680, ff. 147-147v.

— Letters to G. B. Shaw, 1909, 1911. 50515, ff. 242, 243v; 50516, ff. 62v, 64.

Peel (Albert), *editor of 'The Congregational Quarterly'*. Letter to G. B. Shaw, 1939. *Signed*. 50522, f. 193.

Peel (*Sir* William), *K.B.E.; K.C.M.G.; Governor of Hong Kong*. Invitation to G. B. and C. F. Shaw, 1933. Partly *printed*. 56493, f. 59.

Peel (William Robert Wellesley), *2nd Viscount Peel*. Letter to, of Sir M. Bone, copied to G. B. Shaw, 1925. *Copy*. 50519, f. 264.

Pelosio (Anselmo A.), *of Buenos Aires*. Letter to G. B. Shaw, 1946. *Signed. Span*. 50525, f. 275.

Penfield (Mary), *American journalist*. Letter to G. B. Shaw, 1898. 50513, f. 180.

People's Front Propaganda Committee. Statement, 1936. *Copy*. 50521, ff. 214-216.

People's Theatre, *Newcastle-upon-Tyne*. Broadcast speech by G. B. Shaw rel. to, 1939. *Draft*. 50698, ff. 101-103.

'Percy (Edward)', *pseudonym*. *v.* Smith.

Percy (Harry W.), *of 'One and All'*. Letters to G. B. Shaw, 1879. 50508, ff. 166, 167.

Percy (Saville Esmé), *actor*. Letter, etc., to G. B. Shaw, *circa* 1912. 50527, f. 184.

— Lecture on G. B. Shaw, *circa* 1912. *Draft*. 50527, ff. 185-194.

— Photograph of Esmé Percy, 1926? *Newsprint*. 50585, f. 14.

— Letter to Dr. F. E. Loewenstein, 1948. 50565, f. 192.

Performing Animals Defence League. Notice of public meeting, 1921. *Printed*. 50701, f. 248.

Peri (Peter), *of Camden Town*. Entry in alphabet design competion, 1958. 79494 B, ff. 7-9.

Perinbanayagam (S. H.), *of Manipay, Ceylon*. Letter to G. B. Shaw, 1948. *Signed*. 50533, f. 115.

Phipson (Emma), *author*. Letters, etc., to G. B. Shaw, 1882. Partly *printed*. 50509, ff. 109, 229, 239.

Phonetics. Letters and papers rel. to phonetics and spelling reform, *circa* 1852-1969. Partly *duplicated, printed,* and *copy*. Partly *Germ*. Partly in phonetic scripts. 50554-50556; 50679, ff. 325-374; 54576 A, f. 145; 71615; 79492-79494 B.

— Correspondence and papers of Sir R. F. Harrod concerning the will of G. B. Shaw, 1955-1957. Partly *signed, printed* and *copy*. 71615.

Photographs. Photograph of Barry Sullivan, 1860? 50585, f. 55.

— Portraits of G. B. Shaw's family, 1860s?-1937? 50583; 50587.

— Group photograph taken at Dalkey, co. Dublin by R. Pigott, *circa* 1865. Two *copies*. 50583, ff. 6, 7; 50587, f. 10.

— Photograph of B. H. Hodgson, 1870? *Signed*. 50584, f. 73.

— Photograph of Mary McNulty, 1875. 50584, f. 129.

— Portrait photograph of Agnes Shaw, 1875? 50587, f. 21.

— Photograph of Hans Richter, 1876. 50525, f. 154v.

— Portrait photographs of G. B. Shaw, 1878?-1950, n.d. Partly *printed*. 50582; 50587, ff. 13, 16, 26-28.

— Photograph of Ada Cavendish, 1879. 50584, f. 24.

— Photographs of Sir Henry Irving, 1879, n.d. 50584, ff. 86, 87.

— Portrait of Ellen Terry as Portia, with notes of her performances on the verso, annotated by G. B. Shaw, 1880. *Printed* signature. 50585, ff. 57-57v.

— Portrait photograph of W. Archer, *circa* 1880-1890. 50584, f. 1.

— Portrait photograph of Jane Lockett, 1881. 50584, f. 120.

— Photograph of Mrs. J. Patterson, 1887. 50585, f. 11; 50587, f. 22.

— Portrait photograph of May Morris, 1889. 50584, f. 141.

— Photograph of Alice and Vera McNulty, 1890? 50584, f. 127.

— Photograph of M. S. Cholmondeley and 'Jack Straw', 1890?-1900? 56524 B, f. 132.

— Photographs of Vera McNulty, 1890?, 1907? 50584, ff. 127, 131.

— Carte-de-visite photograph of Lady Colin Campbell, 1891. 50584, f. 23.

— Photograph of tomb of F. Lassalle by F. Krapp, 1893? 50586, f. 91.

— Photographs of H. Ibsen, 1895, n.d. 50584, ff. 77-85.

— Photographs of Frederick Evans, 1895?, 1915. 50584, ff. 50, 51.

— Portrait photographs of E. F. Fay, S. M. Kravchinsky, T. Macguire, Carrie Martyn and W. Morris on New Year's greeting signed by J. K. Hardie, 1896. *Printed*. 50584, f. 142.

— Photograph of Lucy Carr and Reginald Roberts in 'Shamus O'Brien' by R. L. Dobbie, 1897. 50583, f. 14.

— Photographs of Lucy Shaw, 1897-1937? 50583, ff. 12-14; 50587, f. 20.

— Photographs of Sidney and Beatrice Webb, 1897?, 1942. 50585, ff. 73-81.

— Photographs of C. F. Shaw, 1898-1899. 50587, ff. 15, 29.

— Photograph of Arnold Dolmetsch, 1899. 50584, f. 46.

Photographs (*continued*).

— Portrait photograph, *signed,* of A. M. Janiewski, by T. Sebald of Cracow, 1900. 50584, f. 88.

— Photograph of Rev. and Mrs. J. O. Hannay, 1900? 50584, f. 11.

— Photograph of Lady Gregory, 1900? 50585, f. 56.

— Portrait photograph of Ellen Terry, 1900? 50585, f. 60.

— Photographs of Col. W. Loch, 1900?-1910? 50585, ff. 38, 39.

— Photographs of Maharao Umaid Singh, 1900?-1910? 50585, ff. 38, 39.

— Photograph of Raj Bijey Singh, 1900?-1910? 50585, f. 39.

— Portrait photograph of Jean-Louis Janvier, 1902. *Inscribed.* 50584, f. 98.

— Photographs of H. G. Wells, his son and grandson, 1902, 1946. 50585, ff. 83, 84.

— Portrait photograph of Count L. N. Tolstoi, 1903? 50531, f. 62.

— Photographs of Agnes Sorma, 1904? 50585, ff. 41-46.

— Portrait photograph of G. B. Shaw, 1905. *Inscribed* 'Ole Shaw'. 45296, f. 158.

— Photographic self-portraits by G. B. Shaw, 1905, n.d. 50582, ff. 7, 25.

— Portrait of A. Henderson by E. O. Hoppé, 1905? *Signed* by E. O. Hoppé. 50584, f. 66.

— Photograph of Nancy Price, 1905? *Signed.* 50585, f. 22.

— Photograph of August Strindberg, 1905? 50585, f. 54.

— Photographs of 'Lion' Phillimore taken by G. B. Shaw, 1905?-1915. 50585, ff. 15-21.

— Photographs of Mrs. George Standring and son, 1907. 50585, ff. 50, 51.

— Photograph of H. Vallentin, 1907. *Signed.* 50585, f. 62.

— Photograph of S. L. Clemens, Archibald Henderson and Mitchell Kennerley, 1907. 50584, f. 65.

— Photograph of 'Harrison Hill', 1907? *Signed.* 50584, f. 69.

— Photograph of the home of S. L. Clemens *al.* 'Mark Twain', 1908. 50515, f. 199.

— Portrait photograph of H. Fisher, 1908. 50584, f. 52.

— Photograph of Rev. and Mrs. Ensor Walters and others, 1908. 50585, f. 70.

— Photographs of the Hamer-Pearson 'Candida' Company, 1908. 50588, ff. 49-52.

— Photograph of Herbert Thomas, 1908? 50585, f. 59.

— Photograph of the actor E. Gwenn as G. B. Shaw, 1909. 50584, f. 59.

— Photographs of Anna Bahr-Mildenburg, 1909, 1910, n.d. 50516, f. 71v; 50584, ff. 4, 5.

— Photographs of S. Brett, 1909-1912. *Signed.* 50529, f. 92v; 50584, ff. 17, 18-20.

— Portrait postcard of H. Garland, 1910. 50515, f. 354v.

— Photographs of Hermann Bahr, 1910. 50584, ff. 3, 4.

— Photograph of Richard Strauss, 1910. 50585, f. 53.

Photographs (*continued*).

— Photograph of Mr. and Mrs. T. Konrad, 1910. 50585, f. 105.

— Photograph of — Keeling, 1910?, annotated by G. B. Shaw, 'killed in the Great War 1914-18'. 50584, f. 100.

— Photograph of Brynhild Olivier, 1910? 50585, f. 3.

— Photograph of Frederic Shields, 1910? 50585, f. 26.

— Portrait photograph of A. A. Needham, *circa* 1910. *Inscribed.* 50584, f. 145.

— Portrait photograph of A. H. Beagin, *circa* 1910-1920. *Signed.* 50584, f. 9.

— Letters, with photograph, of H. Garland to G. B. Shaw, 1910, 1921, n.d. 50515, ff. 352-354v; 50527, ff. 76-79; 63183, f. 28.

— Photographs of Charles Rowley, 1910?-1933. Partly *newsprint.* 50585, ff. 26, 28; 50741, f. 65.

— Photograph of C. W. Stetson, bef. 1911. 50516, f. 82v.

— Photograph of Mathilde H. Richter, 1911. 50516, f. 98v.

— Photograph of Fraülein Reuss, 1911. 50516, f. 98v.

— Photograph of Mlle. Van Dyck, 1911. 50516, f. 98v.

— Photograph of Siegfried Wagner, *circa* 1911. 50516, f. 71v.

— Photograph of Hans Richter, *circa* 1911. 50516, f. 100v.

— Description, with photograph, of Sir J. Epstein's sculpture of a lion, 1912. 50516, ff. 277-279v.

— Photograph of Japanese production of Ibsen's 'A Doll's House', *circa* 1912. 50548, f. 64v.

— Portrait photographs of Robert Loraine, 1912, 1915. Partly *inscribed.* 50584, ff. 124, 125.

— Portrait photographs of Gertrude Kingston, 1912?, 1929. *Inscribed.* 50584, ff. 102, 103.

— Portrait photographs of Sylvia Loeb, *circa* 1913-1920. 50516, f. 435; 50584, f. 122.

— Group portrait in cowboy costume of T. E. Scott-Ellis, W. Archer, Sir J. M. Barrie, G. K. Chesterton and G. B. Shaw, 1914. 50582, f. 39.

— Photographs of H. G. Granville-Barker, 1914, n.d. 50584, ff. 56-58.

— Photographs of Grace George in 'Major Barbara', 1915. 50589, ff. 41, 46, 49, 51-55.

— Portrait photograph of W. B. Yeats, by L. Connell, 1915? 50585, f. 93.

— Photograph of L. McCarthy and O. P. Heggie in 'Androcles and the Lion', 1915? 50588, f. 1.

— Photographs of New York production of 'The man who married a dumb wife', 1915? 50588, f. 3.

— Photographs of New York production of 'Captain Brassbound's Conversion', 1915? 50588, ff. 85-118.

— Photograph of W. A. Brady and son, 1915? 50588, f. 119.

— Photographs of C. M. Scott, *circa* 1916. 50527, ff. 266v, 267v.

— Wartime photographs of T. E. Lawrence, 1916?-1918? 50584, ff. 108-118.

— Photographs of T. D. O'Bolger and his daughter, *circa* 1916-1919. 50565, ff. 95-97.

Ratcliffe (Samuel Kerkham), *American writer*. Letters and postcard to G. B. Shaw, 1915-1944. Partly *signed*. 50517, f. 259; 50520, f. 255; 50524, f. 183; 50528, f. 82.

Rathbone (Alfred S.), *London agent for the Dunedin 'Star'*. Correspondence with G. B. Shaw, 1887. Partly *shorthand draft*. 50511, ff. 325-328.

Rathbone (Basil), *actor*. Letter to G. B. Shaw, 1945. 50524, f. 308.

Ratton (*Mrs.* K. Holroyd), *of Oxford*. Letter to G. B. Shaw, 1944. 50524, f. 49.

Raum (William), *insurance agent, of Chester, Pennsylvania*. Letter to G. B. Shaw, 1946. *Signed*. 50526 B, f. 328.

Raverat *née* Darwin (Gwendolen Mary), *wood-engraver*. Woodcut, 'Sheep', 1925. *Printed*. 50697, f. 221v.

Rawnsley (David), *of Production Facilities (Films) Ltd.* Letter, etc., to G. B. Shaw, 1946. *Signed*. 50526 A, f. 178.

Ray (Tridib Nath), *advocate, of Calcutta*. Letter to Constable and Company, publishers, 1939. *Signed*. 50522, f. 222.

Raybould (*Mrs.* H. E.), *of Birmingham*. Letter to G. B. Shaw, 1946. 50525, f. 198.

Rayner-Wood (Algernon Cockburn). *v.* Wood.

Rayz-Shaer (Adolf Edgar), *of Göttingen, Germany*. Letters and poems to G. B. Shaw, 1946. *Germ.* 50525, ff. 58, 164-170v.

Read (E. J.), *socialist, of Cardiff*. Letter, etc., to E. J. Read of F. Palmer, 1909. *Signed* and partly *printed*. 50515, f. 203.

Read (*Sir* Herbert Edward), *author and art critic*. Letter to G. B. Shaw, 1943. *Signed*. 63186, f. 181.

Reading Radical Club. Advertisement for open-air meeting, 1891. *Printed*. 50701, f. 108.

Reaney (Hamilton), *singer and composer*. Recital programme, etc., 1937? Partly *printed*. 50742, ff. 190-193.

'Recreation in Ancoats'. Programmes of meetings, 1897-1905. *Printed*. 50701, ff. 172, 188, 199.

Redford (George Alexander), *Examiner of Plays*. Licensing reports on plays of G. B. Shaw, 1909, 1910. Partly *dictated*. L.C.P. Corr. 1909/80; L.C.P. Corr. 1910/223; L.C.P. Corr. 1916/91.

Redmond (John Edward), *M.P.* Letter to G. B. Shaw concerning United Irish League of Great Britain, 1901. 50514, f. 12.

Reed (Bonnie), *of Dallas, Texas*. Letter to G. B. Shaw, 1946. *Signed*. 50525, f. 29.

[Reed?] (E. M.). Postcard to A. M. Collet, 1919. 56492, f. 17.

Reed (Edward Charles), *author; manager of the Ruskin Institute, Cardiff*. Documents relating to action for debt against E. C. Reed brought by W. T. May, 1909. Mainly *printed*. 50515, ff. 204-207.

Rees (Hugh) Ltd., *booksellers*. Memorandum to G. B. Shaw, 1927. 63186, f. 43.

Ridgway (Alfred), [*screenwriter?*]. Letter to G. B. Shaw, 1943. 50523, f. 111.

Rieu (Emile Victor), *editor of the Penguin Classics.* Letter to G. B. Shaw, 1935. *Signed.* 50521, f. 4.

Right to Work National Council. Notice of demonstration, 1906. *Printed.* 50701, f. 208.

Rilke (Rainer Maria), *poet.* Letters to F. S. Fischer, 1906. *Typewritten copies.* Partly *Germ.* 50548, ff. 134, 135.

— Letters to his wife, 1906. *Imperf. copies. Engl. transl.* 50548, ff. 135, 136.

— Letter to Mrs. E. der Heydt, 1906. *Imperf. copy. Engl. transl.* 50548, f. 136.

Rinder (Michael), *of Richmond, co. Surr.* Letter to G. B. Shaw, 1946. 50525, f. 158.

Risdon (Elisabeth), *actress.* Portrait photographs from the Theatre Guild New York production of 'Heart-break House', taken by I. D. Schwarz, 1920. 50589, ff. 31-38.

Ritchie (W.), *of 'Picture Post'.* Letter to B. H. White Publications Ltd., 1947. *Signed.* 50565, f. 126.

Rivers (*Rev.* Charles). Letter of G. B. Shaw to, 1910. *Typewritten copy.* 50562, f. 65.

Rivers (Walter Courtenay), *M.R.C.S.* Letter to G. B. Shaw, 1902. 50514, f. 80.

Robbins (A. C.), *of Watford, co. Hertf.* Letter to G. B. Shaw, n.d. 50527, f. 206.

Robbins *afterw.* **Wells** (Amy Catherine).

v. Wells *née* Robbins.

Robbins (*Sir* Edmund), *Secretary of the Admiralty, War Office and Press Committee.* Notice to the Press concerning C. H. Norman, 1915. *Copy.* 50517, f. 304.

Roberts (Denys Kilham).

v. Kilham Roberts.

Roberts (*Sir* Frank Kenyon), *at the Foreign Office.* Letter of the Lord Chamberlain to, 1939. *Copy. L.C.P. Corr.* 1938/1857.

Roberts (George), *publisher.* Letter to G. B. Shaw, 1914. *Signed.* 50517, f. 192.

Roberts (*Sir* James Reginald Howard), *clerk of the London County Council.* Letter to J. P. Blake, 1949. *Signed.* 50526 B, f. 455.

Roberts (Lewis Euron), *vicar of Peasmarsh, co. Suss.* Letter to G. B. Shaw, 1946. 50525, f. 334.

Roberts (Morley), *novelist.* Letters to G. B. Shaw, 1903, n.d. 50514, ff. 160, 168; 50527, f. 208.

— Letter to C. F. Shaw, 1903. 56491, f. 38.

Roberts (Reginald), *actor.* Photograph with Lucy Carr in 'Shamus O'Brien' by R. L. Dobbie, 1897. 50583, f. 14.

Roberts (Richard Ellis), *writer.* Letters of G. B. Shaw to R. E. Roberts, 1900. *Typewritten copies.* 50561, ff. 136, 146.

Roberts (William), *R.A.* Portrait of Lord Lloyd, 1927? *Photographic copy.* 56499, f. 50.

— Chalk portrait of Sir R. R. Wingate, 1927? *Photographic copy.* 56499, f. 51.

Rodd (James Rennell), *1st Baron Rennell.* Letter, etc., to G. B. Shaw, 1938. Partly *printed.* 50522, f. 114.

— Letter to 'The Times', 1938. *Printed.* 50522, f. 115.

— Letters to B. Patch, 1938. 50522, ff. 116, 124.

Rodin (François Auguste René), *French sculptor.* Correspondence with C. F. Shaw, 1906-1907. Partly *signed* and *draft. Fr.* 50548, ff. 155-176.

— Bust of Shaw, photographed in 1906 and 1910. *Photogr.* 50582, ff. 30, 34.

— Correspondence with G. B. Shaw, 1906-1914. Partly *dictated, signed* and *draft. Fr.* 50548, ff. 137v-154.

Roe (Frederick H.), *speech therapist, of Derby.* Letter, with prospectus, to G. B. Shaw, 1914. Partly *printed.* 50517, ff. 133, 138-140.

Roeder (Ralph), *actor.* Portrait photographs from the Theatre Guild New York production of 'Heartbreak House', taken by I. D. Schwarz, 1920. 50589, ff. 31-38.

Rogers *née* **Gurly** (Charlotte), *aunt of G. B. Shaw.* Letters, etc., to G. B. Shaw, circa 1920-1933. 50518, f. 234; 50520, f. 217; 50527, f. 167.

Rogers (*Miss* Constance), *of Streatham Hill, London.* Letter to G. B. Shaw, 1943. 50523, f. 4.

Rogers (Douglas), *editor of 'Socialist Leader'.* Letter to G. B. Shaw, 1946. *Signed.* 50525, f. 138.

Rogers (Eames), *cousin of G. B. Shaw.* Letter to his mother, 1933. 50520, f. 218.

Rogers (John William), *journalist, of Dallas, Texas.* Letter to G. B. Shaw, 1938. *Signed.* 50522, f. 143.

Rogers (Kathleen Doreen), *nurse, of Stoke-on-Trent.* Letter to G. B. Shaw, 1946. 50525, f. 389.

Rokotov (T.), *editor of 'International Literature', Moscow.* Letters to G. B. Shaw, 1938, 1940. *Signed.* 50522, ff. 139, 271.

Rolfe (Ethelwyn), *retired school teacher.* Letter to G. B. Shaw, 1943. *Signed.* 50523, f. 162.

Rolland (Marie Romain), *wife of R. Rolland.* Letter to G. B. Shaw, 1949. *Signed.* 50548, f. 182.

Rolland (Romain), *French author.* Letters, etc., to G. B. Shaw, 1914-1919. Partly *typewritten.* 50518, f. 141; 50548, ff. 177-181.

— 'Déclaration de l'indépendance de l'Esprit', 1919. Mainly *typewritten draft; fragm. Fr.* 50518, f. 141.

Rolleston (Thomas William Hazen), *writer and poet.* Letter to G. B. Shaw, 1920. 63186, f. 29.

Romanovsky-Pavlovsky *née* **Lygon** (Mary).

v. Lygon *afterw.* Romanovsky-Pavlovsky.

Romary (Peggy), *of Glen Rock, New Jersey.* Letter to G. B. Shaw, *circa* 1937. 50527, f. 213.

Roos (Joseph), *of Haskell-Travers Inc., publishers.* Letter to B. Patch, 1934. *Signed.* 50520, f. 254.

Roosen (*Dr.* J.), *of Cologne.* Letter, etc., to G. B. Shaw, 1938. *Signed.* 50522, ff. 78-85.

Roosevelt (Theodore), *President of the U.S.A.* Correspondence between T. Roosevelt and R. L. Wolf, 1917. Partly *copies*. 50518, ff. 61-69v.

Roosevelt (*Brig.-Gen.* Theodore), *son of Theodore Roosevelt, President of the U.S.A.* Letter and card to G. B. Shaw, 1932, 1933, n.d. 50520, f. 143; 63728, f. 12.

— 'Report of the Governor-General of the Philippine Islands', 1933. Mainly *typewritten*. 50742, ff. 45-93.

Root (Benjamin Franklin), *D.D.; episcopal clergyman, of Canutillo, Texas*. Letter to G. B. Shaw, 1945. *Signed*. 50524, f. 346.

Rose (Edward), *dramatist*. Letters to G. B. Shaw, 1886-1903. 50511, f. 224; 50512, f. 131; 50514, f. 155.

Rose (Erle), *New Zealand author*. Letter to G. B. Shaw, 1938. 50522, f. 52.

Rosmini-Serbati (Antonio). Photograph of his tomb, 1926? 56499, f. 46.

Ross (Arthur Leonard), *Counselor at Law, of New York*. Letters to H. Harris, 1937. 50538, ff. 38, 40, 44.

— Letter to, of P. Covici, 1937. *Copy*. 50538, f. 40.

Ross (J. E.), *proprietor of Patent Fitall Steel Tongs Company*. Letter to G. B. Shaw, 1946. 50524, f. 161.

Ross (Robert Baldwin), *literary executor of Oscar Wilde*. Correspondence with G. B. Shaw, 1916. Partly *typewritten copy*. 50517, f. 431; 50562, f. 117.

Rossetti (William Michael), *author and art critic*. Letter to G. B. Shaw, 1887. 50511, f. 355.

Rostron (Thomas A.), *anti-vaccinationist, of Southport, co. Lanc.* Letter to G. B. Shaw, 1939. *Signed*. 50522, f. 233.

Roth (Charles F.), *of Pittsburgh, Pennsylvania*. Letter to G. B. Shaw, 1946. 50525, f. 11.

Roth (Edwin), *of London*. Letter to G. B. Shaw, 1946. *Signed*. 50526 B, f. 283.

Rothenstein (*Sir* William), *Principal, Royal College of Art*. Letters to C. F. Shaw, 1903. 56491, ff. 34, 36.

— Letters to G. B. Shaw, 1903-1943. 50514, ff. 153, 273; 50516, f. 325; 50519, f. 280; 50523, f. 72.

— Self-portrait, 1913. 50516, f. 325.

Rothschild (Lionel Walter), *2nd Baron Rothschild*. Invitation to G. B. Shaw, on behalf of Joint British Committee Ort-Oze, 1930. Mainly *printed*. 50520, f. 20.

Rothstein (Andrew), *London correspondent of T.A.S.S.* Letter to G. B. Shaw, 1943. *Signed*. 50523, f. 102.

Rothwell (J.), *of Bolton*. Letter, etc., to G. B. Shaw, 1934. 63728, f. 3.

Rothwell (John), *of the Malthusian League*. Correspondence with G. B. Shaw, 1882. Partly *shorthand draft*. 50509, ff. 235, 244, 251-255v.

Rouile (Louisa)
v. Huddart (E. L.).

Routledge (George) **and Sons Ltd.**
v. Sonnenschein (William Swan).

Rowley (Charles), *founder of the Ancoats Brotherhood*. Drawing, 'Love and Time', designed for Charles and Mary Rowley's golden wedding by F. J. Shields, 1877. *Printed*. 50585, f. 29v.

— Letter and postcard to G. B. Shaw, 1905, n.d. 50514, f. 274; 50527, f. 205.

— Correspondence with T. B. Moxon, 1906. Partly *signed* and *copy.* 50514, ff. 377-378.

— Photographs of, 1910?-1933. Partly *newsprint.* 50585, ff. 26, 28; 50741, f. 65.

— Testimonial on behalf of, 1911. *Copy.* 50516, f. 116.

— Letter to C. F. Shaw, 1912. 56491, f. 114.

— Invitation and list of guests at 'Rowley's Round Table', 1913. Mainly *printed.* 50711 A, f. 161.

— Letter to G. B. Shaw of A. Mellor concerning, 1935. 50521, f. 56.

Rowley (Jean D.), *widow of Charles Rowley.* Letters to G. B. Shaw concerning, 1935, 1937. Partly *signed* and *draft.* 50521, ff. 56, 250, 251; 50543, ff. 198, 199.

— Letter to G. B. Shaw, 1937. 50521, f. 260.

Royal (Dorothy), *free-lance journalist.* Letters, etc., to G. B. Shaw, 1943-1947. *Signed.* 50523, f. 41; 50524, f. 366; 50526 B, f. 392.

Royal Automobile Club. Notes and reports on motor tours by G. B. Shaw, 1909-1925. Partly *printed* and *typewritten copy.* 50678, ff. 169-230.

Royal Commission on the Arrest and Subsequent Treatment of F. S. Sheehy Skeffington, T. Dickson, and P. J. McIntyre. Report, 1916. *Printed.* 56491, ff. 217-222.

Royal Court Theatre, London. Prompt copies of Shaw productions, 1904-1907. 65156 Q-W.

Royal Dublin Society. Ephemera, 1928-1934. Mainly *printed.* 50711 A, ff. 225-229.

Royal Institute of British Architects. Invitation card to G. B. Shaw, 1898. Partly *printed.* 50513, f. 172.

Royal Opera House, Coventry. Programme of lectures, 1913. *Printed.* 50701, ff. 225-238.

Royal Society of Arts. Programme of Ibsen Centenary Lectures, 1928. *Printed.* 50701, f. 254.

Royds (George S.), *of Wellington House, Strand.* Letter to G. A. Keen, 1941. *Copy.* 50522, f. 367.

Ruggles-Brise (*Sir* Evelyn John), *K.C.B.; Prison Commissioner.* Letter to C. F. Payne-Townshend, 1884. 56490, f. 24.

Ruhr (*Dr.* H. W. von der), *of Berlin.* Letter to G. B. Shaw, 1938. *Signed. Germ.* 50522, f. 40.

Rumbold *née* **Fane** (Etheldred), *C.B.E.; wife of Sir Horace Rumbold, 9th Bart.* Letter to, of R. Cavendish-Bendinck, concerning G. B. and C. F. Shaw, 1951. 52752, f. 321.

Rumford *née* **Butt** (Clara Ellen Kennerley).
v. Butt *afterw.* Rumford.

Rummel (Walter Morse), *pianist and composer.* Letter to G. B. Shaw, 1946. *Signed.* 50526 A, f. 10.

Rumsey (John W.), *President, American Play Company, Inc.* Letter to G. Kingston, 1915. *Signed.* 50539, f. 84.

— Transcript of reception for Bernard Shaw in Trade Union House, Moscow, 1931. *Typewritten.* 50743 B, ff. 424-431.

— Letters to 'The Times' of G. B. Shaw concerning the Soviet Union, 1931. *Printed.* 52752, ff. 306, 313, 317.

v. also Shaw (G. B.).

WRITINGS, ETC., ON THE SOVIET UNION.

Rust (George), *writer of verse.* Letter to G. B. Shaw, 1940. *Signed.* 50522, f. 296.

Rust (William), *editor, the 'Daily Worker'.* Letter to G. B. Shaw, 1946. *Signed.* 50525, f. 85.

Ryan (Helen Louise), *in St. Pancras Hospital, London.* Letter and postcard to G. B. Shaw, n.d. 50527, ff. 215, 217.

Ryan (Maria), *amateur musician.* Group photograph taken at Dalkey, co. Dublin by R. Pigott, *circa* 1865. Two *copies.* 50583, ff. 6, 7; 50587, f. 10.

Rypins (Stanley), *American professor of English Literature.* Letter to G. B. Shaw, 1931. 50520, f. 111.

Ryswyk (John van). Postcard to G. B. Shaw, 1946. Mainly *printed.* 50526 B, f. 371.

S

S (S. D. de), *of Colombo, Ceylon.* Letter, etc., to G. B. Shaw, 1946. *Typewritten.* 50525, f. 23.

— Notes rel. to confusion, 1946. 50525, ff. 24-25.

Saarbach Company, *of Cologne.* Telegram concerning 'Peace Conference Hints' to Constable and Company, 1919. 50518, f. 143.

Sächsische Staatstheater. Photographs of the Sächsische Staatstheater production of 'Candida' taken by U. Richter, 1926. *Signed.* 50588, ff. 55-69.

Šafránek (Karel), *of Hradek Králové, Czechoslovakia.* Letter to G. B. Shaw, n.d. 50527, f. 218.

St. Davids, *Bishop of.*
v. Jones (William Basil Tickell).

'St. John (Christopher)', *pseudonym.*
v. Marshall (Christabel).

St. John Ambulance Association. Certificate awarded to C. F. Payne-Townshend, 1880. Partly *printed.* 56490, f. 4.

St. John Gogarty (Oliver). Invitation to G. B. Shaw, *signed* by W. B. Yeats, O. St. John Gogarty, S. W. Maddock and H. McLaughlin, 1924. Mainly *printed.* 50711 A, f. 128.

St. Pancras Ethical Society. Notice of meetings, 1903. *Printed.* 50701, f. 189.

St. Pancras Vestry. Correspondence and papers of G. B. Shaw rel. to, 1894-1901, n.d. Partly *printed* and *typewritten draft.* 50513, f. 183; 50514, f. 181; 50678, ff. 103-168; 50701, ff. 141, 143-146, 159, 163.

— Letter to G. B. Shaw concerning public lavatory provision, 1898. 50513, f. 183.

— Letter of G. B. Shaw to Sir T. P. Whittaker concerning school provision, 1904. *Copy.* 50514, f. 181.

246 INDEX

50516, f. 99; 50519, f. 55; 50557, ff. 81-237 *passim.*
— Notice of meeting in support of candidature of, 1906. *Printed.* 50701, f. 206.
— Letter to C. F. Shaw, 1912. 56491, f. 84.
Sandford ([W.?]), *of Cork.* Letter to C. F. Shaw, 1912. 56491, f. 111.
Sandhurst, *Viscount.*
  v. Mansfield (William).
Sandrey (Dennis), *director of the Anglo-Persian Institute.* Letter to G. B. Shaw, 1947. *Signed.* 50526 B, f. 386.
Sands (C. Rosemary), *of Cheltenham.* Letter to G. B. Shaw, 1949. *Signed.* 50526 B, f. 474.
Sands (Dorothy), *American actress.* Photographs of C. O. Skinner's production of 'Candida', 1939. 50588, ff. 81-83.
Sanford (Erskine), *actor.* Portrait photographs from the Theatre Guild New York production of 'Heartbreak House', taken by I. D. Schwarz, 1920. 50589, ff. 31-38.
Sansom (*Sir* George Bailey), *G.B.E., K.C.M.G.; diplomatist.* Letter to G. B. Shaw, 1933. 50520, f. 194.
Sansom (Katharine Gordon), *wife of Sir G. B. Sansom.* Letter to C. F. Shaw, 1933. 56493, f. 64.
Sarawak, *Ranee Muda of.*
  v. Brett *afterw.* Brooke (Sylvia).
'Sardonicus', *of New York.* Letter, etc., to G. B. Shaw, 1936. *Typewritten.* Partly *printed.* 50521, f. 150.
Sargent (Louis A.), *artist.* Letters to G. B. Shaw, 1906. 50514, ff. 337, 340.

Sarolea (Charles), *Professor of French, Edinburgh University.* Letters, etc., to G. B. Shaw, 1908-1913. Partly *signed* and *printed.* 50515, f. 130v; 50516, ff. 192, 255, 272, 295; 50527, f. 221.
Saroyan (William), *American novelist.* Letters to G. B. Shaw, 1942-1947. *Signed.* 50522, f. 441; 50524, f. 43; 50526 B, f. 383.
Saumarez (James St. Vincent), *4th Baron De Saumarez.* Correspondence with the Lord Chamberlain's Office, 1910. *L.C.P. Corr.* 1910/223.
Saunders (*Sir* Alexander Morris Carr-).
  v. Carr-Saunders.
Saunders (Fred W.), *of Steventon, co. Berks.* Letter to G. B. Shaw, 1941. 50522, f. 338.
Sawier (Charles G.), *designer and engraver, [of Dublin?].* Photograph of, with plaque for Shaw's birthplace, 1949. *Signed.* 50586, f. 51.
Saxon (E. F.), *Stage Manager, The Royal Court Theatre.* Prompt Book of 'Candida' annotated by, 1904-1905. Mainly *printed.* 65156 Q.
Scarborough (James), *of Downham Market, co. Norf.* 'New World-Alphabet' designed by J. Scarborough, *circa* 1945-1950. *Lino-cut print.* 50556, f. 225.
Scarizza (S.), *Italian engineer.* Letter to G. B. Shaw, 1929. 50519, f. 381.
Schanglies (Jackson W.). Letter to G. B. Shaw, *circa* 1946. 50527, f. 223.
Schappeller (Karl), *Austrian inventor.* Memorandum concerning, 1938? *Typewritten.* 50742, ff. 119-128.

— Photographs of, 1898-1899, n.d. 50582, f. 136; 50587, ff. 15, 29.

— Account of responses to 'Summary of Six Papers', 1899?-1913? 56524 A, ff. 64-69.

— Financial correspondence and papers of and concerning, 1900-1946. Mainly *typewritten* and *printed*. 63183, ff. 25, 26; 63197, ff. 45, 49; 63198 B-63202.

— Annotations to 'Man and Superman', 1905-1907? 65156 U.

— 'Rent and Value' adapted by, from 'Fabian Essays', 1909. *Printed*. 50690, ff. 227-232.

— 'La Femme Seule' by E. Brieux, translated by, *circa* 1913-1916. *Fragm., draft* and partly *shorthand*. 56523, ff. 1-88.

— Correspondence with Society of Authors of and concerning, 1913-1961. 56627, ff. 103, 104; 56633, ff. 98-221.

— Notes on Theosophy and Eastern religions, 1917-1937, n.d. 56508-56517; 63193 E; 63194 A-C; 63195 A-E; 63196, ff. 1-77.

— Correspondence, accounts etc., relating to 'Damaged Goods', 1917-1943. Partly *signed*. 56633, ff. 98-212 *passim*; 63197, ff. 97-103.

— Notes on proof copies of 'Seven Pillars of Wisdom', *circa* 1921. 56498.

— Correspondence with and papers rel. to T. E. Lawrence, *circa* 1921-1935. Partly *typewritten* and *copy*. 45903, 45904, 45922, 56496-56498, 56514, f. 30; 63203, ff. 1v, 2v, 3v.

— Notes rel. to writings of G. B. Shaw, 1931, n.d. 50662, ff. ii-vii;

56492, ff. 127, 142-143, 147, 158-159, 162, 171, 195-196, 215-218.

— Letter to T. Jones, 1931. *Copy*. 56633, f. 214.

— Correspondence, etc., with Incorporated Society of Authors, Playwrights & Composers regarding E. Brieux, 1933-1940. Partly *copy* and *signed*. 63197, ff. 15-33, 42, 58.

— Will of, 1935. Mainly *typewritten*. 63198 A, f. 152.

— Notes on G. B. Shaw's diet, *circa* 1935-1941. 56524 B, ff. 147-148, 155.

— Bequeathed, 45903, 45904.

— Letters from Janet Webb rel. to, 1960. 52752, ff. 300-301.

— List of correspondents, n.d. 63197, f. 95.

v. also

> Correspondence listed under names of individuals, societies and public bodies. Payne-Townsend, *family*.

Shaw (*Capt.* Donald), *editor, 'The Hornet'*. Correspondence with Capt. D. Shaw of G. J. V. Lee, 1877. 50508, ff. 48-107v *passim*..

Shaw (Edward Carr), *son of Edward Bernard Shaw of Tasmania*. Letter to G. B. Shaw, 1946. 50526 A, f. 216.

Shaw (Eleanor Hester), *widow of Frederick William Shaw, 5th Bart*. Letters to G. B. Shaw, 1945. 50524, ff. 354, 356.

Shaw (Elinor Agnes), *sister of G. B. Shaw*. Portrait photograph of Agnes Shaw, 1875? 50587, f. 21.

Shaw (Eliza), [*wife of James C. Shaw*?]. Letters to G. B. Shaw, 1882. 50509, ff. 205, 209, 278v.

Shaw (Ethel).

v. Shaw *afterw.* Davis *afterw.* Walters (Mary Ethel).

Shaw (Frederick C.), *cousin of G. B. Shaw.* Letters to G. B. Shaw, 1933, 1943. 50520, f. 221; 50523, f. 93.

Shaw (George Bernard), *author.*

Arranged as follows:

DRAMATIC WORKS.

DRAMATIC TRANSLATIONS, SKETCHES AND COLLABORATIONS.

NOVELS, POEMS AND SHORT STORIES.

WRITINGS ON ART, LITERATURE AND DRAMA.

WRITINGS ON MUSIC.

FABIAN WRITINGS AND PAPERS.

WRITINGS ON IRELAND.

WRITINGS, ETC., ON THE SOVIET UNION.

GENERAL POLITICAL AND ECONOMIC WRITINGS AND PAPERS.

AUTOBIOGRAPHICAL, BIOGRAPHICAL AND PERSONAL CORRESPONDENCE, NOTES AND PAPERS.

GENERAL CORRESPONDENCE AND MISCELLANEOUS PAPERS.

PHOTOGRAPHS, PORTRAITS, CARICA- TURES, ETC.

DRAMATIC WORKS

The Admirable Bashville:

— *Printed* proof with *autogr.* note, submitted to Lord Chamberlain, 1901. 65567 L.

— Stage Society *typewritten* prompt book with *autogr.* rehearsal notes, 1903. 50613.

Androcles and the Lion:

— *Printed* submission to Lord Chamberlain, 1913. 66026 I.

— Licensing reports, 1913. 66026 I; *L.C.P. Corr.* 1913/1827.

— Letter to 'Daily News and Leader', 1913. *Printed.* 50695, f. 179.

— Programme for performance in Steglitz, *circa* 1913-1933. *Germ.* 50742, f. 169.

— Photographs of productions, 1915?- 1948, n.d. 50588, ff. 1, 2, 4-24.

— Photograph of L. McCarthy and O. P. Heggie in, 1915? 50588, f. 1.

— Rehearsal notes, 1934. 50644, ff. 287-295 *passim.*

— Photographs of Berlin production, 1948. 50588, ff. 4-16.

— *Typewritten* film scenario, 1950. 50627.

— Press reviews of version in the 'Shaw Alphabet', 1962. *Newsprint.* 79493, ff. 75-79.

Annajanska the Wild Grand Duchess:

— *Typewritten* with *autogr.* corrections, 1917. 50630.

— *Printed* submission to Lord Chamberlain, 1917. 66183 G.

— Use of authorial pseudonym 'Gregory Biessipoff', 1917. 66183 G.

— Licensing report, 1917. 66183 G.

— *Typewritten* rehearsal notes, 1918. 50644, ff. 33-35.

The Apple Cart:

— *Typewritten* submission to Lord Chamberlain, 1929. 66656 I.

— Licensing report, 1929. *L.C.P. Corr.* 1929/8971.

— Rough proof, unpublished, 1929. 80805. Published text, 1930. 80806.

— Rehearsal notes, 1929-1937. 50644, ff. 311-313; 50645-50647 *passim.*

Arms and the Man:

— *Autogr.*, 1893. 50601 A-C.

Shaw. DRAMATIC WORKS *(continued)*.

— Licensing report, 1910. *L.C.P. Corr.* 1910/223.

— Rehearsal notes, 1930? 50648.

Mrs. Warren's Profession:

— *Autogr.,* 1893. 50598 A-C.

— *Printed* script with *autogr.* revisions, 1894. 50599, ff. 1-42.

— Preface, *printed*, with *autogr.* and *typewritten* revisions, 1898. 50599, ff. 43-53v.

— Cast list for copyright performance in unknown hand, 1898. 50643, ff. 200-200v.

— *Printed* and *autogr.* 'Expurgated version in 3 Acts', submitted to Lord Chamberlain, 1898. 53654 H.

— *Printed*, with *autogr.* rehearsal notes, aft. 1900. 50600, ff, 96v-131v.

— Rehearsal notes, 1900?, 1926. 50600, ff. 96v-131v; 50644, ff. 182-206; 50730, ff. 5v-6v.

— Letters of Fanny Brough concerning the principal role, 1901. 50514, ff. 37-40.

— Correspondence rel. to reception in Rome, 1909. 56627, ff. 7-13.

— Correspondence etc., of Lord Chamberlain's Office concerning, 1911-1926. *L.C.P. Corr.* 1924/5632; *Deposit* 10014/104.

— Opinion of Sir John Hare, 1911. *Deposit* 10114/104.

— Opinion of Edward Carson, 1911. *Deposit* 10014/104.

— Comments of S. O. Buckmaster, 1911-1922. *L.C.P. Corr.* 1924/5632, ff. 62, 91; *Deposit* 10014/104.

— Opinions of Sir Walter Raleigh, 1911, 1917. *L.C.P. Corr.* 1924/5632, f. 61; *Deposit* 10014/104.

— Opinions of Squire Bancroft, 1911, 1922. *L.C.P. Corr.* 1924/5632, f. 95; *Deposit* 10014/104.

— Review of French production, 1912. *Printed. Fr.* 50740, ff. 97v-99.

— Photographs of French production, 1912. *Newsprint. Fr.* 50740, ff. 97v-99.

— French translation, writer unknown, 1913. *Typewritten.* 63185.

— Correspondence, legal opinions, etc., rel. to a production in Glasgow, 1913. *L.C.P. Corr.* 1924/5632, ff. 1-13.

— Correspondence of G. B. Shaw with the Lord Chamberlain's Office, 1916-1926. *L.C.P. Corr.* 1924/5632, ff. 21-27, 31-33, 121-124.

— Appeal of G. S. King for licence to perform, 1916. *L.C.P. Corr.* 1924/5632, ff. 14, 20.

— Petition, etc., in favour of performance, 1917. *L.C.P. Corr.* 1924/5632, ff. 39, 48-55, 67-68.

— Appeal of E. Heys for licence to perform, 1917. *L.C.P. Corr.* 1924/5632, ff. 37-40v, 47-57, 66-68, 71-74.

— Opinion of Sir E. W. Gosse, 1917. *L.C.P. Corr.* 1924/5632, f. 76.

— Correspondence of Viscount Haldane concerning, 1918. *L.C.P. Corr.* 1924/5632, ff. 78, 79.

— Letter of Beatrice Webb to R. B. Haldane concerning, 1918. *Signed. L.C.P. Corr.* 1924/5632, f. 79.

Shaw. DRAMATIC WORKS *(continued).*
— Licensing report and related correspondence, 1909. *L.C.P. Corr.* 1909/80.

Pygmalion:
— French translation by Augustin and Henriette Hamon, 1912?-1914? *Fr.* 50571.
— Portrait of G. B. Shaw during rehearsals, 1913? 50582, f. 38.
— Photographs of Polish production, 1914. 50590, ff. 6-11.
—*Printed* with additional *typewritten* dialogue for Act II, submitted to Lord Chamberlain, 1914. 66056 F.
— Licensing report, 1914. 66056 F.
— *Printed* performing copy with *autogr.* rehearsal notes, 1914? 50629.
— Rehearsal notes, 1914?-1936. 50629 *passim*; 50644, ff. 36-55, 59-60, 303-308.
— Preface in *typewritten draft* with *autogr.* and *shorthand* amendments, 1916. 50628, ff. 1-4.
— Photographs of the Paris production, 1923. 50590, ff. 31-35.
— Photographs of Moscow production, 1932? 50590, ff. 13-27.
— Film scenario, 1934. 50628, ff. 5-35.
— Transcript of remarks by G. B. Shaw for film trailer, *circa* 1939. 50522, ff. 220-221.
— Discussion of casting requirements, 1946-1948. 56631, ff. 184, 193, 194, 211v; 56632, ff. 68-71; 56634, ff. 103, 124, 150, 152, 188, 190, 212, 233, 245.

St. Joan:
— *Typewritten* and *autogr. fragments* sent for publication, 1923. 50633, ff. 1-28.
— *Shorthand*, 1923-1924. 45923, ff. 1-68.
— *Shorthand* Preface, 1923-1924. 45923, ff. 69-101.
— Correspondence with L. Langner, 1923-1924. Mainly *typewritten copies.* 50539, ff. 124-125, 127-143.
— Miscellaneous correspondence of G. B. Shaw concerning, 1923-1929. 50519 *passim*; 50522, ff. 320-322, 343-344.
— Notes, 1923?-1947? 63182, ff. 1-6.
— *Printed* submission to Lord Chamberlain, 1924. 66385 A.
— Licensing report, 1924. *L.C.P. Corr.* 1924/5376.
— Rehearsal notes, 1924, 1936. 50644, ff. 130-166, 299-302.
— Letter to E. Gosse concerning, 1924. *Ashley* 1525*.
— Photographs of stage sets for the Polish Theatre, Warsaw, 1925. 50590, ff. 40-45.
— Photograph of Moscow production, 1926. *Newsprint.* 50590, f. 63.
— Photograph of Tsukiji Theatre, Japan, production, 1926. 50592, f. 15.
— Published (1927) edition with *autogr.* amendments, 1928. 50632.
— Broadcast talk on Joan of Arc, transcribed by J. R. Power, 1931. *Imperf. Typewritten.* 50520, ff. 77-81.

Shaw. DRAMATIC TRANSLATIONS (*cont.*).
To Be Or Not To Be:
— Parody, 1919? *Typewritten.*
50696, ff. 300-305.

NOVELS, POEMS AND SHORT STORIES
The Black Girl's Search for God,
published as **The Adventures of the
Black Girl in her search for God:**
— *Shorthand,* with *pencil drawings*
by G. B. Shaw, 1932. 50658, ff.
109-154.
— Letters to J. Farleigh (1932)
concerning illustrations. *Newsprint,*
1937. 50658, ff. 155-163v.
— Letter to F. Sobieniowski con-
cerning, 1933. *Ashley* B4019, f. 112.
v. also Short Stories, Scraps and
Shavings.
Cashel Byron's Profession:
— Notes, n.d. 50650, ff. 98-121
passim; 50721 A, ff. 76v-90 *passim.*
— *Shorthand,* 1882-1883. 50655 A, B.
Immaturity:
— Notes, n.d. 50650, ff. 98-121
passim; 50721 A, ff. 110v-112v.
— Macmillan & Co. reader's report,
1880. 55934, pp. 131-133.
— Letter of Macmillan & Co.
inviting revised version, 1880.
55410, ff. 161-162, and (*copy*) f. 189.
— *Typewritten.* 1930, n.d. 50651-
50653.
— *Printed.* 1930. 80807.
The Irrational Knot:
— Notes, n.d. 50650, ff. 98-121
passim; 50721 A, ff. 100v-103.
— Macmillan & Co. reader's report,
1881. 55935, p. 34.
— Preface, 1905. 50654.
Short Stories, Scraps and Shavings:
— Stories Nos. 1-6, partly *type-

written* and *printed,* 1885-1916.
50658, ff. 1-108v.
— Wood engraving blocks by
J. Farleigh for, 1932, 1934. 71451-
71455.
An Unsocial Socialist:
— *Shorthand,* 1883. 50656.
— Macmillan & Co. reader's report,
1885. 55937, pp. 18-19.
Unfinished novel:
— *Typewritten,* n.d., 50657.
**Poems, epigrams and notes on
novels:**
— Partly *shorthand* and *type-
written,* 1883-1946. 50650.
v. also correspondence of
Macmillan and Company.

*WRITINGS ON ART, LITERATURE
AND DRAMA*
— 'The Merchant of Venice at the
Lyceum', 1880. With corrections in
another hand. 50693, ff. 78-107v.
— Lecture on 'Troilus and Cressida'
to New Shakespeare Society, read
by G. Latham, 1884. *Draft.* 50702,
ff. 41-124v.
— Lecture, 'Art', 1885. *Draft.*
50702, ff. 162-190v.
— 'A Socialist's Notion of a Novel',
1886. 50693, ff. 140-143.
— Lecture, 'Fiction', 1887. *Draft.*
50702, ff. 219-246.
— Annotations on 'Masks and
Faces' by W. Archer, 1888. *Printed*
proofs (*fragm.*). 45296, ff. 14v-17.
— Commentary on 'Masks and
Faces', 1888. 45296, f. 17v.
— 'From Dickens to Ibsen', 1889?
50693, ff. 201-222.
— Lecture for Church and Stage
Guild, 1889. *Draft.* 50702, ff. 256-265.

Shaw. POLITICAL AND ECONOMIC WRITINGS *(continued)*.

— Circular letter as L.C.C. Progressive candidate, 1904. *Type-written draft*. 50602, f. 36.

— 'The Class War', 1904. *Draft* and *printed*. 50694, ff. 92-97.

— 'The Queen's coup d'état', 1905. *Draft*. 50694, ff. 117-125.

— Article on Kaiser Wilhelm II, 1908. *Typewritten draft* with *autogr.* amendments. 50695, ff. 31-33.

— 'The Socialist Criticism of the Medical Profession', 1909. Lecture notes. 50703, ff. 188-191.

— Letter to 'The Times' on 'Labor Dissatisfaction', 1910. 50695, f. 71.

— Correspondence with 'Die Zeit' on international affairs, 1911. Partly *duplicated* and *typewritten draft*. 50695, ff. 125-129.

— Lecture, etc., on 'Christian Economics' to City Temple Literary Society, 1913. Speaking notes, *typewritten* transcript and *printed* report. 50704, ff. 23-27, 29-90.

— 'Common Sense About the War', 1914-1915. 50668.

— Article on Belgian Relief, 1914, 1915. *Printed* proof and *typewritten draft*, with *autogr.* amendments. 50695, ff. 232-252.

— Preface to projected reprint of 'Common Sense About The War,' 1915. Mainly *typewritten*. 50483, ff. 78-88; 50668, ff. 146-150.

— Letter to Chairman of International Socialist Bureau, (British Section), 1915. *Printed* proof with *autogr.* corrections. 50557, f. 238.

— Manifesto, etc., in response to that of the German Social Democratic Party, 1915. *Printed* proof and *printed draft* with *autogr.* annotations. 50557, ff. 238-241, 243-249v.

— Lecture, 'The Nation's Vitality', arranged by East London Federation of Suffragettes, 1915. Speaker's notes and *printed* reports. 50704, ff. 122-126.

— 'More Commonsense About the War', 1915. *Typewritten,* with *MS.* annotations of G. B. and C. F. Shaw. 63179, 63180.

— 'More Commonsense About the War', *circa* 1915-1918. *Shorthand, typewritten* and *autogr.* 50669 A, B.

— Letter on conscription to the 'Liverpool Courier', 1916. *Fragm.* 50696, ff. 1-4.

— 'Sir Edward Grey still marks time', 1916. *Typewritten* with *autogr.* amendments. 50696, ff. 77-98.

— 'Joy Riding at the Front', 1917. *Printed* proofs with *autogr.* amendments. 50696, ff. 164-184.

— 'The Effect of the War on Me', 1917. Partly *shorthand* and *typewritten draft*. 50696, ff. 199-201.

— 'The Falling Market in War Aims', 1918. *Typewritten draft* with *autogr.* amendments. 50696, ff. 202-210.

— 'Peace Conference Hints', 1918, 1919. *Shorthand, typewritten* and *autogr.* 50671 A, B.

— 'Are we disarming too precipitately?', 1919. *Typewritten,* with *autogr.* amendments. 50696, ff. 248-252.

Shaw. BIOGRAPHICAL PAPERS (*cont.*).
and *typewritten copy.* 50678, ff.
169-230; 50711 B, ff. 131-170.

— Letter to the Editor of 'The
Morning Post' rel. to Henderson's
biography, 1911. *Copy.* 50564,
f. 107.

— Horoscope by I. M. Pagan, *circa*
1914. 56491, f. 169.

— Opticians' records for G. B.
Shaw, 1916-1945. Partly *printed.*
50711 A, ff. 50-54v.

— Diary entries, 1917. Partly
typewritten. 50711 A, ff. 230-231v;
63181.

— Chapters of a book about G. B.
Shaw, by F. H. Hayward, aft. 1917?
Typewritten. 50577.

— Letters concerning radiograph of
G. B. Shaw, 1923. 50519, ff. 60, 61.

— Letters from A. Henderson rel.
to Shaw *v.* Henderson, 1923-1954.
52721, ff. 82-93.

— Play, 'St. Bernard and St. Joan',
by L. Langner, 1924. *Typewritten.*
50578.

— Invitation and guest list for 70th
birthday dinner, 1926. Mainly
printed and *typewritten.* 50711 A,
ff. 219-222.

— 'Naprapathic Chart Book'
prepared for G. B. Shaw, 1928,
1929. *Printed* with *MS.* insertions.
50711 A, ff. 55-67.

— Preface to the published edition
of his correspondence with E.
Terry, 1929. *Printed* proofs with
autogr. amendments. 50664, ff. 75-
90v.

— Palm reading for G. B. Shaw,
1930. Letter with *photogr.* and

typewritten enclosures. 50743 B, ff.
416-423.

— Accounts, etc., rel. to tenancy in
Whitehall Court, 1934-1943, n.d.
63187.

— Notes rel. to the preservation and
publication of his correspondence
with E. Terry, 1934-1945, n.d.
43800, ff. i, ii; 46172, f. 37; 50664,
ff. 91-105v.

— Notes of C. F. Shaw on G. B.
Shaw's diet, *circa* 1935-1941.
56524 B, ff. 147-148, 155.

— Medical correspondence, etc., of
G. B. and C. F. Shaw with A. G.
Evans, J. S. Hensman, C. E. Dukes
and R. Roche, 1938-1943. Partly
signed, copy and *printed.* 56494, ff.
1-63 *passim*, 101, 163; 63197, f. 47.

— 'Shaw Gives Himself Away',
1939. Galley proofs and *typescript*
with extensive *autogr.* additions.
50706.

— Letters from B. Patch rel. to
G. B. and C. F. Shaw, 1939-1951.
52743, ff. 5-17.

— Correspondence and papers
relating to, 1940-1945. Partly
copies, partly *printed.* 59620 C, ff.
235-298 *passim*; 59620 D.

— Notes on the history of the Shaw
family, 1943?-1950? *Partly typewritten* and *autogr.* 50711 A, ff.
1-4.

— Entry in the 'Biographical
Encyclopaedia of the World'
concerning, 1944. *Printed.* 50524,
f. 14.

— 'What is my religious faith?',
1944. Mainly *typewritten.* 50699,
ff. 23-28.

Shaw. BIOGRAPHICAL PAPERS (*cont.*).

— Notes on the will of C. F. Shaw, 1944? 56494, f. 207.

— 'Sixty Years in Business as an Author', 1945. *Shorthand* and *typewritten draft*. 50679, ff. 375-385.

— Sonnet for G. B. Shaw by Capt. D. S. Hancock, 1946. *Typewritten copy*. 50525, f. 126.

— Statement of the National Executive Committee on G. B. Shaw's ninetieth birthday, 1946. *Typewritten*. 50525, f. 228.

— Poem to G. B. Shaw of P. E. Stangl, 1946. *Germ*. 50525, ff. 352-355.

— Verses on G. B. Shaw by Hamilton Fyfe, 1946. *Printed*. 50525, f. 373.

— Script of radio talk on G. B. Shaw by N. Kazantzakes, 1946. *Signed copy*. 50527, f. 35.

— 'Lines for the Ninetieth Birthday of George Bernard Shaw' by J. E. Masefield, 1946. *Partly printed*. 50543, f. 93; 63728, f. 11.

— Handbill of International Arts Guild announcing first performance of 'Musical Portrait of George Bernard Shaw', 1946? *Duplicated*. 50741, f. 251.

— Letters from S. Winsten rel. to, 1946-1949. 52769, ff. 1-4.

— Letters from A. D. Power rel. to, 1947. 52752, ff. 298-299.

— Note concerning C. F. Shaw's collection of his letters, 1948. *Typewritten* and *signed*. 46505, f. i.

— 'Sixteen Self Sketches', 1949. Preliminary *drafts, typewritten* discarded material, and galley proofs with *autogr*. amendments. 50707-50709.

— Home Office memorandum regarding the British citizenship of G. B. Shaw, 1949. *Signed*. 63186, f. 221.

— Correspondence and papers of Sir R. F. Harrod concerning the will of G. B. Shaw, 1955-1957. *Partly signed, printed* and *copy*. 71615.

— 'An Irish Basset-horn', article by Sir M. K. Tippett on G. B. Shaw, [1956?]. 72045, f. 53.

— Notes, legal opinions, etc., concerning the will of G. B. Shaw, 1957. *Duplicate, copy* and *printed*. 79493, ff. 1-26v.

— Letters from S. Weintraub rel. to, 1959-1961. 52768, ff. 1-5v.

— Letters from J. Musters rel. to, 1960-1961. 52741, ff. 111-162.

GENERAL CORRESPONDENCE AND MISCELLANEOUS PAPERS

— General correspondence, 1857-1950, n.d. 50508-50527, 63186.

v. under names of individuals, societies, and public bodies.

— Letters and papers rel. to phonetics and spelling reform, *circa* 1852-1969. Partly *duplicated, printed*, and *copy*. Partly *Germ*. Partly in phonetic scripts. 50554-50556; 50679, ff. 325-374; 54576 A, f. 145; 71615; 79492-79494 C.

— Lecture on capital punishment, 1884? *Draft*. 50702, ff. 1-40.

— Index slips for an edition of T. Lodge's works, 1885. Partly *shorthand*. 50511, ff. 92-94v.

— 'The Future of Marriage', 1885. 50693, ff. 118-122v.

Shaw. GENERAL CORRESPONDENCE (*continued*).

— Notes for lecture on copyright, 1885-1890? 50702, ff. 252-255.

— 'Asides', 1889. 50693, ff. 188-194.

— Correspondence and papers rel. to vivisection and cruelty to animals; 1892-1950. Partly *printed, copy* and *draft.* 50516, ff. 300, 302; 50521, f. 308; 50522, f. 1; 50526 B, ff. 390, 501; 50678, ff. 1-102; 50701, f. 308; 50743 B, f. 359.

— Collected articles on religion and religions, 1896-1931, n.d. 50663.

— 'Scientific Credulity', 1900. lecture notes. 50703, ff. 32-35.

— 'Twentieth-Century Free-thinking', 1901. Lecture notes. 50703, ff. 40-50v.

— 'On Modern Composition', 1902? *Typewritten.* 50694, ff. 1-4.

— 'Letter on Maternity without Marriage' *dictated* by G. B. Shaw, 1905. In Charlotte Shaw's hand. 56524 A, ff. 20-31.

— Lecture notes on childhood and education, 1905? 50703, ff. 111, 112.

— 'The Religion of the British Empire', 1906. Lecture notes. 50703, ff. 116-123v.

— Speech, 'Some necessary repairs to religion', 1906? 1907? Verbatim report in another hand. 50703, ff. 125-165.

— 'Religion and Credulity', 1907. *Lecture draft.* 50703, ff. 169-179.

— *Draft* article, 'A Nation of Villagers', 1907. 50736, ff. 1-39.

— Answers to printed 'Inquiry into Moral Instruction and Training in Schools', 1907. 50743 B, f. 344.

— Letter recommending the establishment of a German Society of Authors, 1908. *Printed. Germ.* 45296, f. 202v.

— Letter to 'The Freethinker', 1908. *Printed* and *fragm.* 50695, f. 24.

— Note to unidentified recipient, 1908. *Ashley* B1509, f. 5.

— Papers rel. to Society of Authors, 1908-1946. Partly *printed* and *typewritten drafts.* 50679, ff. 1-125.

— 'Draft Letter to Millionaires', 1909. *Typewritten.* 45296, ff. 214-221.

— Correspondence, etc., rel. to permissions and fees for performances, 1909-1950. 50649; 56627-56633 *passim*; 56634-56637.

— 'General Mourning', 1910. Mainly *shorthand draft.* 50695, ff. 51-57.

— Notice, speaker's notes, reports, etc., of address to Heretics (Cambridge University), 1911. Partly *printed.* 50703, ff. 203-214.

— Postcards, etc., of G. B. Shaw from motoring tours in Germany and France, 1912, 1913. 46506, ff. 28-99.

— Notes on 'Idolatry', bef. 1914. *Typewritten.* 50699, ff. 376-379.

— 'The Press', 1914. Speaking notes. 50704, ff. 96-103.

— Letter to 'Liverpool Evening Express' concerning A. Mair, 1916. *Printed.* 50696, f. 16.

Shaw (George Carr), *father of G. B. Shaw*. Letters to L. E. Shaw, 1857. 50508, ff. 1-11v, 15-19, 23-27.

— Group photograph taken at Dalkey, co. Dublin by R. Pigott, *circa* 1865. Two *copies*. 50583, ff. 6, 7; 50587, f. 10.

— Letters to G. B. Shaw, 1879-1884. 50508, ff. 161, 257; 50509, ff. 17, 248v; 50510, ff. 240v, 250, 258, 262.

Shaw (Georgina), *wife of R. F. Shaw*. Letters to her nephew, G. B. Shaw, 1878-1908. 50508, f. 122; 50509, f. 128; 50515, ff. 194, 196.

Shaw (Jack Wingfield), *great grandson of Sir Frederick Shaw, 3rd Bart*. Letter to G. B. Shaw, 1947. 50526 B, f. 400.

Shaw (James Cockaigne *al*. 'Kaffir'), *cousin of G. B. Shaw; commission agent*. Letters, etc., to G. B. Shaw, *circa* 1882-1914. 50509, ff. 196, 199; 50510, f. 190; 50511, f. 114; 50514, ff. 331, 335, 344, 352, 375; 50515, ff. 138, 259, 280, 297; 50516, ff. 35, 225, 243, 262, 339; 50517, f. 168; 50527, ff. 248, 250.

— Letter to, of H. T. Brockman, 1909. 50515, f. 257.

Shaw (John), *of Dublin; son of James C. Shaw*. Testimonials on behalf of J. Shaw, 1904, 1905. *Copies*. 50514, ff. 194-197.

— Letter to L. F. Shaw, 1910. 50515, f. 362.

— Letter of recommendation by A. J. Graves, on behalf of, 1911. *Copy*. 50516, f. 23.

— Letters to G. B. Shaw, 1912. 50516, ff. 138, 223, 236, 245, 271.

— Letter to his father, 1912. 50516, f. 220.

Shaw (John), *of London*. Letter to G. B. Shaw, 1944. 50524, f. 108.

Shaw (Katharine Ceceley), *wife of Sir B. V. Shaw*. Letters to C. F. Shaw, 1940, n.d. 56494, ff. 69, 194.

Shaw (Lucinda Elizabeth), *mother of G. B. Shaw; wife of G. C. Shaw*. Letters to, from her husband, 1857. 50508, ff. 1-11v, 15-19, 23-27.

— Letter to, from Dr. W. J. Gurly, 1857. 50508, f. 12.

— Letter to, from E. Whitcroft, 1857. 50508, f. 20.

— Letter to, from C. J. Johnston, 1857. 50508, f. 38.

— Group photograph taken at Dalkey, co. Dublin by R. Pigott, *circa* 1865. Two *copies*. 50583, ff. 6, 7; 50587, f. 10.

— Letter to, from F. Willett, 1878. 50508, f. 125.

— Letter to, from Capt. R. H. Horne, 1878. 50508, f. 126.

— Postcard and letters to G. B. Shaw, 1880, 1884. 50508, f. 255; 50510, ff. 252, 261, 264.

— Reminiscences of J. B. Logier, 1894. 50513, ff. 33, 39-41v.

Shaw (Lucinda Frances), *actress; sister of G. B. Shaw*. Correspondence with G. B. Shaw, 1880-1918. Partly *draft* and *copy*. 50508, f. 270; 50515, f. 185; 50517, f. 74; 50518, ff. 133, 198.

— Photograph with Reginald Roberts in 'Shamus O'Brien', 1897. 50583, f. 14.

— Photographs of, 1897-1937? 50583, ff. 12-14; 50587, ff. 20.

— Letter to, from J. Shaw, 1910. 50515, f. 362.

— Letter to C. F. Shaw, 1914. 56491, f. 190.

— I.O.U.s to E. M. Schneider, 1916-1919. 50517, f. 440; 50518, ff. 70, 131.

Shaw (Lucy Carr).

v. Shaw (Lucinda Frances).

Shaw (*Miss* Mabel), *missionary in N. Rhodesia.* Letters to G. B. Shaw, 1929, 1940. 50519, f. 375; 50522, f. 312.

Shaw *afterw.* **Davis** *afterw.* **Walters** (Mary Ethel), *cousin of G. B. Shaw.* Letters, etc., to G. B. Shaw, 1912-1946. Partly *signed.* 50516, f. 218; 50523, ff. 1, 184; 50524, ff. 29, 35, 222; 50526 A, f. 155.

Shaw (Mary Margaret), *M.B.E.; daughter of Frederick William Shaw, 5th Bart.* Letter to G. B. Shaw, 1946. 50525, f. 2.

— Letters to B. & H. White Publications Ltd., 1947, 1948. 50565, ff. 123, 189.

Shaw (Mildred B.), *of Palo Alto, California; widow of George Eden Shaw.* Letter to G. B. Shaw, 1943. 50523, f. 88.

— Photograph of, 1943. 50585, f. 37.

Shaw (Richard Frederick), *Chief of the Land Valuation Office of Ireland.* Correspondence with his nephew, G. B. Shaw, 1877, 1885. 50508, f. 88v; 50511, ff. 64-66v, 76.

Shaw (Robert), *son of Edward Carr Shaw.* Letter to his cousin, G. B. Shaw, 1909. 50515, f. 285.

Shaw (Robert), *7th Bart.* Letter to G. B. Shaw, 1944. 50524, f. 6.

Shaw (Stephanie), *of Zyrardów, Poland.* Letter to G. B. Shaw, 1946. *Signed.* 50556, f. 108.

Shaw *formerly* **Lawrence** (Thomas Edward).

v. Lawrence *afterw.* Shaw.

Shaw Fund. Purchased for British Library, in 1992, 71068.

Shaw Memorial Appeal. Minutes, etc., 1952. *Duplicated.* 58493, ff. 108-111.

Shcherbakov (A.), *Secretary, Soviet Writers' Union.* Letter to G. B. Shaw, 1934. *Signed.* 50520, f. 258.

Sheed *née* **Ward** (Maisie).

v. Ward *afterw.* Sheed.

Sheehy (J. S.), *C.M.; priest of St. Joseph's, Blackrock, Dublin.* 'Notes on Reading and Elocution', bef. 1935. *Printed.* 50521, ff. 9-18.

— Letters, etc., to G. B. Shaw, 1935, 1944. Partly *printed.* 50521, f. 6; 50524, f. 111.

— Photographs of J. S. Sheehy, *circa* 1937. 50521, f. 8v.

Shelley (*Mrs.* Marjorie), *of Childs Hill, London.* Letter to G. B. Shaw, 1943. 50523, f. 178.

Shelley (Percy Bysshe), *poet.* Notice of Centenary Meeting at the Hall of Science, 1892. *Printed.* 50701, f. 123.

Shepherd (*Dr.* Michael), *of Cardiff.* Postcard to G. B. Shaw, 1946. 50526 A, f. 88.

Sheppard (Hugh Richard Lawrie), *Canon of St. Paul's (1934).* Letter to C. F. Shaw, 1927. *Signed.* 56492, f. 99.

— Letter of G. B. Shaw to, 1930. *Shorthand* and *typewritten drafts.* 50520, f. 10.

Smith (Wilson W.), *of East Peoria, Illinois.* Letter, etc., to G. B. Shaw, 1946. *Signed.* 50525, f. 203.

— Verses, *circa* 1946. *Copies.* 50525, ff. 204-210.

Smith, Elder and Co., *publishers, of London.* Letters to G. B. Shaw, 1880-1884. 50508, f. 208; 50509, ff. 42, 43, 135, 147; 50510, ff. 22, 171.

Smitt (Gudrun), *Danish [author?].* Letter to G. B. Shaw, 1946. 50525, f. 201.

Smoker (Barbara). Notes, with Sir I. J. Pitman, on G. B. Shaw's Will, 1957. *Copy.* 79493, f. 2.

Smyth (E. Skeffington). Letters to C. F. Payne-Townshend, 1884, 1895. 56490, ff. [37?], 135.

Smyth (Ethel Mary), *D.B.E.; composer.* Correspondence with G. B. Shaw, 1914. Partly *draft.* 50517, ff. 136, 156, 163v.

— ['Radio Times'?] photograph of, 1930? 50585, f. 40.

Snábl (*2nd Major* Frank), *cultural attaché, Czechoslovak embassy.* Letter to G. B. Shaw, 1946. *Signed.* 50525, f. 211.

Snape (J. C.), *of Liverpool.* Letter to G. B. Shaw, 1910. *Typewritten.* 50515, f. 324.

Snowden (Philip), *Viscount Snowden.* Letter to G. B. Shaw, 1913. *Signed.* 63186, f. 8.

Sobieniowski (Floryan), *Polish translator of G. B. Shaw.* Inscribed photograph to W. Hudd, 1926. 71658, f. 59.

— Correspondence with G. B. Shaw, 1933, 1938. 50522, f. 19; *Ashley*

B4019, ff. 111-113v; *Ashley* 5768, ff. 99-100v.

Social Democratic Federation. Notices of meetings, etc., 1887-1897. *Printed.* 50701, ff. 13-262 *passim.*

— Report to the International Socialist Workers' Congress, 1893. *Printed.* 50680, ff. 114-117.

Socialist League. Correspondence with G. B. Shaw, 1885-1887. Partly *draft.* 50511, ff. 62, 157, 272v, 281v-283.

— Notices of meetings and demonstrations, 1887-1891. *Printed.* 50701, ff. 11-105 *passim.*

Socialist Medical Association. Letter, etc., to G. B. Shaw of Dr. S. Hastings, 1938. *Dictated.* Partly *Copy.* 50522, f. 32.

Socialist Unity Demonstrations Committee. Notice of meeting, 1914. *Printed.* 50687, f. 1.

Social Union. Programme of meetings, 1901. *Printed.* 50701, f. 185.

Societatea Compozitorilor Romani, *of Bucharest.* Letter to G. B. Shaw, 1939. *Signed. Fr.* 50522, f. 251.

Society of Authors. Correspondence with and rel. to G. B. Shaw, 1908-1950, n.d. Partly *signed,* partly *copies.* 50679, ff. 1-125; 56627-56632; 56633, ff. 1-97.

— Correspondence with and rel. to C. F. Shaw, 1913-1961. 56627, ff. 103, 104; 56633, ff. 98-221; 63197, ff. 15-33, 42, 58.

Soermus (*Mrs. —*). Letter to, of J. Maxton, 1931. *Signed.* 50520, f. 55.

Somers (*Mrs.* Lee). Letter to G. B. Shaw, 1946. 50525, f. 344.

Somervell (R. U.), *of Waybrook, co. Notts.* Letter to G. B. Shaw, 1944. 50524, f. 194.

Somerville (Edith Anna Oenone), *artist and author.* Letters to G. B. Shaw, 1922, 1944. 50518, f. 295; 50524, f. 197.

Sondhi (G. D.), *of Government College, Lahore.* Correspondence with G. B. Shaw, 1926-1927. Partly *signed* and *shorthand draft.* 50519, ff. 277-278v, 285-286v, 296.

Sonneberg (Walter), *of Philadelphia.* 'The Case of Shaw's Inequality', 1913. Mainly *typewritten.* 50516, ff. 426-430v.

Sonnenschein *afterw.* Stallybrass (William Swan), *publisher.* Correspondence with G. B. Shaw, 1887, 1888. Partly *signed* and *shorthand draft.* 50511, ff. 268-366v *passim*; 50512, ff. 1, 1v.

Sorbonne, *University of.* Lectures on G. B. Shaw's plays by A. F. A. Hamon, given at the Sorbonne, 1910-1912. *Typewritten,* with *MS.* notes. *Fr.* 50574.

Sorma (Agnes), *German actress.* Photographs of, 1904? 50585, ff. 41-46.

Sotheby and Co., *auctioneers, of London.* Letters to G. B. Shaw, 1944-1949. Partly *signed* and *printed.* 50524, f. 67; 50526 B, ff. 467, 469.

Southam (Ethel Armitage), *author.* Correspondence with G. B. Shaw, 1882. Partly *shorthand draft.* 50509, ff. 193, 200, 204, 212.

Southern (Walter Duckett), *M.R.C.S.; L.R.C.P.* Letters to C. F. Shaw, 1940-1941. 56494, f. 82; 63197, ff. 56, 63, 72.

Southgate (Lucienne), *sec. to H. G. Wells.* Letter, etc., to G. B. Shaw, 1930. *Signed.* 50552, f. 56.

Southorn (Bella), *wife of Sir W. T. Southorn.* Letter to C. F. Shaw, 1933. 56493, f. 60.

South Place Institute. Programmes of lectures, 1882-1891. *Printed.* 50701, ff. 3, 95; 50721 B, f. 11v.

South Place Religious Society. Report of the committee, 1887. *Printed* and *fragm.* 50702, ff. 247-251v.

Sowerby (T. W.), *of Lawrence, Graham & Co.* Letters to C. F. Shaw, 1940. *Signed.* 63197, ff. 44, 45.

Sowers (Judith MacKenzie), *Jehovah's Witness, of Los Angeles, California.* Letter to G. B. Shaw, 1946. 50526 B, f. 299.

Sowter (Sissie), *niece of Mrs. William Archer.* Letter to G. B. Shaw, 1946. 50525, f. 222.

Spalding (Lillian), *of Torquay, co. Devon.* Letter to G. B. Shaw, 1946. 50526 A, f. 55.

Sparks (Frank M.), *of King's Somborne, co. Southt.* Letter to G. B. Shaw, 1946. 50526 A, f. 51.

Sparrow (John Hanbury Angus), *Warden of All Souls College, Oxford.* Letter to R. F. Harrod, 1956. *Signed.* 71615, f. 77.

— Affidavit in respect of the will of G. B. Shaw of Sir R. F. Harrod, amended by J. H. A. Sparrow,

1956. *Typewritten draft* with *MS.* amendments. 71615, ff. 78-104.

Speakman (*Mrs.* J. C. G.), *at Siena.* Letters to G. H. Thring, 1909. Partly *typewritten copies.* 56627, ff. 7-13, 18-21.

Speed (James A.), *of Preston, co. Lanc.* Letter to G. B. Shaw, 1946. *Signed.* 50526 A, f. 16.

Spence (Fordham), *author.* Article on musical and dramatic criticism by G. B. Shaw rel. to F. Spence, 1910-1911. *Draft.* Partly *shorthand.* 50695, ff. 106-113.

Spencer (F. A.), *of Liverpool.* Letter to G. B. Shaw, 1946. 50526 B, f. 277.

Spencer (*Flight-Lieut.* G. R. C.), *Commanding R.A.F. Station, Miranshah.* Daily Routine Orders issued by Flight-Lieut. G. R. C. Spencer, 1928. *Typewritten.* 45904, f. 13.

Spencer (Henry), *fruit grower, of Wickford, co. Essex.* Photograph of Essex-grown bananas, 1920?-1930? 50585, ff. 47, 48.

Spencer (Herbert), *philosopher.* Letter to G. B. Shaw, 1896. *Signed.* 50513, f. 107.

Spencer (Herbert), *son of H. Spencer, fruit grower.* Photograph of Essex-grown bananas, 1920?-1930? 50585, ff. 47, 48.

Spender (John Alfred), *journalist.* Correspondence with G. B. Shaw, 1900, 1907. 46391, f. 225; 50513, f. 224.

Speyer (*Sir* Edgar), *Bart.* Letter to G. B. Shaw of Sir E. Speyer, n.d. 50527, f. 256.

Spielmann (Marion Harry), *Editor, 'Magazine of Art'.* Letter to J. T. Harris, 1930. *Copy.* 50538, f. 53.

— Letter, etc., to G. B. Shaw, 1938. *Signed.* 50538, f. 52.

Sponneck (*Count* Frederik Wilhelm), *Danish diplomatist.* Letters to C. F. Payne-Townshend, 1884-1885. 56490, ff. 18-22v, 29-36, 42.

Spooner *afterw.* **Carr** (Geraldine). *v.* Carr *née* Spooner.

Spooner (N. L.), *of the 'Daily Herald'.* Letter to G. B. Shaw, 1932. *Signed.* 50520, f. 171.

Squire (*Sir* John Collings), *Editor, 'London Mercury'.* Letter from G. B. Shaw to, 1913? 59892, f. 141.

Stacey (Francis Newton), *researcher, of Washington D.C.* Letter to G. B. Shaw, 1946. *Signed.* 50525, f. 359.

Stachelschied (Albert), *of the Social Democratic Federation.* Letter to the 'Church Times', 1882. *Drafts.* 50509, f. 269.

— Letters to G. B. Shaw, 1884, 1908. 50510, f. 257; 50515, f. 132.

Stage Society. Letter of G. B. Shaw to Stage Society Casting Committee, 1903? *Draft.* 56524 B, f. 133.

Stallybrass *formerly* **Sonnenschein** (William Swan). *v.* Sonnenschein.

Stamfordham, *Baron.* *v.* Bigge (*Lt.-Col.* Arthur John).

Standring (*Mrs.* —), *wife of George Standring.* Photographs of Mrs. George Standring and son, 1907. 50585, ff. 50, 51.

Standring (George), *printer and publisher.* Correspondence with

Storey (Mary Gladys), *author.* Letter to G. B. Shaw, 1939. *Signed.* 50546, f. 75.

'Stormfield', *Redding, Connecticut, home of 'Mark Twain'.* Christmas greetings to G. B. Shaw from S. L. Clemens, A. Henderson and A. L. Coburn, 1908. 50515, f. 199.

Stout (*Sergeant* John), *former Secretary, Anglo-Egyptian Amateur Dramatic Society.* Letter to Consul General at Alexandria of Sergeant J. E. Jones, M. Abdullah, Sergeant J. Stout and Sergeant J. L. Price, 1916. *Signed.* 56627, f. 185.

Stránská (Marie), *of Prague.* Letter to G. B. Shaw, 1929. 50519, f. 367.

Strauss (Richard Georg), *composer. Draft* 'interview' for 'The Lady's Field' by G. B. Shaw rel. to, 1905? 1906? Mainly *typewritten.* 50694, ff. 126-130v.

— Photograph of, 1910. 50585, f. 53.

— Christmas card to G. B. Shaw, 1926. *Photogr. Germ.* 50563, f. 18.

Streatfield (*Dr.* Raymond). Letters to, of B. Patch, 1942-1943. Partly signed. 74734 P.

Street (George Slythe), *Examiner of Plays.* Licensing reports on plays of G. B. Shaw, 1914-1934. 66056 F; 66118 F; 66356 A; *L.C.P. Corr.* 1915/ 3885; *L.C.P. Corr.* 1921/ 3794; *L.C.P. Corr.* 1922/4288; *L.C.P. Corr.* 1923/4900; *L.C.P. Corr.* 1924/5376; *L.C.P. Corr.* 1924/ 5632, ff. 17, 18, 81-83, 98, 110; *L.C.P. Corr.* 1929/8971; *L.C.P. Corr.* 1932/11312; *L.C.P. Corr.* 1933/12381; *L.C.P. Corr.* 1934/ 12935; *L.C.P. Corr.* 1934/ 13107; *L.C.P. Corr.* 1935/13605; *L.C.P. Corr.* 1924/5632.

Strelling (W. H.), *shopkeeper, of Hull.* Letter to G. B. Shaw, 1938. 50522, f. 117.

Strindberg (Johan August), *dramatist.* Photograph of, 1905? 50585, f. 54.

— Letter to G. B. Shaw, 1910. 63186, f. 5.

Strobl (Kisfalud Sigismund de), *sculptor; Professor, Royal Academy of Art, Budapest.* Photographs of, 1932. 50587, ff. 24, 25.

— Letters to G. B. Shaw, 1932-1949. 50520, f. 172; 50521, f. 166; 50522, f. 53; 50526 B, ff. 428, 438, 446, 448.

Stromberg (Hunt), *American film producer.* Telegram to G. B. Shaw, 1946. 50526 A, f. 26.

Stromeyer (C. E.).

v. Stromeyer (J. P. E. C.)

Stromeyer (Johann Philip Edmond Charles), *engineer and author.* Letter, etc., to G. B. Shaw, 1913. Partly *printed.* 50516, ff. 312-321.

Strong (Anna Louise), *American author and socialist, in Moscow.* Letter to G. B. Shaw, 1931. *Signed.* 50520, f. 110.

Strong *afterw.* **Pattison** *afterw.* **Dilke** (Emilia Francis).

v. Dilke *formerly* Pattison *née* Strong.

Strowd (*Dr.* Alice T.), *osteopath of Glendive, Montana.* Letter, etc., to G. B. Shaw, 1946. *Typewritten* and signed. 50526 B, f. 380.

Struben (Charles), *barrister, of Cape Colony.* Letter to, of E. De Chair, 1931. 56492, f. 222.

T

Tacchi (*Maj.* G.), *spelling reformer.*
Letters, etc., to G. B. Shaw, 1941.
Partly *printed.* 50554, ff. 138-143,
183-186, 192-195.

Tadema (Laurence Alma-).
v. Alma-Tadema.

Tagore (*Sir* Rabindranath), *Indian
poet.* Telegram concerning Annie
Besant, 1917. *Copy.* 50529, f.
66.

— Correspondence with G. B. Shaw,
1927. Partly *draft.* 50519, f. 319.

— Report of R. E. James of interview
with, 1941. *Typewritten.* 50522, ff.
410-417.

Tairov (Alexsandr Lakovelevich),
*Director, Moscow Kamerny
Theatre.* Letter to G. B. Shaw,
1924. 50519, f. 146.

Tait (H. Sinclair), *M.D., of Palmer,
Massachusetts.* Letter to G. B.
Shaw, 1946. 50526 B, f. 310.

Tal (Lucy), *of M.G.M.* Letters to
G. B. Shaw, 1940. *Signed.* 63186,
ff. 133, 138.

Talgeri (Krishna M.), *of Kolhapur,
India.* Letter to G. B. Shaw, 1945.
50523, f. 71.

[Tanguey?] (Elizabeth), *actress.*
Letter to G. B. Shaw, *circa* 1938.
50527, f. 7.

Tara-Pada Vasu.
v. Basu (Tarapada).

Tarapore (Burzorji Pherozshah), *of
Secunderabad.* Letter, etc., to G. B.
Shaw, 1944. *Signed.* 50524, f. 68.

Tarbuth Limited, *booksellers and
publishers, of Palestine.* Correspondence with G. B. Shaw, n.d. Partly

imperf. and *shorthand draft.* 50527,
ff. 44, 44v.

Tarkhad (M. A.), *of Rajkumar
College, Rajkot, India.* Letter to
G. B. Shaw, 1886. 50511, f. 217.

Tarpey (W. Kingsley), *playwright.*
Letter to G. B. Shaw, 1903. 50514,
f. 97.

Tarrida del Mármol (F.), *Spanish
journalist and author.* Letter to,
from G. B. Shaw, 1902. *Draft.*
50527, f. 152.

Tay (Frederick S.), *of Salem,
Massachusetts.* Letters to G. B.
Shaw, 1914. 50517, ff. 41, 62.

Taylor (F. A.), *of Hove, co. Suss.*
Letter to G. B. Shaw, 1944. 50524,
f. 273.

Taylor (G. F. H.), *of Austin Bros.,
picture frame makers, Hoxton.*
Letter to G. B. Shaw, 1928. 50519,
f. 344.

Taylor (G. P.), *of Okehampton, co.
Devon.* Letter [to B. Patch?],
1930?-1940? 63186, f. 241.

Taylor (George Paul), *metropolitan
police magistrate.* Letter to, of
J. Lane, 1910. *Copy.* 50515, f. 443.

Taylor (H. G. F.), *of the 'Pall Mall
Gazette'.* Letter to G. B. Shaw,
1880. 50508, f. 231.

Taylor (P. W. E.), *[barrister?].* Joint
legal opinion on the will of G. B.
Shaw of C. Russell and P. W. E.
Taylor, 1956?-1957. *Typewritten
extract.* 79493, ff. 12-14.

Tchaykovsky (Barbara), *daughter of
N. Tchaykovsky.* Letters, etc., to
G. B. Shaw, 1908-1942. Partly
signed. 50515, ff. 168-174, 282,
308, 381; 50522, f. 458.

Tchaykovsky (Nicholas), *Russian revolutionary.* Letters to G. B. Shaw relating to bail relief funds for N. Tchaykovsky, 1908. 50515, ff. 180, 183v.
— Letters, etc., concerning his imprisonment and release, 1908-1910. Partly *printed* and *signed.* 50515, ff. 104, 168-174, 178-184, 282, 308, 381.

Teachers' Guild of Great Britain and Ireland. Notice of meetings, 1900. *Printed.* 50701, f. 182.

Teall (Cecil George), *M.B.; Ch.B.* Letter concerning radiograph of G. B. Shaw to E. T. Pheils, 1923. 50519, f. 60.

Temko (Allan Bernard), *of Richmond Hill, New York.* Letter to G. B. Shaw, 1946. *Signed.* 50526 B, f. 330.

Tempest (Ted), *policeman, of Deighton Bar, co. York.* Letter to G. B. Shaw, 1946. *Signed.* 50525, f. 213.

Tempest de Blaby (*Capt.* George), *of Pulborough, co. Sussex.* Letter to G. B. Shaw, n.d. 50527, f. 61.

Tempest-Stewart (Edith Helen Vane-).
v. Vane-Tempest-Stewart.

Temple (Thomas), [*undergraduate of Harvard University*?]. Letter to G. B. Shaw, 1946. 50525, f. 223.

Tendulkar (Dinakara G.), *of Bombay, author.* Letter to G. B. Shaw of V.-B. K. Jhaveri and D. G. Tendulkar, 1946. *Signed.* 50525, f. 282.

Tennant *afterw.* **Stanley** (Dorothy).
v. Stanley *née* Tennant.

Tennant *afterw.* **Asquith** (Emma Alice Margaret).
v. Asquith *née* Tennant.

Tenterden, *co. Kent.* Photographs of E. Terry's farm at Small Hythe, 1904. 43802, ff. 149, 150v.

'**Terriss** (William)', *pseudonym.*
v. Lewin (William Charles James).

Terry (Alice Ellen), *G.B.E.; actress.* portrait of, as Portia, with notes of her performances on the verso, *annotated* by G. B. Shaw, 1880. *Printed* signature. 50585, ff. 57-57v.
— Correspondence with G. B. Shaw, 1892-1922, n.d. Partly *signed.* 43800-43802; 46172, ff. 39-49; 46505, f. 33; 71068; *Facs.* 496. Published edition, 1931. 80809.
— Letters to C. F. Shaw, 1898. 56490, f. 166; 56491, ff. 1, 3.
— Portrait of, 1900? 50585, f. 60.
— Photographs of her farm at Small Hythe, 1904. 43802, ff. 149, 150v.
— Preface by G. B. Shaw to the published edition of his correspondence with E. Terry, 1929. *Printed* proofs with *autogr.* amendments. 50664, ff. 75-90v.
— Notes rel. to the preservation and publication of G. B. Shaw's correspondence with E. Terry, 1933-1945, n.d. 43800, ff. i, ii; 46172, f. 37; 50664, ff. 91-105v; *Ashley* A4011, f. 113.
— Letter to G. B. Shaw of C. St. John rel. to, 1947. 50526 B, f. 387.

Thackeray (Arthur G.), *insurance agent, of Tunbridge Wells.* Letter to G. B. Shaw, 1945. 50524, f. 300.

Theatre Royal, *Richmond, co. York.* Verses written on the re-opening of

Political Union. Letter to M. Cunningham, 1914. *Copy.* 50517, f. 142.

United Arts Club, *Dublin.* Card, with verse and cartoon portraits presented to G. B. Shaw, 1931. Mainly *printed.* Partly *Gaelic.* 50711 A, f. 166.

United Irish League of Great Britain. Letter to G. B. Shaw of J. E. Redmond concerning United Irish League of Great Britain, 1901. 50514, f. 12.

United Whalers Ltd. Letter to G. B. Shaw, 1946. *Imperf.* 50526 A, f. 168.

Unity Theatre Club. Letter to G. B. Shaw of P. Robeson, Sir L. Casson and W. H. Thompson concerning Unity Theatre Club, 1937. *Signed.* 63186, f. 95.

University Students Maltese Association of Pieta, Malta. Letter to G. B. Shaw, 1946. *Imperf.* 50526 A, f. 108.

Unwin *née* **Cobden** (Emma Jane Catherine), *daughter of Richard Cobden; wife of T. F. Unwin.* Letter to C. F. Shaw, 1907. 56491, f. 53.

Unwin (*Sir* Stanley), *K.C.M.G.; publisher.* Letters to G. B. Shaw, 1936-1946. *Signed.* 50522, ff. 204, 404; 50524, f. 120; 50525, f. 156; 63186, f. 85.

Unwin (Thomas Fisher), *publisher.* Correspondence with G. B. Shaw, 1888-1902. Partly *signed* and *printed;* partly *typewritten copy.* 50512, ff. 19v, 27, 65v, 92, 102-108, 207, 210, 227; 50514, f. 49; 50561, ff. 7, 35, 82, 83, 88, 90.

Unwin Brothers, *printers and publishers.* 'What is Underpaid Labour?', 1889. 50512, ff. 104-107v.

— Letters to G. B. Shaw, 1889. 50512, ff. 112, 125v.

Upper Chelsea Institute. Programme of lectures, 1888. *Printed.* 50701, f. 38.

Urdu Academy Jamia Millia, *of New Delhi.* Letter to Constable and Company, publishers, 1939. *Signed.* 50522, f. 223.

Usborne (Richard A.), *Assistant Editor, 'Strand Magazine'.* Letter to F. E. Loewenstein, 1948. *Signed.* 50565, f. 171.

Uspensky (Petr Demyanovich), *theosophical writer.* Notes by C. F. Shaw on, 1934-1936, n.d. 56508, 56509.

U.S.S.R.

v. Russia.

Shaw (G. B.). WRITINGS , ETC., ON THE SOVIET UNION.

V

Vaccination. Notices of meetings protesting against vaccination, 1901, 1915. *Printed.* 50701, ff. 184, 239-240v.

— Correspondence rel. to, 1901-1944. Partly *printed.* 50514, ff. 35, 36, 69, 302-304; 50516, f. 144; 50517, ff. 367-371, 376, 390; 50524, f. 15.

— Notes on vaccination, 1902, n.d. 50729, ff. 1-14; 50730, ff. 1-4.

'Vaccination Inquirer and Health Review'. Issue for December 1902, 1902. *Printed.* 50740, f. 40.

Valantine and Carr, *brass founders and music smiths.* Letters to G. B. Shaw, 1880. 50508, ff. 218, 221.

Valerio (Edith), *of Brussels.* Letter to G. B. Shaw, 1938. 50522, f. 140.

Vallentin (Hugo Ferdinand), *Swedish writer.* Correspondence with G. B. Shaw, 1906-1917. Partly *type-written copy.* 50515, f. 89; 50517, f. 288; 50562, ff. 43-47, 83, 134, 140; *Ashley* A5019, ff. 62, 63, 63v.

— Photograph of H. Vallentin, 1907. *Signed.* 50585, f. 62.

— Letter to C. F. Shaw, 1912. *Signed.* 56491, f. 86.

Vallon (Josef), *secretary of the Thomas Paine Society, New York.* Letter to G. B. Shaw, 1938. *Signed.* 50522, f. 155.

Vance (Hart), *draughtsman, of Chicago.* Letters to G. B. Shaw, 1913, 1914. *Signed.* 50516, f. 374; 50517, f. 57.

Vance (Wilson J.), *American author.* Letter to G. B. Shaw, 1931. *Signed.* 50520, f. 35.

Vandercom & Co., *solicitors, of London.* Letter to Sir F. D. Acland as Under-Secretary at the Foreign Office to Sir F. D. Acland, 1912. *Copy.* 50516, f. 204.

Van Dyck (—), *[daughter?] of Ernest M. H. Van Dyck, Belgian tenor.* Photograph of Mlle. Van Dyck, 1911. 50516, f. 98v.

Vane-Tempest-Stewart (Edith Helen), *al. 'Sidonia'; wife of Charles, 7th Marquess of Londonderry.* Letters to G. B. Shaw, 1939, 1940. 50522, ff. 175, 258.

Van Nosdall (George A.),. *American book collector.* Letter to G. B. Shaw, 1942. *Signed.* 50522, f. 470.

Vansittart (Robert Gilbert), *1st Baron Vansittart of Denham.* 'Vansittartitis'; letter to 'Tribune' of G. B. Shaw, 1942. *Typewritten draft.* 50698, ff. 213-215.

— Letter to 'Tribune' of H. G. Wells rel. to R. G. Vansittart, 1942. *Copy.* 50698, ff. 216-217.

Varsanyi (Irene), *of Budapest.* Letter to G. B. Shaw, 1923. 50519, f. 67v.

— Photograph of I. Varsanyi, 1923. *Signed.* 50585, f. 63.

Vassie (William C.), *Relieving Officer, no. 7 ward, St. Pancras.* Letter to G. B. Shaw, 1913. 50516, f. 355v.

Veall (A. D.), *President of the Student's Union at the L.S.E.* Correspondence with C. F. Shaw, 1941. Partly *draft* and *signed.* 63197, ff. 76, 77.

Vedrenne (John E.), *theatrical manager.* Prompt copies of Shaw plays produced at The Royal Court Theatre by H. Granville-Barker and J. E. Vedrenne, 1904-1907. *Printed,* with *MS.* annotations. 65156 Q-W.

— Correspondence with G. B. Shaw, 1905-1912. *Signed;* partly *typewritten copies.* 50515, ff. 446, 447; 50516, f. 195; 50562, ff. 37, 38-42, 50.

Veer (Willem de), *Dutch novelist.* Letter to G. B. Shaw, 1912. *Signed.* 50516, f. 176.

'Vegetarian News, The'. Issue for July 1936, 1936. *Printed.* 50741, f. 75.

Vivisection. Correspondence and papers of G. B. Shaw rel. to vivisection and cruelty to animals, 1892-1948. Partly *printed, copy* and *draft.* 50516, ff. 300, 302; 50520, ff. 44-50; 50521, f. 308; 50522, f. 1; 50525, f. 190; 50526 A, f. 187; 50526 B, ff. 390, 501; 50678, ff. 1-102; 50701, f. 308; 50743 B, f. 359.

Vocadlo (Otakar), *head, English Dept., Komensky University, Prague.* Letter to B. Patch, 1933. *Signed.* 50520, f. 216.

— Letter to G. B. Shaw, 1935. *Signed.* 50521, f. 1.

Vogel (*Prof.* E.), *of Prague; Zionist.* Letter to G. B. Shaw, 1946. *Signed. Germ.* 50526 A, f. 5.

Vogt (C.), *German socialist.* Letter to G. B. Shaw, 1925. *Dictated.* 50519, f. 225.

Volz (*Mrs.* Luise), *of Wanasari Estate, Bandung, West Java.* Letter to G. B. Shaw, 1933. 50520, f. 184.

Vox (Maximillien). Letter to, of Sir I. J. Pitman, 1957. *Typewritten extract.* 79493, f. 36.

Voynich *née* **Boole** (Ethel Lilian), *author and translator.* 'The Gadfly', dramatised by G. B. Shaw, 1898. *Typewritten* with *autogr.* stage directions. 50608.

W

Wachter (A. E.), *socialist, of Cheshire.* Correspondence with G. B. Shaw, 1909. Partly *copy, signed* and *shorthand draft.* 50515, ff. 295, 296.

Waddams (Ronald), *of Thayer St., London.* Entry in alphabet design competition, 1958. 79494 B, ff. 10-13.

Wadsworth (Edward Alexander), *A.R.A.* Letter of P. W. Lewis, E. A. Wadsworth, F. Etchells and C. Hamilton concerning Omega Workshops, 1913. *Signed.* 50534, f. 93.

Wagner (Norman), *schoolboy, of East London, South Africa.* Letter, with three other schoolboys, to G. B. Shaw, 1946. *Signed.* 50526 A, f. 195.

Wagner (Richard).
v. Wagner (Wilhelm Richard).

Wagner (Siegfried Helferich Richard), *composer; son of Richard Wagner.* Photograph of Siegfried Wagner, *circa* 1911. 50516, f. 71v.

Wagner (Wilhelm Richard), *composer.* Letter of G. B. Shaw rel. to translation of his prose works, 1905. 50514, f. 241.

Wakefield (Percy V.).
v. Rock (Percival S. Wakefield).

Walberg (Fred), *medical student, of Oslo.* Letter to G. B. Shaw, 1946. 50526 B, f. 358.

Walbrook (Henry Mackinnon), *writer and critic.* Speech introducing H. M. Walbrook by G. B. Shaw, written for M. Halstan, 1911. *Typewritten copy.* 50562, f. 78.

Waldman (Ronald Hartley), *of the B.B.C.* Letter to G. B. Shaw, 1946. *Signed.* 50525, f. 44.

Walker (*Dr.* A. H.), *at the Waldorf Astoria Hotel, New York.* Letter to G. B. Shaw, 1942. *Signed.* 63186, f. 180.

Walker (Dorothy), *daughter of Sir Emery Walker.* Postcards to C. F. Shaw, 1929-1933. 63197, ff. 12, 34, 35.

— Letters, etc., to G. B. Shaw, 1932, 1944. 50520, f. 182; 50524, f. 263.

Walker (*Sir* Emery), *engraver and typographer.* Correspondence with G. B. Shaw, 1889-1932. *Partly copy.* 45347, f. 73; 50512, f. 179; 50514, f. 84; 50515, f. 326; 50517, f. 18; 50519, f. 317v; 50520, ff. 18, 34, 132, 183.

— Letter to S. J. Webb, 1908. *Signed.* 50515, f. 155v.

— Letter to C. F. Shaw, 1912. 56491, f. 89.

—Portrait photograph of R. S. Bridges, taken by O. V. A. Morrell, engraved by Sir E. Walker, 1924. 50529, f. 136.

Walker (Harry), *of Northenden, Manchester.* Letter, etc., to G. B. Shaw, 1946. 50525, f. 315.

Walker (Jimmy), *of New York.* Letter to G. B. Shaw, 1939. *Signed.* 50522, f. 202.

Walker (Mary Grace), *wife of Sir Emery Walker.* Letter to G. B. Shaw, 1886. 50511, f. 248.

Walkley (Arthur Bingham), *dramatic and literary critic.* Correspondence with G. B. Shaw, 1888-1906. Partly *typewritten copy.* 50512, f. 59; 50514, f. 110; 50562, f. 48.

— Letter to Mrs. C. F. Shaw, 1900. 50513, f. 234.

Wallace (Alfred Russel), *naturalist.* Letters to A. R. Wallace and F. T. Bond of E. Beckett, 1902. *Printed.* 50514, ff. 69, 69v.

Wallas (Audrey *al.* Ada), *wife of Graham Wallas.* Letter to C. F. Shaw, 1912. 56491, f. 116.

Wallas (Graham), *political psychologist.* Letters to G. B. Shaw, 1889?-1929. 50553, ff. 1-29.

Waller (Lewis), *manager of the Imperial Theatre.* Letter to G. B. Shaw, bef. 1907. 50514, f. 389.

Walling (William English), *American socialist.* Letter to, of Upton Sinclair, 1917. *Typewritten copy.* 50549, f. 96.

Wallis (*Sir* Whitworth), *F.S.A.; director, the Corporation Museum and Art Gallery, Birmingham.* Letter and telegram to G. B. Shaw, 1912, 1914. *Signed.* 50516, f. 285; 50517, f. 94.

— Letter to C. F. Shaw, 1926. 56492, f. 96.

— Letter to G. B. Shaw, n.d. 50527, f. 276.

Walpole (S. C.), *of Chapman and Hall, Ltd.* Letter to G. B. Shaw, 1880. 50508, f. 201v.

Walsh (Andrew T.), *of Dublin.* Letter, etc., to G. B. Shaw, 1946. 50525, f. 121.

— Poems, 1946. *Typewritten copies.* 50525, ff. 122-123.

Walsh (J. J.), *editor of the 'Munster Express', Waterford.* Letter to G. B. Shaw, 1946. *Signed.* 50525, f. 336.

Walshe (Christina), *theatre designer; lover of R. Boughton.* Portrait photograph of C. Walshe, 1917. 50518, f. 54v.

— Postcard and letter to G. B. Shaw, 1917, 1938. 50518, f. 54; 50522, f. 22.

American production of 'The Devil's Disciple', produced by M. Webster, 1950. 50589, ff. 1-10.

Weekes (George), *member of Bromley Borough Council.* Letter, etc., to G. B. Shaw, 1906. *Dictated; partly copy.* 50514, f. 356.

Weichmann (Louis), *of Berlin; writer on G. B. Shaw.* Letter to G. B. Shaw, 1919. 50518, f. 192.

Weintraub (*Dr.* Stanley), *of 'The Shaw Review'.* Letters to S. C. Cockerell, 1959-1961. 52768, ff. 1-5v.

Weir (George), *secretary of the National Anti-Vaccination League, Leeds branch.* Letter to G. B. Shaw, 1912. 50516, f. 144.

Weiser (Allen), *store manager of Philadelphia, Pennsylvania.* Letter to G. B. Shaw, 1946. 50525, f. 15.

Welch (Reginald Stuart), *musician.* Letter, etc., to G. B. Shaw, 1910. 50515, f. 405.

Wellesley (Arthur), *1st Duke of Wellington.* Memorial of Col. T. C. Kirby, as Lt.-Col., to A. Wellesley, 1844. *Copy.* 56526, f. 4.

Wellington, *Duke of.* v. Wellesley (Arthur).

Wellock (Wilfred), *author.* Letter, etc., to G. B. Shaw, 1939. 63186, f. 105.

— 'The Mystery of Germany and Russia', 1939. 63186, ff. 106-113.

Wells *née* **Robbins** (Amy Catherine), *2nd wife of H. G. Wells.* Letter to E. R. Pease, 1906. *Copy.* 50557, f. 78.

— Description of Mrs. Wells's funeral by C. F. Shaw, 1927. *Partly type-written copy.* 45922, ff. 26-30, 87-91; 56497, ff. 30-34.

Wells (Carolyn), *author.* Poem, 'With Trumpets and also with Shawms', 1906. *Printed.* 45296, f. 170.

Wells (Gabriel), *of New York; dealer in books and manuscripts.* Owned orginals of 50561, 50562.

Wells (Geoffrey Harry), *al. 'Geoffrey West'; writer; son of H. G. Wells and Rebecca West.* Letters to 'Geoffrey West' from B. Patch on behalf of G. B. Shaw, 1925. *Signed.* 60571, ff. 150, 151.

Wells (George Philip), *son of H. G. Wells.* Letter to G. B. Shaw, 1946. 50552, f. 69.

Wells (Herbert George), *author.* Correspondence with G. B. Shaw, 1901-1941. *Partly copy* and *draft.* 50518, f. 152; 50552, ff. 1-11, 15, 17-19, 21-27, 33-55, 60-68; 50682, ff. 27-30; 60571, ff. 150, 151.

— Photographs of H. G. Wells, his son and grandson, 1902, 1946. 50585, ff. 83, 84.

— Letters to C. F. Shaw, *circa* 1906-1909. 50552, ff. 13, 16, 31; 56494, f. 204.

— Letter from G. B. Shaw to S. J. Webb and H. G. Wells, 1907. *Draft.* 50682, ff. 27-30.

— Letters, etc., with G. B. Shaw to G. H. Jackson, 1907. *Partly type-written.* 62992, ff. 9, 13-23.

— Memoranda on the Fabian Society and politics, 1907-1908. *Type-written drafts.* 50681, ff. 27-28; 62992, ff. 19, 21.

— Letter to S. J. Webb, *circa* 1909. 50552, f. 20.

— Review by G. B. Shaw of 'What is Coming', 1916. Partly *printed;* partly *typewritten* with *autogr.* amendments. 50696, ff. 101-118.

— Letter to G. H. Thring, 1930. *Copy.* 50552, f. 57.

— 'Declaration of Rights', 1939. *Typewritten* and *duplicated.* 50557, ff. 298-300.

— Letter to 'Tribune' rel. to R. G. Vansittart, 1942. *Copy.* 50698, ff. 216-217.

— Letter to, of J. MacClamroch, 1943. *Copy.* 50555, f. 63.

Wells (Jane).
v. Wells *née* Robbins (Amy Catherine).

Wells (John Carveth), *F.R.G.S.; author.* Letter to G. B. Shaw, 1943. 50523, f. 112.

'Well wisher', *friend of Mrs. A. L. Dodd.* Letter to G. B. Shaw, 1911. 50516, f. 113.

Welton (*Lieut.* Norman A.), *the Royal Fusiliers.* Letter to G. B. Shaw, 1943. 50523, f. 103.

Welty (Ruth), *American playwright.* Letter to G. B. Shaw, 1944. *Signed.* 50524, f. 196.

Wentworth, *Baroness.*
v. Lytton (Judith Anne Dorothea Blunt).

Wesendonck (Mathilde), *poet; friend of Wagner.* Letter to G. B. Shaw, 1892. 50512, f. 275.

West (*Major* George Frederick Myddleton Cornwallis-).
v. Cornwallis-West.

West (Julius), *Fabian.* Letter, as editor of 'Everyman', to G. B. Shaw, 1916. *Signed.* 56627, f. 180.

— Letters to E. R. Pease, 1917. *Copies.* 50557, ff. 263-267.

'West (Rebecca)', *pseudonym.*
v. Andrews *née* Fairfield (Cicily Isabel).

Westbourne Park Institute. Programmes of lectures, 1894, 1908. *Printed.* 50701, ff. 135, 213.

Western Federation of Miners, *of the U.S.A.* Draft circular with alterations by G. B. Shaw, 1902. *Copy.* 50557, ff. 64-66.

Westley (Helen), *actress.* Portrait photographs from the Theatre Guild New York production of 'Heartbreak House', taken by I. D. Schwarz, 1920. 50589, ff. 31-38.

West London Social and Political Reform Association. Programme, 1888. *Printed.* 50701, f. 28.

West Southwark Liberal and Radical Club. Programme of lectures, 1889. *Printed.* 50701, f. 48.

Weymouth (Anthony), *of the B.B.C.* Note to, concerning the cancellation of G. B. Shaw broadcast, 1940? *Typewritten.* 50705, f. 113.

Whall (R. Henry), *horn player, of Stroud, co. Glos.* Letter to G. B. Shaw, 1934. 50520, f. 252.

Wheeler (Alexander), *L.R.C.S.* Letter to C. Gane, 1901. 50514, f. 36.

Wheeler (Horatio F. de Courcy), *secretary, Shaw Society, Dublin.* Postcard and letters to G. B. Shaw, 1944. 50524, ff. 160, 218, 232.

Wheeler (Margaret), *of Workington, co. Cumb.* Letters to G. B. Shaw, 1946-1949. Partly *imperf.* 50526 A, f. 17; 50526 B, ff. 406, 447.

Williams (G. Radford), *language and spelling reformer, of Coventry.* Mailing list and shorthand system, 1945?-1950? *Signed* and *duplicated.* 50556, ff. 226-242.

Williams (George Emlyn), *C.B.E.; actor and playwright.* Letter to C. F. Shaw, 1939. 56494, f. 29.

Williams (Howard). Letter to G. B. Shaw, n.d. 50527, f. 277.

Williams (James Thomas), *son-in-law of A. de Candole, vicar of Ayot St. Lawrence.* Postcard to G. B. Shaw, 1941. 50522, f. 358.

Williams (*Maj.-Gen. Sir* John Hanbury-).
v. Hanbury-Williams.

Williams (Joseph) **Ltd.,** *music publishers, of London.* Letter to the editor of 'The Hornet', 1877. 50508, f. 75.

Williams (*Flight-Lieut.* Lawrence), *Royal Canadian Air Force.* Letter to G. B. Shaw, 1946. 50526 B, f. 287.

Williams (Robert), *Secretary, National Transport Workers' Federation.* Account of a visit to the Soviet Union, 1920. *Duplicated.* 50518, ff. 204-207.

Williamson (Henry), *novelist.* Letter to G. B. Shaw, 1924. 50519, f. 134.

Williamson Hill and Company, *solicitors.* Letter to G. B. Shaw, 1882. 50509, f. 126v.

Willis (Dorothy Treherne), *of Putney.* Letter to G. B. Shaw, 1905. 50514, f. 251.

Willock (Laura), *musician.* Letter to G. B. Shaw, 1878. 50508, f. 120.

Wills. Wills of G. B. Shaw, 1901-1950. *Copies* and *drafts,* with

autogr. notes. 50712; 56524 B, ff. 135-141.

— Will of Mrs. C. F. Shaw, 1935. Mainly *typewritten.* 63198 A, f. 152.

— Notes on the will of C. F. Shaw, 1944? 56494, f. 207.

— Correspondence and papers of Sir R. F. Harrod concerning the will of G. B. Shaw, 1955-1957. Partly *signed, printed* and *copy.* 71615.

— Notes, legal opinions, etc., concerning the will of G. B. Shaw, 1957. *Duplicated, copy* and *printed.* 79493, ff. 1-26v.

Wills (Frederick Alexander), *author.* Letter to G. B. Shaw, 1946. *Signed.* 50525, f. 124.

Wilmot (M.), *A.B, H.M.S. Zest.* Letter to G. B. Shaw, *circa* 1945. 50527, f. 278.

Wilshire (Gaylord), *American socialist writer and publisher.* Photographs of G. Wilshire, 1925? Partly *signed.* 50585, ff. 86-90.

Wilson (*Col.* Arthur Harry Hutton-).
v. Hutton-Wilson.

Wilson (Charlotte Martin), *editor of 'Freedom'.* Letters to G. B. Shaw, 1884-1889. 50510, f. 310; 50511, ff. 96, 99, 112, 174, 176, 215, 284, 345; 50512, f. 161.

Wilson (Frederick J.), *editor of 'Ideas'.* Letters to G. B. Shaw, 1883-1885. 50510, ff. 105, 164; 50511, f. 78.

Wilson (George T.), *of Leyton.* Letter to G. B. Shaw, 1946. 50525, f. 139.

Wilson (J. Hay), *accountant, of Honolulu.* Letter to G. B. Shaw, 1937. 50521, f. 294.

Wilson (*Sir* James Steuart), *singer and musical administrator.* Letter, etc., to G. B. Shaw, 1937. 50529, f. 77.

— Letter to A. N. Chamberlain concerning civil list pension for R. Boughton, drafted by Sir J. S. Wilson, signed by G. B. Shaw, 1937. *Draft.* 50529, f. 78.

Wilson (John Gideon), *C.B.E.; chairman and managing director of J. and E. Bumpus, Ltd., booksellers.* Letters and Christmas card to C. F. Shaw, 1936-1941. Partly *signed* and *printed.* 56493, f. 190; 56494, ff. 106, 107, 110, 114; 63197, f. 38.

Wilson (Ormond), *of Bulls, New Zealand.* Letter to C. F. Shaw, 1934. 56493, f. 120.

Wilson (Richard Albert), *Canadian author.* Letters to G. B. Shaw, 1941-1945. Partly *signed* and *imperf.* 50522, ff. 340, 439, 442, 475, 477; 63186, f. 199.

Wilson Taylor (John), *secretary of the Bath Club.* Circular letters, 1941. 63197, ff. 80, 83.

Wimbledon Literary Society. Programme of lectures, 1894. *Printed.* 50701, ff. 150-152.

Windsor, *Duke of.* v. England.

Wingate (*Gen. Sir* Francis Reginald), *1st Bart.* Chalk portrait by W. Roberts, 1927? *Photographic copy.* 56499, f. 51.

Winsten (Clare), *sculptor.* Letter, etc., to G. B. Shaw, 1944, n.d. *Signed.* 50524, f. 251; 50563, f. 37.

Winsten (Stephen), *at Ayot St. Lawrence.* Letters to S. C.

Cockerell rel. to G. B. Shaw, 1946-1949. 52769, ff. 1-4.

Wintersgill (A. T.). Letter to G. B. Shaw, n.d. 50527, f. 279.

Wise (Thomas James), *book collector.* Correspondence with G. B. Shaw, 1908?-1933, n.d. Partly *signed* and *copy.* 50520, f. 213; 59621 B, f. 47; *Ashley* B1517, ff. 6, 6v; *Ashley* B1518, f. 7; *Ashley* A1525, f. 118; *Ashley* B1529, f. 15; *Ashley* A1968(3), f. 106; *Ashley* A4011, f. 113; *Ashley* B4019, ff. 114-119.

— Letter to, of B. Patch, 1924. *Ashley* B1521, f. 8.

Wise (William H.), *publisher, New York.* Materials rel. to propectus of his Collected Edition, 1929-1931. 50664, ff. 106-116.

— Letter, etc., to G. B. Shaw, 1931. *Signed.* 50520, f. 23.

Witcop (Rose), *of 'The Spur'.* Letter to G. B. Shaw, 1916. *Signed.* 50517, f. 394.

Witherow (James M.), *attorney, of Moorhead, Minnesota.* Letter to G. B. Shaw, 1939. *Signed.* 50522, f. 201.

Witney (John Humphrey), *Assistant Sec., British Museum.* Letter to C. F. Shaw, 1940. *Signed.* 56494, f. 74.

— Letter to G. B. Shaw, 1945. *Signed.* Mainly *printed.* 50524, f. 316.

Witt (Martin), *German playwright.* Postcard to G. B. Shaw, 1905. 50514, f. 264.

Wolf (Robert L.), *American author.* Correspondence between T. Roosevelt and R. L. Wolf, 1917. Partly *copies.* 50518, ff. 61-69v.

— Letter, etc., to G. B. Shaw, 1917. Partly *copies*. 50518, f. 81.

Wolf (Sadye), *of New York.* Letter to G. B. Shaw, 1914. 50517, f. 31.

Wolfenden (J. R.), [*land agent?*]. Letter to Col. T. C. Kirby, 1840. 56526, f. 2.

Wolff-Metternich (*Count* Paul), *German Ambassador in London.* Letter of Lord Chamberlain to, 1913. *L.C.P. Corr.* 1909/80.

Woll (Nanny), *of Torrington Square, London.* Letter to G. B. Shaw, 1892. 50512, f. 281.

Wolpert (Roland H.), *of Brooklyn, New York.* Lettter to G. B. Shaw, 1946. *Signed*. 50525, f. 72.

Wolverhampton Fabian Society. Notices of meetings, 1891. *Printed*. 50701, ff. 100, 112.

Wolverhampton Trades and Labour Council. Programme of lectures, 1891. *Printed*. 50701, f. 100.

Women's International League for Peace and Freedom. Notice of meeting on mothers' pensions, 1917. *Printed*. 50701, f. 242.

Women's International Progressive Union. Programme of meetings, etc., 1899. 50701, f. 177.

Women's Progressive Society. Programme of meetings, etc., 1894. *Printed*. 50701, f. 155.

Women's Social and Political Union. Account of prison experiences of 'Jane Warton' and Lady Lytton by Lady C. G. Bulwer-Lytton, distributed by Women's Social and Political Union, 1910. *Copy*. 50515, ff. 318-322.

— Letters to M. Cunningham concerning Women's Social and Political Union, 1914. *Copies*. 50517, ff. 141-155.

Wontner (Arthur), *actor.* Letter to G. B. Shaw, 1935. 50521, f. 34.

Wood (Algernon Cockburn Rayner-), *Housemaster at Eton.* Letter to G. B. Shaw, 1937. *Signed*. 50521, f. 293.

Wood (*Sir* Henry Joseph), *C.H.; conductor.* Note by G. B. Shaw rel. to, 1944? *Typewritten*. 56429, f. 33.

Wood *formerly* **Linton** (Lady Jessie). *v.* Linton (Jessie).

Wood (*Mrs.* Maeve Evelyn), *at Bombay.* Letter to C. F. Shaw, 1933. 56493, f. 55.

Wood (Peggy). *v.* Weaver.

Woodruff (Caroline S.), *president, National Education Association.* Letter to G. B. Shaw, 1937. *Signed*. 50521, f. 332.

Woodruff (George B.), *of Brighton.* Correspondence with G. B. Shaw, 1883. Partly *shorthand draft*. 50510, ff. 46, 84, 87, 92.

Woods (Katherine), *typist, of Dublin.* Letter to G. B. Shaw, 1944. 50524, f. 158.

Woolf *née* **Stephen** (Adeline Virginia), *novelist.* Letter and postcard to G. B. Shaw, 1940. *Signed*. 50522, ff. 293, 318.

— Photograph of Monk's House, home of Leonard and Virginia Woolf, 1940. 50522, f. 318v.

Woolf (Julia), *composer.* Letter to the Music Editor, 'The Hornet', 1876. 50508, f. 44.

'**Wynne** (Lewis)', *literary forger.*
　v. Bostock (John Stuart Louis Wynne).

Wynyard (Diana), *actress.* Letter to G. B. Shaw, 1937. 50521, f. 277v.

X

Xiong (Shiyi)
v. Hsiung (Shih I).

Y

Yager (Thomas M.), *postal employee, of Anthony, Kansas.* Postcard, etc., to G. B. Shaw, 1946. *Signed.* Partly *printed.* 50526 B, f. 362.

Yao (Hsin-nung), *Chinese author and dramatist.* Letter to G. B. Shaw, 1937. *Signed.* 50521, f. 297.

Yao (Xinnong).
　v. Yao (Hsin-nung).

Yates (Charles), *son of E. Yates.* Letter from G. B. Shaw to, 1894. *Draft.* 50513, f. 47v.

Yates (Edmund), *novelist and founder of 'The World'.* Letter to W. Archer, 1886. 50528, f. 40.
— Letters to G. B. Shaw, 1887-1890. Partly *signed.* 50511, ff. 310, 349; 50512, ff. 186, 208, 225.

Yeats (William Butler), *poet.* Correspondence with G. B. Shaw, 1901-1932. Partly *signed* and *copy.* 50553, ff. 142-163, 165-167.
— Letter to, of C. H. O'Connell O'Riordan, 1909. *Typewritten extract.* 50534, f. 175.

— Letter drafted, with T. S. Moore, on behalf of 'English Review', 1911. *Copy.* 50538, f. 61.
— Portrait photograph of, by L. Connell, 1915? 50585, f. 93.
— Invitation to G. B. Shaw, signed by W. B. Yeats, O. St. John Gogarty, S. W. Maddock and H. McLaughlin, 1924. Mainly *printed.* 50711 A, f. 128.
— 'Roger Casement', 1937. Proof *copy,* with *MS.* amendment. 50521, f. 244.

Yevonde (*Madame —*　), *photographer, of London.* Portrait photographs of G. B. Shaw, 1920? 50582, ff. 45, 64-67.

York (Jack), *of Colliers Wood.* Letter, with R. E. Scott, to G. B. Shaw, 1946. *Signed.* 50526 A, f. 82.

Yorke (Ursula), *of London.* Letter to G. B. Shaw, 1946. 50525, f. 104.

Young (Edward Hilton), *1st Baron Kennet.* Letter to G. B. Shaw, 1948. *Signed.* 63186, f. 207.

Young (*Maj.* Hubert Winthrop). Note to T. E. Lawrence, with proofs of his 'Makik', 1926. 56499, ff. 13-32.

Young *formerly* **Scott** *née* **Bruce** (Kathleen), *sculptor; widow of Capt. R. F. Scott; wife of Edward, 1st Baron Kennet.* Correspondence with G. B. Shaw, 1923-1944. Partly *draft.* 50519, f. 29; 50522, f. 298; 50524, f. 252.

Young (Wayland Hilton), *2nd Baron Kennet.* Letter to G. B. Shaw, 1943. 50523, f. 140.

Yount (David Leroy), *pipe organ builder, of Grensburg, Pennsylvania.* Letter to G. B. Shaw, 1946. *Signed.* 50526 B, f. 265.

Z

Zangwill (Israel), *author and Zionist.* Letter to C. F. Shaw, 1902. 56491, f. 27.

— Correspondence with G. B. Shaw, 1903-1919. *Partly signed* and *copy.* 50514, f. 158; 50517, ff. 307-310, 313-314; 50518, f. 185.

Zara (Louis), *American author.* Letter to G. B. Shaw, 1939. *Signed.* 50522, f. 240.

Zerkalova (Daria), *Soviet actress.* Photographs of Moscow production of 'Pygmalion', 1932? 50590, ff. 13-27.

Zhang (Xueliang).
 v. Chang (Hsueh-liang).

Zhu (Xiang).
 v. Chu (Hsiang).

Zil'ber (Georgy).
 v. Silber (Georges).

Zimmerman (Louis A.), *of New York.* Letter, etc., to G. B. Shaw, 1946. Partly *printed.* 50526 B, f. 302.

[Zirner-Zwieback?] ([Ella?]), *of Bayswater, London.* Letter to G. B. Shaw, 1941. 50522, f. 324.

Zoor (*Dr.* Syed Mohiuddin Qadri), *Head of the Department of Urdu Literature, Osmania University, Secunderabad, India.* Foreword to Urdu translation of 'St. Joan', 1944. *Typewritten copy. Engl. transl.* 50524, f. 70.

Zubov (Konstantin), *Soviet actor.* Photographs of Moscow production of 'Pygmalion', 1932? 50590, ff. 13-27.

Zuchardt (*Dr.* Karl), *author and playwright, of Dresden.* Letter to G. B. Shaw, 1946. *Germ.* 50525, f. 240.

Zucker (Leopold), *of Cologne.* Letters to G. B. Shaw, 1936. Partly *Germ.* 50521, ff. 187, 188-190v.